D1154095

LAWYERING FOR THE RAILROAD

LAWYERING FOR THE RAILROAD

BUSINESS, LAW, AND POWER IN THE NEW SOUTH

William G. Thomas

DISCARDED LIBRARY

LOUISIANA STATE UNIVERSITY PRESS
Baton Rouge

BOWLING GREEN STATE
UNIVERSITY LIBRARY

Copyright © 1999 by Louisiana State University Press
All rights reserved
Manufactured in the United States of America
First printing
08 07 06 05 04 03 02 01 00 99
5 4 3 2 1

Designer: Glynnis Weston
Typeface: Galliard
Typesetter: Coghill Composition
Printer and binder: Thomson-Shore, Inc.

Extracts from the correspondence between various Baker & Botts attorneys and other
attorneys in Texas concerning their work for the Southern Pacific Railway, held in the
Baker & Botts History Collection at Rice University Library, are reproduced by permission
of Baker & Botts, Houston, Texas.

Library of Congress Cataloging-in-Publication Data

Thomas, William G., 1964–
    Lawyering for the railroad : business, law, and power in the New
South / William G. Thomas.
        p.   cm.
    Includes bibliographical references and index.
    ISBN 0-8071-2367-6 (cloth : alk. paper). — ISBN 0-8071-2504-0
(pbk. : alk. paper)
    1. Railroad law—Southern States—History.   2. Railroads and
state—Southern States—History.   3. Corporate lawyers—Southern
States—History.   I. Title.
KF2289.T48   1999
343.7509'5—dc21   99-28125
                                                        CIP

The paper in this book meets the guidelines for permanence and durability of the Committee
on Production Guidelines for Book Longevity of the Council on Library Resources. ∞

I think a good lawyer is about the best man in the world,
and a mean lawyer is probably about the meanest man in the world.

—Alexander Hamilton
Vice-President and General Counsel, Atlantic Coast Line

Contents

Illustrations

This book is about lawyers, in particular those who represented the railroads. Some of them were mean as hell, sacrificing any moral obligation before their duty to protect their clients. Others saw their way clear to a moral vision of the law, making difficult choices along the way. Many felt deep inner conflict about their role in the New South political economy, wondering about their own dependence on big, northern-owned corporations. Some of them acted in ways that we might find reprehensible. Most viewed their surroundings in plainly pragmatic ways. Whatever their choices, many of them participated in key decisions about the direction, shape, and character of the New South political economy. This book attempts to find out who they were and what kinds of choices they made.

This book is also about the ways that monopoly power worked in the everyday legal struggles between the interstate railroads and southern citizens. Railroad development became a hot political issue for the Populists in the 1880s and 1890s and for the Progressives later, and railroad attorneys as lobbyists often are found in the middle of the action. Most historians have focused on the issues of rates and the development of state regulatory commissions. Nearly every railroad-corporation history has an obligatory chapter with a title like "The Railroad in Politics," in which there is some accounting of the free pass and the relative amount of bribery that railroad attorneys used to keep the legislature under wraps. This book accounts for railroad monopoly power in other ways. It locates the source of the railroad problem in the South's political economy in the activities of the lawyers. Their regular litigation-settlement patterns did as much to make the railroad a live political issue as the free pass. The monopoly power of the railroads was more pervasive than legislative electioneering; it was present in the daily attempts of everyday southerners to use the legal system to seek redress for railroad-corporation wrongs and inequities. It was also evident in the retainers that interstate railroads offered their southern attorneys, who found their choices restricted and their professional independence threatened. If the free pass was emblematic of the railroads' monopoly power, it had resonance because of all the other less visible ways that railroads, through their lawyers, tried to control the political economy.

Since by 1890 virtually every corner of the South had heard the rumble of the locomotive wheels and the shriek of the train whistle, the New South was defined as much by the paths of the railroad tracks as by the lines of state boundaries, the courses of rivers, and the ridges of mountains. Interstate railroads ran through the political boundaries of states, cities, and counties. They united and divided the region in new ways, imposing their own system and design on the old landscape. They recognized and respected the traditional boundaries of the region, appointing state counsels for handling the political-legal business defined within states. At the same time, though, the interstate railroads set their own standards for considering the South as a region. Freight classification, for example, assigned only certain states to a regional southern section.

This book follows the sources of some of the largest interstate railroad companies in the South—the Southern, the Norfolk & Western, the Illinois Central, the Louisville & Nashville, the Gulf, Colorado & Santa Fe, and the Southern Pacific. These railroads together networked the South's major subregions—the Atlantic seaboard, Appalachia, the Delta, the Upcountry, and the Southwest—and reached every southern state. And their cars carried each subregion's major products—lumber, coal, cotton, grain, and livestock. This book carries its main themes into all of the major subregions of the South, following the tracks of the primary interstate railroads that serviced them. Some states receive more attention in the book, but only because their material was more applicable than others.

Historians have only recently begun to write about the less visible ways that lawyers shaped the political economy for large industrial enterprises. Two recent important works in legal history help shape this new scholarship. First, Edward Purcell's *Litigation and Inequality* demonstrates the crucial difference between what he calls the "formal process of the law," such as courts, laws, and doctrine, and the "informal process of the law"—out-of-court settlement patterns, distance to court, and level of court. To understand the ways corporation attorneys, especially railroad and insurance lawyers, gained such advantages over their opponents, Purcell argues, we have to take account of not just the highly visible formal process but also the murky arena of informal process. Second, R. W. Kostal's *Law and English Railway Capitalism* traces the role of England's railroad lawyers in the development of the English political economy. He emphasizes the numerous ways that private negotiation and litigation shaped the English experience with large railroads. Kostal shows how railroads invaded the English landscape, supplanted local priorities and practices, ran over and killed passengers, employees, and bystanders, and in the process generated booming business for the railway lawyers and a great deal of public resentment. In the end, Kostal points out, such drama brought more uniform and national regulation and the end of the free-for-all days of the litigation-busy railroad lawyer, as railroads moved to in-house counsel, regular settlement, and a more developmental-less monopolistic approach to their business.[1]

Railroads brought a great deal of legal business to the South, just as they did in England, and they also helped spawn a similar sequence of abuse, reform, and reconstituting of the legal and constitutional order. This book attempts to follow that sequence. Chapter 1 follows the build-

---

1. Edward A Purcell Jr., *Litigation and Inequality: Federal Diversity Jurisdiction in Industrial America, 1870–1948* (New York: Oxford University Press, 1992), and R. W. Kostal, *Law and English Railway Capitalism, 1825–1875* (Oxford: Clarendon Press, 1994). These books also highlight important developments in legal history theory. Some legal scholars emphasize the law as a derivative of social and economic historical changes, not at all "constitutive" or an independent actor on them. Other scholars, such as Robert W. Gordon, disagree, suggesting that the law is not merely "reflective" of social and economic change, but a force for change on social groups. Both Purcell and Kostal offer a more "interactive" view—that law and legal processes both shape and derive from social and economic change. William E. Forbath's recent work on law and the labor movement also takes this approach, at the same time trying to ground the debate in more empirical study. William E. Forbath, *Law and the Shaping of the American Labor Movement* (Cambridge, Mass.: Harvard University Press, 1991). For a thorough account of these divisions in the scholarship of legal theory, see Robert W. Gordon, "Critical Legal Histories," *Stanford Law Review* 36 (1983–84), 57–125; see also Mark V. Tushnet, "Perspectives on the Development of American Law: A Critical Review of Friedman's 'A History of American Law,' " *Wisconsin Law Review* (1977), 81–109.

ing of the interstate railroads in the 1880s. Every railroad began with acquiring right-of-way, and this process did a great deal to anger some southerners before a railroad was even built. Lawsuits over right-of-way and condemnation cluttered the courts when a railroad was built in the 1880s. Contests over county and city stock subscriptions pitted the interstate railroads against citizens who saw their control over formerly local lines slipping away. Chapter 2 traces the beginning of the corporate bar in the South and the interstate railroads' role in reshaping the law business. It examines a crucial development in the political economy of the region: the division in the bar between corporation and anti-corporation, or "personal injury," lawyers. Some railroad attorneys expressed unease about the new circumstances; they could not help but feel less independent. Chapters 3 and 4 explain how the railroads litigated increasingly numerous personal injury suits and lobbied increasingly antipathetic legislatures. Of central importance in these chapters is the high accident rate for southern railways, a brutal fact that stood in stark contrast to the lobbyists' persistent claims of progress and economic development. Chapters 5 and 6 follow these same themes through the Progressive period, as southern reformers focused on railroad abuses in the legal, political, and humanitarian arenas. Chapter 7 turns to the development of regulatory commissions as a means for railroads to gain stability and predictability and for shippers, businessmen, and citizens to have a forum for their views. Railroad lawyers, especially state level and general counsel, disagreed initially over whether to fight the commissions, but eventually they came to see regulation by commission as an opportunity to gain stability, away from increasingly unpredictable courts and legislatures. Chapter 8 follows the themes of the previous chapter into the area of employers' liability and personal injury, where railroad attorneys eventually sought more federal regulation and predictability. Finally Chapter 9 returns to the interstate railroad corporation legal department, its development, and its consequences. The division of the bar that began in the 1880s widened into a gulf in the 1900s. Local attorneys for the railroads found that progressive changes did not always bring them business; commissions and uniform laws meant less business and restricted opportunities for them. If commissions could resolve all of the problems, if corporation general counsels succeeded in getting predictability through the law, some may have wondered, will there be any lawsuits? Corporate attorneys were by no means united. They still represented the views and interests of their clients, but they were troubled by the new circumstances.

Finally, this book tries to draw a social history of the southern political economy and of the lawyers themselves. The legal departments of these large interstate corporations served as a kind of clearinghouse for nearly all of the ways that the railroads brought change to southern communities. Within the world of the lawyers we can see how the railroads tried to use the law and the legal process to mold the political economy to their ends and what kind of opposition they faced. While boards of directors set policy and made financial deals, the railroad lawyers in the legal departments struggled with the everyday consequences of the railroads' operations. If we hope to survey the landscape of the southern political economy, the tensions surrounding the interstate railroad corporations, the controversies that they sparked, the movements that they gave rise to, and the trail that they blazed, the legal departments provide the best vantage point.

This book tries to stand right at the crossroads where business, law, and politics intersected. I wanted to see how the region as a whole changed and adapted to the process of industrialization, as guided by large interstate corporations—what costs were incurred, what bargains struck, and what chits called in. I wanted to chronicle the southern experience with large-scale industrial economic development. And I wanted to understand whether the lawyers of the New South acted as blind facilitators without regard for the moral choices in their work or as more enlightened brokers, aware of the costs and inequities before them.

Acknowledgments

This book would not have been possible without the support and assistance given me by many people, foremost among them being Edward L. Ayers of the University of Virginia. Were it not for his careful guidance, thorough readings, expert counsel, and good humor, this book would not have been the same. I owe more than acknowledgments to this wonderful teacher, friend, and colleague.

Charles W. McCurdy at the University of Virginia deserves great thanks for his advice and critical readings along the way, as do Michael F. Holt and Mark W. Thomas at the University of Virginia, who helped me focus this work at an early stage. The University of Virginia Department of History supported the research for this book through a Southern Fellowship. Without this support I would not have been able to travel to the archives in Houston and Chicago.

Several historians and law professors read the book in its manuscript form and offered valuable suggestions and support. Among them my thanks go especially to Dan Ernst of Georgetown Law School, Tom Green of Michigan Law School, and Dirk Hartog of Princeton University's Department of History. I am particularly grateful to Dirk Hartog for his early support of my manuscript and his thoughtful suggestions on how to improve it. I would also like to thank the anonymous readers for Louisiana State University Press, who carefully read the manuscript and offered sound advice for its improvement.

Many archivists gave me invaluable assistance on this project, guiding me through the sometimes labyrinth-like railroad records. Laura Katz Smith at Virginia Polytechnic Institute helped me on my many trips to work in the tremendous Norfolk and Southern Railroad Collection. Dale Patterson helped me through the Louisville & Nashville records at the University of Louisville. Mark Cedek steered me about the state of records of the Mid-West and Southern lines and helped me through the Barriger Collection at the Mercantile Library in St. Louis. All three have my thanks. I would also like to thank the staff archivists who helped me in my research at the Newberry Library, the Southern Historical Collection at the University of North Carolina–Chapel Hill, Rice University, and the Houston Metropolitan Research Center.

My thanks also go to the firm of Baker & Botts for its permission to use material from the Baker & Botts History Collection at Rice University. I wish more law firms would consider placing their old records in libraries for use in research. Ken Lipartito at the University of Houston gave me help and guidance on my research trip at Rice University's collection, and I extend my thanks to him also.

Many others have helped me along the way, either reading my work or talking about it with me. I would like to thank George H. Gilliam for his thoughtful reading and good friendship, and for his bringing to my attention the quotation that stands as the epigraph for this book; Lindsay Robertson for his support and friendship; and Alan Howard, Rebecca Edwards, Brad Mittendorf, Alice Carter, Jack and Julia Corrado, and Scot French.

Finally, I want to thank my family. I come from a family of lawyers and educators, and they were never very far from my mind as I wrote this book. My father, brother, uncle, and grandfather, lawyers all, have at one time or another represented big corporations, including railroads, lobbied in the legislature and city council, and struggled to build up their practices. My father and brother encouraged me every step of the way, shoring up my resolve when on rare occasions it lagged. My mother, a teacher and social worker, provided the balance and perspective that I needed for this work, not to mention the model for determination and grit that every scholar needs to survive. My sister's example of fortitude showed me what perseverance was all about. They all have provided me with encouragement and have greeted this project at every turn with enthusiasm and support.

My wife, Heather, gave her generous spirit to this work, listening to me when I needed it most and always offering her support.

Abbreviations Used in Notes

BBHC-RU   Baker & Botts History Collection, Rice University Library

GPRR-VPI   Georgia Pacific Railroad Company Records, Virginia Polytechnic Institute

ICRR-NL   Illinois Central Railroad Company Records, Newberry Library

L&NRR-UL   Louisville & Nashville Railroad Company Records, University of Louisville Archives and Records Center

N&W-VPI   Norfolk & Western Railway Company Records, Virginia Polytechnic Institute

PRAC   *Proceedings of the Railroad Attorneys' Conference* (followed by year of publication), in John W. Barringer III National Railroad Collection, St. Louis Mercantile Library

R&DRR-VPI   Richmond & Danville Railroad Company Records, Virginia Polytechnic Institute

SFRR-HMRC   Gulf, Colorado & Santa Fe Railroad Company Records, Houston Metropolitan Research Center

SHC-UNC   Southern Historical Collection, University of North Carolina–Chapel Hill

Abbreviations Used in Notes

SRy-VPI   Southern Railway Company Records, Virginia Polytechnic
               Institute

UVA   Alderman Library, University of Virginia

VHS   Virginia Historical Society

VPI   Virginia Polytechnic Institute

LAWYERING FOR THE RAILROAD

ONE

Building the Interstate Railroads:
Right-of-Way and Construction

In nearly every nineteenth-century southern county seat, two buildings stood at the center of the landscape—the courthouse and the railroad depot. The courthouse was often highly visible, its neoclassical architecture evoking the principles of justice, truth, and resolution. Every month citizens of the county gathered to take their grievances to their peers and to hear their officials prosecute those who violated the law. Around the corner from the courthouse, usually within a block or two, was "lawyers' row," a street of townhouses where the lawyers resided when court was in session. In the larger towns, such as Staunton, Virginia, or Greenville, Mississippi, the more prominent attorneys had offices in town close to the court. In these places the railroad depot sat low on the horizon, usually only a few blocks from the courthouse and always abuzz with activity day and night. Its architecture spoke of the more pedestrian virtues of efficiency and business. There was more than a connection of proximity between the courthouse and the train station. They were where most of the business of the New South took place—lawsuits and traffic.

Lawyers traveled between these buildings regularly, doing a brisk business in the New South, since more and more traffic seemed to spawn more and more lawsuits. In each county, town, and state through which their lines ran, railroad corporations retained attorneys to represent their interests. These corporate attorneys became a powerful group of pro-growth advocates, and many became the most articulate and effective proponents of the new business economy in the region. "With the abolition of slavery," one North Carolina railroad lawyer explained in an address before the Alabama Bar Association, "the commanding power of the planter class in the South came to an end." In its place, this attorney contended, lawyers succeeded to the mantle of power and influence in the region: "Probably in no State or country is the influence of lawyers more deeply felt than in the South."[1]

The railroad lawyers worked from within localities to open communities to economic development, build support for the new business economy, and extend the reach of their interstate corporate clients. The coming of the interstate railroad to virtually every corner of the South in the 1880s promised growth and opportunity. At the same time it threatened the independence and power of localities. By 1890 nine out of ten southerners lived in counties serviced by a railroad; their isolated communities became connected with distant markets, cities, and industries. What the interstate railroad brought to southern towns and counties in newer products and broader markets, it also took away in autonomy and stability. In this conflict-prone and fluid situation, tension over the terms and implications of railroad expansion pulled southerners in different directions. Those who profited or benefited from the railroad seemed willing to overlook its ugly consequences of property damage and inequity. But many southerners could ignore neither the railroad's ill effects nor its apparent manipulation of the democratic process. Whatever their specific reactions

---

1. Fabius H. Busbee, "Duty of Southern Lawyers Toward Negro Question," *Alabama Bar Association Proceedings* (1904), 107. Gail Williams O'Brien, *The Legal Fraternity and the Making of a New South Community, 1848–1882* (Athens: University of Georgia Press, 1986), 139, accords lawyers the role of influential brokers in the New South. Peter W. Bardaglio also views lawyers as part of a governing elite in the New South. See Peter W. Bardaglio, "Lawyers, Lynching, and Governance in the New South, 1880–1900," paper presented at the Annual Meeting of the Southern Historical Association, Louisville, Kentucky, 12 November 1994. National studies have accorded lawyers a significant role in the development of big business: see Morton Keller, *Affairs of State: Public Life in Late Nineteenth Century America* (Cambridge, Mass.: Belknap Press of Harvard University Press, 1977), 350. Keller describes lawyers as "the chief engineers of the new business economy." One recent account of the Houston firm of Baker & Botts examines the role of lawyers in the formation and development of business in the New South. Kenneth Lipartito and Joseph Pratt, *Baker and Botts in the Development of Modern Houston* (Austin: University of Texas Press, 1991). See also Kenneth Lipartito, "What Have Lawyers Done for American Business? The Case of Baker and Botts of Houston," *Business History Review* 64 (autumn 1990): 489–526.

to the railroad's transformative effects, many voiced great unease about the place of the interstate corporation in their society.[2]

Attitudes toward railroads among jurors, judges, local lawyers, and businessmen varied from one locality to another, leaving railroads with the unenviable task of attending to these unstable boundaries. In each county, town, or city, local power emanated from "courthouse cliques"—groups of attorneys, judges, and active government officials. These people controlled the levers of the democratic process by which businesses and individuals negotiated their goals. The local leaders approved plans, adjudicated disputes, negotiated settlements, proposed and weighed changes in ordinances. By no means did they do so without debate or faction, but they controlled the process. From the 1880s well into the twentieth century, no railroad corporation could afford to ignore these people, their friends, or their concerns.

If localities demanded the railroads' attention, so did the states. A long tradition of states' rights in the South combined with a highly federalized constitutional structure in the 1880s to present interstate railroads with a variety of state issues and personalities. Like localities writ large, southern states expected to have some degree of control over corporations that operated inside their borders. As non-southerners came to dominate railroad corporate boards, many states enacted legislation requiring board of directors' meetings to take place within the state. Government officials invited railroads into their states and localities only to find that the reality of the railroad business often pushed aside their expectations of favorable rates, responsive policies, and sympathetic management. Fears of outside control and of its consequences fed state-wide opposition to the railroads' way of doing business. Nearly every southern state at some point after 1880 acted on its frustration and tried to tame the power of large interstate railroad corporations.

2. For a comprehensive analysis of this growth and its social, economic, and political effects on the region, see Edward L. Ayers, *The Promise of the New South: Life After Reconstruction* (Oxford: Oxford University Press, 1992). See p. 9 for data on county railroad growth. For an account of the railroads' transformation of the South's local political economy, see Steven Hahn, *The Roots of Southern Populism: Yeoman Farmers and the Transformation of the Georgia Upcountry, 1850–1890* (New York: Oxford University Press, 1983). See also Ronald D. Eller, *Miners, Millhands, and Mountaineers: Industrialization of the Appalachian South, 1880–1930* (Knoxville: University of Tennessee Press, 1982), and Altina L. Waller, *Feud: Hatfields, McCoys, and Social Change in Appalachia, 1860–1900* (Chapel Hill: University of North Carolina Press, 1988).

In this highly charged environment southern railroad companies initiated unprecedented expansion and development. Although the southern roads east of the Mississippi River laid only 2,650 miles of track in the seventies, an increase of 25 percent, they built 14,396 miles in the eighties—more than doubling the total mileage. For the South as a whole, railroad mileage increased in the 1880s by 135 percent, outpacing the national average of 86 percent. This boisterous growth represented the beginnings of large-scale industrial development in a predominantly agrarian region. Not only was this growth far stronger and broader than that of the 1870s, but it was of a wholly different character. In the 1870s southern railroad promoters rushed to develop local lines and territories. Designed to serve a town or city, these lines often tied a local product to a distribution point and allowed local capitalists to control transportation costs. The depression of the seventies, though, cast doubt on the viability of these disconnected, local schemes. Many southern railroads began to seek non-southern capital and to expand beyond their territories. In the process of expansion and consolidation, most of the region's large railroads became national corporations whose major stock- and bondholders resided in the North or abroad. The shift from local to outside control in the years around 1880 did not go unnoticed among corporate attorneys. James T. Weatherly, assistant general counsel for the Georgia Pacific in the 1880s, referred to it in a bar association speech in 1884. "The local railroads of former times," he told his fellow Alabama bar members, "have become parts of great systems, traversing the length and breadth of this continent. They have introduced into our judicial system new causes of legal controversy."[3]

To many southerners, interstate railroad corporations displayed all of the ugly characteristics of monopoly power. In their search for through

---

3. C. Vann Woodward, *Origins of the New South, 1877–1913* (Baton Rouge: Louisiana State University Press, 1951), 120. See also John F. Stover, *The Railroads of the South, 1865–1900: A Study in Finance and Control* (Chapel Hill: University of North Carolina Press, 1955), 61, 125, for detailed accounts of the slow growth in the 1870s. Maury Klein and Kozo Yamamura, "The Growth Strategies of Southern Railroads, 1865–1893," *Business History Review* 41 (winter 1967): 358, 375–76. See also Maury Klein, *The Great Richmond Terminal: A Study in Businessmen and Business Strategy* (Charlottesville: University Press of Virginia, 1970), 16–29; and Maury Klein, "Southern Railroad Leaders, 1865–1893: Identities and Ideologies," *Business History Review* 42 (autumn 1968): 288–310. James T. Weatherly, "Judicial Delay in Alabama," *Alabama Bar Association Proceedings* (1884), 48.

traffic after 1880, southern railroad managers viewed small, independent lines as threats to stability, so they swallowed them up, creating huge monopolies. For the larger systems, managers moved to build new lines and consolidate others to protect their traffic from instability. Southern citizens and businessmen, often connected to local enterprises, expected both rate stability and railroad competition when the railroad came to their town, but the nature of the railroad business demonstrated throughout the period the inherent contradiction in their demand. Competition fostered wildly unstable rates, and only railroad pools seemed to maintain rate predictability—and even then only for the short life span of most agreements. Pooling limited competition and smacked of unfairness, so it was never popular with the public, even if it kept rates stable.[4]

As southern railroads developed after 1880 into interstate systems, expanded to more than double their mileage in the decade, and came under the control of non-local interests, these companies turned to the region's lawyers as negotiators. These railroad-corporation attorneys developed legal and political strategies for their expansionist clients. In effect they were the first corporate attorneys in the region, representing an entirely new class of citizens. When the Houston & Texas Central Railway Company's receivership, for example, brought a change from local to non-southern ownership of the company in 1886, the parties turned to prominent Texas railroad attorneys to mediate their differences. W. B. Botts urged William Pitt Ballinger, a fellow Texas railroad-corporation lawyer, to attend the road's reorganization meeting: "It is his [the new owner's] desire to co-operate with his colleagues in all things proper and as he is comparatively a stranger to them he, in a great measure, relied upon your presence and your good counsel in avoiding any unpleasantness or misunderstanding." Fearing the partisanship that such reorganization might generate, the new owners sought Ballinger as a "peacemaker" whose "presence was desirable in the event that any differences should arise between the non-resident counsel."[5]

Most southern railroad-corporation lawyers had little interest in retard-

---

4. Maury Klein, *A History of the Louisville & Nashville Railroad* (New York: Macmillan, 1972), 316–20. See also Klein, "Competition and Regulation: The Railroad Model," *Business History Review* (summer 1990): 311–25; and Klein, *Great Richmond Terminal*, 287–88.

5. W. B. Botts to William Pitt Ballinger, 29, 3 June 1886, Ballinger Letter Book, BBHC-RU.

ing industrial growth in their communities and states, and stepped easily into the role of brokering for the railroads. They welcomed the growth of interstate railroad systems in the eighties and put together a capitalist consensus to promote railroad development within southern towns, counties, and states. In towns and small cities throughout the South, attorneys vied for the business that the railroads brought with them. They were motivated largely by their own need for steady work, seeing the railroad as the milking cow of the legal business in their area. Though non-locals owned and operated most lines, railroad attorneys suggested that what was good for the railroad was good for the region, and indeed good for the locality. The consequences of their advocacy, then, included not only jobs, expansion, and growth for the South but also a business and legal environment overtly favorable to railroads.

Some sacrifices were necessary, the lawyers suggested, in the successful promotion of regional economic development. By equating their companies' growth with that of the region, railroad lawyers hitched their futures to the promise of this economic development. Public criticism of the southern corporate lawyer as a dependent slave of northern executive officers stung sensitive nerves in these attorneys. They did not need the criticism of others to apprehend their anomalous position. Just as they facilitated the introduction of outside power in their localities, they experienced a distinct loss of control over their own practices. Easily labeled as accomplices to further regional servitude, railroad-corporation lawyers saw themselves as independent brokers, pushing the region to grow its way out of dependence. Practical notions governed most attorneys' thoughts and actions, but some heard poignant reminders of their conflicting circumstances in orders passed down the legal department hierarchy, in newspaper editorials, in legislative committee discussions, and even in bar association speeches. Their personal struggles over the terms of corporate dependence in their practices mirrored those of the South's inner war over the development of large-scale industrial capitalism.

In the mid–nineteenth century southern lawyers took advantage of their position close to the action of business and economic growth. They were more than just facilitators for entrepreneurs. They personally invested in mines, slaves, land, railroads, factories, banks, foundries, and other local enterprises. After the Civil War young southern attorneys continued to use their practice of law to bring themselves business opportunities. They associated themselves with the Democratic Party and infused it with a program of aggressive economic growth. Practicing in small firms of two or three partners, these young lawyers linked local business growth with social and political conservatism. In many cases, they orchestrated their communities' economic development by connecting business interests with governmental and social institutions.

When interstate railroads evolved in the 1880s from local businesses, young lawyers in cities, towns, and counties across the South stood ready to help these corporations negotiate the terms of their expansion and growth. Railroads brought a large volume of legal business with them into any locality: title work, right-of-way negotiation, casework for claims. Lawyers in small towns were first and foremost small businessmen, and they welcomed the new clients. Many of these nascent corporation attorneys came from privileged families, fought in the Civil War at a young age, and then immediately after the war read law or attended law school. As young practitioners, they combined Democratic Party activism and local entrepreneurship with the practice of law. Active in their local and regional economies before the arrival of interstate railroads, many made a transition from local business attorney to interstate corporation counsel. One young attorney in Virginia, for example, "was despairing of success when the way was opened for an active career of honor and success." The Richmond & Danville Extension Company retained him to work in its legal office for the new Georgia Pacific line. This young attorney's qualifications blended skill with expertise: "it is difficult to say which was most needed, the scientific engineer, the shrewd man of business, the keen lawyer, or the courageous and skillful negotiator." For these lawyers the new circumstances of railroad-corporation growth provided precious opportunities for career advancement and for combining law and economic growth with local, state, and regional development. One southern attorney summed up, "Today the most important litigant in the courts is the corporation, and the most lucrative field in legal attainments is the study of corporation law."[6]

Young, aggressive, and politically active, corporation lawyers in the South grew with the rise of interstate railroad companies in the 1880s. As general solicitor for the Chesapeake & Ohio from 1886 into the 1920s,

6. Memorial sketch of Bernard Peyton, general counsel for the Georgia Pacific Railroad Company, *Alabama Bar Association Proceedings* (1886), 59–62; W. S. McCain, "Railroads as a Factor in the Law," *Alabama Bar Association Proceedings* (1886), 10.

Henry T. Wickham, for example, linked politics with corporate law practice. His father, Williams C. Wickham, was a "lawyer, planter, soldier, and railroad president." In 1874 Henry T. Wickham took a position as assistant attorney with the Chesapeake & Ohio Railroad, which his father had consolidated out of two local Virginia roads and served as president. Five years later, young Wickham was elected to the Virginia House of Delegates. Promoted to assistant counsel, Wickham earned a $2,400 salary, as much as most southern states' circuit court judges. As general solicitor in 1886, Wickham earned $3,540, and in 1887 $3,833, a salary more than Virginia's Supreme Court chief justice. The following year Wickham's value to the C&O increased when he was elected to the Virginia Senate and became chairman of the powerful finance committee. His salary jumped to $5,000, and by 1900 Wickham received $9,000 for his services. Few lawyers in Virginia could boast of such retainers.[7]

Across the South's legislatures and judicial benches, railroad lawyers sat in powerful positions; Wickham was no exception. In Alabama, Thomas Goode Jones, a Louisville & Nashville attorney, served in the state legislature, became Speaker of the Alabama House, governor of the state, and eventually a federal district court judge. Other lawyers in Alabama shared his career path. A. M. Tunstall, one of the Southern Railway's attorneys in Alabama, became Speaker of the Alabama House, and Joel Goldsby, another railroad attorney, became president pro tempore of the Senate. In other southern states the pattern of railroad-attorney Democratic Party legislative power looked much the same. In Virginia, for example, W. Gordon Robertson, Norfolk & Western attorney in Roanoke, served as a delegate to the Virginia House. In Tennessee, James Holmes Cummins served as general attorney for the Chesapeake, Ohio & Southwestern and as a legislator from 1872 to 1876. Cummins served on every Democratic state committee between 1867 and 1896. In Mississippi, Leroy Percy and his law partner William G. Yerger represented the Illinois Central in the Delta, but Percy also represented Washington County at the Democratic conventions, was appointed to fill a vacant U.S. Senate seat, ran for U.S. Senate, and tangled with Mississippi demagogue Theodore G. Bilbo. In Florida, Stephen M. Sparkman, prominent railroad attorney for Henry B. Plant, controlled Democratic Party politics as the party's executive committee

---

7. Williams C. Wickham Family Papers, Box 24, VHS. See also the entry for Henry T. Wickham in Lyon G. Tyler, ed., *Men of Mark in Virginia: Ideals of American Life* (Washington, D.C.: Men of Mark Publishing Co., 1908), 1:254.

chairman. In Texas, George Clark lobbied for the railroads, held the office of secretary of state and attorney general, and ran for governor against James Stephen Hogg.[8]

It seemed that in every southern state railroad lawyers held political office and wielded political power. Railroad-company legal departments grew into tiered hierarchies in which lawyers at the local, state, and national levels represented their companies. In the South, local and state-level attorneys played a crucial role in the introduction and development of large interstate railroads. General counsels, such as Henry T. Wickham, presided over the legal needs of the company, supervised all of the company's attorneys, and monitored important casework. State and local attorneys performed these same functions in their respective jurisdictions. Landing an interstate railroad company retainer required their law practices to secure "the confidence of the most influential and best business men of that section of the country."[9]

In general, railroads found eager southerners when they proposed a new line through a region without railroad service, but construction brought conflict, and completion created opposition. According to one Illinois Central official, "the people are in favor of building a new road and do what they can to promote it, [but] after it is once built and fixed then the policy of the people is usually in opposition." This sequence repeated itself across the South in the eighties. Localities and states wanted railroad growth, but both also expected the railroad corporations' priorities to resemble to their own. They were disappointed to discover that the large interstate railroads often had vastly different priorities. Even more disconcerting to many southerners was the increasingly apparent fact that railroads set their interests according to forces over which localities and states had little control.[10]

---

8. For Jones's career in politics, see Sheldon Hackney, *Populism to Progressivism in Alabama* (Princeton: Princeton University Press, 1969), 11–23; Albert D. Kirwan, *Revolt of the Rednecks: Mississippi Politics, 1876–1925* (Lexington: University of Kentucky Press, 1951), 109–21, 191–210, 310–11. Obituary, unidentified newspaper clipping, 1896, on James Holmes Cummins. I would like to thank Sara C. Flatau for sending this obituary to me. See Robert C. Cotner, *James Stephen Hogg: A Biography* (Austin: University of Texas Press, 1959).

9. Memorial sketch of Edward L. Russell, general counsel for the Mobile & Ohio Railroad, *Alabama Bar Association Proceedings* (1907), 199–201.

10. Quoted in Robert H. Wiebe, *The Search for Order, 1877–1920* (New York: Hill & Wang, 1967), 46.

Before any railroad could be built or extended, it needed to acquire right-of-way through its projected course. Each railroad company hoped to secure valid title to its right-of-way at minimal cost, both in terms of dollars and offended or angry landowners. As the southern railroads expanded to double their mileage in the 1880s, their attorneys worked feverishly to keep up. They rushed into all corners of the South to gather and clear titles for right-of-way. Often they were the first railroad-company representatives in an undeveloped area. The lawyers bargained with landowners, trying to mediate their needs and concerns with those of the railroad.

Railroad corporations derived extraordinary power from the law. Of particular utility was the railroads' right of eminent domain, and it punctuated nearly all property negotiations between railroad lawyers and southerners. Under this legal principle the state bestowed its public power of property condemnation upon its railroad corporations. If, after a railroad offered bona fide compensation for property necessary for the development of the road's tracks and a landowner still refused to relinquish deed, the railroad retained the power to condemn the property for a fair value determined by the courts.[11]

Because most southern railroads expanded through private property without a land grant or subsidy from the state or federal government, they relied on negotiation with landowners for title to their right-of-way. Once a railroad company established a favored line for development, it needed to secure good title to the right-of-way before construction went forward. The entire future of the line depended on clear, undisputed title, but a briar patch of personalities, laws, and rights threatened to undermine any such venture. When the Illinois Central considered buying the Memphis, Selma & Brunswick Railroad in 1883, for example, the president dispatched general counsel James Fentress to examine the title to the roads' right-of-way. "This hurried review," Fentress reported, "shows that it is full of lawsuits to any solvent party who may buy it. My advice is to have nothing to do with it." A revenue-producing railroad, such as the Illinois Central, became an attractive target for unsatisfied parties who might use a title suit to get some return from worthless stock. The Illinois Central

11. Nearly every railroad law treatise or manual treats the concept of eminent domain. For example, see Simeon E. Baldwin, *American Railroad Law* (Boston, 1904), 81; and Charles F. Beach Jr., *The Modern Law of Railways* (San Francisco, 1890).

steered clear of ownership, preferring in this case to work out a traffic arrangement to tap into the Memphis market. Referring to Fentress's report, the Illinois Central president concluded, "You will see . . . to secure a perfect title . . . would require time, expense, and litigation." Large railroads, such as the Illinois Central, tried to avoid all three of these.[12]

Sometimes local railroad attorneys in charge of securing titles for a new line performed sloppy work. When the Richmond & Danville initiated a takeover of the Oxford & Clarksville Railroad in 1888, the road's officials requested the original deeds and right-of-way documents from the responsible local attorney, Robert Watson Winston. Winston, though, failed to respond promptly. When he finally sent his documentation weeks later, O&C officials returned the deeds with a stern reprimand: "they seem to be in very bad form. Next to none of them recorded; some are witnessed but not acknowledged."[13]

Poorly crafted and weakly documented right-of-way titles threatened to dog the originally incorporated railroad as well as any subsequent owners. The initial job of securing proper title required diligence, careful attention to detail, and diplomacy on the part of the negotiating attorneys. Local knowledge, though, made these negotiations more successful, so large railroads retained local attorneys for this often delicate work. The small firm of Anderson & Edmondson, for example, in Lexington, Virginia, performed the title work necessary for the construction of the Richmond & Allegheny Railroad in the early eighties. The road from Richmond to Clifton Forge opened in 1881, and construction was under way on other sections. William A. Anderson and his partner were strong backers of regional economic development and the extension of railroad service into southwestern Virginia. They negotiated a variety of obstacles and challenges to their northern-owned, New York–financed railroad client.[14]

---

12. J. C. Clarke to Stuyvesant Fish, 15 September 1885, Board Supporting Documents, ICRR-NL. For a similar case, see Baker & Botts to William Pitt Ballinger, 22 September 1887. Baker & Botts to William Pitt Ballinger, 11 October 1887, William Pitt Ballinger Letter Book, 1886–87, BBHC-RU; James Fentress to J. C. Clarke, 16 June 1883, Board Supporting Documents, ICRR-NL.

13. E. D. Christian to Robert W. Winston, 15 May 1888, Robert Watson Winston Papers, SHC-UNC.

14. For the Richmond & Allegheny's history, see Henry Varnum Poor, *Manual of the Railroads* (New York: H. V. & H. W. Poor, 1883), 410.

Property owners, according to local attorneys such as Anderson & Edmondson, stood to gain from the entrance of the railroad into the region. Land values would rise and distant markets become more easily accessible, these attorneys insisted, as they trumpeted the railroad's economic-development benefits to the neighboring landholders. Anderson typically negotiated with the landowner for an "option" on the land at a certain price; only if unsuccessful did he turn to condemnation proceedings. The condemnation process brought the landowner and the railroad company before a commission of local citizens, which heard arguments on valuation and made a binding determination on the damages. For the railroad, favorable relations with the commissioners became an essential element in this process. The railroad considered it the responsibility of the local attorney to ensure a railroad-friendly commission. In practice this goal proved elusive for the local attorneys, and commissions often inflated local land values.

Local railroad attorneys preferred, therefore, to deal directly with landowners and tried to avoid settling right-of-way disputes before the commissions of citizens. In the case of Luther Watts's land, the Richmond & Allegheny attorneys worried that an old canal right-of-way might not carry full rights with it. The railroad acquired only oral permission from the previous owner of the Watts property; in other words, the railroad had not obtained a deeded right-of-way. Anderson visited Watts at his home and negotiated a settlement of $335 for the right-of-way—the personal solicitation brought a favorable settlement for the railroad. "From our subsequent experience," Anderson revealed in his report, "we are inclined to think a commission would have allowed Mr. Watts double this sum."[15]

Fewer parties involved in the negotiation usually translated into more favorable settlements for the railroad. One landowner along the Richmond & Allegheny considered his option price too low and petitioned the board of directors of the railroad for an increase. He explained to the attorneys his signature of the original option: "I did not wish to do an act or be charged with being a stumbling block in the way of said railroad being built. I gave the option for this reason, at a less amount than I would have done." Ideally, of course, the local railroad attorneys fostered exactly such a herd mentality, sweeping up large chunks of right-of-way at once.[16]

15. William A. Anderson, "Title Report for the Richmond & Allegheny Railroad, March 1881–March 1882," William Alexander Anderson Papers, UVA.
16. John J. Gillock to J. K. Edmondson, 20 July 1881, ibid.

Competition from other railroad promoters spoiled the chances for favorable options, as Anderson and the Richmond & Allegheny discovered in 1882. Representatives of the Shenandoah Valley Railroad entered the area and started bidding up the land. "The estimates of the land owners of the value of their lands, and of the damages occasioned by the building of a railway through them, became enlarged," Anderson reported to the Richmond & Allegheny president, "and public sentiment in the county which had been decidedly opposed to the allowance or claim of anything like excessive damages, and had been very favorable to all railroad enterprises, shifted over to the other side." Anderson found that his job changed almost overnight, from securing easy deals to extracting difficult compromises. For the local citizens along the proposed right-of-way, the advantages of railroad competition and the costly features of railroad monopoly became obvious. From the first negotiation of a railroad for right-of-way through a town or county, southerners learned the sheer power of monopoly.[17]

It took only one landowner along the right-of-way to interrupt a title windfall and cause complications for the railroad attorneys. It was no surprise to the attorneys that the most difficult negotiation along the Richmond & Allegheny's right-of-way involved a large landowner and local businessman, John Davidson. The projected line of the railroad cut through Davidson's extensive dairy operation, passing through a tenant house and near another. Worse, the line divided prime agricultural land and separated Davidson's large flouring mill from the bulk of the property. "We were practically in Mr. Davidson's power," Anderson confessed in his report. After "repeated and protracted interviews" between Anderson and Davidson, they achieved a negotiated settlement. Davidson proposed several options to the railroad. In the end the company agreed to pay $10,000 for the land right-of-way, and Francis French, the road's president, personally bought the flouring mill for $8,500.[18]

The proposed line of the Richmond & Allegheny also threatened to divide the property of Anderson's law partner, J. K. Edmondson. Ander-

17. William A. Anderson to Francis French, 24 March 1882, ibid. See Charles P. Jones to William A. Anderson, 12 January 1891, for a similar complaint.

18. Anderson, "Title Report," ibid. For more correspondence on the Davidson lawsuit, see Richmond & Allegheny Railroad Papers, Leyburn Library, Washington and Lee University.

son's title report revealed that the attorneys expected the commission to value the property at $2,400, but the company's president paid Edmondson $5,250 for the land. In this case as well, Francis French's personal account accumulated assets surrounding the railroad's right-of-way. French expected to sell the property later or develop it in some way after the railroad had been built. However, connections and business with the railroad paid off for local attorneys and large landowners immediately, as they took advantage of insider information and knowledge. Such deals were commonplace. Their cumulative effect was to secure initial loyalty from local attorneys to the corporation and bring about resentment on the part of landowners who may have gotten wind of these deals.

Protests emerged from unlikely sources to contest the Richmond & Allegheny's effort to secure title for its right-of-way. According to Anderson's title report, "a comparatively young widow and a number of children" threatened to disrupt the road's extension into the North River valley near Lexington, Virginia. The sudden death of the title holder, Mr. Hartsook, with whom the attorneys had negotiated but not exercised an option, prompted the railroad to notify the widow of its acceptance of the contract on the terms. According to Anderson, the widow "repudiated the contract, and under the advice of counsel insisted that the option . . . was not binding upon his heirs."[19]

The stakes were high for the railroad. "We were very apprehensive," Anderson confessed, "that the Court would give her dower in kind [the house] in which event she would have the company practically in her power. . . . in this contingency the last dollar which could be extorted from the company would be extracted." To build his case, Anderson tracked down the adult children heirs, some of whom lived out of the state, and "turned" them against the widow. As it turned out, Anderson discovered the real title belonged to another woman and successfully defended a suit by the widow to evict the railroad company from the property without using the testimony of the children.[20]

Savvy landowners understood that severe engineering considerations, especially in the Appalachian Mountain region, constricted the railroad and gave them bargaining power in their negotiations over the right-of-way. Like the Hartsook widow, Walter S. Gunn recognized the Rich-

19. Anderson, "Title Report," Anderson Papers, UVA.
20. Ibid.

mond & Allegheny's desperation for right-of-way through his property, but Gunn, a New York resident, carried the power of valid title and strong local connections. Anderson relied on the Richmond & Allegheny's acquisition of an old canal company's right-of-way through Gunn's estate, but Gunn challenged this title. "Through his counsel, Judge Sheffey," Anderson reported, Gunn "claims that he is entitled to damages on account of the change of the use of the canal land." Represented by a former judge and other local railroad lawyers, Walter Gunn mounted a serious challenge to Anderson and the Richmond & Allegheny. Anderson forwarded the problem to John W. Daniel, Richmond & Allegheny counsel and prominent attorney in southwestern Virginia, and to the road's general counsel with the observation: "The question is a vital one for the company." Though the terms of this settlement remain unclear, Gunn's local connections, strong legal representation, and proper title combined to make the railroad compromise.

Railroad attorneys worked to solve these vital questions of title and right-of-way with as little trouble and hard feelings as possible. When necessary, these attorneys brought corporation power to bear on recalcitrant locals. They resorted to condemnation proceedings only as a last measure. They understood that in the long run their corporations did not benefit from leaving behind battered and bruised feelings among the local citizens. When the Alabama Great Southern built an extension near Eutaw, Alabama, for example, the local attorneys there orchestrated an arbitration to resolve conflicting damage assessments between some landowners and the railroad. Two landowners held out against the railroad's offers for right-of-way, hoping to secure a station on their property. The railroad's local attorneys, Thomas C. Clark and J. Pickens McQueen, proposed a binding arbitration board to assess damages instead of condemnation proceedings. The arbitration, they argued in a letter to the road's chief engineer, "saves the delay and expense of a petition to condemn the land before the Probate Court, and settles the matter amicably."[21]

Time, money, and good local relations added up to valuable commodities for a developing railroad corporation, none of which railroad attorneys wanted to lose. With proper title the property owner commanded a powerful base in the law in any contest with a railroad company. If the property

---

21. Clark & McQueen to Cabell Breckinridge, 9 October 1881, Alabama Great Southern Railroad Records, VPI.

owner was prominent, local citizens backed his cause. If he was wealthy, he could afford to hire good counsel. A landowner with clear title, even without strong local influence, posed a considerable obstacle to the railroad.

Some attorneys could see that the railroads went from hero to goat in southern communities in the time it took to build them. "We have entered upon a new era," W. S. McCain told the Alabama Bar Association in 1886, "—an era of jealousy, mistrust and hostility. Both the people and the [railroad] corporations have taken counsel as to their legal rights." McCain outlined several reasons why the railroads found such antagonism, including their complete dominance over their employees, their violation of the Sabbath, and their monopolistic tendencies. "The truth is," he declared, "our railroad corporations have become a vast *imperium in imperis*." McCain pointed to the right of eminent domain as an example of railroad power gone too far. He suggested that only the state could exercise this right for the public good and that privately owned railroad corporations were making a mockery of the concept of eminent domain. "At every term of the court," McCain pointed out, "we find suits brought in the name of railroad companies to condemn to property of citizens." The practice should be stopped, he suggested, "for no other reason than to inculcate among the people the true idea, that no one but the State can take the property of a citizen."[22]

Nevertheless, the lawyers' negotiations often engendered hard feelings and inequity, as widows found their land taken without compensation, or farmers had their fields cut in half, most at well below market prices. Only a few prominent or well-represented men were able to squeeze an equitable settlement out of the company. Some of the inequity and hard feelings were part and parcel of the process, but it went beyond that too often, and aggrieved locals throughout the South watched the right-of-way cleared through their property, a harbinger of railway construction and operation.

As large railroads across the South expanded and consolidated in the 1880s, they found new forms of opposition to their operations. Negotiation for right-of-way brought some opposition even when locals called for railroad expansion in their area. Construction and completion spurred more opponents. When the Norfolk & Western Railroad Company investors took over the old Atlantic, Mississippi & Ohio in 1881, they discov-

22. W. S. McCain, "Railroads as a Factor in the Law," 9–30.

ered construction contractors waiting to be paid. The contractors' attorneys wrote to the Norfolk & Western chairman that his clients were "men of character, position and influence, largely engaged in business which makes them customers of your road." Moreover, they pointed out, "they are men whose hearty good will, commercially and politically, will be an important factor in the success of your enterprise." Large railroads entered localities and states populated by "men of influence" whose opposition came from many sources. Most southern railroads used their local and state attorneys to develop their own commercial and political ties and their best legal defenses to meet this opposition.[23]

A mix of legal difficulties over property rights bedeviled the Richmond & Allegheny Railroad Company as it plodded through construction. Building a railroad seemed to generate disaffected parties on both sides of a right-of-way. Landowners, though generally supportive of railroad development in their area, defended their property against damage from construction and operation of the railroad. When the Richmond & Allegheny construction crews began taking gravel and ballast from a small island in the North River, for example, the property owner informed the railroad of her intentions to "take the proper steps to protect myself." The railroad's right-of-way negotiations had proven "fruitless" with this landowner, and the company had resorted to condemnation proceedings. After some investigation, Anderson concluded that the island "was not condemned or acquired by the company but still belongs to Mrs. Johns." He advised his client "to order the work to stop. Your company has no rights upon that island."[24]

In another incident, the Richmond & Allegheny's construction caused severe damage to an adjacent county road. "We have been apprehensive," Anderson explained, "lest the matter of the obstruction of this road would be brought before the grand jury, or other steps adopted which would embarrass the company, but so far have been able to suppress and repress such inimical measures." When the county authorities filed motions in court, Anderson recommended quick compromise and railroad payment for the construction of a new road.[25]

23. John Lyon to Clarence H. Clarke, 16 March 1881, N&W-VPI.

24. E. G. Johns to Decatur Axtell, 13 June 1882, Anderson Papers, UVA; Anderson, "Title Report," ibid.; W. A. Anderson to G. W. Agee, 22 June 1882, ibid.

25. W. A. Anderson to Decatur Axtell, 24 March 1882, ibid.

Once railroad corporations completed construction and started to operate, they often faced joint suits from landowners along the right-of-way when railroad-related events caused property damage. Engine sparks caused fires and crop damage, for example. One landowner along the Richmond & Allegheny informed Anderson that the railroad company ought to buy his tobacco barn near the tracks before it accidentally sets fire to it and has to pay damages, not only for the barn but for its contents. Railroad construction, especially abutments, dikes, and bridges, sometimes resulted in flooding from overflow water. In all of these cases landowners needed unity and strong representation to challenge the railroad. "It seems that the people along the right-of-way have determined to get some money out of the company," one Louisville & Nashville Kentucky attorney explained to the general counsel. In this instance flood damage provided the cause. "Leonidas Redwine has subsidized the attorneys branch of the business. . . . At the present rate we will have more suits in this county in a short time than we can chin."[26]

William A. Anderson and other local railroad lawyers realized the potential dangers of trampling over local citizens' property rights. Callous disregard and manipulative legalities spawned resentment and hostility. For many railroad promoters in the New South, locals as often as outsiders, the railroad tracks served as a vehicle for widespread plunder, and, they suggested, public opinion merited little attention. Land companies, mining concerns, hotels, mountain resorts, and manufactories accompanied railroad extension in these visionary promoters' schemes. On these projects railroad promoters often realized huge profits. Southern developers secured options on large tracts of land along or near the planned railroad extension, before selling to speculators and other investors, or to railroad companies. When promoters exploited local citizens' ignorance of the law of contracts, often the corporate railroad attorneys were left to clean up the legal difficulties and deal with the long-term effects of misrepresentation.[27]

26. Echols to William A. Anderson, 2 May 1881, ibid.; O. H. Pollard to F. S. Jouett, 10 April 1912, L&N Railroad File #209, Samuel Wilson Papers, University of Kentucky Library. For a similar set of suits on the Santa Fe, see S. T. Bledsoe to J. W. Terry, 11 April 1908, Box 31, Folder 16, SFRR-HMRC. See also these cases: *Emery et ux. v. Raleigh & Gaston Railroad Company*, 102 N.C. 209; *Mississippi Home Insurance Co. v. Louisville, New Orleans & Texas Railway Co.*, Mississippi Supreme Court, 28 November 1892.

27. On land development, see Justin Fuller, "History of the Tennessee Coal, Iron, and

When the Richmond & Danville Extension Company built the Georgia Pacific Railroad in the early eighties, it inherited legal controversy from the original local syndicate. The Georgia Pacific, its promoters hoped, would unlock the vast coal lands of northern Alabama. General John B. Gordon, Confederate veteran and Georgia Redeemer-era governor, initiated the scheme for a western railroad extension from Atlanta and secured option contracts on nearly 100,000 acres of Alabama mineral lands. Gordon, his brothers, and Georgia governor A. H. Colquitt acquired the rights to the Columbus, Fayette & Decatur Railroad in 1880. Later, when these local promoters sold their interests to the Richmond & Danville Extension Company at a huge profit, Gordon left behind angry citizens and poor legal documentation.[28]

In a special report, the Georgia Pacific general counsel reviewed the titles to the coal lands. Having secured proper title to 56,523 acres, the general counsel halted negotiations: "I found that great and unexpected difficulties stood in the way of carrying these mineral contracts into grant. Outrageous frauds had in numerous instances been practiced on the makers (generally ignorant people) by the agents who secured the contracts, and I found among those people a wide-spread feeling of dissatisfaction and an almost universal determination to resist any attempts to procure the deeds. It was only by continued, expensive and troublesome efforts that we made any headway at all in this work."[29]

According to general counsel Bernard Peyton in 1884, the Georgia Pacific, as an "innocent" purchaser of the deeds through the Richmond & Danville Extension Company, stood to lose the most. Many of the contracts relied on the railroad's meeting certain conditions, such as deadlines

Railroad Company, 1852–1907" (Ph.D. diss., University of North Carolina–Chapel Hill, 1966), and Ethel M. Armes, *The Story of Coal and Iron in Alabama* (1910; reprint, New York: Arno Press, 1973); and on a New South railroad development scheme, see William G. Thomas III, " 'Under Indictment': Thomas Lafayette Rosser and the New South," *Virginia Magazine of History and Biography* (April 1992): 207–32; see also William Way Jr., *The Clinchfield Railroad: The Story of a Trade Route Across the Blue Ridge Mountains* (Chapel Hill: University of North Carolina Press, 1931), and Eller, *Miners, Millhands, and Mountaineers*.

28. See Ralph Lowell Eckert, *John Brown Gordon: Soldier, Southerner, American* (Baton Rouge: Louisiana State University Press, 1989), 244–47, for an account of Gordon's development of the Georgia Pacific Railroad.

29. Bernard Peyton to Jonathan W. Johnston, 20 December 1884, Box 3, GPRR-VPI.

for construction and location of the projected line. In a large number of cases, the railroad did not meet these preconditions and the options became invalid. As a result, these landowners refused to execute the contracts, according to Peyton, "relying on various grounds for defence, generally (and I believe truthfully) that fraud had been practiced upon them in the procurement of the contracts." In sum, the Georgia Pacific general counsel concluded: "I have gotten in about all the deeds that can be secured by personal solicitation. If any others are obtained, it will only be as the consequence of litigation now pending." The suits, he admitted, might lead some "weak-kneed" landowners to settle; in fact, he was counting on it to "secure several thousand acres more."[30]

The sale of the Columbus, Fayette & Decatur to the Georgia Pacific generated other problems as well for the new owners and their attorneys. When the Georgia Pacific expanded its line in 1886 from Birmingham, Alabama, across Mississippi, it ran into opposition from some city and county councils. The city council of Columbus, Mississippi, in particular, objected to the transfer of the city's bonds from the original holder, the Columbus, Fayette & Decatur Railroad, to the Georgia Pacific. According to the city council, the original stockholders of the Columbus, Fayette & Decatur Railroad Company represented local interests, and the subsequent owners—Gordon, his brothers, and Colquitt—agreed in the transfer contract to protect local concerns. The Georgia Pacific, it appeared to the city council, threatened to discriminate against Columbus. Worse, locals did not control the new company, outsiders did.

The city council addressed the issue to the Georgia Pacific in early 1886 in a public letter. It enclosed the contract between the original stockholders of the Columbus, Fayette & Decatur Railroad and the Gordons-Colquitt investors who bought the decrepit company in 1881. As an original investor in the road, the city of Columbus bought shares of stock in 1872 when the citizens voted by the necessary two-thirds majority to invest in the local enterprise. Upon the sale of the company to the Gordons-Colquitt investors, the contract bound the new owners and their successors not to discriminate against Columbus. After the sale to the Gordons-Colquitt investors, the Columbus city council issued $100,000 in new bonds to the CFDRR without holding a public referendum. The bonds came due in 1886, and early in that year the new city council queried

30. Ibid.

the Georgia Pacific management on its intentions: "And as we have been informed that the Georgia Pacific Railway Company has sold or transferred to the Richmond & Danville Extension Company and they to the Pennsylvania Central Company, we would like to know if this contract here inclosed was made a part of and incorporated into these two last named transfers also."[31]

In its letter the city council feared a loss of local control three times removed. As evidence for its charges, the city council cited several prominent citizens who alleged they could prove the Georgia Pacific discriminated against Columbus in rates. According to the council, the Georgia Pacific's lease of the Columbus branch of the Mobile & Ohio effectively ruined Columbus as a terminus of two competing lines, instead leaving it a station on one line. To demonstrate its seriousness of purpose, the city council voted to withhold interest on the railroad bonds until given satisfactory assurance of non-discrimination from the Georgia Pacific.

Georgia Pacific president Jonathan W. Johnston's reply only exacerbated the city's fears of the loss of local control over its investment. Johnston indicated his need to consult with the company's officials in New York before fully answering the council's concerns. "We are very far from desiring any unfriendly controversy," Johnston concluded. "On the contrary we desire to have and cultivate the most friendly relations with [Columbus's] officials and people, and to consult and advance its interests in all reasonable ways." To the locals on the city council his response underscored their point that control no longer rested close to home but instead with some faceless manager in New York.[32]

The Georgia Pacific relied on the efforts of its local attorneys in the city, Orr & Simms, to cultivate friendly relations. The firm used its local connections to influence the struggle over both the issue of discrimination and the city council's decision to withhold bond payments. J. A. Orr's family's control over one of the city's newspapers, the *Democrat*, ensured that the railroad had a prominent voice in the community. The *Democrat*'s editor, C. H. Orr, opposed from the beginning the city council's bond-interest withholding. "If the Georgia Pacific Railroad has discriminated against Columbus we are thoroughly in favor of driving a peg there; but

---

31. *Columbus Dispatch,* 3 February 1886, Box 4, GPRR-VPI (newspaper clippings in notes 30–39 found in this source).
32. Ibid.

to repudiate an honest, moral obligation would not only be ruinous to the city's future welfare, but it falsifies the promise of a majority of her citizens." Moreover, the editors warned, tangling with the railroad meant expensive litigation, something the Orrs understood would cost the city taxpayers.[33]

Some citizens, however, agreed with the city council's maneuvering. One supporter, calling himself "Columbus" in a letter to the *Dispatch*, considered the transfer of the city bonds from the Columbus, Fayette & Decatur to the Georgia Pacific void. Because the constitutionally necessary two-thirds vote in 1872 applied to the former road, and because the bonds were never issued to that failed enterprise, the latter company needed, according to this argument, its own vote to acquire city bonds. In 1881 the city council had authorized $100,000 in bonds issued to the Georgia Pacific in obligation to its 1872 promise to the predecessor company, and "Columbus" considered this transference null and void.[34]

Another citizen, calling himself "Business" in a letter to the *Dispatch*'s editor, supported this argument and elaborated on the reasons behind the city's efforts to bind the Georgia Pacific. The stock of the original Columbus, Fayette & Decatur, he pointed out, "was owned altogether by Columbus men, its officers and directors were Columbus men—in fact it was a Columbus enterprise." In addition, the route of the proposed original road joined Columbus with Decatur and the coal and iron deposits of Alabama. "This was the Company, this the route," he pointed out, "that the people voted $100,000 to! No legislative enactments, no legerdemain of consolidations." The transfer of the original road included a contractual obligation on the part of its successors not to discriminate against Columbus, thereby preserving the local interests' objectives for the line. The Georgia Pacific, according to "Business," broke this binding contractual agreement and discriminated against Columbus. What irked "Business" was Georgia Pacific president Johnston's response to an initial inquiry of rate discrimination. According to him, Johnston responded, "Columbus is too provincial." "It was a real funny remark, and it cut the town to the core," he bitterly reminded the newspaper's readers. The city council, he suggested, should defend local citizens against the Georgia Pacific's discrimination.[35]

33. *Columbus Democrat*, 14 February 1886.
34. *Columbus Index*, 13 February 1886.
35. *Columbus Dispatch*, 7 March 1886.

The Georgia Pacific through its local attorneys orchestrated a citizen campaign to overturn the city council's decision to withhold the bonds' interest payments and to defend its rate structures. First, it worked through a prominent and sympathetic local businessman, R. W. Banks, to broadcast its position. Banks wrote an open letter to the mayor and city council, published in the Columbus *Dispatch*. The thrust of Banks's objection to the council's actions rested on three points, neither of which too closely identified him as a railroad company puppet. Banks's tactics directed public attention to his position in the city as a businessman and taxpayer. The bond-interest withholding, according to Banks, smacked of repudiation and threatened to jeopardize further railroad growth in the area. In addition, the city's fight with the railroad would cost the taxpayers, especially if it engaged in protracted litigation. Moreover, Banks intimated that the council's heavy-handed action betrayed a kind of insecurity that infected the locals' relations with the large interstate railroad company. "Did you expect the president of a large corporation to carry in his hand and head all the papers and all the information touching the company's interest?" asked Banks rhetorically, in defense of Johnston's off-the-cuff response to the initial inquiry.[36]

Meanwhile, the *Democrat*'s editorials and letters continued to support the railroad in the bond fight. The editor printed letters from citizens opposed to the city council's actions. One considered the bond-interest withholding a "lawless use of the people's money." "We need other railroads," this citizen urged. "We may have use for a good name, and fair credit. Railway projects are now being discussed by our enterprising citizens, and he would be a bold fool who would say that we have not a vital self-interest in preserving our character in railway circles." This observer counseled against making "war" with the Georgia Pacific. Businessmen of Columbus, he suggested, should "cultivate good feeling with the only railroad which can bring us coal; the only road that can enable us to compete with Aberdeen, West Point, or Starkville." Praising this and other letters, the *Democrat* editor warned its readers: "The baneful effects of THE OLD REPUDIATION caused our commonwealth to too long 'stink in the nostrils of the world,' and it is to be hoped that no INFANTILE repetition of the curse will ever be forced upon our people."[37]

36. Ibid., 3 March 1886.
37. *Columbus Democrat*, 5 March 1886.

Banks went to work, probably with the help of Orr & Simms, gathering support from the city's businessmen for his fight with the council. Over fifty businessmen signed a letter to the city council published in the city's newspapers in support of Banks's position on the bond-interest-withholding issue. They pointed out that the city collected the tax for the railroad bonds and it should therefore pay the interest. "The credit of the city should not be rashly jeopardized or wantonly sacrificed," they concluded. At the same time, one businessman and member of the city's Board of Trade, M. Brownrigg, disputed the city council's version of the board's request to investigate the nature of the railroad transfer contract between the Columbus, Fayette & Decatur and the Gordons-Colquitt group. According to Brownrigg in a letter to the Columbus *Index*, the Board of Trade asked the city council to investigate the contract, not repudiate the interest on the bonds. Brownrigg emphasized his and the board's opposition to the city council's actions and asked "how is it that our city government could have so far mistaken our best interests as to commence a war upon the only railroad that promises soon to give us the long hoped for connection with the great eastern and northern markets." Brownrigg concluded that the "town was dead" before the arrival of the Georgia Pacific and that the railroad "caused the building of at least one hundred homes and several stores."[38]

Despite this opposition to their actions, the city council stood by its decision to withhold interest payment on the bonds and to hire its own attorneys to investigate the validity of the bond transfer to the Georgia Pacific. In response, Banks organized a citizens' committee and presented to the city council a resolution to pay the bond interest. After the resolution's failure, the city council and the committee came to an agreement: the committee had twenty-four hours to gather signatures for a petition asking the council to rescind its bond-intrest-withholding action. Meanwhile, the city council's attorneys recommended after considerable investigation that the council drop its effort and pay the bond interest. Upon this news, the Columbus *Democrat* increased its opposition to the council and threatened an injunction to prevent the council members from contracting any other lawyers at the city's expense.[39]

Eventually, the city council backed down under the pressure generated by Banks, the *Democrat*, and the railroad attorneys. They authorized pay-

38. *Columbus Index*, 3 March 1886.
39. *Columbus Dispatch*, 2 April 1886.

ment of the interest on the bonds, and the *Democrat* deemed it a "grand victory." Indeed, the paper's editor, C. H. Orr, considered bond-interest payment a matter of local, collective honor. "A senseless cry of 'DIS-CRIMINATION' was raised against our only railroad friend," he pointed out. Moreover, when the railroad attorneys brought a bondholder from Baltimore to testify before the council that he paid money for them in good faith, the council turned him away without a hearing. The newspaper considered this rebuff a despicable affront to a legitimate bondholder and a reckless display of arrogance on the part of the city's representatives.[40]

The controversy revealed the fissures that the development of interstate railroads caused in a southern community. As the Georgia Pacific changed hands, slipping out of local control into that of distant owners, it betrayed new priorities in Columbus. Originally chartered to connect the town with the Alabama coalfields, the road had become something entirely differ-ent—a large, interstate line dependent on through traffic. Citizens became divided over how to deal with this change. Some did not want to offend their only connection to larger markets and were willing to give the corpo-rations leeway. Others, less friendly and not at all trustful, viewed the rail-roads as large-scale schemes in which lawyers and promoters make money while everyone else in the community suffers under the burden of railway financing. In this struggle over the terms of economic development, the railroad's local attorneys manipulated social, political, and business con-nections to protect and promote the new railroad's interests.

The South's divided mind over railroad development had a history. During Reconstruction many Republican politicians used state and local railroad aid schemes as a centerpiece in their political effort to convert southerners to their party's ideals. They engineered state loans and aid packages to railroads, arguing that the railroads would foster prosperity and growth. The depression of the 1870s and the fall of Reconstruction governments across the South dampened the "gospel of prosperity" rail-road aid as a Republican Party program. Democrats and Redeemers, though chastened, continued state and local aid to railroads in the 1880s. Aid from Democrats came mostly in the form of tax advantages and favor-able charters, but convict leasing and local government stock subscriptions also contributed to railroad development.[41]

40. *Columbus Democrat*, undated clipping.

41. On the "gospel of prosperity" see Mark W. Summers, *Railroads, Reconstruction, and the Gospel of Prosperity: Aid Under the Radical Republicans, 1865–1877* (Princeton: Princeton University Press, 1984). See also Eric Foner, *Reconstruction: America's Unfinished*

The desperate hope of economic development in the South and the vision of the railroad as the great salvation continued unabated in the 1870s. While states no longer offered direct aid to railroads, localities and counties stepped up their efforts to attract railroads. Stock subscriptions and other forms of direct railroad aid continued in the South on the county level well after the demise of the Reconstruction Republicans' "gospel of prosperity." In Columbus as elsewhere, the Georgia Pacific retained local attorneys to secure county and city stock subscriptions and rights-of-way. In Starkville, Mississippi, local attorney Wiley N. Nash assured Georgia Pacific president Jonathan W. Johnston that "no stone will be left unturned to carry the vote in the county" for stock subscription. Each county required separate special elections, and under Mississippi's constitution, passage required a two-thirds majority of registered voters. The Georgia Pacific, so its officers alleged, needed local capital to complete the road. The local attorneys orchestrated the time-consuming and tedious effort to canvas the county, organize an election, and campaign for a two-thirds majority. They ran into organized, fierce opposition in some counties and cities.

Fearing the accusation of underhandedness, Johnston questioned local attorneys Fox & Beckett about the "validity or regularity" of the Clay County subscription elections, which resulted in a decision favorable to the Georgia Pacific. "Some rumors have come to our people," Johnston wrote the attorneys, "that the election was barely carried after severe purging of the registration books, and that questions are likely to be raised." The attorneys vigorously assured Johnston that they carried the vote "in accordance with the law" and that they purged from the county voter-registration books only the dead and those citizens who moved. They pointed out that in West Point, Mississippi, the vote for a $50,000 subscription carried by a margin of 473 to 0, out of only 530 registered voters. In the surrounding county, however, the election ended with just eleven votes more than the necessary two-thirds majority in favor of a $40,000 subscription. The local attorneys, in a letter to Johnston, challenged the "world, the flesh and the devil to show that two-thirds of the qualified voters of this county did not vote for this donation." The attorneys con-

Revolution, 1863–1877 (New York: Harper & Row, 1988), 379–92. Michael Perman, *The Road to Redemption: Southern Politics, 1869–1879* (Chapel Hill: University of North Carolina Press, 1984).

sidered the matter beyond dispute, but as if in admission of something to hide, they urged Johnston to hurry up the construction through the county. The vote totals were enough to make anyone nervous and some flabbergasted that the railroad had such solid support in these communities.[42]

Southerners eagerly awaited the arrival of the railroad in their town or county in the eighties, and boosters rushed to promise the prospective lines extraordinary benefits. Railroads often gained the luxury of attractive aid from competing towns and counties that hoped the corporation would choose them for the location of their line or even a depot, repair yard, or shop. Unfortunately for the railroads, a choice often made enemies in the bypassed locality. Even in a chosen town, the railroad stood to offend. Illinois Central general solicitor James Fentress traveled to Starkville, Mississippi, to negotiate the location of the proposed Canton, Aberdeen & Mississippi Railroad. He found "the people unanimous for the railroad and the only difference between them was as to which of the surveyed lines . . . was best for the town." No doubt whichever the side of town the railroad chose, the other would be angered.[43]

Even a town that already had some railroad service could be offended—railroad officials seemed to go out of their way at times to insult townspeople's intelligence and create antagonism. Several citizens of Amite City, Louisiana, petitioned the Illinois Central to create a stop for one of its passenger trains in their town. The railroad replied with careful courtesy that it could not stop one of its passenger trains there. "While the delay incident to making the stop at Amite may seem to be a small matter to you it would be rather a serious one to us in connection to making the schedule with such a train." The railroad official elaborated on this issue in an effort to educate the citizens of Amite how through-passenger traffic might work to their advantage. Speed and dispatch meant first-class service, and "when first-class service is furnished [to] through passengers

---

42. Jonathan W. Johnston to Fox & Beckett, 6 May 1888, Fox & Beckett to Johnston, 12 May 1888, Fox & Beckett to Johnston, 19 April 1888, and 12 May 1888, Box 4, GPRR-VPI. See Stuart Daggett, *Chapters on the History of the Southern Pacific* (New York: Augustus M. Kelley Publishers, 1966), 32, for a similar account, in this case of the Central Pacific's fight with San Francisco over the city's subscriptions to company bonds and the use of underhanded methods to secure the vote for bond subscription.

43. James Fentress to W. H. Osborne, 10 October 1882, Fentress Out Letters, ICRR-NL.

they naturally think better of the county which they pass than if the service was indifferent." The citizens of Amite probably failed to see the logic of the railroad's response—how could passing through the town be more beneficial than stopping? Development for Amite, the railroad suggested, would be hindered by a passenger stop. The Illinois Central official closed his response with a reminder of the railroad's economic development efforts: "You know of the efforts our Company is making to build up the country through which the road passes and I trust will feel that we are at all times disposed to do what we can to accommodate the local communities."[44]

This kind of imperious and arrogant response echoed throughout the South, as railroads argued that almost anything they did benefited "the local communities." Choices like the one in Starkville more often depended on engineering considerations than on which party promised more benefits for the railroad, just as the one in Amite depended on traffic patterns between Chicago, St. Louis, and New Orleans. Local interests, though, were not satisfied and instead expected more favorable prioritizing. The consequences of these railroad-management decisions gathered momentum, and many southerners, neither understanding nor agreeing with the priorities of the interstate railroad corporations, came to distrust these powerful entities. After well-financed public relations campaigns and allegedly fair 473–0 vote margins on stock subscriptions, citizens had more reason to distrust the railroads than ever.

Opposition to railroad expansion came not just from bypassed communities but also from powerful interests within railroad localities. In Columbus, Mississippi, for example, Georgia Pacific president Jonathan Johnston relied on the local law firm Orr & Simms to handle securing the right-of-way for a depot. Town property holders speculated on the road's route and the depot's placement. "My experience with property owners," J. A. Orr warned Johnston, "teaches me that the average citizen has little conscience when dealing with a railroad company." Orr feared that the property owners might use opposition to the road to extort bigger concessions from the railroad. Orr considered the railroad's local negotiator, R. W. Banks, unlikely to secure right-of-way through the town: "Some of the

---

44. O. M. Dunn to Robert R. Reid, 22 December 1898, Robert R. Reid Papers, Louisiana State University Library. I would like to thank Edward L. Ayers for sharing this quotation with me.

parties he has to deal with are men of means and influence and will in all probability strenuously oppose the project per se."[45]

Railroads needed right-of-way not just through the sparsely populated, remote lands of Appalachia and the Wiregrass but through places populated much more densely. When railroads sought to expand operations in the South's cities and large towns, their plans required balancing sometimes powerful property interests. In Atlanta, Georgia, no one wanted a railroad track through his backyard, particularly the rector of St. Phillip's Episcopal Church. The L&N's subsidiary, the Atlanta, Knoxville & Northern Railway Company, needed the church's property badly. It also needed the church's support before the city council when it requested expansion of its line into a city street and changes in the use of buildings there. The church's reluctance to sell the property to the L&N prompted the AK&N attorneys to enlist powerful support to convince it otherwise— former governor Henry D. McDaniel, a Georgia Railroad director and a prominent attorney and businessman in Atlanta.[46]

The church committee demanded $25,000 for its prime real estate, and the Episcopal bishop backed his parish. The railroad considered the price ridiculous. According to the company vice-president, "the whole difference lay in the purely speculative question of damage to . . . the Church property by reason of the proximity of the railroad." With the mediation of McDaniel, whose "services . . . in this matter were certainly invaluable," the railroad's attorneys executed an $18,000 settlement. "The determination of the Church, from the Bishop down," reported one railroad executive officer, "to actively oppose us in the City Council . . . in which body it was readily conceded the Church would have strong influence, was the chief reason to induce us to accept the onerous terms. . . . The Church people are now pledged to support us; and since the Church is the principal property holder concerned, outside of the Railway Company itself, this support will certainly be of value." The price shocked the railroad officers, but they relented to the pressure and accepted the contract, the vice-president admitting he had "since been trying to believe that it was the wise thing to do."[47]

45. J. A. Orr to Jonathan W. Johnston, 29 October 1888, Box 4, GPRR-VPI.

46. *Atlanta Journal*, 27 July 1926, obituary. McDaniel served as governor from 1883 to 1886 as a Democrat. He was a Baptist and a member of First Baptist Church in Atlanta. McDaniel's connection to the L&N came through the Georgia Railroad, a subsidiary of the L&N.

47. J. H. Ellis to M. H. Smith, 18 January 1904, Miscellaneous President's Office, Box 102, Folder 2105B, L&NRR-UL.

Two months later, however, the railroad came to the conclusion that it did not need the St. Phillip's Church property after all. It dispatched its attorneys to get out of the contract. The church mustered its own attorney into action and warned the railroad company that it planned to hold it to the terms of the contract. The railroad attorneys, after careful scrutiny, concluded that "assuming . . . proper title . . . the Church has an enforceable contract with the Company." As for the church, the bishop's attorney contacted former governor McDaniel, the railroad's mediator in the deal: "I am hardly prepared to believe that it is necessary to take steps looking towards forcing the railroads to carry out their part of the contract. I hope that you will use your good offices to see that the church is not put to any more trouble than is necessary in closing this transaction."[48]

Although it is not clear whether the church succeeded in holding the railroad to the contract, the church brought all of its considerable influence to bear on the railroad corporation. The AK&N general counsel requested "specific instructions as to the extent of resistance" to put up in the fight with the church. They construed L&N president Milton H. Smith's response "to mean that we are not expected to co-operate in furthering the consummation of the deal, but are not to actively resist it, if the title and proposed conveyance are good and in proper form." In these contests of power and property, of title and right-of-way, railroads in the South worked to manipulate local power to their advantage. Even with the mediation of a former governor, though, the L&N attorneys could not leverage the legal process to their advantage in the fight over the church's property. Their attempts to do so, though, reveal the lengths to which the railroads would go to win—not even the Episcopal Church deserved favorable treatment.[49]

Neither thorough attorneys nor careful attention to titles prevented large systems such as the L&N from becoming entangled in title disputes and contract litigation. As larger roads consolidated poorly built, weakly financed, smaller lines throughout the South in the late nineties, disputed titles took on greater significance. For the larger systems, many of these contests involved minority stockholders of subsidiary companies who sued to recover the value of their stock. Minority stockholders possessed considerable legal weapons to prevent or delay transfer of title.

48. Ellis to Smith, 14 March 1904, Robert C. Alston to Governor H. D. McDaniel, 1 March 1904, ibid.

49. Smith, Hammond & Smith to J. H. Ellis, 11 March 1904, ibid.

Local considerations often led railroad attorneys to seek removal to federal court in these cases. When railroad corporations faced a suit in a state other than the one in which it was domiciled, they could seek removal to federal court under diversity of citizenship rules. In some cases removal to federal court depoliticized a trial. Railroad attorneys considered federal judges, appointed with life tenure, less likely to concern themselves with political issues than popularly elected state judges. They favored federal courts in stockholder suits and some other cases, such as bond repudiations, that threatened to divide a local community or that carried political potential beyond the courtroom. Illinois Central general solicitor James Fentress summed up the reasons for removal in an 1882 Mississippi stockholder suit:

> My impression is that it would be wiser to have all the McComb cases tried in New York than in Mississippi. . . . If any part of the facts in the case is to be submitted to a jury it would be much easier to get an intelligent jury in New York than in Oxford, Miss. 2nd while Judge Hill is a good, kindhearted old gentleman he is hardly the equal of a New York judge in the intricate questions involved in these cases. . . . 3rd General West lived in Oxford for a long time and has relations and warm personal friends there and as our success depends in large measure upon showing a wicked and fraudulent breach of trust on his part it is but natural that influence would be developed against us which would not arise if the cause were heard before strangers.[50]

Railroad lawyers weighed the competence and sentiments of juries and judges, as well as the local power and influence of their opposition. Any adversity—a contract not fulfilled, a child killed on the tracks, a right-of-way disputed—often led attorneys to escape to more favorable terrain in

50. James Fentress to W. H. Osborne, 16 March 1882, Fentress Out Letters, ICRR-NL. For an analysis of McComb's management of the New Orleans, Jackson & Great Northern and Mississippi Central railroads, especially his attempt to abscond with $100,000 before the roads' receiverships and his fraudulent scheme to build McComb City, see Stover, *Railroads of the South*, 162–76.

federal court under their special consideration as interstate corporations. The tactic remained a powerful line of defense, one that spoke volumes about the way the railroads did business.[51]

Interstate railroad corporations, often headquartered in distant cities or other states or regions, appeared faceless to many Southerners whose ties to local men and institutions were strong. During the 1880s railroad officers confronted an increasingly antipathetic public. At the state and local level, it seemed that every mile of built railroad added another aggrieved party. By the early nineties the great railroad construction boom in the South reached its apogee, and the vast majority of southerners lived in counties served by a railroad. They had witnessed the underhanded methods of securing title, the arrogance displayed by distant railway officers who characterized their locality as "too provincial" to deserve any sort of priority, and the slippery logic of federal removal to escape local legal action. From the beginning of interstate railroad involvement in the South, inequities surfaced in the legal process.

As the promoting and building of the great lines gave way to their operation, many southerners grew opposed to the railroads' priorities. When public opposition hardened, railroad attorneys faced an increasingly challenging environment. The Georgia Pacific's president summed up the legal situation in 1889: "Our train men and laborers have of course imbibed more or less of the prevailing sentiment of the people. Considering this, the attitude of the legislatures, the commissions, courts, and juries and the number of shyster lawyers in every city and country town, it is hardly to be wondered that our general litigation has been so large and costly, and we will be fortunate indeed if the years to come do not show a marked increase."[52]

---

51. Edward Purcell pointed out the prevelance of local prejudice in such cases. See Edward A. Purcell, *Litigation and Inequality: Federal Diversity Jurisdiction in Industrial America, 1870–1948* (New York: Oxford University Press), 138.

52. Jonathan W. Johnston to James T. Worthington, 26 January 1889, Box 1, R&DRR-VPI.

TWO

The Making of the Railroad
Legal Department

At the same time as railroad lawyers began to work for interstate corporations, brokering right-of-way deals for their powerful clients, moving aside weaker plaintiffs, and bringing in heavy-hitting allies when needed, many southerners began to raise concerns about the bar. Some of those who questioned these tactics and voiced apprehension were fellow lawyers. Some of them were members of the growing plaintiff's, or personal injury, bar that the railroad helped to spawn. Others were old-style lawyers who saw immorality on both sides of an increasingly divided bar. Even some railroad-corporation attorneys became disillusioned with their clients and saw themselves sliding down a slippery slope into a world of shady deals and power plays. The rise of the railroad legal department and the corporate lawyer in the South came with opposition, defiance, and self-doubt.

At the third annual meeting of the Virginia Bar Association in 1891, William C. P. Breckinridge gave the keynote speech. He chose to talk about the direction of the legal profession and the moral compass of his state's lawyers. A congressman from Kentucky and a lawyer, Breckinridge saw a distinction between the statutory laws of a state and the law as a "rule of conduct." The latter he valued as essential to the legal profession, an ideal to which all lawyers should aspire. The lawyer's duty, Breckinridge observed, was to navigate a course through the tricky waters of economic growth and change. These economic forces, in his opinion, posed the greatest threat to the morality of the legal profession: "It is his function to be at once counsellor, guide and umpire; that to capital free scope and ample protection be given; to the plain people pure Courts and vested rights be preserved; to the Commonwealth freedom and purity be continued."[1]

Breckinridge, like many other bar association lawyers, grappled with what historian Robert W. Gordon calls "the ideal and the actual in the law." Gordon tries to understand lawyer reform movements in the late nineteenth century not just as cynical efforts to serve specific material interests, but instead as valid attempts to resolve an increasingly puzzling tension in the legal profession. Gordon sees lawyers as "double-agents" with duty to the law as an abstract principle and to their clients' concrete interests. "The lawyer's job," Gordon points out, was "to mediate between the universal vision of legal order and the concrete desires of his clients, to show how what the client wants can be accommodated to the utopian scheme."[2]

Such accommodation often failed in practice, as lawyers put aside their ideals to serve the interests of their clients. For Breckinridge, standing before the bar association, the problem he saw was a lack of professional standards. The bar association, he counseled, needed to take responsibility for itself. The trouble was that bar association members and lawyers, in general, remained deeply ambivalent about the choice between the ideal and the actual. Practicing lawyers, whatever they heard or said at bar association meetings, found these conflicts in real, everyday choices. Too many of them in towns across the South needed business, and their ideals remained a distinctly lower priority.[3]

Breckinridge aimed his criticism not at ambulance-chasing personal injury attorneys but the corporation lawyers, specifically those serving railroads. These lawyers, he suggested, ignored principles and sold their souls to their greedy clients. Great economic change, Breckinridge asserted, produced "a type of thought and a type of man that shall respond to that development, where greatness of enterprise shall take the place of fidelity to principle." Breckinridge conceded that "we can not stop the

1. William C. P. Breckinridge, "The Lawyer: His Influence in Creating Public Opinion," *Virginia Bar Association Proceedings* (1891): 164.
2. Robert W. Gordon, " 'The Ideal and the Actual in the Law': Fantasies and Practices of New York City Lawyers, 1870–1910," in *The New High Priests: Lawyers in Post–Civil War America*, ed. Gerard W. Gawalt (Westport, Conn.: Greenwood Press, 1984), 53.
3. Breckinridge, "The Lawyer," 167.

growth—we ought not to stop it. In all this development there is good." For the lawyer who represented the great developers, however, Breckinridge reserved skepticism. "In a bad sense railroads do sometimes 'hire a lawyer,'" Breckinridge stated matter-of-factly, "not merely as counsellor but as servant; not to give advice but to obey; not to counsel, guide, inform, protect, but to carry out plans to which he was not privy; to make legal that which is devious, to devise means for ends which are doubtful. Here is the generic difference between the counsellor and the servant."[4]

Other turn-of-the-century bar association speakers addressed this problem. Many of them concluded that the corporation attorney surrendered his independence and with it any public interest principle. A corporate lawyer, according to these critics, replaced such principles with devotion to his clients' interests. An American Bar Association speaker echoed Breckinridge nearly a decade later, observing that "instead of client and lawyer the relation of employer and employee has been substituted." According to Theron Strong, a prominent turn-of-the-century New York lawyer, lawyers on annual retainers to corporations "become little more than . . . paid employee[s] bound hand and foot to the service of" the corporation. The lawyer "is almost completely deprived of free moral agency and is open to at least the inference that he is virtually owned and controlled by the client he serves."[5]

Bar associations in the late nineteenth century were notoriously conservative, led and controlled by representatives of the elite, corporate bar. Most engaged in constant admonishing of "shyster lawyers" or "ambulance chasers" for undignified and unprofessional solicitation of business. The concern over the rise of personal injury specialists began in the mid-1890s and reached widespread proportions around the turn of the century. In 1895 Virginia's legal fraternity reflected those of other states, denouncing the "blood sucking generation" of new personal injury specialists. Criticism of the personal injury lawyers, though, mirrored similar concern over corporation lawyers whose rigid devotion to their clients'

---

4. Ibid., 168–69.

5. James D. Andrews, address before the American Bar Association, 1906, quoted in Wayne Hobson, "Symbol of the New Profession: Emergence of the Large Law Firm, 1870–1915," in *The New High Priests*, ed. Gawalt, 4; Theron Strong, quoted in Marc Galanter and Thomas M. Palay, *Tournament of Lawyers: The Transformation of the Big Law Firm* (Chicago: University of Chicago Press, 1991), 16.

material interests seemed to cloud their moral bearings. As early as 1891, bar members such as Breckinridge exhibited great dismay over the ethics of corporation lawyers and the specialized practice of the new corporate law firm. For the next twenty years, lawyers engaged in a public dialogue about the ethics of their profession. The lines along which this debate fell reflected the division of the bar into two competing groups: corporation lawyers and "anti-corporation" lawyers.[6]

The rise of the corporate lawyer at the bar has led historians to investigate the emergence of the large law firm, its corporate-client basis, and its effect on the legal profession. Most chart the development of the large law firm with the emergence of the "Cravath system." Relying on the monumental, three-volume chronicle of Paul Cravath's firm by his partner, historians located the emergence of the large, corporate-client-oriented firm in New York around the turn of the century. At this time Cravath instituted a systemized practice and established the model for many large law firms to follow. The principle elements of the what became known as the "Cravath system" included a largely corporate clientele, a host of associ-

6. For conservative addresses by southern railroad attorneys, see I. E. Shumate, "Professional Responsibility," *Georgia Bar Association Proceedings* (1887): 99–107, and Joseph B. Cumming, "Lawyers, The Trustees of Public Opinion," *Georgia Bar Association Proceedings* (1886): 88–97. See John A. Matzko, " 'The Best Men of the Bar': The Founding of the American Bar Association," in *The New High Priests*, ed. Gawalt, for a balanced treatment of that organization's character. See also Mark E. Steiner, " 'If We Don't Do Anything but Have an Annual Dinner': The Early History of the Houston Bar Association," *Houston Review* (1989): 95–110, for an analysis of the "shyster problem" and the efforts of the Houston bar to clean up the profession after one citizen shot a policeman over a matter of honor on advice of counsel. See "To Weed Out the Shysters," *Law Notes* (November 1898), 154; also *Law Notes* (November 1901), 144, (March 1902), 223, on "ambulance chasers." See Edward A. Purcell, *Litigation and Inequality: Federal Diversity Jurisdiction in Industrial America, 1870–1948* (New York: Oxford University Press, 1992), 150–54, for an analysis of the emergence of the plaintiffs' personal injury bar. Purcell suggests that a specialized personal injury bar did not emerge until the mid-1890s and achieved stature only around 1900. In the South, at least, it appears that the development of a divided bar and a specialized personal injury practice took shape earlier, in the 1880s, but that it did not develop fully until around 1900. See also Lawrence M. Friedman, *A History of American Law* (New York: Simon & Schuster, 1985), 650–51. On corporation lawyers, see Jerold S. Auerbach, *Unequal Justice: Lawyers and Social Change in Modern America* (New York: Oxford University Press, 1976), 32–39. Public journals responded to this effort by referring in the early 1890s to lawyers as either "corporation" or "anti-corporation" attorneys. See *The Railway and Corporation Law Journal* (21 May 1892), 241.

ates out of law school, promotion to partner after demonstrated success in the firm, and specialized practice.[7]

Although most historians agree that the large firm first appeared in turn-of-the-century New York, historians have not established a clear reason why the large firm emerged when it did and why it developed in the way that it did. New York firms such as Cravath & Swaine, Stetson, Jennings & Russell, and Dillaway, Davenport & Leeds specialized in mergers, acquisitions, and receiverships, all legal work attending the great economic changes at the turn of the century. Their work facilitated the financiers' efforts in the great consolidation movement between 1897 and 1903, the activities of Standard Oil, the Pennsylvania Railroad, and U.S. Steel. The large firm followed the national trend of consolidation, systemization, merger, and big business. As a product of those inexorable changes, the large firm, according to this argument, mirrored other societal and economic developments.[8]

Outside of New York City, though, the day-to-day legal work of large interstate corporations inspired significant changes in the legal profession. Across the South the corporate-client-based law firm emerged when it did for specific reasons and in a particular fashion, not simply as a result of large, impersonal trends in the economy and society. The interstate railroad companies in the late nineteenth century played a significant role in these firms' development. As the first interstate corporations in the South, railroads demanded new legal services. Lawyers on a daily basis lived and worked in troubling circumstances, confronting difficult choices between their ideals and interests, between their understanding of what the practice of law meant and their clients' specific needs. Railroad employment often secured stability, guaranteed income, provided benefits, brought prestige at the bar, and allowed practice in an exciting field of law. At the same

---

7. Hobson, "Symbol of the New Profession." See also Kenneth Lipartito and Joseph Pratt, *Baker & Botts in the Development of Modern Houston*. See Robert T. Swaine, *The Cravath Firm and Its Predecessors, 1819–1947*, 3 vols. (New York: Ad Press, 1946–48). For a description of the main features of the emergence of the large law firm, see Galanter and Palay, *Tournament of Lawyers*, 4–19.

8. Though Hobson, like Galanter and Palay, clearly explains the features and patterns of the emergence of the large firm, he gives little indication of why the large firm developed when it did and as it did. He points to the organizational trend in American business, as described by Alfred D. Chandler Jr. in *The Visible Hand: The Managerial Revolution in American Business* (Cambridge, Mass.: Belknap Press of Harvard University Press, 1977).

time, however, lawyering for the railroad corporation made them more and more dependent on the railroad company for business. More than any other consequence, southern railroad attorneys feared sole dependence on the corporation. They expressed this fear in pleas for larger salaries, in reports of increasing litigation, and in personal letters and diaries. For most railroad attorneys their corporate clients crowded their business and by their nature demanded special attention. As outside business dwindled, railroad attorneys lost personal security and came to depend on the corporation for support.

For southern lawyers who took on railroad clients, a precarious balancing act ensued. Solicitous of new economic development in their states and localities, these attorneys respected the power of the railroad companies to transform the economy. As they assisted these interstate railroad systems in breaking down the barriers of local and state power, railroad attorneys grew fearful of losing their own professional autonomy. Most railroad attorneys tried to retain their independence as well as their specialized corporate practice. Dependence emerged in part as a function of a new legal landscape that the railroads created and perpetuated. Its outstanding feature was a divided bar, separating those lawyers with corporate clientele from those who represented plaintiffs confronting corporations.

Nationwide, most lawyers continued to work in small, two- or three-partner firms even as late as 1915, and although some large firms emerged after 1900, they were concentrated in the eastern financial centers, especially New York City. These were transition years, historian Wayne Hobson has pointed out, in the development of large law firms in the United States. In the rapidly developing South, railroads provided the impetus for the transformation of the legal profession. Their daily legal business brought law firms into corporate practice. Many small southern firms hitched their practice to the railroad in the 1880s and early 1890s only to discover that the changes in the profession dictated by the railroad's needs produced great tension in their vision of legal practice. Not all resolved that tension without conflict and loss.[9]

9. Hobson, "Symbol of the New Profession," 10. Robert W. Gordon concludes that without any new unifying ideology to resolve the tension between the ideal and the actual, lawyers generally split along three lines: those that reverted to the principles of classical legal science, those that fell into "institutionalized schizophrenia," and those that withdrew into apolitical technical service to the client's interests. Most, he suggests, followed the last path. Gordon, "The Ideal and the Actual," 66.

In the early 1880s railroad lawyers experimented with the systemization of railroad legal departments. As once locally owned and controlled railroads slipped into the hands of distant capitalists and were joined into larger systems, legal departments expanded across jurisdictions and needed local legal representation loyal to the corporation and protective of its varied interests. General counsels tightened operations. Their law departments evolved from one or two attorneys who were paid on a fee basis for each case into a hierarchy of lawyers on retainer. On small, local roads and on some territorial roads in the seventies, the first vice-president or another general officer did double duty as the road's general counsel. With minimal litigation, little regulation, and small territories, these local companies hired attorneys as they needed them. When these roads either came under control of larger systems or grew into interstate companies in the eighties, they experimented with different systems of hierarchy for the legal department.

Beginning in 1880 railroads in the South underwent sweeping changes. Consolidation of railroads into larger "interterritorial" systems affected the legal demands of roads. Legal departments changed because consolidation extended the business of a large corporation through many jurisdictions. Location-specific changes in litigation affected the organization of legal departments as well. In general, railroads faced rising litigation across the South in the 1880s and 1890s and responded with greater levels of representation. As litigation demands overburdened railroad lawyers, they pushed for better systemization in their client's legal affairs. Beyond this, though, patterns shifted over time, and one county, state, or city's litigation rate often fluctuated. Railroads met such shifts with flexibility—whole districts were eliminated or redrawn to meet changes in litigation loads.

The pattern of railroad legal departments developed along predictable lines. It did not include, for example, the retention of in-house counsel at each level of the hierarchy; in fact, only the top level of general counsel and general solicitor qualified as in-house, that is, working exclusively for the corporation as an employee. In a period of increasing business consolidation and vertical integration, it might seem curious that railroad corporations did not internalize this area of operations. At first glance, such failure appears an oversight or, worse, an inefficient mistake. Railroad companies, though, had good reasons for using outside legal services.

In-house representation for all legal matters lacked efficiency, and railroad companies perceived the benefits of using outside lawyers to represent them. Their demand for legal services fluctuated greatly over time and across region, and outside counsel on "fee contingency" or on retainer satisfied their needs without sacrificing revenue or burdening operations. Just as important, though, railroads confronted the determined independence of their attorneys who balked at exclusive work for one master.

It turned out that federalism and localism emerged as the most significant considerations in the evolution of legal departments for southern railroad companies. According to legal historian Harry Scheiber, "great areas of policy, not least economic policy, remain[ed] in the hands of state legislatures and state judges."[10] In the 1880s and 1890s states retained considerable power over business activities, eclipsing the minimal interference of federal courts and law. The variance of state statutory and common law across the South led railroads to secure legal representation for each state. Local considerations prompted equally decentralized retention. Railroads needed lawyers on-the-ground, close to the courthouse, and sensitive to the local legalities. In-house counsel oversaw the operations, but southern railroad corporations operated in a highly decentralized legal environment, one shaped in every respect by federalism.

The Georgia Pacific's attorneys, for example, responded to changing legal needs in their early efforts to initiate and direct greater systemization in the company's legal department. From construction under the Richmond & Danville Extension Company to operation in the early eighties, the Georgia Pacific Railroad traversed three Deep South states, running from Atlanta, Georgia, through Birmingham, Alabama, to Greenville, Mississippi. Never a local road, the Georgia Pacific developed an interstate corporation legal department from scratch. In 1883 as the Georgia Pacific shifted from construction to operation, Bernard Peyton, the road's assistant general counsel, petitioned president Jonathan W. Johnston on his requested plan for the "organization of [the] legal bureau." Peyton pointed out the steadily increasing litigation as the main reason for his new mea-

10. Harry Scheiber, "Public Economic Policy and the American Legal System: Historical Perspectives," in *The Law of Business and Commerce: Major Historical Interpretations*, ed. Kermit Hall (New York: Garland Publishing, 1987), 734, and Scheiber, "Federalism, The Southern Regional Economy, and Public Policy Since 1865," in *Ambivalent Legacy: A Legal History of the South*, ed. David J. Bodenhamer and James W. Ely Jr. (Jackson: University Press of Mississippi, 1984), 69–106. See also Kenneth Lipartito, "What Have Lawyers Done for American Business? The Case of Baker and Botts of Houston," *Business History Review* 64 (autumn 1990), 492–93.

sures to reorganize the legal department. Specifically, he recommended that the general counsel be given "*entire* charge" of the department, that "all officers and employees of the company should be instructed to report claims, service of process, etc. . . . directly to his office," that "local counsel should be retained in each county through which the road runs," and that "all expenditures for legal matters should pass under his supervision." Peyton stressed repeatedly the necessity of clear definition of authority for the general counsel. Nine months later, though, he had not received any indication of the company's intentions.[11]

Peyton formally appealed to the president again to consider "the pressing necessity" for reorganization of the legal department. He cited the road's litigation, "which has assumed such proportions" that he doubted whether it was being carefully handled. To make his point Peyton set out some conditions for remaining on the staff without reorganization in what he called an "anomalous position." He requested an accurate definition of his duties "so that I may not be held accountable for the negligence and misdoing of others in matters where I have no (or at any rate inadequate) authority." Peyton felt that he was limited by the extraordinary power of the local attorneys, in particular, who "have been prompt to discover the weakness of my position." These attorneys, who were retained on a fee basis by the president to complete title and right-of-way work for the Richmond & Danville Extension Company, ignored Peyton as they handled legal business for the Georgia Pacific. Moreover, he was often held accountable for their and others' legal errors, despite his lack of authority to correct them. After a year of considerable lobbying, Peyton secured authorization for a reorganization of the legal department under his administration. He replaced the loosely monitored and indifferently regulated legal department with clear lines of authority and procedure.[12]

One young attorney in Georgia reported similar law department organization efforts in which the railroad gave him considerable leeway. Alexander R. Lawton Jr. opened a new law firm in Savannah, Georgia, and benefited from his father's extensive legal, political, and railroad-company connections. Doing legal work for the Central of Georgia Railroad, Lawton informed his father "we have the work well in hand now, and are proceeding to 'organize' the Law Department in accordance with the views

11. Bernard Peyton to Jonathan W. Johnston, 16 September 1883, Box 2, GPRR-VPI.
12. Peyton to Johnston, 20 June 1884, Box 3, ibid.

of the new administration."[13] The new owners asked Lawton & Cunningham to reorganize the department, but the young lawyers retained considerable control over the form and detail of reorganization. According to Lawton, for example, the president, General E. P. Alexander, allowed them great latitude: "He puts the whole responsibility on us, and does not want us to go into details. . . . Says he looks to us to protect the company's interest. I like that . . . it puts me more on my mettle and makes me more particular." As a young attorney, Lawton found responsibility for the company's legal affairs thrust on his small firm.[14]

Peyton, Lawton, and other lawyers understood that establishing a law practice in the South demanded great effort, and the railroad represented steady, lucrative employment. By the turn of the century, bar association speakers and journal editors were commenting regularly on the "overcrowding" at the bar. Observers in the South noted the financial difficulties for young lawyers in the profession who tried to build up an active practice. One young attorney in Danville, Virginia, described his financial difficulties to a colleague from whom he hoped to borrow $100. "I've been here just 18 months and have just commenced to make a living. During the first twelve months that I was here I only made $150, and out of that paid $75 in license taxes." For a young attorney, railroad work often boosted revenues and led to important and valuable connections. For Henry Jackson, who later became division counsel for the Georgia Pacific, his business with Alexander R. Lawton, general counsel for the Central of Georgia, resulted in much-appreciated assistance "in building up my law practice."[15]

As their needs changed, railroad companies were not afraid to experiment in their legal departments. Consolidation and increasing amounts of litigation, for example, inaugurated new concerns. It is tempting to view the relationship between outside capital and legal department systemization as one of one-way cause and effect. In this view the railroads as the great business organizers extended their model of management down

13. Alexander R. Lawton Jr. to Alexander R. Lawton, 18 December 1887, Alexander R. Lawton Family Papers, SHC-UNC.

14. Ibid.

15. See Eugene Ray, "Young Lawyers and Some of the Obstacles They Encounter," *Georgia Bar Association Proceedings* (1904): 164–73; C. W. Throckmorton to W. T. Sutherlin, 14 January 1884, William Thomas Sutherlin Papers, SHC-UNC; Henry Jackson to Alexander R. Lawton, 30 March 1885, Lawton Family Papers, SHC-UNC.

onto the legal department, imposing its order and efficiency on an otherwise disorganized, loose chain of authority. In fact, legal departments evolved not because of imposed system but because of specific, outside demands. Railroad attorneys themselves played a role equal to that of management in this process and set the pace and character of legal department organization. The direction of suggestion for reform flowed as much up as down the hierarchy from the lawyers who recognized the benefits and necessities of reorganization. Railroads' managerial reforms provided the model, no doubt, but the lawyers many times initiated and usually shaped the process.[16]

When an intrastate southern railroad evolved into an interstate system, its legal department developed into a more hierarchical, federalized chain of firms and attorneys. General counsels and their officers oversaw the road's legal business, while district and local attorneys represented the road before state and county courts. Only the general counsel and their assistants worked as in-house attorneys on salary as a general officer and exclusively for the railroad company. Although state and district attorneys could take outside business, many came to share with their superiors a similarly exclusive relationship with their corporate client. Railroad corporations retained these attorneys on a salary basis, sharply differentiating them from local attorneys on fee contingency. For most of these partnerships, railroad business represented the largest segment of their work, and it increasingly monopolized their time.

As a first step in legal department organization, most railroads retained local counsel in each county through which their lines ran. In vast, desolate stretches of the South, these lawyers often represented the company only in name. The general counsels' strategy called for the monopolization of the best attorneys in the distant, rural counties in which their lines operated. If the railroad company retained the best of the local attorneys, especially in towns where it located depots, shops, or repair and switching yards, weaker attorneys represented their opponents—employees, accident

16. For this process in management, see Chandler, *Visible Hand*, 100–40. Olivier Zunz in his recent study of corporate culture addresses this issue: "This multilayered transformation was not simply imposed from the top down by a corporate elite. . . . Rather, corporate goals were simultaneously adopted and devised by an aspiring new salaried class." Olivier Zunz, *Making America Corporate, 1870–1920* (Chicago: University of Chicago Press, 1990), 4–5. Zunz focuses on the "distinctive culture and social milieu of the growing managerial class and the formation of a new white-collar culture."

victims, local property owners. Unfortunately for the local attorneys, retention by a railroad company did not always bring corporation business.
The railroad wanted these attorneys' influence in the community as much
as their litigation skills. Division and state counsel almost always litigated
the important cases. In putting together a railroad legal department, Alexander R. Lawton Jr. explained the strategy: "Judge Lyon is to get us a
local in every one of his counties when he can. These are to have an annual
pass as a retainer, and we are to be under no obligation to employ them in
cases . . . as Judge Lyon says he wants no local counsel for litigation."
Using the free pass as a retainer, railroad general and state counsel locked
up local attorneys on a fee basis but avoided employing them for anything
other than routine courthouse paperwork.[17]

To guarantee loyalty, railroads required local attorneys to forswear cases
against the company. This arrangement appeared fair, but it turned out
that most railroads shunned local attorneys when it came to litigation. As
a result, the local attorneys were retained, in effect, to do no business but
to champion the railroad and salve its local constituency. One small-town
local attorney complained about these conditions: "If you still insist that I
am not to take any case against you brought here in Danville, and yet do
not think it necessary for me to appear in the cases, you ought to agree to
pay me a fair retainer by the year. . . . I know you can see at a glance that
it will not be justice to one to continue declining to take claims against
you and you not employing me in the suits." Eventually railroads required
local attorneys to take no damage cases against any railroads under any circumstances. The benefits of corporate legal work, then, trickled down only
marginally below the level of division or district attorney. Local attorneys
faced the unenviable choice of doing little business for the railroad or
scraping for business against a powerful corporation armed with legal
talent.[18]

The bar at the local level became increasingly divided between railroad-
corporation attorneys and anti-corporation attorneys. Railroads enforced
and perpetuated this division in an effort to monopolize the best legal talent and leave their opponents at a disadvantage. The railroads achieved
only marginal success with this strategy. They divided the bar but did not

17. Alexander R. Lawton Jr. to Alexander R. Lawton, 18 December 1887, Lawton Family Papers, SHC-UNC.
18. E. E. Zouldin to W. T. Sutherlin, 9 January 1884, Sutherlin Papers, SHC-UNC.

necessarily eliminate legal talent servicing plaintiffs, especially in the growing cities of the region. As early as 1888 James Weatherly reported somewhat self-servingly to his executive officers on the Georgia Pacific: "As the company's counsel I am frequently opposed to the best lawyers in the State, such men, for instance as Judge Samuel F. Rice . . . [and] Messrs. Hewitt, Walker & Porter. Against me in other cases are Lane, Taliaferro, Pearson, Webb & Tillman, Smith & Lowe, and others, all the principal lawyers of Birmingham."[19] Railroads created a lucrative business for both sides of an increasingly divided bar. Especially in southern cities, such as Birmingham, railroads witnessed the emergence of a specialized and successful personal injury bar in the eighties.

By the nineties railroad-company officers wanted total loyalty from their local and state counsel. In 1896 the three-partner Chattanooga firm of Cooke, Swaney & Cooke faced a loyalty test from their railroad client, the Southern Railway Company. Accused by the Southern's general counsel of bringing a $25,000 personal injury suit for the death of a fireman against the Cincinnati Southern, a Southern Railway subsidiary, the firm protested that it "has not, either directly or indirectly, brought suit or participated in the bringing [of] suit against the Cincinnati Southern Road or any other railroad since our employment by you as attorneys for the East Tennessee, Virginia & Georgia Railway Company." The firm noted that their only suit against a railroad company originated in 1892, when they "were not employed as counsel for any Railroad Company." They also reminded the Southern's attorneys that their contract allowed them to follow through with all cases taken before their retention as railroad attorneys. The realities of the retainer, though, complicated the matter:

> In connection with this matter, while our firm has complied strictly with its contract with reference to not bringing suit against the R.R. Co., the Cincinnati Southern Road has not yet sent passes for any members of our firm except myself, and the Nashville, Chattanooga & St. Louis Ry. Co. have not sent any passes for any of us. While the terms of our contract were that the different members of our firm should be furnished with annual passes over all the roads entering into Chattanooga, and

19. James Weatherly to Jonathan W. Johnston, 7 January 1888, Box 4, GPRR-VPI.

> although this has not been done by those roads . . . we
> have determined that we would not bring suits against
> these railroads anyway, but that was a matter of our own
> choice while the terms of the contract were not being
> complied with by the Railroads.

Cooke, Swaney & Cooke vociferously defended themselves against accusations of disloyalty. Railroad business was too profitable and too secure to gamble away on one high-damage suit.[20]

In addition to enforcing loyalty within their own railroad company system, railroads often secured formal agreements from their attorneys to turn down all casework against railroad corporations in general. Free passes again served as the glue in this binding arrangement. For a local attorney, an annual pass brought considerable freedom to his practice, allowing him mobility and access to other jurisdictions. "It has been customary for a number of years in Chattanooga," one railway official explained, "for the attorneys representing the various railways at that point to have an understanding amongst themselves that they will not accept any damage suits against other railways centering there." Such an agreement monopolized local counsel on the side of the railroads, enforced a divided legal fraternity, and fostered a form of loyalty for the railroads even at the lowest level of representation.[21]

Railroads, moreover, expected their work to receive top priority. Retainer contracts emphasized these expectations. Railroad companies defined and enforced loyalty by demanding that their attorneys never take cases against them. Even a local attorney retained with a free pass and paid on a contingency fee basis faced certain firing for such a breach. As Texas Central state counsel, Baker & Botts of Houston had the responsibility for taking action in such a situation. "Mr. W. L. Hall has been representing the company in cases originating in the justice courts of Wharton County," Baker & Botts reported to the Texas Central officers, "but as we notice he accepts employment against the company in district court cases, we believe it to the interest of the company to discontinue this arrange-

20. Thomas H. Cooke to Col. W. A. Henderson, 11 April 1896, Vice-President's Correspondence, Box 1, Folder 15, SRy-VPI.

21. S. M. Felton to W. H. Baldwin, 4 February 1896, Vice-President's Correspondence, Box 1, Folder 9, ibid.

ment, as we hardly think that an attorney can represent a client, especially a railroad company, in one court and fight it in another and do full justice to either client in either case."[22]

While local attorneys labored under these circumstances, wanting business but finding the scraps too paltry to satisfy them and the rules too stiff to comply with, railroad state and district counsel became the centerpiece in the railroad legal department hierarchy. They developed extraordinary authority in their clients' legal affairs but were subject to intense partisanship as railroads consolidated and merged in the 1890s. When railroad corporations changed ownership, attorneys often felt the consequences of lost autonomy. David Schenck's experience with the Richmond & Danville in North Carolina demonstrated the vagaries of corporation legal work and the uncertainties of railroad legal business.

As a young judge, David Schenck found a railroad offer both attractive and timely. He hoped to gain appointment to the state supreme court, but the governor overlooked him. State judges' salaries, at less than $2,500 a year, barely allowed for comfort on the circuit, and Schenck faced reelection as a Democrat in 1882 when he predicted Democratic failure. These circumstances pushed him "to seek for something of a more certain character" and to accept the Richmond & Danville's offer of North Carolina general counsel. The uncertain politics and substandard salary of judgeship induced Schenck to take the three-year appointment at $3,000 per year. At the time he profusely thanked God for the railroad appointment, playfully alluding to the Twenty-third Psalm: "It delivers me from the degradation of political life and the disappointments, apprehensions and despondency of such uncertain and unsatisfactory life."[23]

After only a few months on the job, Schenck cheerfully recorded in his diary, "I am rapidly accomplishing myself in my profession, especially as a corporation lawyer and when the time comes I expect to make some reputation." For the ambitious attorney, railroad law offered the opportunity to specialize in a lucrative field. An early case gave Schenck the opportunity to demonstrate his ability. "I prepared this case with great care and labor," Schenck admitted, "feeling the importance of the suit and knowing that

22. Baker & Botts to G. G. Kelly, 2 November 1902, Box 11L, Folder "Wharton Local Attorney," BBHC-RU.
23. David Schenck Diary, 14, 24 April 1881, SHC-UNC.

all the railroad magnates would be present. . . . [victory] will strengthen my position and make me more secure."[24]

Within his first year Schenck faced an important decision in his railroad work—whether or not to practice exclusively for the railroad. "If inducement enough is offered," Schenck determined that he would devote all of his time to the railroad. Offered full-time railroad work for $5,000, Schenck took the position with thanks and broke with his partnership. Although Schenck undoubtedly feared losing his independence, he must have been willing to barter it for the salary offered. The average lawyer, especially in the western North Carolina rural counties where Schenck practiced, earned far less than $5,000. With ten children to house, clothe, and feed, Schenck praised every dollar. After a few years in his new position Schenck quantified the benefits of his full-time railroad work. No longer in debt, financially secure, owner of a beautiful home, an office, and a good library, Schenck also witnessed his reputation rise. Comfortable in his position, Schenck now even rejected a gubernatorial offer to sit on the state supreme court. He cited the "necessities of my family" that prevented him from accepting a "pecuniary sacrifice."[25]

In early 1884 Schenck's health began to deteriorate and with it his confidence in the wisdom of corporate-counsel practice. Schenck, after much solicitation, finally received assurance from the railroad's vice-president that his position as state general counsel was "secure." In addition to his own health problems, Schenck faced troublesome relations with several railroad officials. The general manager of the Richmond & Danville, Schenck confidently concluded, was "a narrow-minded pompous little Virginian who holds everything in contempt that does not emanate from that state. . . . wherever [he] has authority he curtails my privileges and ignores my services." Under fire from officials within the company and mindful of his questionable health, Schenck confessed, "I chafe under the idea of being dependent on any one person or corporation and at times I am sorely tempted to resign but prudence and interest are both against my action."[26]

24. Ibid., 12 August 1881, 6 March 1885.
25. Ibid., 30 September 1883. In 1884 North Carolina's supreme court justices, as well as circuit court judges, received only $2,500 in salary. For all state judges' salaries, see *Georgia Bar Association Proceedings* (1884), 105.
26. Schenck Diary, 27 March 1884, 24 January, 1 February 1885.

His dependence on the corporation became more precarious and disturbing to him when the Richmond & Danville's controlling syndicate collapsed in 1886. For some reason Schenck developed an antagonistic relationship with the Richmond & Danville general counsel in New York, James Worthington. Taking advantage of the syndicate change, Schenck broke his relationship with Worthington and concluded that "if he continues in I will go out." In communication with his friends in the R&D, Schenck received assurances that Worthington would not last the syndicate's reorganization. Worthington retained powerful allies among the R&D stockholders and began what Schenck perceived to be a quest to subvert his authority. According to Schenck, Worthington ordered local counsel Fabius H. Busbee and Schenck's legal assistant, Charles Price, to divide the North Carolina work between them. Schenck, Worthington decided, suffered from such poor health that he was ineffective as R&D counsel. The plot failed, however, and Worthington lost his position as general counsel in the syndicate's shake-up.[27]

Such internecine corporate struggles left Schenck disillusioned and insecure. Though Worthington was out and he in, Schenck confessed to his old law partner, "with ill health and surrounded by strangers and worried with the detestable ways and manners of my Yankee superiors in office there is but little of pleasure." Schenck further despaired, "If I only had my health and strength . . . I would resign and declare war against corporations and monopolies, the great curses and tyrants of the age." Whether the civil war with Worthington or the increased northern control of the company caused Schenck's loss of faith, he clearly regretted his dependence on the corporation. "I am inside," he confessed, "and have to see the oppression and imposition and soulless operations of these railroads upon the people . . . until I can scarcely refrain from crying out against it." When the Interstate Commerce Act passed, Schenck took the opportunity to record his views on corporations in his diary:

> It is not of choice that I serve the Rail Road Company professionally. But I do not depart from my professional duty to defend their wrongs or abuses nor shall I use any personal influence to restrain the righteous indignation of the people against them. . . . They grieve the poor,

27. Ibid., 17 December 1886, 5, 7 January 1887.

they defy the law, they corrupt the courts, and legislatures, and bring distress to the land, where if used hon-
estly and lawfully they would be a blessing to the people.
Everyday experience teaches me the truth of these assertions and I do pray that I may one day be free to proclaim
them.

Schenck lived the tension between the ideal and the actual, as he confronted his own troubled spirit over his retainer. "The parsimonious Yan-
kees, who control the R&D syndicate," he fretted, refused to retain his
son as his clerk, took away his phone allowance, and reclaimed his free
family pass, all in an effort to cut costs. Schenck concluded not to "exert
any personal or political influence on their behalf" and to build up his private practice to decrease his dependence on the company. "The corporation yoke begins to gall me," Schenck confessed.[28]

A year after his triumph over Worthington, Schenck received word of
the reorganization of the legal department. "The fact is that the company
is embarrassed and has watered its stock and bonded its interests until the
property will not pay and in addition to this the owners are divided." To
Schenck's dismay, the legal department's reorganization brought the return of his nemesis, James Worthington, as general counsel. Worthington
reduced Schenck's jurisdiction and cut his salary to $3,500. Schenck re-
mained with the company, however, for reasons of security. For his part
Schenck labored as a railroad attorney but distracted himself with amateur
historical work.[29]

In the end Schenck's feud with Worthington played no role in his demise as counsel for the R&D; instead, his unresolved conflict over corporate work values finally erupted into the open. In the midst of the 1890s
depression years, Schenck failed to receive his salary for three months. Un-
beknownst to Schenck, the R&D officials, busy reorganizing into the
Southern Railway, kept Schenck on the payroll only to keep him from
causing them problems elsewhere. In 1894 they paid Schenck "until the
legislature should be in session in January, as Judge Schenck would be a
very dangerous man against us and is of such a nature that he would be

28. Ibid., 9 January 1887, 25 January, 2 February 1887.
29. Ibid., 25 December 1887.

inclined to initiate us if he were set down too suddenly."[30] Fearing his imminent removal from office, Schenck searched for the possible explanations. He blamed the road's president for his troubles: "I would not do dirty and degrading work for him—I would not swear to the petitions for the removal of the Bostian Bridge wreck cases to the . . . States Court because they contained falsehoods. Mr. Price [Schenck's assistant] swore to them and I was turned off as Division Counsel and Charles Price took my place."[31] Unwilling to violate his ideals concerning the practice of law, Schenck was left to mull over Thomas Fortune Ryan's letter of dismissal, which stated plainly for Schenck "the road is run on purely business principles and no personal feeling can be allowed."[32]

A similar process characterized the growth of the legal department on the Gulf, Colorado & Santa Fe in Texas. William Pitt Ballinger served as general counsel of the railroad in the early 1880s when it expanded across Texas. He developed a legal department hierarchy for the Texas line similar to that evolving on other large systems. As general counsel for the road, Ballinger devoted over 60 percent of his time to railroad work, monitored a network of fourteen district and local attorneys, and received a $12,000 salary. In addition, though, Ballinger received $7,000 for representing both the Galveston, Harrisburg & San Antonio and the Galveston, Houston & Henderson, and an additional $2,000 as local counsel in Galveston for the Missouri Pacific.[33]

As general attorney of the Santa Fe, Ballinger had considerable autonomy in directing the legal department. He set policy, retained attorneys, and advised the road's executive officers. In 1886, though, Ballinger's independence diminished as the Texas line consolidated with the larger Atchison, Topeka & Santa Fe system. Ballinger became Texas general counsel with a $15,000 retainer, but his authority to set policy suffered under the new arrangement. The Santa Fe's general counsel directed Ballinger that the new rules and procedures for the legal department "be put into effect immediately." Instructed to have his "arrangements with local attorneys conform to those which have been made on the Atchison sys-

30. Samuel Spencer to Baldwin, 6 August 1894, President's Correspondence, SRy-VPI.
31. Schenck Diary, 17 December 1894.
32. Ibid.
33. John Moretta, "William Pitt Ballinger" (draft manuscript), 1100 I would like to thank John Moretta for letting me read this manuscript.

tem," Ballinger faced a new hierarchical environment in which all "final decisions [were] to be made through the office of the General Solicitor."[34]

Not all lawyers cherished this managerial role. Outside counsel, especially state or district attorneys, betrayed the most ambivalence about their changing roles in the legal profession. William Pitt Ballinger's loss of autonomy and greater managerial responsibilities left him lukewarm. "At first I felt very affronted by the new policies," he confessed to his associate after a company legal department meeting in Boston, "but upon more dispassionate and rational examination, I have concluded them to be based on sound deliberation among the company's directors and lawyers. Times have changed, my dear friend,—the practice of law is going forward at such a rate that if we don't try to 'change with the times' as they say, then we will be left behind." General counsels found themselves reprimanding their subordinates, defining lines of authority, and outlining proper policy.[35]

Other railroad attorneys experienced similar tension in their relationship with the corporation, though few diaries remain as testament to their feelings. Like Schenck, most railroad lawyers initially guarded their independence carefully and resisted linking their future solely to the corporation. Like him, too, many gave up their independence when offered a position as general counsel. For example, James Weatherly, assistant general counsel for the Georgia Pacific, faced the decision in his practice of whether to work full-time for the railroad. Weatherly demanded a significant increase in salary and a title change to general counsel in exchange "for being withdrawn *entirely* from the general practice of my profession, and being forced to rely for a livelihood and professional success upon the good will of one client—a corporation—whose officers and servants are subject to change at any moment." For emphasis, Weatherly informed his officers of the increased litigation all along the line and the increased strength of his opposition counsel. He asked for $3,000 as a salary and explained, "I can earn that much in my general practice and sooner or later

34. Ibid., 1114.
35. Quoted ibid., 1115. Other railroad general counsels also found themselves managing rather than practicing law: "I endeavored to impress you," James Fentress wrote a local attorney, "with the idea that . . . the habit of attending to a thing while it was convenient and then when it wasn't turning it over to the General Solicitor's or other Department was wrong. . . . It is your duty as local attorney to complete what you begun [*sic*]." James Fentress to Frank Fentress, 7 July 1887, Fentress Out Letters, ICRR-NL.

I must quit the company's service rather than remain with the present salary, feeling as I do than I am gradually losing my hold upon the legal business of the general public."[36]

His terms met, Weatherly abandoned his remaining general practice to become general counsel of the Georgia Pacific Railway Company in 1888 and immediately submitted his plan for the reorganization of the legal department. Like Bernard Peyton, his predecessor, Weatherly took the opportunity of his change of position to further the legal department's efficiency and success. He requested a clerk and a sizable office space, but his final request demonstrated the power of the lawyers in directing their departments' corporate organization. "The operation and work of the department," he suggested, "should be thoroughly systematized." All legal documents, deeds, contracts, briefs, case files, and stock subscriptions should be held in the legal department and indexed for ease of reference. All state, county, and city tax records and payment schedules should also be managed by the legal department. Weatherly suggested as well that the legal department institute a current address record for all present and past employees. Cases dragged on for years, Weatherly pointed out, and former employees remained key witnesses. The company needed their testimony. Through these and other suggestions, Weatherly hoped to bring system into the legal department. His plan revealed the importance of building an institutional memory for a railroad legal department. Railroad attorneys recognized that strong institutional memory translated into power before commissions, courts, and legislatures, as well as in conference rooms, private arbitrations, and settlement meetings. [37]

Lest his managers think his requests unnecessary, Weatherly summarized the growing litigation problem. He conceded that his requests constituted a significant increase in legal department expenditures, but he maintained that the result would be a bottom-line decrease in expense for the company. Fewer cases lost and even fewer taken to court added up to significant savings for the company through the legal department. Increased litigation, he argued, was responsible directly for his requests for increased spending. Weatherly drew attention to one startling comparison for the Georgia Pacific officials: "There are now [in 1888] pending in the City and Circuit Courts at Birmingham alone nearly as many suits against

---

36. James Weatherly to Jonathan W. Johnston, 7 January 1888, Box 4, GPRR-VPI.
37. Weatherly to Johnston, 22 September 1888, ibid.

the company as were pending in all the Courts of Georgia, Alabama, and Mississippi on October 1st 1885."[38]

In addition to this deluge of lawsuits, Georgia Pacific attorneys struggled with problems in the legal department brought on by the road's consolidation into the Richmond & Danville system in 1888. R&D general counsel James Worthington set about re-restructuring the Georgia Pacific's legal department and, in the process, angered both that road's officers and its attorneys. The change from a loosely managed to a highly structured legal department lay at the heart of the tension. For years the Georgia Pacific's legal department reflected the unstructured environment of a small "interterritorial" road. In a long report Georgia Pacific president Jonathan W. Johnston confessed to Worthington his method of operations: "In building and operating the Georgia Pacific road—now about seven years—I have been in the habit . . . of myself in effect doing much— many things—ordinarily incumbent upon the Legal Department. On several matters of great importance I relied not only upon our office lawyer—Mr. Peyton and afterwards Mr. Weatherly—but upon Hopkins & Glenn, Orr & Simms, Percy & Yerger, and Col. W. W. Gordon . . . as occasion required."[39]

Johnston's lax organization and his "habit" of transgressing the bounds of formal procedure characterized many 1880s southern railroads not yet part of a greater system. The president, in this case Johnston, often retained local attorneys for specific assignments without consulting his general counsel. Even on an interstate system such as the Georgia Pacific, legal department organization remained flexible and indefinite in the eighties and nineties. Worthington's mishaps in reorganizing the department demonstrated the difficulties of restructuring a functioning legal department and the tensions brought on by the consolidation of large railroads.

Problems first surfaced in Atlanta in late 1888 when the Georgia Pacific attorneys there, Jonathan L. Hopkins & Sons, submitted their letter of resignation. Hopkins gave little indication of his reasons for stepping down except for citing the "recent changes, in reference to the Georgia Pacific,"

---

38. Ibid.

39. Jonathan W. Johnston to James T. Worthington, 26 January 1889, Box 1, R&DRR-VPI. For a description of the Georgia Pacific's complicated ownership, see Maury Klein, *The Great Richmond Terminal: A Study in Businessmen and Business Strategy* (Charlottesville: University Press of Virginia, 1970), 191.

but clearly some personal bitterness polluted his relationship with the Richmond & Danville general counsel James Worthington. The president of the Georgia Pacific, Jonathan W. Johnston, soon to be fourth vice-president of the Richmond & Danville, was caught by surprise and sought to resolve the matter quickly, as the road's heavy caseload demanded attention. Johnston wanted the R&D to retain Hopkins, who had handled the Georgia Pacific business in Atlanta for years. "He has been diligent, faithful and efficient," Johnston wrote the R&D's second vice-president, "and, indeed, has given much more of anxious attention, time and thought to our concerns than is at all usual with lawyers representing corporations." Moreover, Johnston remarked, "he is not a lawyer to hunt up cases against corporations."[40]

Johnston was convinced that Hopkins had not sold out to become an anti-corporation lawyer but instead retained a genuine interest in railroad work. He concluded that Hopkins needed more compensation for the increased caseload in Atlanta. "It is true, too," observed Johnston, "that many of our employees, though running on our lines in Alabama and Mississippi, live in Atlanta, and, being acquainted with Atlanta lawyers ready and anxious to take cases against us, much of our outside litigation has been localized there." Before the finalization of the roads' consolidation, Johnston planned to increase Hopkins's $3,000 salary, "so as to have his entire time, or, at least, his entire time to the exclusion of any and all other Railroad practice."[41]

The merger of the two railroads' operations was not easy. Johnston confessed to Worthington that he was "much perplexed about matters pertaining to the adjustment of the new relations" between the two companies and singled out the legal departments as the source of his bewilderment. As for Hopkins in Atlanta, Johnston reassured Worthington that Hopkins held no "such feelings as would debar him from undertaking services with us." Job security for railroad lawyers depended on loyalty toward the corporation, and railroad attorneys were expected to demonstrate such loyalty by refusing to take cases against railroad companies.[42]

40. Jonathan W. Johnston to W. G. Oakman, 24 December 1888, Box 1, R&DRR-VPI. Jonathan L. Hopkins to James Weatherly, 2 January 1889, ibid., referred to putting "behind us all merely personal matters."

41. Johnston to Oakman, 24 December 1888, Johnston to James T. Worthington, 17 January 1889, ibid.

42. Johnston to Worthington, 25 December 1888, Worthington to Johnston, 27 December 1888, ibid.

Pressured no doubt by impending appointment of Johnston as an R&D vice-president, Worthington offered Hopkins a place in the new legal department. For Atlanta, where the litigation load was heaviest, Worthington created a new title in the legal department organization and called it "assistant division counsel." Hopkins, who had served as the Georgia Pacific's special counsel in Atlanta, balked at the terms of the new position, especially the restrictions on his practice:

> Up to the time of leasing the Road to the Richmond and Danville, I did not feel that we were prevented from bringing suits against the latter company; now, nearly all of the roads here appear to be part of one system. The litigation of the Georgia Pacific is heavy, many suits being brought here for Alabama injuries. $3,000 is low pay for the Georgia Pacific business as heretofore conducted, and is not enough if I am to be precluded from suing other companies. I do not think it best . . . to be partly for and partly against railroads. I like to be all on one side . . . $3,000 is not adequate compensation for giving up the opportunity of employment against the other roads.

As railroads consolidated into single, large systems, local counsel, such as Hopkins, faced a "with us or against us" situation.[43]

Worthington stood up for his authority in a personal letter to Johnston. He stated bluntly that Hopkins's record "does not commend him to this office or to other executive officers of the Richmond & Danville Co." Worthington voiced his own lack of trust in Hopkins, fearing that he "would act entirely independent of regulation, or any departmental authority." As for the salary, Hopkins's sticking point, Worthington informed Johnston that the R&D regularly retained attorneys with similar caseloads and responsibilities for one-third the salary offered Hopkins. Hopkins's demand that he attend only to Georgia Pacific cases in Atlanta, Worthington pointed out, flew in the face of the law department's organization. "You see therefore," Worthington lectured, "the appointment of Judge Hopkins, confined alone to business at Atlanta, with a salary excessive in proportion to that paid to other counsel of the Company, is entirely

43. Oakman to Johnston, 29 December 1888, Jonathan L. Hopkins to James Weatherly, 4 January 1889, Johnston to Oakman, 14 January 1889, ibid.

subversive of the organization and methods upon which it has been found necessary to conduct the business of the Law Department."[44]

As for Hopkins's protestations concerning his inability to take other railroad suits, Worthington declared it "a bad argument." "Counsel employed by the Law Department," he pointed out, "are considered counsel of the Richmond & Danville RR Co, and of no special or specific part of it, and therefore are expected to be loyal to it in all matters, whether belonging to the Division they are attached to or others." Finally, Worthington informed Johnston of his recent meeting with the R&D president about the reorganization of the Georgia Pacific law department, "especially in regard to Judge Hopkins and other counsel who were demanding large fees." The president backed Worthington's authority "to organize the Georgia Pacific Division in strict accordance with the present organization and regulations of the Law Department." The position stood as offered, Worthington concluded—Hopkins could take it or leave it. Declaring the $3,000 offer "not just," Hopkins cut his ties with the railroads.[45]

The consolidation of the Georgia Pacific into the Richmond & Danville system created bruised egos and contested turf. Worthington administered his department "by strictly enforced regulation, method and system." Although he was perhaps an extreme stickler for the rules, Worthington was otherwise not an exception: he represented the new development of in-house corporate counsel. The values and qualities associated with this system included loyalty to the company, respect for strict lines of authority, and serious evaluation of performance above personality. For the Georgia Pacific officers and attorneys, the consolidation inaugurated a new era in corporate relations. No longer a railroad president, Johnston became a link in the chain of command and found the situation unfamiliar. Local attorneys, such as Hopkins, faced new and severe choices. In Atlanta, for example, all but two railroads—small railroads—came under control of the Richmond & Danville. In these circumstances local attorneys either worked for the railroad or against it. Consolidation of the largest, most powerful corporations in the region brought with it, then, an increasingly dichotomous legal profession.[46]

44. Worthington to Johnston, 21 January 1889 (marked "personal"), ibid.
45. Jonathan L. Hopkins to James Weatherly, 21 January 1889, ibid.
46. Worthington to Johnston, 21 January 1889 (not marked "personal"). Worthington considered the law department responsible for only the operating areas of the road; for all other property under Johnston's authority he should hire local attorneys. Johnston wanted

In the case of the Georgia Pacific, consolidation with the Richmond & Danville initiated deep change in the structure of the legal department. In the early 1880s, under the management of Bernard Peyton and James Weatherly, the road's legal department hired local counsel along the line on a fee basis. In particular cities, Birmingham and Atlanta for example, the general counsel retained attorneys on a salary to secure the necessary attention that ever-increasing litigation at those points demanded. Hopkins in Atlanta, for example, met those needs in mid-1880s.

When the Georgia Pacific came under control of the larger R&D system, Johnston wanted to maintain the Georgia Pacific's legal department intact. As he explained to Worthington, "the idea is to operate the Georgia Pacific Road as a Division, or, if it may be so called, a Grand Division, of the Richmond & Danville Railroad Company; and this involves, among other things, the appointment of Division Counsel for the Georgia Pacific, whose jurisdiction shall extend over all the lines of that Road." Initially, it appears Worthington organized the new division in this way. As general counsel, Worthington controlled a network of in-house division attorneys, including James Weatherly on the Georgia Pacific division, who hired local attorneys on a fee basis. The Georgia Pacific, and probably other previously independent lines, constituted one division in the R&D legal system. This initial scheme of organization reflected the patchwork conglomeration of independent railroad lines into larger systems, but it failed to fit the needs of the new corporation.[47]

The problems associated with trying cases in many different jurisdictions threatened to unbalance the Georgia Pacific and R&D system. In his lengthy report to general counsel Worthington, former Georgia Pacific president Johnston noted the problems that federalism posed for the reorganization of the legal department: "It is apparent, however, that the divisions are unequal in mileage and unequal also in the number of counsel assigned to each. . . . I notice that the mileage of some of the divisions is wholly within one state, and of others, mainly in one state. Also, that in some instances the mileage is largely made up of branch lines, and of lines possibly without a great amount of important litigation."[48]

to rely on the law department proper to satisfy these properties' legal needs. Worthington to Johnston, 31 January, 1 February 1889, Johnston to Worthington, 9 February 1889, ibid.

47. Johnston to Worthington, 25 December 1888, ibid.

48. Johnston to Worthington, 26 January 1889, ibid. For analysis of similar reorganizations in administrative offices, see Chandler, *The Visible Hand*, 175–84. Chandler explained

Within the circumstances of rapid consolidation and increasing litigation, southern railroads, such as the Georgia Pacific, struggled to develop legal departments that could respond to their needs. They experimented with several methods of organization. Some railroads, including the Georgia Pacific and the Richmond & Danville, grafted newly consolidated lines' legal departments onto those of the larger system, leaving intact a divisional structure insensitive to state and local jurisdictional boundaries. Others developed a system-wide legal department hierarchy with a general counsel, state or division counsel, and local attorneys. A few large systems used only general counsel and local attorneys, a select few of which were retained on a salary. Railroad legal departments experimented with different hierarchical methods of organization, but in the 1880s and early 1890s southern railroad companies settled on no uniform system. These were years of rapid growth, consolidation, and change, and legal departments were similarly in flux.

For railroad lawyers, the increasingly wide division of the bar brought as much tension and ambivalence as security and business. The railroad expansion throughout the South in the eighties fostered a highly competitive business environment for the railroads. For every lawyer, such as David Schenck, who refused to lower his professional standards when the company's interests demanded, there was another lawyer in the hierarchy that complied with the request. Schenck and other attorneys struggled in these circumstances to take advantage of the specialization that railroad work offered without slipping into complete dependence on the corporation.

Interstate railroad corporations seemed to bear a desire to exercise inordinate control over every factor affecting their business. In the case of retainers for legal counsel, these corporations could be found moving silently through the South in the 1880s and 1890s securing the best legal talent in each town and county and forcing them to refuse cases against railroads. Exercising monopoly power in Atlanta the Richmond & Danville could tell Jonathan L. Hopkins to work either for the railroads or against them. For the railroads the division of the bar served the short-term goal of weakening their opposition and reshaping the legal profes-

the decentralized system of the Pennsylvania Railroad Company, which planned its administration as it expanded. Chandler pointed out that the centralized model, favored by large banking houses, became the standard by 1900.

sion's boundaries. But the myopic view of railroad managers and some general counsels helped bring about a whole new field of lawyers—the personal injury or anti-corporation bar—allied in their common struggle against the monopolistic and powerful forces of the interstate railroad corporation.

THREE

The Consequences of Growth

Wrecks and delays were so bad on the Georgia Pacific that one passenger felt compelled to write a letter to the editor of the Birmingham *Age-Herald*. "As the trip from Anniston here was made in daylight," he pointed out, "I amused myself by counting the cars scattered along the track and turned over by recent wrecks, and got tired when the number reached twenty-five." The outspoken passenger continued, "Having seen what I did, I felt on my arrival here that I had cause for thankfulness in getting through with my whole bones. . . . Again necessity compelled me to risk myself on the Georgia Pacific." Curiously, this critic blamed the road's owner, the Richmond & Danville, and its management in Washington, D.C., not the Georgia Pacific's local management. These distant operators were to blame, he concluded, for they could not possibly control events on their Georgia properties with any degree of precision. The following day's paper carried a follow-up on the letter reporting that "prominent" railroad men from Birmingham agreed with the commentary, especially with the assessment of blame for the Georgia Pacific's safety record.[1]

As railroads grew in size and scope, they posed enormous danger for those who worked and rode on them. Passengers could not help but feel concern for their safety. From construction to operation, the Georgia Pacific carved a path of death, destruction, delay, and deposition through the heart of the New South. From Atlanta, Georgia, to Greenville, Mississippi,

---

1. Letter to the editor from "Observer," *Birmingham Age-Herald*, 2 October 1890.

the railroad, like its counterparts elsewhere in the South, found itself in circuit and supreme courts fighting against southerners seeking damages for personal injuries. At a local level these trials became contests of social and economic power between citizens and corporations.[2]

In courtrooms and lawyers' offices southerners challenged the power of large railroad corporations but with only limited success. In the 1880s and 1890s railroads held significant advantages over individuals seeking damages. Railroad companies benefited, first of all, from able and experienced legal counsel. These lawyers tried dozens of cases each year in defense of railroads and mastered both the law and courtroom tactics. They perfected the process of settlement in cases of company liability, developed experience in federal district and appellate courts, and built up the resources of their legal departments.[3]

Railroad companies also enjoyed the advantage of economy of scale over individuals. No one case carried the importance for the railroad company that it did for the individual plaintiff. As a plaintiff's personal injury bar grew up in the 1880s to service the large numbers of accident victims, railroad attorneys adopted new tactics and started to employ agents, surgeons, and experts to tilt the informal legal process in their favor. Distance to court, trial delay, and corporate diversity jurisdiction all favored the railroad company in the 1880s and 1890s, and railroad lawyers used these advantages at every opportunity. And as if these were not enough, legal doctrine under common law, especially the fellow-servant rule, contribu-

---

2. Accidents and the litigation arising from such trials have received little attention from historians. Most railroad historians conceded the dangers surrounding the nineteenth-century railroad but bypassed the subject in the effort to understand the financial and business history of the road. For a general treatment of accidents, see Robert B. Shaw, *A History of Railroad Accidents, Safety Precautions and Operating Practices*, 2nd ed. (Potsdam, N.Y.: Northern Press, 1978). For a treatment of accidents in business histories of single lines, see Maury Klein, *A History of the Louisville & Nashville Railroad* (New York: Macmillan, 1972); and Allen W. Trelease, *The North Carolina Railroad, 1849–1871, and the Modernization of North Carolina* (Chapel Hill: University of North Carolina Press, 1991), 237–39.

3. See Randolph E. Bergstrom, *Courting Danger: Injury and Law in New York City, 1870–1910* (Ithaca, N.Y.: Cornell University Press, 1992), 97. Bergstrom points to experienced counsel as an important advantage railroad defendants held over individual plaintiffs. In New York City, he discovered, over 40 percent of defendant lawyers represented appeared in ten or more personal injury suits, while the same percent of plaintiff counsel appeared in only one such case. See also Marc Galanter, "Why the 'Haves' Come Out Ahead: Speculations on the Limits of Legal Change," *Law and Society Review* 9 (1974): 95–160.

tory negligence, and assumption of risk, provided a wall of railroad-company defenses before the turn of the century.[4]

Any examination of New South court records reveals a highly litigious society. Railroad attorneys commented on the region's appetite for lawsuits. Bernard Peyton, general counsel for the Georgia Pacific, explained the large number of personal injury suits against his company: "In these Southern states it seems to be the custom to go to law instead of endeavoring to effect a private settlement; when a person is injured on the Road, the Co. generally receives notice of suit through some Atty. just about as soon as it gets in the Accident Report." Peyton assured his executive officers that "every possible effort is made to keep down this dangerous class of litigation."[5]

Newspaper reporting confirmed the hazards of southern train travel in the late nineteenth century. The Birmingham *Age-Herald* reported almost daily accidents and wrecks on various southern railroads and the large volume of litigation they spurred. For example, in October 1890 alone the newspaper noted twenty-four accidents or wrecks involving area trains. Most of these reports gave details on accidents that claimed the lives of railroad employees who were killed or severely wounded on the job. A typical entry revealed the gruesome account of body parts severed and cars smashed.[6]

In addition, the papers followed accident litigation carefully. When a Kansas City, Memphis & Birmingham Railroad wreck killed two employees and injured at least twenty-four passengers, the paper carefully reported the resulting court cases. Similarly, the newspaper reported individual, non-wreck-related personal injury cases and higher-court deci-

---

4. See Edward A. Purcell, *Litigation and Inequality: Federal Diversity Jurisdiction in Industrial America, 1870–1948* (New York: Oxford University Press, 1992), 153, 138.

5. Bernard Peyton, "Annual Report," 1 October 1885, Box 3, GPRR-VPI. In the only docket study of a southern circuit court, James L. Hunt finds that while "the function of criminal law was to control Durham's poor, especially its poor blacks," the ultimate objective of the legal system was to protect property. In civil courts, moreover, Hunt discovered that individuals sued corporations, not each other, and in particular sued "only certain types of corporations, primarily those with out-of-state ownership." In these cases, Hunt asserts, plaintiffs experienced uniform success in front of a jury. James L. Hunt, "Law and Society in a New South Community: Durham County, North Carolina, 1898–1899," *North Carolina Historical Review* 68 (October 1991): 446, 452, 455.

6. See *Birmingham Age-Herald*, 9, 21, 22 October 1890.

sions on appeals. One black plaintiff, Mary Thompson, obtained a circuit court verdict of $8,000 damages for the wrongful death of her husband, an employee of the East Tennessee, Virginia & Georgia Railroad. In a common scenario, Nollie C. Hill, in a suit against the Alabama Great Southern Railroad Company for injuries suffered in a wreck, obtained an $8,000 verdict in circuit court only to have it overturned in the state supreme court on technical grounds. The paper reported on settlements as well as verdicts. "Mr. T. N. Jones, attorney for the International and Great Northern Road was in the city for the purpose of settling with Mr. C. H. Carlisle for injuries received by the latter in the accident coming out of Galveston," the *Age-Herald* reported, describing the $750 personal injury settlement. "Drs. Lockett and Hynes examined Mr. Carlisle's injuries and they say that the railroad company got off easy."[7]

It seemed to many southerners that the railroads always escaped responsibility for their actions. Built ostensibly to serve a community, the railroads too often killed or injured local citizens with impunity. In the view of many southerners, railroads undermined the legal and judicial process through friendly judges, stacked juries, powerful attorneys, special agents, and sympathetic expert witnesses. When these conditions proved insufficient for victory, railroads fled local justice by removing their personal injury cases to federal court in another state.

Below the surface of appellate court litigation, personal injury suits against railroads flooded southern district courts. The number of these suits increased between 1880 and 1900, according to railroad lawyers. David Schenck, Richmond & Danville's North Carolina counsel, hinted at the sheer volume of personal injury cases in his diary: "The balance of the day is spent in examining papers, studying the cases, writing instructions, preparing legal briefs, and numerous duties incident to taking care of the legal affairs of 750 miles of Railroad. The accident reports now reach me every morning and my Special Agent James D. Glenn is directed to investigate the facts and make report." Smaller railroads, too, faced significant personal injury litigation.[8]

---

7. *Birmingham Age-Herald*, 22, 5, 7 October, and 30 January 1890. In Wisconsin, of 307 personal injury cases before the state supreme court, two-thirds had been ruled in favor of the worker in lower courts, but in the supreme court only 20 percent were decided in favor of the worker. Lawrence M. Friedman and Jack Ladinsky, "Social Change and the Law of Industrial Accidents," *Columbia Law Review* 67 (1967): 50–82.

8. David Schenck Diary, 11 January 1890, SHC-UNC. For example, the superintendent of the Knoxville, Cumberland Gap & St. Louis Railroad resigned "to have ample time to

Railroad lore is full of stories of bad wrecks and accidents, of engineers jumping from trains, of brakemen slipping from the tops of the cars, of conductors making heroic attempts to save passengers. Songs and poems dedicated to the railroad and its dangers abound. Even amateurs wrote such verse about the railroad. One engineer on the Shenandoah Division of the Norfolk & Western Railroad wrote a poem, entitled "His Wonderful Care," referring to the presence of God throughout his career on the railroads:

> While I was a Locomotive Enginneer
> I never dreamt of the danger that lurked so near,
> But after crossing one hundred and fifty bridge
> Between East Lexington and Timber Ridge;
> Around a curve I could not see
> A landslide that was facing me.
> Without a warning we struck this slide,
> A way to safety, no time to decide.
> "Oh! Lord, save us," silently, I cried,
> Engine 2044 turned on her side.
> But, thanks to God, no one injured or nobody died.[9]

When most engines turned on their sides, though, people did die, and in the South these kinds of deaths occurred with remarkable frequency. From its inception in 1887 the Interstate Commerce Commission compiled statistical data on railroads, each year publishing its findings on matters ranging from ton mileage to operating expenses and accident rates. From the data in these reports, observers detected distressing trends on accidents.

Railroad employees assumed terrible risks in their workplace. In one of its early reports, for example, the ICC noted 1,972 deaths and 20,028 injuries to railroad employees in the United States. The data reflected 1 death for every 357 employees and 1 injury for every 35 employees in the

attend to the personal injury cases." Clarence Coary to J. W. Wilson, 23 December 1890, William Carson Ervin Papers, SHC-UNC.

9. Rockbridge Historical Society Manuscripts, Frank Royce Collection, Leyburn Library, Washington and Lee University.

year 1888. For trainmen (engineers, firemen, brakemen, and conductors), the ratios worsened to 1 death for every 117 and 1 injury for every 12 employees in a year. A later report summarized the statistical dangers: "While trainmen represent but 20 percent of the total number of employees, the casualties sustained by them represent 58 percent of the total casualties. A passenger riding continuously on a train [at 30 miles per hour] might expect immunity from death by railway accident for 158 years, but an engineer, a brakeman, or a conductor, under the same conditions, must expect a fatal accident at the expiration of 35 years [of eight-hour days]. At the end of the century, the data for trainmen continued to demonstrate serious risks. One trainman died in 1899 for every 155 employed and 1 sustained injuries for every 11 employed.[10]

As early as 1890 the ICC considered regional variation in accident rate data. In that year the commission concluded that the South and West lagged the rest of the country in overall safety. The following year's report ventured some possible reasons: "These facts seem to indicate that density of traffic has little to do with rate of casualties, but that the character of the equipment and the degree of intelligence among employees are the most important factors." Shoddy construction and poor human capital, the ICC concluded, represented the obvious differences in the regional rail networks.[11]

By 1892 the data began to reveal a pattern: Southern railroads were the most dangerous roads in the country for employees and passengers alike. Even when the data were adjusted for mileage, the South proved the most dangerous region to work on and ride. Southern-railroad safety remained consistently poor throughout the nineties despite the increased use of automatic couplers and continuous power air brakes. After Westinghouse Company's invention of air brakes in 1869, public pressure for improvement in railroad safety prompted railroad management to convert to newer, safer technologies. By 1877 most passenger trains were equipped with air brakes, but freight trains remained unconverted until the end of the century. The invention obviated the need for brakemen to climb on top of the moving train to turn manually the brakes on each car. Brakemen experienced a high rate of accidents from falls, as they moved from the top

10. *Interstate Commerce Commission: Statistics of Railways in the United States* (Washington, DC., 1889), 36–38, (1890), 76; (1899), 108.
11. *ICC: Statistics* (1890), 80, (1891), 97.

of one car to the next setting brakes (24 percent of employee deaths and 11 percent of the injuries in 1892).[12]

The ICC reports clearly demonstrated that coupling and uncoupling cars accounted for the most prevalent casualties to trainmen (15 percent of deaths and 37 percent of employee injuries in 1892). Automatic couplers replaced the manual link and pin coupler, which required trainmen to move in between the cars on the track. The ICC reports consistently called for improvement in brakes and couplers and for national legislation to mandate the adoption of safer technologies. Although the Safety Appliance Act of 1893 fulfilled the ICC's requests, it did not require full compliance until the end of the century. Most companies, particularly those in the South, delayed the costly conversion for as long as possible.[13]

Incompatibility of new and old technologies elevated the dangers inherent in the work of the trainmen and brakemen. Without federal mandates, companies were free to adopt new technologies as they pleased. Because railroads often hauled other companies' freight cars over their lines, any given train had the potential for a jumble of technologies. In addition, the vast number of patented couplers in use presented trainmen with an array of different situations each time they stepped between the

12. In 1892, for example, one trainman was killed for every 83 employed, and one injured for every 6 employed in the southeastern states. In New England and the middle Atlantic states, the ratio for trainmen killed stood at 1:124 and 1:105, respectively, and 1:12 and 1:9 for trainmen injured. The Deep South appeared equally dangerous, and the commission concluded that "the high rate of mortality among railway employees of these groups is probably due to the quality of labor which it is necessary for the railways in this part of the country to take into their employ." *ICC: Statistics* (1892), 78. As late as 1899, in the Southeast one employee was killed for every 234,043 freight train miles run. In the Deep South the ratio was similarly high, at 1:217,820, but in New England and the middle Atlantic states it stood at 1:180,411 and 1:192,633, respectively. Passengers on southern railroads faced the same regional disparity as trainmen. For example, in 1897 in the southeast one passenger was killed for 40,620,518 carried one mile; in the Deep South the ratio was a dismal 1:19,399,335. In comparison, New England experienced a 1:166,961,626 ratio, and in the United States as a whole the ratio was 1:55,211,440. *ICC: Statistics* (1899), 100–105. See Henry Varnum Poor, *Manual of the Railroads* (New York: H. V. & H. W. Poor, 1899), for freight train mileage data for each group—1899 was the earliest year for which freight train mileage was available.

13. See *ICC: Statistics* (1891), 92–93; Steven W. Usselman, "Air Brakes for Freight Trains: Technological Innovation in the American Railroad Industry, 1869–1900," *Business History Review* 58 (spring 1984): 30–50; *Interstate Commerce Commission Third Annual Report* (1889), 90.

cars to work the coupling. The ICC summarized the results of this technological incompatibility. The figures on trainmen casualties from coupling cars and falling "form the basis in fact of the argument in favor of the universal use by railway companies of some form of train brake and automatic coupler of uniform device. . . . railways are making practically no progress in the equipment of their cars and engines with uniform safety."[14]

Even new technologies posed dangers when mishandled. Automatic couplers required careful attention on the part of the trainmen, or the results could be fatal. The ICC found in 1900 that 20 percent of the automatic couplers failed from improper maintenance. "While in such a condition," the commission reported, "it is agreed that they are far more dangerous to the men employed . . . than the old link and pin coupler. When an accident in the coupling now occurs, it is said there is more probability of its resulting fatally." New power brakes also posed new dangers, as workers failed to comprehend their proper use and as engineers, confident in the new brakes' ability to stop trains more quickly, drove their trains at higher speeds. The ICC took note of this unintended result in 1901 and stated its concern that the increased speeds "neutralized" the benefit in safety from new brakes. Improper maintenance of both the new couplers and brakes, the ICC concluded, increased with the introduction of these new technologies and led directly to defects in performance.[15]

14. *ICC: Statistics* (1891), 92–93.

15. *ICC Fourteenth Annual Report* (1900), 82; *ICC Fifteenth Annual Report* (1901), 76. See also *ICC Sixteenth Annual Report* (1902). In a recent study of the 1893 Safety Appliance Act's effectiveness, Philip Hersch and Jeffry Netter concluded that its results were "at best mixed." Hersch and Netter set out to measure the effectiveness of the act in promoting a safer workplace for railroad employees. Using the data on accidents in the ICC reports and regression analysis, they found that automatic couplers "significantly reduced injury rates but had no impact on fatality rates"; that air brakes had "little effect" on overall accident rates from falls; that "lack of experience was a source of accidents"; and finally that "accident rates in general were higher in the south." Philip L. Hersch and J. M. Netter, "The Impact of Early Safety Legislation: The Case of the Safety Appliance Act of 1893," *International Review of Law and Economics* 10 (May 1990): 72–75. Note that this conclusion contradicts the ICC's speculation on the increased fatalities from the new coupler technology. For an account of the New South's labor market and its relation to the economy as a whole, see Gavin Wright, *Old South, New South: Revolutions in the Southern Economy Since the Civil War* (New York: Basic Books, 1986), especially Chapter 6. For an account of race and labor on one line, see Trelease, *North Carolina Railroad,* 231–32. Trelease found that African Americans constituted the overwhelming majority of train crews and road departments with the exception

Although railroad employees and passengers suffered high rates of casualty in these years, others met death and injury on the tracks as well. Railroad attorneys classified these people as "trespassers" and often referred to them as "tramps" or "hobos." Unlike passengers, whose business the railroads solicited, and employees, whose skills and labor the railroads needed, trespassers simply got in the way.

Railroad officials and attorneys knew that trespassers posed a serious problem, a problem whose solution lay in reform. As early as 1893 Illinois Central president Stuyvesant Fish ordered the fencing of all tracks "in order to exclude the public from committing suicide at our expense." In nearly a year's compilation of accident reports on the Southern Railway, officials determined that 93 "trespassers" and 12 "citizens" were killed in 1897–1898 versus 29 employees and 3 passengers. Not only were many more trespassers killed than either employees or passengers, but when involved in an accident trespassers were more likely to die. Typical entries in an accident report were as follows:

- "#11,890—Pete Parker, a small white boy at Atlanta, Ga. January 1st, 1898 attempted to board train, fell under cars and had left hand and foot cut off."
- "#11,955—David Garlic, colored, at Richmond, Va., January 18th, 1898., drunk on track, was run over and killed."
- "#11,926—Pearl Shorter, colored girl eight years of age, picking up chips under a car was run over and killed. Macon Yard, Ga., January 10th, 1898."
- "#11,368—M. P. Sorenson, white, residence Spartansburg, S.C. . . . ran along side of postal car to mail some letters, fell and had his right leg mashed November 2nd. He died from the effect of injuries the following day."[16]

Over time railroad attorneys found that most trespassers were not "tramps" or "hobos" but instead, as the foregoing sampling suggests, residents in a locality who for various reasons crossed or used the railroad

---

of skilled or prestigious positions, such as conductor or engineer, which were reserved for whites.

16. Stuyvesant Fish to James W. Scott, 12 April 1893, Fish Out Letters, vol. 12, p. 265, ICRR-NL; "Statement of Personal Injuries for November, 1897, January, 1898," SRy-VPI.

tracks. Stories of horrible deaths on the tracks filled southern newspapers as old and young, drunk and sober, black and white, male and female, wealthy and poor fell victim to the railroad. In Paris, Texas, for example, "a prominent farmer, J. Q. Peppers" on his way to pay his taxes "missed the regular passenger train and secretly boarded a through freight. The freight train did not stop, and he jumped off and was instantly killed."[17]

Often disturbing for their banality, these deaths hit southern communities at all socioeconomic levels. One study of trespasser deaths concluded that "the great majority are not of the class of aimless wanderers who might be expected to be careless of their lives, but are business or professional men, regularly employed workingmen, and members of their families, whose deaths are a distinct loss to the community." This report observed that many trespassers "use the right-of-way between streets or highways in going to or from their work . . . [or] when public highways are wet and muddy, or difficult to walk upon."[18]

Railroads brought new products, services, and technologies to southern communities, but the social costs remained high. With the most dangerous rail network in the country, the region witnessed daily injury and death. It is not improbable that most southerners knew someone killed or injured in a railroad accident. Southern newspapers covered the most spectacular accidents and the deaths of local men, but it is railroad company records that describe the full extent of employee, passenger, and trespasser death and injury.[19]

- -

When victims or their families brought a suit for personal injury damages against the railroad, they found that the formal processes of the law in most states favored the railroad corporations. Courts required plaintiffs to prove the defendant railroad negligent. In general terms, negligence meant "the neglect of the use of ordinary care or skill toward a person to

17. *Brenham Daily Banner*, 16 January 1890.

18. *Railway Age Gazette*, 8 March 1912. See also " 'Safety First' the Slogan," in *Railway Library* (1912), 158, for an address by ICC commissioner C. C. McChord on this subject. See also "Why 5,000 Trespassers Are Killed Yearly," *Railway Library* (1912), 189.

19. For a detailed compilation of one railroad's accidents, see the Nashville, St. Louis & Chatanooga Railway Company Accident Record Book, Filson Club, Louisville, Kentucky. See also Norfolk & Western Railroad Records, Baker Library, Harvard Business School.

whom the defendant owes the duty of observing ordinary care and skill, by which neglect the plaintiff, without contributory negligence on his part, has suffered injury to his person or property." Both common law and statutory law defined the duty of one party to another. For railroads these duties ordinarily involved a reasonably safe place to work, reasonably safe machinery and appliances on which to work and ride, reasonable company rules and regulations, and responsibly selected, competent employees.[20]

As a bulwark against local bias and growing litigation, railroad attorneys in the South exploited a triad of defenses against personal injury suits: contributory negligence, the fellow-servant rule, and assumption of risk. Armed with these defenses, railroad lawyers were able to fend off legal attacks from all quarters—employees, passengers, trespassers, and crossers. Each of these doctrines developed in the judge-made common law, rather than by legislative statute. As a result they were very difficult to overturn or circumvent. They were flexible enough to provide defendant railroads some protection in nearly every instance of personal injury.[21]

The contributory negligence defense was most commonly used in the multitude of crossing cases. Christopher Patterson stated the general rule in his 1886 manual on railroad accident law: "It is the duty of travellers on the highway, when approaching a grade crossing, to exercise a prudent care for their own safety, and to that end to look and listen, in order to satisfy themselves that it is safe to cross the line." Contributory negligence doctrine located the cause of an accident and held that if a plaintiff contributed to the cause in any way, he could not recover. If the engineer performed all his requisite duties of driving at a safe speed, using the headlight at night, blowing the whistle at the required distance from the crossing, and braking to avoid collision, the plaintiff often failed to prove negligence. In addition, if the railroad attorneys could show that the plaintiff failed to "look and listen" at the crossing or did not demonstrate reason-

---

20. *M. R. Brett, Heaven v. Pender,* 11 Q.B.D. 507, in Christopher S. Patterson, *Railway Accident Law: The Liability of Railways for Injuries to the Person* (Philadelphia: T. & J. W. Johnson, 1886), 7. See also Edward J. White, *The Law of Personal Injuries on Railroads,* vol. 1, *Injuries to Employees* (F. H. Thomas Law Books Co., 1909).

21. Lawrence M. Friedman, *A History of American Law* (New York: Simon & Schuster, 1973), 475. According to Friedman, "What they added up to was also crystal-clear. Enterprise was favored over workers, slightly less so over passengers and members of the public. Juries were suspected—on thin evidence—of lavishness in awarding damages; they had to be kept under firm control."

able care, the judge often dismissed the case on contributory negligence grounds. If the railroad attorneys could secure a friendly local judge, either with a free pass, a personal favor, or reelection money, they might be able to count on his throwing out these cases on a regular basis.[22]

The fellow-servant rule complemented contributory negligence as a railroad defense but applied only to employee suits. The doctrine emerged out of several American cases in the 1840s and held that a servant (employee) could not sue a master (employer) for injuries resulting from the negligence of a fellow servant. The rule prevented workers from recovering against their employers and left them to sue one another. Assumption of risk allowed railroad lawyers another defense. Under common law, workers assumed certain risks in the workplace—the negligence of competent fellow servants, the dangers incidental to the business, and the dangers arising from the existing condition of the premises which are known or ought to be known to the servant. Over time the fellow-servant rule weakened as the hierarchies of workplaces demanded a more sophisticated approach to the definition of fellow servant, and common law adapted to the changing circumstances.[23]

Despite these limitations, railroad attorneys used the fellow-servant rule again and again to deflect employees' suits. By the early 1900s some authorities, such as Frank Dresser, deemed the rule inequitable: "The burdens of the fellow-servant rule have pressed more heavily upon railway employes than upon any other class of servants, and the reasoning upon which the doctrine is founded has in no other business proved more fallacious."[24]

Some southern state bar associations debated the merits of these employer defenses. As chairman of the Texas Bar Association's 1889 Committee on Jurisprudence and Law Reform, Robert G. Street submitted an annual report to the association recommending reform of the fellow-servant rule. Referring to personal injury cases, Street directed attention "to the defective condition of the law of our State in a single matter,

22. Patterson, *Railway Accident Law*, 168.

23. Frank F. Dresser, *The Employers' Liability Acts and the Assumption of Risks in New York, Massachusetts, Indiana, Alabama, Colorado, and England* (St. Paul: Keefe-Davidson, 1903), 393, 262. See also William M. McKinney, *A Treatise on the Law of Fellow-Servants* (Northport, N.Y.: Edward Thompson, 1890), 112–79. For the gradual weakening of the fellow-servant rule in common law, see Friedman, *History of American Law*, 480–84.

24. Dresser, *Employers' Liability Acts*, 231.

whose practical importance is testified by the very large number of cases now and for several years past occupying a great part of the time of our courts." As far as the committee was concerned, personal injury negligence cases resulted directly from the expansion of the railroad and multiplied to mammoth proportions as the railroad spread its tracks across the state. The committee recommended legislative action to correct the "unsatisfactory state" of the law as it evolved in the courts of the nation: "While the danger is greatly augmented, the supposed ability of the employes by acquaintance with all the dangers of their employment to protect themselves becomes a heartless fiction."[25]

England's passage in 1880 of an Employers' Liability Act exemplified the type of reform the committee sought. The act removed the fellow-servant defense in employees' personal injury claims. At the same time, it allowed all other defenses and limited the amount of damages. Street concluded that "it was adopted as a concession to the sentiments of humanity that revolted at the barbarity and the untruth in fact of the legal presumption that one engaging in a dangerous employment contemplated the acceptance of all the risks of the negligence of his fellows."[26]

The Texas committee recommended that the bar association petition the governor and legislature. They hoped that the legislation would include, first, a limitation of recovery for personal injury cases to a sum not exceeding five thousand dollars, and second, a restriction of recovery against fellow-servant defenses (all other defenses allowed) to three years' wages. Together these innovations, the committee hoped, would promote settlements and "restrain speculative litigation." As a whole the committee's recommendations sought limits—on the number of cases, on the amounts recovered, on the ability of defendants to escape through the fellow-servant rule, and ultimately on the vagaries of jury trials. Following England's 1880 example, several state legislatures limited the fellow-

25. Admitted to the Alabama bar in 1865 after serving four years in the Confederate army, Street moved to Galveston, Texas, in 1867. He served a term in the state senate, wrote a treatise on the law of personal injuries, and eventually sat as a district judge. *Who Was Who in America*, vol. I, 1897–1942 (Chicago: Marquis Who's Who, 1968), 1198 (*S.V.* "Street, Robert G."). Robert G. Street, "Report of the Committee on Jurisprudence and Law Reform," *Texas Bar Association Proceedings* (1889), 59, 62.

26. Street, "Report," 63. The fellow-servant doctrine, Street reminded the association, evolved in the American courts in *Murray v. Railroad Co.*, 1 McMull (1841), and *Farwell v. Boston & Worcester Railroad Co.*, 4 Met. (1841), and spread to England in 1850.

servant defense in the late nineteenth century with the passage of employers' liability acts.[27]

Not all state bar association members, though, recommended restriction of the fellow-servant rule. Indeed, many sought to protect its power to defend corporations. Railroad lawyers participated actively in most state bar associations and contributed to the conservative tone of the proceedings. Chesapeake & Ohio Railroad local attorney Robert L. Parrish, for example, defended the fellow-servant rule in front of the Virginia Bar Association in 1892. Considered by many "the ablest lawyer in Western Virginia," Parrish practiced in Covington, where the C&O maintained a large number of employees in its yards. He considered the fellow-servant doctrine fundamentally sound and blamed the courts of last resort for the rule's shaky foundations. These courts, he determined, "by their various and conflicting opinions, have placed what is known as the 'Fellow-Servant Doctrine,' in a state of decided unrest, and, if they keep up their present pace, it will not be many years before the whole doctrine will be abolished." Parrish stated his view of the rule simply to the Virginia Bar in 1892:

> If the master is without fault, I regard it as a wise rule of law that frees him from responsibility for an injury to a servant, inflicted by the negligence of a fellow-servant. And even if the master is at fault . . . it is not a harsh rule that frees the master from liability for an injury . . . to which a fellow-servant contributed. For if the servant, knowing the master's faulty, elects to do the work, or, in other words, to take the risk of the situation in which he is placed, he is himself guilty of contributory negligence.[28]

27. Street, "Report," 63. See Alabama Employers' Liability Act (Civ. Code Ala. 1896, c. 43, sections 1749–1751), Massachusetts Employers' Liability Act (Rev. Laws 1901, c. 106), Indiana Employers' Liability Act (Burns' Rev. St. Ind. 1901), Colorado Employers' Liability Act (Mills' Supp. Ann. St. Colo. 1891–1896), Texas Employers' Liability Act (1891), and New York Employers' Liability Act (Laws 1902, c. 600).

28. Robert L. Parrish, "Master and Servant," *Virginia Bar Association Proceedings* (1892), 131, 135; Lyon G. Tyler, ed., *Men of Mark in Virginia: Ideals of American Life* (Washington, D.C.: Men of Mark Publishing Co., 1908), 4:322; *Charlottesville Daily Progress,* 14 July 1904, obituary.

Railroad attorneys such as Parrish considered the doctrine sound not only in theory but also in practice. They argued that the rule prevented accidents because it forced all employees to act more carefully. Without recourse in the courts for the negligent actions of a fellow, this logic concluded that workers guarded their and others' safety. After a thorough examination of the fellow-servant principle, Parrish concluded, "If these principles are founded in reason . . . it would seem to follow that they should be preserved and maintained, both by the bar and the courts, rather than be frittered away and substituted by matters of sentiment only."[29]

While legal doctrine kept many personal injury suits from reaching the courts and frustrated others, procedure contributed equally to railroad success in these cases. Taking advantage of their corporations' diverse citizenship, railroad attorneys sometimes used a powerful tactic to deflect personal injury suits: removal to federal court. Removal not only offered railroads more favorable common law and supposedly less prejudicial juries but also burdened plaintiffs with distance and their lawyers with different procedural rules and law. Railroads retained counsel with experience in federal courts, and they used the larger, more complex federal system to frustrate and intimidate plaintiffs and their attorneys.[30]

Railroad lawyers in the South expressed particular concern for the adverse bias of the juries. These attorneys comprehended that for jurors each case represented a one-time incident and that therefore jurors were disposed to sympathize with the plaintiff. Harsh doctrines such as the fellow-servant rule and contributory negligence were necessary tools in the hands of the judges, these attorneys thought, to offset juries' supposedly pro-plaintiff leanings. Railroad attorneys thought they faced jurors who viewed the corporation with skeptical disdain and harbored deep resentment toward large, impersonal organizations. Juries, though, did not constitute either the entirety of the legal system or its most decisive component, nor were they uniformly antagonistic to railroad corporations in the 1880s and 1890s.[31]

29. Parrish, "Master and Servant," 150.

30. For the definitive examination of corporate diversity, see Purcell, *Litigation and Inequality*. Purcell discounts local prejudice in the railroad attorneys' decisions to remove, instead emphasizing the burdens both procedural and physical removal laid on the plaintiffs. Southern railroad attorneys testified to all of these reasons, citing local prejudice, better judges, smaller awards for damages, better juries, favorable procedural rules, and burdens of distance and delay.

31. "During those years I had represented corporations. I naturally lost a number of

----

In a study of New York courts, the first jurisdictions to deal extensively with accident litigation, historian Wex Malone discovered the impetus for the doctrine of contributory negligence, which was a virtually unused concept before the emergence of the railroad. Malone found that "the available evidence indicates that the jury tended to break down as an effective administrative arm in the railroad crossing cases." The jury, he discovered, became "plaintiff-minded" in railroad accident cases. Increasingly, judges distrusted the juries. They sought a new method for trying these volatile cases and a new means to restore balance to the courts and eliminate the anti-corporate bias of the juries. In the underutilized concept of contributory negligence, the New York courts developed an "ingenious device which gave the court almost complete freedom to accept or reject jury participation at its pleasure."[32]

Throughout the South railroad lawyers actively tried to turn local prejudice into favoritism. For example, James Fentress won a damage case in Mississippi in 1882 and reported to his superiors that "this decision is considered very important in Mississippi—as heretofore the unbridled license of the jury was the rule of damages in such cases." Fentress went on to reveal his strategy for the Illinois Central in Mississippi: "I am endeavoring gradually not only to get the good will of the people but to get decisions of the courts of last resort, in favorable cases, as protection against robbery under the guise of the law." In his annual report of 1884 Fentress observed that lower court victories seemed to indicate "the good will of the people conserved, and the company redeemed from the legacy McComb's administration left us of being a 'soulless corporation.'" A year later Fentress again remarked that the "results of suits as shown by this report indicate a steady improvement in the direction of the good will of the States and people and a diminution of that popular prejudice which prevents fair trails." Fentress, it appeared, considered juries' sympathies to be mallea-

cases and became gun-shy of juries." Robert Watson Winston, *It's a Far Cry* (New York: Holt, 1937), 240. See also Winston, *Talks About the Law* (Raleigh, N.C.: Edwards & Broughton, 1894), 42.

32. Wex Malone, "The Formative Era of Contributory Negligence," *Illinois Law Review* 41 (1946): 157.

ble, subject to local condition and to railroad company behavior in a community.[33]

Juries responded to local, even case-specific, circumstances in the 1880s, and 1890s, and to label them pro-plaintiff or anti-railroad oversimplifies their understanding of the law and its application. The Georgia Pacific, one of the South's most dangerous railroads, experienced remarkable success in courts along its line in the 1880s (see table). In both justice of the peace and lower courts of record, the Georgia Pacific attorneys used a careful mixture of settling bad cases, removal to federal court, non-suits on contributory negligence grounds, and the fellow-servant rule to achieve minimal losses at the local level. Of the twenty-one personal injury cases in 1888, for example, the Georgia Pacific general counsel reported settling eight claims totaling 90,500 for $11,360, winning eight cases, and losing five cases. Justice of the peace courts tried cases involving small sums, but railroad lawyers suspected these justices of greater anti-railroad bias than higher courts. "In view of the fact that Justices of the Peace, like necessity, know no law, and are invariably biased against corporations and

GEORGIA PACIFIC IN TRIAL COURTS

Justice of the Peace Courts (all cases)			
Year	% settled	% for	% against
1885	31	37	32
1886	41	37	22
1887	35	12	53
1888	42	16	42
Courts of Record (all cases)			
1885	40	52	8
1886	52	26	21
1887	57	38	5
1888	35	39	25

Source: Annual Reports of the General Counsel, Georgia Pacific Railroad Company Records, Boxes 3 and 4, VPI.

33. James Fentress to W. H. Osborne, 8 June 1882, Fentress Out Letters, ICRR-NL; James Fentress, Annual Report of the Law Department, 31 December 1884, Annual Report of the Law Department, 8 January 1885, Board Supporting Documents, ibid.

in favor of their neighbors, and against the party who can best pay the costs of the suit," James Weatherly concluded, "I think the above a remarkably fine showing."[34]

On the Illinois Central in Mississippi, railroad attorneys strove for favorable public opinion. Their efforts seemed to have worked. In 1899 James Fentress reported the aggregate personal injury statistics, finding that only 30 percent of the cases resulted in a judgment against the railroad. In another 30 percent the railroad company settled, and the company won 37 percent of the cases. In all the company made some payment in 67 percent of the cases and no payment in 33 percent. Moreover, out of a total of $2,481,920 sued for in these cases, the railroad company's payments amounted to $138,688, or 5.59 percent of the total. Based on these numbers company president Stuyvesant Fish remarked to his general solicitor that "there seems to be a disposition on the part of the people and juries on the line to treat the Company fairly."[35]

In most cases railroad lawyers scoffed at the amounts claimed by personal injury plaintiffs. All cases pending against the Georgia Pacific in 1888, for example, totaled $1,119,758 in amounts claimed, and personal injury claims constituted the bulk of the aggregate. Commenting on the significant amount of claims at stake in these cases, the Georgia Pacific general counsel assured his superiors: "In the majority of the cases, I believe the Company will be victorious. Some will be lost, of course, but with reasonably good fortune, the amounts recovered . . . will probably be very small, compared with the amounts claimed." The Illinois Central general counsel explained his views on these large claims in his 1900 report to the

---

34. James T. Weatherly, Annual Report, 13 October 1888, Annual Report, 8 December 1886, Box 4, GPRR-VPI. For an examination of the railroad's lack of success before juries, see W. S. McCain, "Railroads as a Factor in the Law," *Arkansas Bar Association Proceedings* (1886), 16. McCain states, "In the course of my practice I have witnessed jury trials in railroad cases by the score, but I have never yet known a disputed issue of fact to be decided by a jury in favor of a railroad corporation." National law journals continually referred to juries as pro-plaintiff in these years. "The twelve good and true men are commonly reputed to have a habit of giving a verdict against a railway company when an individual claims to have suffered at its hands." *Railway Law and Corporation Journal* (31 October 1891): 341. A year later the journal reflected on the changed sentiments among jurors in railroad damage cases, commenting that "while the old prejudices are by no means weak, they are undoubtedly weakening." *Railway Law and Corporation Journal* (18 June 1892): 289.

35. S. Fish to James Fentress, 26 July 1899, Fish Out Letters, vol. 42, p. 57. S. Fish to James Fentress, 27 July 1899, Fish Out Letters, vol. 42, p. 106, ICRR-NL.

president: "the *ad damnum* [amount sued for] depends entirely upon the lawyer who brings the suit, and some of them delight in suing for large amounts and thus having their names connected with ostensibly large cases. We have sometimes paid the smallest amounts in the largest claims."[36]

Railroad lawyers, though, consistently expressed concern for "dangerous" or "serious" personal injury cases that often resulted in large verdicts. The death or injury of a child always worried railroad attorneys. Not only did juries show great sympathy in these cases, but more importantly, the contributory negligence defense broke down. Large amounts claimed translated into large verdicts in these cases. The death of Richard D. Blanton's two-year-old daughter on the tracks of the Georgia Pacific, for example, brought a suit against the company for $25,000 in 1887. In his annual report on these cases, the general counsel warned, "She was playing on track unaccompanied by nurse—Engineer claims he did not and could not have seen her in time to avoid collision—a serious case." The next year's report showed the case tried and the jury's judgment of $5,500 paid to the family. Summing up the loss, the Georgia Pacific general counsel James Weatherly reported to his superiors, "Our own evidence showed negligence on the part of our Engineer and Fireman. Only a day or two after the killing, I made personal efforts to effect a settlement with the child's parents, who were poor, but they had already given the case to their lawyers." The case, he thought, "showed the great importance of having someone to interview claimants and bring about economical settlements, in proper cases, before the lawyers have been retained." Sometimes, though, Weatherly conseled, "it is best not to settle or compromise while the injury is fresh, but, by a determined and patient resistance, to work the plaintiff down."[37]

Even employee personal injury suits threatened large verdicts where company negligence could be proven. Despite the limitations of the fellow-servant rule and contributory negligence, employees often found grounds for action in cases where they could prove the company failed to provide a safe work environment. In the case of W. H. Dooley, for exam-

36. James T. Weatherly, Annual Report, 13 October 1888, Box 4, GPRR-VPI; J. M. Dickinson to Stuyvesant Fish, 17 August 1900, Fish Out Letters.

37. James T. Weatherly, Annual Report, 24 November 1887, Annual Report, 13 October 1888, Box 4, GPRR-VPI.

ple, the Georgia Pacific freight conductor "was thrown from his caboose against a rock cut, his face disfigured, jawbone broken, five teeth knocked out, two ribs broken, leg cut, shoulder dislocated, and internally injured." The general counsel reported the prospects for the $25,000 suit: "Assigned cause: defective track and rotten cross-ties. A bad case. You may expect heavy damages in this case." In sum, the Georgia Pacific general counsel confessed to his superiors that "it may appear, after fuller investigation of the facts, that some of the cases included in the foregoing statement as dangerous, are not so in fact, while others may develop into serious ones. It is difficult to predict, with any degree of certainty, what the result of any personal injury suit may be."[38]

Unpredictable local circumstances led many railroad attorneys to seek shelter in federal court. They removed dangerous cases whenever possible. Georgia Pacific general counsel Bernard Peyton, for example, removed a $10,000 personal injury suit into federal court in 1885. After achieving a $250 settlement, Peyton commented in his annual report: "A very dangerous case, severe injuries to the lady in a run-off, due to defective track, could not have been successfully defended, and such a favorable compromise only secured by the removal." Similarly, local attorneys for the Illinois Central recommended removal to federal court in a personal injury case, pointing out to James Fentress that "a jury in the federal court is likely to give smaller damages than juries in the state court."[39]

Judges, both federal and state, provided an important bulwark against local prejudice in personal injury cases. Appointed for life terms by the president of the United States upon confirmation by the Senate, federal judges stood apart from the kind of local politics that state judges experienced. In these years federal judges, for the most part, sympathized with the railroads' predicament in prejudicial localities and favored these interstate corporations. Moreover, the federal judges intimidated plaintiffs' attorneys with their high level of expertise and low level of tolerance for mistakes. Unfamiliar with the judges, the rules, and the procedures in federal courts, plaintiffs' attorneys often had little influence and labored at a distinct disadvantage to their corporate adversaries.

Railroad lawyers such as David Schenck in North Carolina expected

---

38. James T. Weatherly, Annual Report, 13 October 1888, ibid.

39. Bernard Peyton, Annual Report, 1 October 1885, Box 3, GPRR-VPI; Humphrey & Davie to James Fentress, 13 December 1893, Fish Out Letters, vol. 14, p. 215, ICRR-NL.

state judges to subscribe to conservative business interests. Schenck, like many railroad attorneys, served as a state judge at one time. In his compilation of North Carolina railroad law, he reinforced the judiciary's economic development sympathies in the many cases involving individuals seeking damages. In the multitude of cases arising from the loss of livestock, Schenck quoted an appellate judicial opinion: "The railroad system, traversing the country in all directions, contributes largely to the development of its agricultural, commercial, and other resources. . . . this inconvenience [of injury to straying cattle] is greatly outweighed by the benefits conferred on the whole country by railway transportation, and it would be an unwise policy to hamper the latter and diminish its usefulness by needless restraints." Appellate judges across the South generally conformed to this reasoning through the 1880s and 1890s.[40]

State trial judges stood for election in many southern states and, as a consequence, weighed decisions in these cases with more accountability than their appellate brethren. Railroads convinced most state trial judges that favoritism to capital made good practical as well as personal sense. Free passes, election funds, and local economic growth kept most judges in the railroads' corner. William Pitt Ballinger, Texas railroad attorney, relied on a local judge for consistent pro-railroad decisions. As the Santa Fe Railroad state counsel, Ballinger explained to a local attorney that he was rarely "disappointed by any of the judge's decisions. He has proven himself to be a friend of the Railroads, and believes their interests and positions must be protected and promoted for the advancement of our State."[41]

Delay proved perhaps the most effective and most widely used method for defeating personal injury suits. Railroad lawyers recognized the advantages they held as defendants. An unresolved case was, in their view, a case not lost. In addition, they knew the burden that delay placed on poorer individuals seeking damages. The tactic often brought eventual settlement in the railroad's favor. In his annual report, Georgia Pacific general counsel James T. Weatherly explained the reason for the long list of cases pending:

40. *Dogget v. Railroad Company* 81 (1879), in David Schenck, *North Carolina Railroad Decisions, 1837–1883* (Richmond: William Ellis Jones, Book and Job Printer, 1883), 459.

41. Ballinger, quoted in John Moretta, "William Pitt Ballinger" (draft manuscript), 1071.

> The courts are naturally slow, lawyers love continuances and the policy of a railroad attorney must frequently be to postpone and delay. It often happens that suits which at first seemed to be meritorious can be exposed by course of time, and besides, plaintiffs sometimes take a very different view of the merits of the cases after having had a long time for reflection. Again, in suits for personal injuries, wounds and injuries at first deemed to be permanent, often become entirely healed, leaving the plaintiffs at the time of trial sound and healthy. Again, *recent* injuries make so much deeper an impression upon the sympathies of jurors.[42]

In some personal injury cases, however, delay tactics hurt the railroad's defense. Local attorneys complained to their general counsels that long-delayed trials often left them without key witnesses. Railroad employees moved regularly in the 1880s and 1890s. Railroad lawyers were unable to maintain current addresses for employee witnesses who moved. Without these key witnesses, many local attorneys simply hoped that delay weakened the oppositions' case more than their own. A $5,000 suit by a Georgia Pacific employee, for example, disturbed the railroad's general counsel. "This would not be anything serious," he explained in his annual report, "were it not for the fact that no claim was made, nor suit brought, until all the witnesses to the transaction had gone away. It will be difficult to defend only for this reason."[43]

Railroad corporations relied on their local and state counsel to defend them against personal injury lawsuits. They discovered that anti-corporation bias infected some localities, and they worked to counter this bias with public relations efforts. In some places they succeeded; in others they faced entrenched opposition. State and local counsel needed to pay attention to these changing boundaries, removing cases when necessary and

---

42. James T. Weatherly, Annual Report, 24 November 1887, Box 3, GPRR-VPI.

43. For example, see Sidney F. Andrews to James Fentress, 31 October 1894, ICRR-NL; James T. Weatherly, Annual Report, 13 October 1888, Box 4, GPRR-VPI. For a similar statement, see Sidney F. Andrews to James Fentress, 31 October 1894, ICRR-NL: "The older the cases are, the more difficult they are to defend, because often our witnesses are gone."

taking advantage of local favor toward railroads when possible. Corporate attorneys, through their extensive practices, grew familiar with state and federal judges, rules, and procedures. Experience benefited the railroads in these cases.

If most personal injury cases remained one-on-one affairs and limited in their scope, most legislative issues involving railroads were public and potentially explosive in their consequences. Railroads could run over someone, quietly remove the case to federal court, acquire a favorable verdict, and move on to the next case. In the public arena of the legislatures they had to consider political opposition and the public's view of their actions. The two arenas were separate, though not far removed from one another. Railroad lawyers saw that over time their actions in one affected their reception in the other.

So, in addition to litigating personal injury cases, southern railroad lawyers represented their companies before the state legislatures and town and county councils. Their lobbying activities received mixed reception from many contemporary observers who considered *lobbying* another word for *corruption*. One bar association speaker saw extremes of vice and virtue in the lobby: "The lobby consists of two distinct parts, the honorable, dignified, skillful counsellor, making a dignified and skillful argument before a committee; and under the shadow of his wing, as it obscured the rays of the sun of justice and of light, the other lobby, the lobby of night and of darkness, corrupts not the committee only, but the Legislature." The local struggles of the Reconstruction years tarnished the railroad lobby, as southern legislatures handed out special benefits to solicitous railroad corporations. Critics decried railroad power and special privilege and labeled all lobbying activities corrupt.[44]

The large, interstate roads of the eighties needed lobbyists to help carry out their expansionist policies. They turned to their lawyers. Railroad lawyers appeared in the halls of the state legislatures across the South with the

---

44. William C. P. Breckinridge, "The Lawyer: His Influence in Creating Public Opinion," *Virginia Bar Association Proceedings* (1891), 165. See Mark W. Summers, *Railroads, Reconstruction, and the Gospel of Prosperity: Aid Under the Radical Republicans, 1865–1877* (Princeton: Princeton University Press, 1984).

arrival of these large railroad corporations, pawning influence, suggesting modifications of statutes, seeking special acts of the legislature, and disabling others that threatened the railroads. In the 1880s southern railroads acquired the financial power to expand their operations from non-local capital, but they needed locals to represent them before the legislatures. Ownership and control of most southern railroads shifted to northern financiers, most of whom had no railroad experience and few local connections. Just as this shift of ownership brought a more distinct separation between financial and operational control, it prompted the need for local representatives of the corporation's interests. After all, the New York or Philadelphia financiers who came to own many southern railroads in the 1880s could not appear in the legislative lobbies of all the states in which their sprawling lines did business. As their systems grew across territories to interstate railroads, these financiers were ill-equipped to perform the task of lobbying. Most lived outside of their railroad's region, knew little about the increasingly specialized field of railroad law, and knew even less about the complicated differences from state to state through which their lines ran. Perhaps most important, they possessed no personal contacts and little direct influence in the region.[45]

Railroad lawyers, by contrast, fit easily into the role of lobbyist. Lobbying required knowledge of state law, familiarity with state legislators and executives, persuasive rhetorical skills, and an understanding of parliamentary procedures and the political process. Lawyers naturally possessed many of these qualities. Paid a flat salary for these duties, general counsel and district attorneys kept an eye on the legislatures while they managed the companies' litigation and other legal affairs. From time to time rail-

45. See Edgar Lane, *Lobbying and the Law* (Berkeley: University of California Press, 1964), 5, for a general treatment of lobbying in the "railway period in our legislative history." Lane concludes that the railroads were responsible for the important changes in lobbying as a profession, but he links the lobbyists' reputation for corruption and bribery with public outrage against them (20–25). By definition, Lane points out, lobbying came to mean corruption or bribery (47–56). On the change from local to non-local ownership, see Maury Klein, *A History of the Louisville & Nashville Railroad* (New York: Macmillan, 1972), 172–78. See also Allen W. Moger, *Virginia: From Bourbonism to Byrd, 1870–1925* (Charlottesville: University of Virginia Press, 1968), 14–15, and Allen Moger, "Railroad Practices and Policies in Virginia After the Civil War," *Virginia Magazine of History and Biography* 59 (October 1951): 423–58. See also Joseph T. Lambie, *From Mine to Market: The History of Coal Transportation on the Norfolk & Western Railway* (New York: New York University Press, 1954) and Nelson M. Blake, *William Mahone of Virginia* (Richmond: Garrett & Massie, 1935).

roads might request local attorneys to lobby in their county or before the legislature, especially the local representatives. These attorneys charged a fee for their work, whether lobbying or litigating. When southern railroads looked for lobbyists, they turned to their district and local attorneys, most of whom were already influential brokers in their respective regions.[46]

In the legislative lobbies across the South, in the press, in any public forum, railroad executives and attorneys articulated an avowedly apolitical vision of economic development for the South. These leaders claimed that their only interest lay in expanding the southern economy, increasing their companies' business, and, of course, multiplying their revenues. Railroads, they argued, provided an indispensable agent for economic growth. Southern legislators generously extended benefits to railroads in an effort to boost economic development. The railroads, for their part, opposed any hostile legislation on the grounds that it would slow economic growth, and they consistently reminded the legislators of their fealty to the new economic development.

This economic development argument resonated powerfully among southerners in general and state legislatures in particular. Southerners welcomed economic prosperity and growth in the 1880s, but they expected both to remain under their control. They often fought over the spoils, such as the location of a railroad line in their town or county. One western North Carolinian expressed his beliefs to a railroad attorney on the possibility of a road's extension into his county: "One thing is plain as noon day sun, a railroad passing through any county or state generally adds millions of dollars. . . . It is a public good." North Carolina railroad attorney David Schenck repeated this optimism in his diary: "It will soon be that every county in North Carolina will have a Rail Road in it."[47]

---

46. Unlike in other southern states, state railroad lawyers in Texas appeared to demand a separate lobbying retainer, distinguishing these duties from those of their general practice on behalf of their clients. Baker & Botts, for example, represented the Southern Pacific lines only once in the period 1880–1900 before the Texas legislature, yet during those years it handled all of the lines' Texas legal work. In 1893 Governor James Stephen Hogg's railroad regulation proposals culminated with a stock and bond law that the Southern Pacific wanted killed. The odd nature of the $5,000 separate retainer remained in the firm's records for reference, and later in the early 1900s Baker & Botts consulted it for some indication of how to arrange future lobbying contracts. Edwin Parker to H. M. Garwood, 30 April 1921, Box 11L, Folder 4, BBHC-RU.

47. T. Worman to William T. Sutherlin, 7 January 1884, Sutherlin Papers, SHC-UNC; David Schenck Diary, 18 April 1884, SHC-UNC.

Railroad lawyers themselves debated the definition of the term *lobbying*. Not all shared a common understanding of what it meant to lobby a legislature. As general solicitor for the Illinois Central, James Fentress, for example, tried to distinguish his road's efforts to defeat some Kentucky legislation from those of the Louisville & Nashville. He instructed his district attorneys in Kentucky not to engage in bribery or corruption, nor "to give the slightest coloring to the idea that we were adopting the well-known policy of the Louisville & Nashville Road, in maintaining a lobby, or attempting improperly to influence legislation." Much later, Edward Baxter, the southern railroads' attorney for ICC matters, wrote Fentress to suggest establishing a congressional railroad lobby. "I know you too well," he clarified, "to suppose for a moment that you would act the part of a lobbyist." Fentress drew a distinction between improper influence—bribery and illegal electioneering—which he labeled "lobbying," and proper efforts to prevent adverse legislation, namely, committee appearances and arguments before public officials.[48]

Lobbying in the New South, in fact, embraced both the Louisville & Nashville's and the Illinois Central's methods. It involved any activity on the part of a private company or individual to affect public policy. Generally, lobbyists made persuasive arguments before legislative committees, in the halls of the legislatures, or at a lower level at county board meetings. They did so as well in men's clubs, at dinners, at parties, and in offices. Lobbyists also participated in elections, backing candidates favorable to their interests and buying newspapers to promote their candidates. The hidden nature of these private routes to power and influence troubled some and gave lobbying evil overtones. Even a few railroad lawyers, such as James Fentress, voiced some discomfort over any lobbying that did not take place in the public view.

Interstate railroads had the problem of managing lobbying efforts in several states, usually on the same issues. If their efforts failed in one state, it could spell disaster for the whole line. When the Illinois Central took over the New Orleans, Jackson & Great Northern Railroad and the Mississippi Central Railroad in 1882, for example, James Fentress orchestrated legislative lobbying in four states, "Louisiana, Mississippi, Tennessee, and

---

48. Fentress, quoted in David L. Lightner, *Labor on the Illinois Central Railroad, 1852–1900: The Evolution of an Industrial Environment* (New York: Arno Press, 1977), 369; Ed Baxter to James Fentress, 9 December 1897, Fish Out Letters, vol. 33, p. 675, ICRR-NL.

The Consequences of Growth

Kentucky, each of which had different laws, policies, and traditions." Fentress wanted to be sure that the new incorporation would "enable us to operate the roads as one line without conflict with the laws of either." In his report on the lobbying efforts, Fentress said that not only were there "the natural differences in the policies of these four states, but the people were aroused against the two railroads. . . . The foregoing legislation has been secured without one farthings [*sic*] cost to this company." An experienced southern lawyer, Fentress understood the necessity for planning legislation, for developing a comprehensive systematic approach, and for laying the groundwork for such legislation before a legislative session opened. It was the latter, he thought, that differentiated the best lobbyists from the ones that made a bad name for them all. For railroad lawyers such as Fentress, the real work of lobbying took place before any legislative session ever convened, before the issues were hammered out in committee, in the summer, out of session, before making their way to the floor for a vote.[49]

Railroad companies, though, bought insurance against unfavorable legislation. They littered southern state and local elections with railroad money, supporting friendly candidates and opposing hostile ones, and in this way they tried to ensure their interests against adverse political circumstances. Railroad companies had good reason to buy such insurance. The southern railroads watched the Granger movement sweep through the Northwest in the 1870s. Farmers in that region of the country grew dissatisfied with the railroads' rates, which they saw as unfairly high and onerous. They pushed for a political change, and several state legislatures enacted "granger laws," which regulated the rates railroads could charge farmers to ship their products to market. As it gathered momentum, the movement met opposition from the region's railroads, whose attorneys contested the "granger laws" in the courts. The dispute centered on the rates railroads charged shippers and farmers and the laws designed to limit them. The railroad attorneys argued that rate regulation deprived their corporations of their rights without due process. The Supreme Court of the United States, however, decided to support the right of states to regulate rates in its 1877 decision in *Munn v. Illinois.*[50]

49. James Fentress to W. H. Osborne, 8 December 1882, Fentress Letter Book, ICRR-NL.
50. See Moger, *Virginia*, Chapter 5, for an excellent description of the Virginia railroads' control of the legislature. For a thorough examination of the tactics used by lobbyists

The railroads suffered an overwhelming defeat in the Granger cases not only because the Court upheld the constitutionality of state regulation but, more importantly, because the Court removed the judiciary from even ruling on the reasonableness of rate regulation. The legislature, the Court determined, possessed the authority to regulate railroad rates, and appeals for reasonableness of rates must be made there. "The people must resort to the polls, not to the courts," Chief Justice Morrison Remick Waite recommended to those business interests desirous of amending state rate regulation. The southern railroads took Justice Waite's advice seriously. Left without the alternative of appeal to the courts, southern railroads in the 1880s made it their business to ensure "friendly" legislatures. They financed election campaigns, hosted dinners, and reminded all willing to listen that the railroads brought strong economic development. It was an expensive insurance policy but one that proved reasonably effective for the region's railroad corporations.[51]

Railroad lawyers feared that if left on their own, legislators might enact "hostile" or "adverse" legislation. General solicitor James Fentress performed the watchdog function for the Illinois Central lines in the South. In one report to the railroad, he described his activities: "I made another dead set at Jackson, Miss., with the Governor and Legislature as to the two new bills of adverse legislation that are pending. . . . unless the Governor violates his faith with me, he will veto any bill that is passed of that character." Fentress's personal appeals also neutralized two key senators who had been voting for "adverse" legislation. After his experience he concluded that "if let alone, 4/5 of both Houses would vote for extreme legislation against railroads." For Fentress, as for many railroad lawyers, this required a consistent effort to watch state legislatures and to appear in defense of

and railroad corporations to ensure a friendly legislature, see David J. Rothman, *Politics and Power: The United States Senate, 1869–1901* (Cambridge, Mass.: Harvard University Press, 1966), 191–220; Richard C. Cortner, *The Iron Horse and the Constitution: The Railroads and the Transformation of the Fourteenth Amendment* (Westport, Conn: Greenwood Press, 1993), 3–4.

51. Cortner, *Iron Horse and the Constitution*, 8. Cortner points out (p. 9) that "the holding by the Court in the Granger Cases that the reasonableness of state-imposed railroad rates was beyond the power of the courts to review remained a much more permanent threat to the roads than the original Granger laws had proven to be, since that constitutional principle appeared to foreclose any challenge in the courts of any railroad rates that legislative majorities saw fit to impose."

the corporation's interests when necessary. Left to their own desires, these attorneys concluded, legislators would succumb to demagogic impulses against corporations.[52]

When state legislators proposed anti-railroad legislation, they often found a solicitous railroad offering them a position in the company's legal department. B. B. Munford, for example, sponsored an unsuccessful bill to regulate railroads in the 1886–1887 Virginia legislative session. Within a few years he had become counsel for the Richmond & Danville Railroad. The power to hire these legislators as attorneys appeared a threat to the democratic process, and many southerners came to view these relationships as underhanded. The practice extended through each southern state in the eighties and continued through the twentieth century; railroads retained several legislators in most states as local or district attorneys.[53]

Railroads cooperated in lobbying southern legislatures only on issues that evenly affected all of the companies. Still highly competitive and cutthroat, railroad managers would not interfere if a legislative body went after one of its competitor roads. The L&N, in particular, promoted cooperation among railroad lobbyists to prevent adverse legislation in its geographical area of operations, but it always kept its eye on its own interests and the competition. In 1888 L&N president Milton H. Smith worried about Alabama's legislature. The previous year's session passed two pieces of "unfriendly" legislation: the color-blind and licensing bills for railroad engineers. Smith viewed these measures as unwarranted interference with the railroad management's business. To acquiesce in these fights, he suggested, would jeopardize resistance to other, more objectionable measures.

Not all railroad men agreed with Smith's adamant opposition to legislative encroachment of any kind. When in 1888, for example, the L&N led the opposition to Alabama's proposal to stop rail traffic on Sundays, the Georgia Pacific chief engineer disagreed with the effort. "There seems to be an impression among some railroad men," he wrote company president Jonathan Johnston, "that any attempt to legislate on the affairs of railroads

---

52. James Fentress to W. H. Osborne, 6 March 1882, Fentress Out Letters, ICRR-NL.

53. Thomas Gay, "Virginia State Corporation Commission," (master's thesis, University of Virginia, 1965), 27. For example, Alabama's legislature included, among other railroad attorneys, the L&N's Thomas Goode Jones and Jefferson Falkner. Each southern state legislature contained at least a handful of railroad lawyers.

is a direct encroachment on invested rights and as such should be promptly resisted"; however, he approved of the sabbatarian measure, and considered the L&N's brand of outright opposition to railroad legislation not only unwarranted but also detrimental.[54]

If the passage of unfriendly legislation in Alabama in 1887 bothered Milton Smith, that none of the railroads opposed this legislation or even knew that it was pending offended him. "Past experience in Alabama as well as experience in Kentucky and Tennessee is such," Smith wrote the Georgia Pacific president, "as to show the necessity of making an efficient organization for the purpose of watching legislation and using all proper means to prevent unfriendly legislation." Smith proposed dividing the expenses of lobbying the Alabama legislature: "In Kentucky and Tennessee, we have an organization which provides for a division of such expenses on the basis of gross earnings of the railroads within the states."[55]

Accepting Smith's suggestion, Jonathan Johnston turned to his general counsel for advice on whom the Georgia Pacific should promote as its lobbyists. Johnston asked general counsel James Weatherly to compile a list of House and Senate members along the line of the Georgia Pacific, and asked, "Do you know anyone who would be likely to have influence with them or any of them? If so, we ought to bring this influence to bear at once in a quiet way." Weatherly took the opportunity to list the most influential person in each county through which the Georgia Pacific ran, and his list included nearly all of the road's local attorneys. These men, according to Weatherly, possessed the influence Johnston requested—they were the lobbyists Johnston needed.[56]

The successes of the railroad lobbyists only drew further attention to their power and influence. In the 1880s and 1890s railroad attorneys stymied hostile legislation across the South; In the 1880s in particular, southern states passed remarkably little general legislation affecting railroads. Texas and Arkansas led the region, with twenty-three and twenty-four general acts relating to railroads, while Virginia, Tennessee, Alabama, Mississippi, and North Carolina all passed fewer than fifteen such general acts in the decade. Most of these measures related to railroads as common carriers and did not burden the companies. Many statutes reflected the

54. I. Y. Sage to Jonathan W. Johnston, 7 December 1888, Box 4, GPRR-VPI.
55. Milton H. Smith to Jonathan W. Johnston, 16 July 1888, ibid.
56. Jonathan W. Johnston to James Weatherly, 29 November 1888, ibid.

demands of growing interterritorial competition and its consequent burgeoning rail network. Indeed, much of the general legislation in the 1880s favored railroad corporations. Most states adopted legislation to prevent vandalism, shooting at trains, or otherwise destroying railroad property. In 1886, Virginia's legislature, a notoriously pro-railroad body, allowed for the employment of convict labor on railroads. In a nod to economic development, Virginia provided that the first lines supplied with convict labor must be railroads projected to run through counties without railroads and through those having the least number of taxable railroad miles.[57]

Although southern legislatures passed few general acts affecting railroads in the 1880s, they approved hundreds of special acts for railroad corporations. Mostly incorporation acts or acts to change the terms of a charter, these special pieces of legislation betrayed the proactive nature of railroad lobbying in these years. In North Carolina, for example, railroad-company incorporation required a special act of the legislature. In 1881 the legislature incorporated or amended the charters of thirty-one railroad companies; in 1885 it passed forty-six such acts. By 1887 the North Carolina legislature handled over sixty of these special acts. Although Georgia passed a general incorporation act for railroads in 1880, many southern states continued to accept special acts of the legislature for establishing or amending railroad-company charters. Railroad lobbyists appeared in the halls of legislatures across the South when their clients wanted something accomplished.[58]

57. Acts of Alabama, 1880–81, pp. 95–96; Acts of Georgia, 1882–83, p. 145. Acts to provide for the free flow of shipments over connecting lines and to require trains to stop at crossing points so passengers and freight might change passed in Alabama in 1881 and Georgia in 1883. Acts of Georgia, 1882–83, p. 132, 1884–85, p. 131; Acts of Texas, 1889, p. 36; Acts of Virginia, 1886, p. 539. North Carolina used similar means—convict labor—to achieve economic development in its western counties.

58. See Acts of North Carolina, 1883–89. For detailed analysis of the shift from special legislative charters to general incorporation acts in the nineteenth century, see James Willard Hurst, *The Legitimacy of the Business Corporation in the Law of the United States, 1780–1970* (Charlottesville: University Press of Virginia, 1970), 132–39; Simeon Baldwin, *Modern Political Institutions* (Boston: Little, Brown, 1898), 194–96; Victor Morawetz, *A Treatise on the Law of Private Corporations* (Boston: Little, Brown, 1886), Chapter 1, paras. 14–15, for a prominent railroad attorney's observation that general incorporation acts did not preclude special acts to amend the charter; also Arthur Webster Machen, *A Treatise on the Modern Law of Corporations* (Boston: Little, Brown, 1908), Chapter 1, paras. 14–16. See also the report of the Interstate Commerce Commission, "Railways in the United States in 1902," part 4,

Railroad lobbyists employed various means of persuasion. Perhaps, the most effective method was the free pass. Over time southerners came to view the free pass as the symbol of railroad abuse of power and of legislative dependence on these powerful corporations. Railroads lavished free transportation on influential people in an unwritten, quiet exchange of favors. The tangible results of such a policy defied easy measurement, for the link between a case dismissed in a railroad's favor or an unfriendly bill killed and the free pass handed a judge or a legislator proved difficult to connect. The concrete costs of the practice, however, added up to hundreds of thousands of dollars in lost ticket purchases. The free pass, in addition, contributed in large measure to the railroads' growing public relations problem.[59]

In the 1880s most southern railroads distributed free passes to influential people from whom in return they expected favorable treatment, or at the very least passive indifference. The legal department assumed the burden of distributing and monitoring free passes for most railroads, and the legal records of southern railroads contain voluminous lists of annual free passes. The Norfolk & Western Railroad, for example, compiled an annual, alphabetical listing of free pass recipients. In 1882 the list ran eight pages long and included approximately 240 beneficiaries. Because the N&W operated almost exclusively in Virginia, it compiled a relatively short list. Nonetheless, it covered nearly all the members of the state legislature, all of the judges in counties through which the road ran, all of the state supreme court justices and members of Congress, the governor, major newspaper editors, fire chiefs, the Catholic bishop, the Episcopal bishop, and the road's attorneys, engineers, directors, and their families as well. The N&W tailored the list to ensure that men of influence received passes, and each year it tried to update it to reflect the changing influence of its recipients. In 1881 the N&W reevaluated its list in light of recent elections. "The new legislature," wrote N. M. Osborne, the road's master of transportation, "will change a great many of the officials this winter so I venture

"State Regulation of Railways," for a complete compilation of state laws passed from 1890 to 1902 regarding railroads.

59. Klein, *History of the Louisville & Nashville*, 378. "This giving of free passes is all wrong," wrote Collis Huntington about the U.S. Senate. He reminded doubters that the Central Pacific carried 6,186 non-payers for a total loss in revenue. See Rothman, *Politics and Power*, 200.

to suggest that in filling out the passes . . . the full official position be shown, for some of them when shorn of their offices will become very small people indeed."[60]

The railroads expected some reciprocity for this outlay. Williams C. Wickham, general counsel for the Chesapeake & Ohio Railroad, explained to Collis P. Huntington the benefits that such passes were intended to accrue. Wickham sought a recommendation and a pass for the son of a judge whose jurisdiction in the western Virginia coalfields the C&O operated. "It will be of material advantage to us," Wickham pointed out, "to oblige him by aiding as far as we can his views in regard to his son. A general letter of recommendation of the young man . . . and a pass . . . will naturally increase the present friendly feeling of Judge Holt towards the Company."[61]

The difficulty of monitoring the "prominence" of free pass recipients often led to blunders of omission. The tangible consequences of offending an influential citizen were as difficult to measure as those of securing their favor. Nonetheless, railroads strove to avoid such mistakes. When the Illinois Central carried a title dispute to the Mississippi Supreme Court, it was surprised to find the court decide against it. James Fentress concluded that the decision "was so monstrous that it is difficult to believe it was honest." Moreover, according to Fentress, "the fact that [the railroad] had refused a pass to Judge Chalmers (who had applied for it) with some asperity just before this decision gives it a still worse look for Chalmers." Fentress explained further that the good Judge Chalmers was mistaken in application for a Congressman Chalmers, who had railed against the railroad in the recent campaign and in the legislature. A mix-up like this might offend important people, like Judge Chalmers, and the results could be as politically dangerous for the offended judge as they were materially dangerous for the bumbling railroad.[62]

As a young judge in North Carolina, Robert Watson Winston came face-to-face with the insidious quality of the free railroad pass. He was presiding over a case in which a North Carolina Railroad conductor had

60. Report of N. M. Osborne, 16 December 1881, Box I-83, N&W-VPI. For the list of annual free pass recipients, see Box I-82, N&W-VPI.
61. Williams C. Wickham to Collis P. Huntington, 10 November 1881, Box 10, Wickham Family Papers, VHS.
62. Fentress to W. H. Osborne, 26 September 1882, Fentress Out Letters, ICRR-NL.

ejected a drunken passenger. On cross-examination of the conductor, the plaintiff's attorney attacked the witness's character on the grounds that as an employee the conductor held a free pass, and "what else is a pass but a bribe?" Winston sat in judgment with "no less than twenty-five free passes, over every railroad and every steamboat in the state" in his pocket. As he put it, "I was in the fix of the train conductor—I, too, had come to court on a free pass." Later, a conscience-stricken Winston helped abolish passes and institute state-funded traveling money for judges, but he did decide the case for the railroad defendant.[63]

In effect, the railroad free pass served as a subtle form of blackmail. Politicians and judges risked the ire of powerful corporations with refusal. One young solicitor turned down a Southern Railway free pass because he "thought it improper for me to accept so much to do so little and thus place myself as a public servant under obligation."[64] His refusal, however, did not go unnoticed. As he explained, "the railroad's opposition to my political ambitions stood from that day." Samuel Spencer, president of the Southern Railway, enclosed a free pass in a personal letter to the editor of the Atlanta *Journal*, and took the opportunity to comment on some of the newspaper's recent editorials. "I must say that I was a little surprised," Spencer reprimanded the editor, "a few days since to see the statements in the Journal with reference to the agitation of consolidation [of the Southern Railway] before the Legislature." The adverse commentary prompted Spencer to remind the editor of the railroad's position as the harbinger of economic growth: "I was in hopes that the work which we are doing in the South and which will greatly benefit the State of Georgia, would be sufficient reason for no one of influence suggesting the putting of any obstacles in our way. . . . Of course, if the Southern Railway is to be attacked politically on the subject, it must at once discontinue the consideration of anything involving the expenditure of money, or improvements of any kind within the State of Georgia until it knows how far its interests there are to be affected."[65] For Spencer the railroad deserved reciprocal favors,

63. Winston, *It's a Far Cry,* 206–207.

64. Aubrey Lee Brooks, *A Southern Lawyer: Fifty Years at the Bar* (Chapel Hill: University of North Carolina Press, 1950), 61–62. Fabius H. Busbee offered the pass in 1900, then Charles Price, state counsel for the Southern, called on Brooks to make a personal offer. Price succeeded David Schenck in the post of state counsel.

65. Samuel Spencer to H. Williams, 7 September 1892, President's Correspondence, SRy-VPI.

and he undoubtedly viewed the free pass as a reminder to the editor of the tenuous nature of their relationship.

What began for the railroads as a basic form of insurance against hostility from people with influence evolved by the 1890s into a monstrous headache. Anyone with any degree of influence peddled their allegiance into a free pass for business and personal trips, gouging the railroad, littering legal files with one-time applications, and setting expensive precedents. "It has always been . . . customary," wrote Charles H. Roads, Internal Revenue Service collector for the Eighth District of Kentucky, to a Southern Railway attorney, "for the railroads in my district and state to furnish me . . . with free transportation." Even attorneys for distant lines appealed for free passes for personal use, exploiting their limited influence where possible. When a Florida railroad attorney's mother died, he wrote the Southern Railway for a pass to her Philadelphia funeral. Unable to procure one before he left Florida, he had to pay the cash fare, and so wrote the Southern for reimbursement, enclosing the receipt. "My expenses in connection with my Mother's death and burial have been very heavy," he explained with a thinly veiled threat, "Aside from the above I am also editor of the Miami *Metropolis*."[66]

Railroads did little in the eighties to curb excess largesse, and by the 1890s faced a growing problem of free pass entitlement. Competition among railroads only promoted the issuance of free passes, as no railroad wished to alienate a potentially influential client. The general manager of the Georgia Railroad, for example, worried about not receiving a pass application from a Standard Oil executive. "While I would not initiate the practice of issuing annual transportation to [him]," he wrote his superiors, "I will, of necessity, be compelled to follow suit if our competitors and other roads do so." The frenzied distribution of free passes worried some Southern Railway managers, who witnessed the haphazard results of an increasingly cumbersome system. They hoped to curb the practice and restore some order but confronted the callousness of an entrenched entitlement system.[67]

66. Charles H. Roads to Hon. C. H. Hudson, 12 December 1894, Vice-President's Correspondence, Box 1, Folder 5, ibid.; W. S. Graham to G. E. Mauldin, 21 April 1897, Vice-President's Correspondence, Box 1, Folder 15, ibid.

67. Thomas K. Scott to W. W. Finley, 25 January 1897, Vice-President's Correspondence, Box 1, Folder 63, ibid.; S. M. Fenton to W. W. Finley, 11 November 1896, Vice-President's Correspondence, Box 1, Folder 9, ibid. Milton H. Smith complained that the

One southern attorney in Kentucky understood the reciprocal relationship that came with the free pass. He described the pass as "a personal kindness which when the opportunity offers I shall be glad to return." As if to confirm his understanding of reciprocity, he explained to the Southern Railway officials his recent generosity: "I expect I sometimes worry my Southern [Railway] friends by bringing damage suits, but somebody will bring them, and elsewhere, outside of the particular cases I bring, I am for you. . . . The Railroad Commission of Kentucky sent for me to advise about the method and manner of taxation. During the conversation your road came up and I was able . . . to present some facts which I think resulted in the reduction of the tax list to a very considerable amount." In conclusion, the grateful attorney offered his services "before the Railroad Commission, the Legislature, or anywhere else, I could have any influence or be of any benefit to you." This attorney appreciated the value of the free pass, for with it he could freely consult witnesses, take depositions, and travel to distant courts, and he was willing to bargain his influence for these valuable benefits.[68]

When the free pass failed to attain the desired results, some railroads made the bribe more straightforward. In North Carolina the Richmond & Danville fought a mighty battle with the Raleigh & Gaston over the route of an extension to Henderson. A local lawyer wrote railroad attorney Robert Watson Winston, "The Richmond & Danville are stirring. I fear the use of money to corrupt votes. Rail road is red hot." The coming of a railroad created interested parties on all sides. Some railroads did use corrupt tactics to secure or kill special pieces of legislation, but more often railroad lobbyists merely employed the art of persuasion spiced with a strong reminder of their considerable financial weight in reelection campaigns. Heavy-handed tactics of bribery proved expensive, and often ineffective. Railroad companies, interested in gaining the most results for the least expenditure of resources, employed lobbyists to cajole, persuade, and lead legislators toward an enlightened, friendly relationship.[69]

free pass had become viewed by many as a "vested right." Klein, *History of the Louisville & Nashville*, 379.

68. Bennett H. Young to W. W. Finley, 22 April 1897, Vice-President's Correspondence, Box 1, Folder 15, SRy-VPI.

69. W. W. Fuller to R. W. Winston, 9 August 1887, Robert Watson Winston Papers, SHC-UNC. On the aversion of railroad companies to use bribery for votes and the relative ineffectiveness of railroad attempts to control legislatures, see Rothman, *Politics and Power*,

In the 1880s railroad expansion in the South generated allies as well as enemies. Citizens across the region fought with one another for access to the railroads, and the railroads responded with great schemes for development of the areas they served. Railroad corporations, though, acquired local enemies with every move they made, and the attorneys both in the courtroom and in the halls of the legislature negotiated with these adversaries. Railroad attorneys quickly recognized that much of the animosity was grounded in the nature of the railroad business but that a large portion of it stemmed from railroad corporations' behavior. They hoped to arrest this negative effect through active lobbying, and they used the economic development argument as the cornerstone of their efforts.

Some railroad attorneys were convinced in the 1880s that public opinion need not be adversarial, that railroads could generate and sustain favorable public relations. David Schenck, for example, began his lobbying work for the Richmond & Danville with optimistic predictions on his effort to amend the incorporation act of the Western North Carolina Railroad in 1883. "Lobbying is a new business to me," Schenck recorded in his diary. "I did not however indulge in any art or dissimulation but called all the Western members together and made frank, candid and truthful statements . . . without stating details I will say that the manly manner in which I approached the members won their confidence and that I feel very hopeful of securing the legislation required by the company." Schenck's performance before the committee on internal improvements generated enough support for his bill to make it onto the floor of the legislature, but there political considerations weighed heavily. With Governor Zebulon Vance actively opposing the bill, Schenck thought he could rely on several members who owed their reelection success to the active support of the Richmond & Danville. Their notable silence prompted Schenck to report that "such is the ingratitude and heartlessness of politicians." Schenck did not hesitate to employ heavy-handed tactics in these circumstances. Politi-

---

Chapter 7. Rothman points out the coincidence of railroad lobbyists' ineffectiveness with two-party strength (219). At times of intense competition, legislators reserved their fealty to their parties, not to certain corporations. This observation holds for the South. Railroads lost whatever slim hold they had on state legislatures when an opposition party or faction seriously challenged the Democratic ruling Redeemers. In the South, party competition in the 1880s and 1890s remained unusually low, and as a result contributed to the security of railroad power. See also Summers, *Railroads, Reconstruction, and the Gospel of Prosperity*, 98–117.

cians who accepted railroad reelection funds owed the company some gratitude. Schenck reminded them of their debt, and the legislators passed the special act.[70]

Later, when the Richmond & Danville chose not to construct a promised section of road in Western North Carolina, Schenck faced the fallout from this broken promise. "It raised a storm of indignation at what western people denounce as breach of faith . . . treachery railroad faith," Schenck commented in his diary. Broken promises angered the western North Carolinians, especially the railroad's allies, who hoped for railroad expansion and its consequent economic development. Schenck considered the reversal a public relations blow from which he doubted the railroad could recover: "Col. Andrews made a very great mistake when he determined to abandon the Murphy branch and risk results. He can never regain the confidence he has lost or reconcile those people to him. They had exaggerated notions already of the bad faith and crooked ways of railroad men and this breach of promise, as they allege, has confirmed their wildest notions on this subject."[71] The immediate result of this fateful decision, Schenck reported, came in the form of "hostile legislation" introduced by western representatives and designed to force completion of the railroad's Murphy branch. After two all-night negotiation sessions, Schenck pacified the hostile feelings and struck a bargain with the angry western legislators: the railroad would complete the western branch with 150 state convicts paid for in the bonds of the railroad company.

Decisions about location of a line seemed bound to offend, but everyday decisions bore equal responsibility for generating adverse public opinion. Albert Fink wrote Georgia railroad attorney Alexander R. Lawton as early as 1882 on the subject: "It is the shortsighted and arbitrary policy that has so much prevailed with Railroad managers in the past that has led to so many difficulties with the people, resulting in hostile legislation. . . . The full force of this ruinous policy has not yet been felt." Fink accurately assessed the future for railroads. Railroad managers and officials made decisions about freight classification and rates every day on the basis of the

70. David Schenck Diary, 14 January 1883, SHC-UNC. North Carolina Laws, 1883, p. 396 (Chapter 241), amended the Western North Carolina Railroad's charter to provide for the sale of the state's interest and to provide convict labor for construction.

71. Schenk Diary, 27 February 1885, SHC-UNC.

company's priorities and needs, with little regard for their possible public consequences.[72]

As James Fentress orchestrated the Illinois Central's consolidation with various Mississippi railroad companies, he, like David Schenck, concluded that with some effort he could salvage the railroad's poor public relations record. "My own conviction is that there is no good reason why a railroad company should ever get into the fix that this railroad was in under [the previous] management. I am unable to see why a railroad company may not from its beginning and all through its life receive as well as deserve the good will and friendship of the community which is benefitted by it." For Fentress the solution to antagonistic feelings toward the railroad involved organizing new legal departments for the various roads with local attorneys who actively solicited the "good opinion of the people."[73]

Local attorneys found themselves soliciting the good opinion of the people at the same time that they used contributory negligence and federal removal to avoid losing personal injury suits. They manipulated legal doctrines while their companies ran over stock, passengers, bystanders, and employees. It is difficult to measure the animosity that these actions generated, but southerners began to ask themselves, "Is this progress?" For a while after interstate railroads came to town, southerners seemed willing to tolerate their excesses, but the cumulative effect of rampant accidents, undervalued properties, unequal rates, free passes, shady deals, and slippery lobbying began to take a toll on southerners' faith in the interstate railroads' version of progress.

72. Albert Fink to Alexander R. Lawton, 13 December 1882, Lawton Family Papers, ibid.

73. James Fentress to W. H. Osborne, 9 March 1882, Fentress Out Letters, ICRR-NL.

FOUR

The Consequences of Monopoly Power

Beginning in the early 1890s, railroad officials across the South wondered why the public viewed their companies with suspicion and skepticism. When the Georgia Pacific Railroad came under control of the Richmond & Danville in 1889, its president, Jonathan W. Johnston, wrote a detailed report on his road's legal affairs to the R&D general counsel, James Worthington. Complaining that the Alabama legislature considered several anti-railroad bills that year, Johnston wrote, "The courts and juries in Alabama are beginning to make for themselves a record as against railroads, but little behind those in Georgia." He went on to suggest that "the liberal State policy and generous public sentiment which stimulated the building of railroads in Alabama" was "slowly but steadily undermined by agitation and the arts of the demagogue." Johnston recognized that the political and legal environment for his railroad in the towns and counties along its line began to change with the road's completion. No longer the great developer, worthy of broad leeway in the conduct of its affairs, the Georgia Pacific experienced a significant change of circumstances. Johnston, though, evinced optimism that "with a just policy and an efficient, watchful organization . . . railroads may be able measurably at last to stem and turn the tide of prejudice, which seemingly more and more threatens to embarrass and injure them."[1]

By 1890, nine of ten southerners lived in counties serviced by a railroad;

1. Jonathan W. Johnston to James T. Worthington, 26 June 1889, Box 1, R&DRR-VPI.

with the network so complete, even railroad officials expected the political atmosphere to swing from pro-development to pro-regulation. The Georgia Pacific president recommended to his road's new general counsel that "it behooves the railroads to have and maintain just dealings and at the same time to keep up our active, vigilant, and efficient organization in all departments, not forgetting the importance of local friends and influences." The national railway industry magazine, *Railway Age,* noted the sweeping legislative challenges beginning to affect the railroads. "The legislative mills are grinding out law for the railways with the utmost liberality, as will be seen from the carefully compiled epitome given in this journal each week," its editor wrote in 1887. "Prohibitory legislation is abundant and it is directed chiefly against special rates, discrimination, stoves in cars, and passes; but affirmative legislation is still more plentiful, and it proposes to establish railway commissions, fix rates, require the maintaining of crossing gates, fences, public records of stock killed."[2]

With the rail network virtually complete, southerners faced a new set of economic development questions. A major depression beginning in the early nineties exposed the railroads' visions of economic growth and prosperity as false dreams and cursed hopes. Many railroads went into receivership, businesses collapsed across the South, and credit grew tight. For many southerners the depression of 1893 began earlier, around 1890. Depression conditions helped spark political upheaval in the South and Midwest. The Populists became the most active political movement in the South in a generation. They aimed their fire at the pro-business, conservative, Democratic leadership of the New South, especially at the local level. The movement was largely an agrarian protest, but it resonated with those southerners whose livelihoods seemed threatened by the new railroads, towns, and businesses that grew up the eighties. These southerners witnessed local control over the terms of economic growth slip away, as interstate railroads, insensitive to any one locality's particular needs, imposed a new and rigorous economic order that seemed to favor others.[3]

2. *Railway Age,* February 18, 1887.
3. Edward L. Ayers, *The Promise of the New South: Life After Reconstruction* (Oxford: Oxford University Press, 1992), 252–53 on the economic depression of 1890 in the South, and 265–66 on what motivated the Populist protests. The literature on the Populist movement is voluminous—the best review of the movement and the literature is in Ayers, *The Promise of the New South.*

The Populist critique, born of tarnished promises and unfulfilled expectations, challenged the way business and government worked in the Gilded Age South. One of the objects of its vociferous protest was the railroad lawyer. An 1889 *Southern Mercury* editorial summed up the Populist view: "the lawyer . . . furnishes the power, the railroad . . . corporation the wedge, and the farmers of Texas are 'split wide open' by the combined power of one driving the other."[4] One 1892 *Texas Farmer* cartoon, called "How We Are Ridden," showed the people on the bottom of a pile, crushed under a fat George Clark, railroad attorney and lobbyist, with Jay Gould sitting on Clark's shoulders. Everything about the interstate railroads' manipulation of the political and economic levers of power—from the use of free passes to the running of fast trains through towns—offended Populists.[5]

For their part most railroad attorneys arrogantly thought the Populists' view of the world was backward. The editor of the leading railroad corporation law journal stated the matter plainly for his railroad attorney readership: "When corporations get full justice in the courts, they will not be compelled to interest themselves so much in legislatures." Nothing could have been further from the truth. Railroads monitored state elections closely in the early nineties, as Populist candidates threatened to win seats in many southern legislatures. In reports from the field, railroad lobbyists demonstrated little concern for party; instead, they looked for unswerving fealty to their company. Correspondence between railroad lawyers and railroad officials characterized "safe" and "dangerous," "reliable" and "unreliable" candidates, candidates who were "friends" or "enemies" of the corporation. In a typical report, one lobbyist listed each probable candidate for the Georgia legislature in 1894. One Democratic candidate, a former law partner of a railroad lawyer, received a candid appraisal of his possible worth: "He is very friendly to our company and is under obligations to it." This candidate could have been obliged to the railroad for any number of typical courtesies: a personal loan, a campaign contribution, a

---

4. *Southern Mercury*, 31 January 1889, quoted in Robert L. Patterson, *State Regulation of Railroads in Texas, 1836–1920* (Ph.D. diss., University of Texas, 1960), 82.

5. Ayers, *The Promise of the New South*, 281–82. Ayers quotes Tom Watson, whose wide definition of "monopoly" included "monopoly of power, of place, of privilege, of wealth, of progress." By the actions of their local, state, and general attorneys, the interstate railroads in the New South manipulated the business and government institutions to protect their interests—they were the foremost example of "monopoly" for Watson and the Populists.

free pass, a sinecure for a son or relative. Another, however, did not fare as well: "He is local counsel [for a railroad] but is looked upon as a dangerous man. That company ought to nurse him."[6]

Many railroad attorneys spoke of a need in the 1890s to "educate the people" about the railroad business. They hoped to do this, one railroad official explained, "not only in legislation, but also in court house trials, showing the injustice of the many outrageous verdicts that are obtained in the courts against corporations." The Populist campaigns in the 1890s provoked some railroads to try to redirect public opinion. Stuyvesant Fish, president of the Illinois Central, explained to James Fentress that the inequitable national banking structure was the real culprit inhibiting the South's economy in the nineties, not monopolies, railroads, or foreign capital. He instructed Fentress to "get up a general correspondence among the railroad attorneys of our Company and others, on this subject." Fish hoped the joint effort would develop "wise counsels" and "turn public attention from its usual point of attack on railroad corporations to the real source of the evil." Like Fish, Milton H. Smith, president of the L&N, railed in the press against the Populists for misrepresentations about the railroad business. Railroad presidents often used their lobbyists to cultivate favor with the major newspaper editors. New South editors trumpeted economic growth, and railroad executives, such as Smith, reminded them that railroads carried the region's economy. Often, a free pass accompanied the reminder.[7]

In the face of rising anti-railroad public sentiment, railroads in the nineties continued to finance the election campaigns of friendly legislators. In 1894 the Richmond & Danville listed political contributions in the recent Virginia elections on its receivership expense sheets. In a letter to the circuit court judge overseeing the reorganization, the R&D receivers explained the expense: "The property and franchise rights of the railway companies might be seriously involved in questions likely to arise in the State Legislature and that all rail road companies were necessarily and

6. *Railway Law and Corporation Journal* (31 October 1891), 341. See, for example, letter to Samuel Spencer, 27 April 1894, Samuel Spencer Papers, SHC-UNC.

7. H. M. Comer to Samuel Spencer, 1 June 1894, Spencer Papers, SHC-UNC; Stuyvesant Fish to James Fentress, 28 November 1896, Fish Out Letters, vol. 27, p. 110, ICRR-NL. Maury Klein detailed the L&N's attempts to produce favorable press in Tennessee in the early eighties in *A History of the Louisville & Nashville* (New York: Macmillan, 1972), 376–77.

deeply interested in the election of a Legislature of intelligence and character." In the minds of many southerners, court-appointed receivers, usually a railroad-friendly lawyer, former judge, or businessman, were suspect of hiding railroad rate inequity, obscuring railroad debt structures, and generally favoring the companies above the public. That a railroad receiver, appointed because the company was unable to meet fiscal payments, would approve spending on elections represented a double indemnity for many southerners.[8]

Sometimes railroads cooperated to accomplish their officers' goals for holding adverse public opinion at bay, but they all sought to keep their lobbying activities quiet. At the height of Populist Party strength in Georgia, Southern Railway officials weighed the possibilities in the 1894 elections. They decided to coordinate with other railroads in an effort to shape the legislature "to at least modify the objectionable railroad laws." To defend against adverse legislation, the railroads agreed "to work quietly . . . with a view to securing . . . the election of good men, who would aid us." The Southern relied on its attorneys to carry out this kind of delicate mission, and the executive officers repeated, "Let us all go to work . . . in a quiet way, so as to avoid the antagonism which would be almost sure to arise in some quarters." The Illinois Central preferred to keep its political efforts quiet out of fear that pronounced partisanship in local elections might come back to haunt it in the jury box. Efforts on the part of lobbyists to keep some actions covert extended by the turn of the century to acts amending railroad charters, which in the 1880s flowed effortlessly out of state legislatures. Private legislation for a charter required public notice, but a North Carolina railroad attorney assured his client "this can be arranged without exciting comment, as the law is silent as to how or where the notice shall be given."[9]

Once a railroad confirmed pending "hostile" legislation before a legislature, it dispatched a local or district attorney to kill the bill. James Fentress, for example, directed his local counsel in New Orleans: "I beg also to call your attention to H.B. No. 126 [a fellow-servant defense limita-

8. R&D Receivers to Hon. Nathan Goff, 24 February 1894, Spencer Papers, UNC-SHC.
9. H. M. Comer to Samuel Spencer, 4 May 1894, ibid.; Stuyvesant Fish to James Fentress, 6 October 1896, Fish Out Letters, vol. 26, p. 638, ICRR-NL; W. C. Ervin to W. A. Barber, 14 April 1900, William Carson Ervin Papers, SHC-UNC.

tion] . . . and request that you will do what every good citizen ought to do, all in your power to prevent the passage of such vicious and partial legislation." As if to buttress his attorney's faith, Fentress even explained his position: "The law as to fellow-servants is founded upon reason and right, and the attempt to become the guardian for employees as against the corporation is wrong in principle and in reason." Armed with this logic, the local attorney appealed to the legislators and killed the measure.[10]

A loose understanding among the southern lines dictated that railroads take the lead in opposing or promoting legislation where they stood the most to lose or gain relative to others. This informal division of responsibility suggests that railroads retained territorial notions long after the advent of interterritorial competition. For example, in 1893 the Kentucky legislature considered a domiciliary bill designed to prevent railroad companies incorporated in other states from removing cases to federal court, and railroads were alarmed at the prospect of passage. The L&N, incorporated in Kentucky and therefore seemingly unaffected by the bill, nevertheless took the lead in active opposition, dispatched Basil W. Duke at a cost of $17,000, and lavished 2,200 free passes on legislators and their friends. Milton H. Smith reported to his counterpart at the Illinois Central, Stuyvesant Fish: "General Duke . . . has been actively at work endeavoring . . . to bring out candidates not unfavorable to railroad interests and doing everything possible to secure a friendly legislature." Smith asked the Illinois Central and other railroads to help defray the costs of lobbying the Kentucky legislature. In response general solicitor James Fentress recommended to Fish that the Illinois Central refrain from such payment. He pointed out: "The L&N is accomplishing some good, and that, if we could repay them in some other way, it would be a pleasure to do so. Doubtless what we do in Mississippi more than offsets any benefit we can possibly get through their efforts in Kentucky, as we have only 40 miles of railroad in that state." In all matters affecting railroad interests in Mississippi the Illinois Central assumed the full burden of intercession, and it expected the L&N to behave in a similar fashion in Kentucky.[11]

10. James Fentress to Thomas J. Kernan, 18 June 1896, Fish Out Letters, vol. 26, p. 249, ICRR-NL.

11. In 1889, for example, the L&N orchestrated the lobbying effort in Alabama, requesting other roads' presence at a meeting "for the purposes of organization and a determined fight." John W. Johnston to James T. Worthington, 26 June 1889, Box 1, R&DRR-VPI; Milton H. Smith to Stuyvesant Fish, 13 August 1893, Fish Out Letters, vol. 13, p. 308,

Railroad lawyers approached state legislatures not only to kill undesirable legislation but also correct and clarify existing laws. Obsolete laws frustrated railroad lawyers and executive officers, and they sought every opportunity to reform them. Many of these laws reflected the local origins of railroad corporations, and efforts to overturn them often pitted interests favoring local control against interstate railroads pushing further development. In early 1895, for example, these forces clashed when a county sheriff served 208 subpoenas on the Illinois Central station agent at Abbeville, Mississippi, for 100 instances of running the train through town at a speed over six miles per hour. At the next legislative session the Illinois Central appealed for modification of the slow-train law. Bogged down in subpoenas, the Illinois Central made the case for faster trains: "If Mississippi is to develop as other western states have, the railroads must not be hampered by petty vexations of the sort which the old law about slowing trains, adopted years ago when we had nothing but handbrakes, may have justified." The Illinois Central tied the company's interests to regional development and local custom or preference had to give way to growth. The corporation's leadership, Fish seemed to say, understood economic development better than any state legislature or town council. The legislature left the speed limit intact, although it abolished the $100 penalty and empowered the railroad commission to issue exemptions upon application.[12]

Using similar arguments, the Illinois Central's legal department waged a decade-long struggle to retain its tax exemption in Mississippi, which it held through its subsidiary's charter. Stuyvesant Fish explained to his southern counsel, "We can afford to pay the taxes, if need be, but can hardly afford to continue the attempt to build up a country, in which the sanctity of contracts is to be constantly repudiated." Fish took an opportunity to speak with the Illinois Central's local counsel and lobbyist in Mississippi. "While Mr. Mayes [IC lobbyist] was too courteous to show it," Fish summarized, "I think he must have been a little shocked at the very plain way in which I spoke about the bad faith which has been shown by the State of Mississippi in this and other transactions, and . . . [I] only wish

ICRR-NL; James Fentress to Stuyvesant Fish, 8 August 1893, Fish Out Letters, vol. 13, p. 304, ICRR-NL.

12. E. L. Mathers to James Fentress, 10 February 1895, Fish Out Letters, vol. 19, p. 954, ICRR-NL; Stuyvesant Fish to James Fentress, 2 January 1896, Fish Out Letters, vol. 23, p. 869, ibid.; Acts of Mississippi, 1896, p. 76.

to have him carry back to Mississippi an appreciation of how these things are thought of by others, and how they affect, and will hereafter affect, the investment of foreign capital in the State." Fish was convinced that the entire effort on the part of the Mississippi revenue agent, Wirt Adams, to take away the tax exemption stemmed from the 20 percent retainer of whatever amount he recovered from the railroad companies. He thought that most courts could be counted on to back the railroads and support their charters. So, when the Mississippi Supreme Court decided against the railroad and to strip away the tax exemption, Fish viewed their decision as corrupt, so corrupt that he hoped to expose it. "It is possible," he instructed James Fentress, "we may not be able to prove the corruption of the court, but I do think it would be worth while to set some intelligent and adroit men at work on the sole business of ferreting this thing out. What I want to get at is, with whom has Adams agreed to divide the money?"[13]

The Mississippi district attorneys, Mayes & Harris, were not deaf to Fish and Fentress's economic development position. They understood the consequences of attacking the railroads, and they worked from within the state's leadership to influence it toward growth and development. "Our people are beginning to see that Mississippi is left behind in the march of progress," they wrote James Fentress, "and we have taken pains in a skillful way to call attention to this fact . . . and to suggest that the cause must be found in the character of legislation, especially as affecting investments of capital. . . . We hope in this way to bring about a state of feeling that will result beneficially and prevent oppressive legislation measures going through." For Fish, only corruption explained the court's rejection of his economic development position. "I cannot believe," Fish wrote Fentress, "that the people of Mississippi, in view of what we are doing for the state, have sunk so low as to repudiate their contract in regard to taxation. . . . While it would be inexpedient, at this time, to make any threats, it . . . would both hamper our capacity, and diminish our inclination to develop the material interests in the state."[14]

13. Stuyvesant Fish to James Fentress, 11 November 1898, Fish Out Letters, vol. 38, p. 449, ICRR-NL; Stuyvesant Fish to James Fentress, 23 December 1898, Fish Out Letters, vol. 39, p. 207, ibid.; Stuyvesant Fish to James Fentress, 13 July 1898, Fish Out Letters, vol. 36, p. 808, ibid.

14. Mayes & Harris to Fentress, 10 February 1896, Stuyvesant Fish to James Fentress, 8 February 1896, quoted in Robert L Brandfon, *Cotton Kingdom in the New South: A History*

Other states too began to challenge the railroads' version of regional economic development. When the Tennessee legislature considered creating a more powerful railroad commission in 1895, the Illinois Central's response was similarly rhetorical: "The question for our friends in Tennessee to consider is whether they also wish to stagnate." Tennessee, like other southern states, eventually rejected the very premise of the Illinois Central's question. As early as 1889, though, the Georgia Pacific Railroad's president summarized the changing political environment in the region: "I apprehend that when our line is complete to Greenville still more determined efforts will be made to subject us to ordinary taxation and otherwise to regulate us."[15]

Railroad presidents and their attorneys generally denied any interest in partisan politics. In 1899 Milton H. Smith, president of the L&N, summarized his position on whether the L&N engaged in "politics": "The management of the L&N Railroad Company has never been active, and has no desire to be active in what is termed 'politics,' except to protect, so far as possible, these important interests against oppressive legislation and unjust enforcement of the law. It will at once be eliminated as a factor in politics when assured by all parties that its interests will be treated fairly and given reasonable protection."[16] For many southerners, Smith simply hid the true depth of his political involvement. Smith, though, revealed the broad outlines of railroad politics. Railroads, through their lobbyists, exhibited a uniform and preeminent concern for their company's interests, regardless of party or personality. Smith's maxim fit other southern railroads. Stuyvesant Fish, president of the Illinois Central, despised party politics and vehemently maintained that the Illinois Central had no political objectives.

Railroad lawyers, whether lobbyists or not, carried political baggage. Even hiring a new district attorney brought political consequences. When the Illinois Central legal department needed a new district attorney for Illinois, Stuyvesant Fish worried about the political considerations of the hire.

of the Yazoo Mississippi Delta from Reconstruction to the Twentieth Century (Cambridge, Mass.: Harvard University Press, 1967), 180.

15. Stuyvesant Fish to James Fentress, 16 February 1895, Fish Out Letters, vol. 19, p. 915, ICRR-NL; Jonathan W. Johnston to James T. Worthington, 26 June 1889, Box 1, R&DRR-VPI.

16. Klein, *History of the Louisville & Nashville*, 384.

He wrote James Fentress, "While I would not allow such a thing absolutely to control the selection, I think it would be well, in view of the fact that you and Mr. Ayer [general counsel] are both Democrats, and that our two District Attorneys in Iowa (a Republican State) are of the same political faith, to appoint as District Attorney a Republican." When his general solicitor objected to such criteria, Fish quickly made clear his views on the matter:

> [I] agree with you perfectly . . . we should select our officers for their fitness, without regard to their political affiliations. . . . we have sometimes been criticized, in Republican states, for having a large number of Democratic Local and District Attorneys. . . . You and I do not attach importance to these matters, but others do. . . . if the two men were equally fit, it might be wiser to appoint the Republican than the Democrat in Illinois. The same considerations in the South would lead to the appointment of Democrats there. I do not care to ask of any man in the Company's service what his politics or religion are, provided he does his duty.

Fish's non-partisan hiring criterion showed the importance he attached to local political considerations. The company, he seemed to suggest to his southern solicitor, benefited from hiring lawyer-lobbyists on the majority side of the state legislatures.[17]

The neat distinction that both Smith and Fish tried to draw between partisan politics and business practices often suffered from the realities of the political process. The Illinois Central's Mississippi counsel and lobbyists, Mayes & Harris, pointed out the difficult position they were in as the Illinois Central's lawyer-lobbyists in the political atmosphere surrounding the road's long-standing suit with the state over taxes. They reminded James Fentress that Mississippi governor Anselm J. McLaurin "proposes to picture the railroads in the worst light possible and in a way which will appeal strongly to the prejudices of the people." Moreover, they observed,

17. Stuyvesant Fish to James Fentress, 30 June 1898, Fish Out Letters, vol. 36, p. 617, ICRR-NL; Stuyvesant Fish to James Fentress, 11 July 1898, Fish Out Letters, vol. 36, p. 719, ibid.

"anything done by the railroad companies or their attorneys will be treated by him as a part of a concerted scheme by the railroad companies to down him." When a Mississippi congressman asked Fentress whether in fact his road was using its attorneys for electoral ends in the political arena, he replied that the political preferences of the Illinois Central attorneys were "wholly of their own motion and in their capacity as private citizens and not at all representing the railroad companies." Many southerners found such protestations disingenuous at best.[18]

The fight in Florida over the establishment, then the dissolution, and finally the reestablishment of the state railroad commission reveals the distrust that many southerners came to have for the interstate railroad companies' political activities. Ironically, a former railroad attorney for the Florida Atlantic & Gulf Railroad, Wilkinson Call, became the standard-bearer of the anti-railroad wing of the Democratic Party in the 1880s and 1890s. Call became a United States senator in 1879, when the railroad issue was hardly a ripple on the pond of Florida politics. The sale of four million acres of Florida's public lands in the Disston Land Purchase to outside capitalists and railroad builders in 1881 became the catalyst for anti-railroad sentiment across the state. Homesteaders, squatters, marginal settlers came to view the railroad companies as the beneficiaries of political connections and the proponents of their dislocation. The free passes, railroad-company tax exemptions, federally approved reclamation of hundreds of thousands of acres of false "swamplands" by railroad companies, and the legislature-approved land grants—25,000 acres of land for each of the 170 miles on the Pensacola & Atlantic Railroad—helped focus antagonism on the railroad power in state politics.[19]

Call's reelection in 1885 positioned him as the spokesman for the anti-railroad faction in the Democratic Party. Call was supported by the Pensacola *Commercial*'s editor, Dennis Wolfe, who gave prominent place to anti-railroad sentiment. One letter to the editor, for example, from the Pensacola Knights of Labor demanded that "the public lands, the heritage of the people be reserved for actual settlers; not another acre for railroads

18. Mayes & Harris to James Fentress, 10 January 1899, Fish Out Letters, vol. 39, p. 792, ICRR-NL; James Fentress to John M. Allen, 24 January 1899, Fish Out Letters, vol. 39, p. 799, ibid.

19. Edward C. Williamson, *Florida Politics in the Gilded Age, 1877–1893* (Gainesville: University Press of Florida, 1976), 77–78.

or speculators." The paper's editorial attacks focused on the Pensacola & Atlantic's outrageous land grant and its political mastermind, William Chipley. Chipley founded a paper, the *Daily News*, to counter the *Commercial*'s attacks. Chipley branded Wolfe "a wilful [*sic*] and malicious liar and libeler . . . [devoid] of a single sentiment of honor." For his part Wilk Call considered "railroad morality" to be "just about equal to that of the ordinary brigand."[20]

By 1887, after a major citrus freeze brought high railroad rates and after continued land speculation drove wiregrass settlers off their land, many Floridians were ripe to listen to Call's rhetoric. The Fort Myers *Press* editor spoke for many small shippers and communities, claiming the railroads were nothing more than "old robber barons exacting ransom from beleaguered cities." The Florida legislature took up the issue of a proposed railroad commission in 1887. Both the leading pro-railroad paper, the Tallahassee *Floridian*, and the leading anti-railroad paper, the Jacksonville *Times-Union*, expressed support for some kind of commission. The legislature responded to the public pressure and enacted the commission law.[21]

After a brief honeymoon, the new commission found some opposition. The Palatka *Daily News*, for example, decided that the commission was failing "to bring the roads to terms—to investigate the management and earnings of the roads and to keep these bloated corporations from growing dangerously fat on the blood of a suffering people." The Ocala *Star Banner* called the "weak or something worse" commission an agent of the "greedy cormorants . . . fed to bursting." The Agrarians, who had long considered the commission too expensive and ineffective, redoubled their criticism of the commission when the pro-railroad governor threatened to fill a vacancy on the commission with one of his most conservative supporters. The *Times-Union*, speaking from the Agrarian Viewpoint, called the appointment "distasteful" and thought it better to not have a commission than have one controlled by the railroads. Thus the Agrarians and the pro-railroad forces, each for different reasons, voted to repeal the commission act and dismantle the railroad commission.[22]

20. *Pensacola Commercial*, 19 May, 22 September 1886; *Fort Myers Press*, 11 July 1885. I would like to thank Timothy O'Brien, whose "Tracks to Progressivism: Railroads and Florida Politics, 1879–1891" (bachelor's thesis, University of Virginia, 1992), 59–60, provided me with much of the research on Wilkinson Call and Florida railroad politics.

21. *Fort Myers Press*, 11 July 1885.

22. *Palatka Daily News*, 25 September 1887; *Ocala Star Banner*, 18 November 1887; *Jacksonville Times Union*, 22 May 1891.

As for Wilk Call, his railroad politics came under attack from former state Democratic Party chairman William Chipley, who tried to down him in 1890 with the publication of *A Review of the Record of Hon. Wilkinson Call.* Chipley personified all of the attractive power of development by railroads. According to many supporters, he had saved Western Florida, especially Pensacola, from economic oblivion through the promotion and building of the Pensacola & Atlantic Railroad. He could even be considered responsible or pulling the region back from the brink of secession from the state of Florida, an act widely discussed and advocated in the early 1880s, when Mobile was booming and Pensacola stranded. Chipley embodied the growth of Pensacola to the second-largest city in the state. It was his P&A's parent company, the L&N, that dredged Pensacola harbor and rebuilt its wharfs.

Chipley criticized Call for his failure to recognize the power of railroad development. "He thanks God," Chipley wrote, "in his speeches that he is under no obligations to corporations, and then he travels on free passes." As for Call's attacks on the P&A land grants, Chipley recalled Call's public comments during construction of the line: "This road is worth every acre of public land in western Florida." To finish his attack on Call's railroad politics, Chipley turned to Call's early involvement in the Pensacola & Georgia Railroad: "What was the P&G Railroad? It was the railroad upon which Mr. Call and others made the first payment with a bogus check, which was never repaid. . . . It was the railroad upon which Mr. Call . . . compromised the 'rights of the state and the people,' and for his treachery received the Littlefield $8000. It was the railroad which . . . put its blight upon northern Florida for nearly twenty years."[23] Where Wilk Call saw deception and deceit, William Chipley claimed growth and promise. What Call called stealing from the public, Chipley called economic development. Chipley's strong opposition helped put nearly every paper in the state against Call's reelection in 1891. Despite these long odds, Call managed to survive and return to the U.S. Senate, after his opponents canceled themselves out in a three-way race.

In other southern states, anti-railroad politicians gained an audience among Agrarians. Frank Burkitt in Mississippi campaigned against corporate interests in politics. In Texas, John H. Reagan and James S. Hogg considered the best ways to limit railroad-corporation power. Reagan

23. William D. Chipley, *Review of the Record of Hon. Wilkinson Call* (1890), 7, 85, 34–35.

thought it "a time when public demoralization is so prevalent that railroad-corporations notoriously control state legislatures and courts, and exercise undue influence in the Congress of the United States; and when they impudently and audaciously violate and defy constitutions and laws and plunder the public with impunity."[24]

Railroads seemed to control legislatures in the South, but they also seemed to control the courts. Bringing suit against a railroad corporation for its wrongs was difficult and expensive. The railroad companies, such as the Southern, the Illinois Central, or the L&N, had enormous resources at their disposal. Some of them employed nearly as many people as the U.S. government and had budgets nearly as large. To take such a large company to court required courage and good reason. Many southerners had both, as tens of thousands of them filed suit each year against the railroads.

Most often the reason for these suits was personal injury. Railroads found themselves in court defending these cases more than any other kind. Pro-plaintiff decisions began to add up for railroads in the nineties. For the Norfolk & Western, a coal line with little passenger business, accidents cost $98,023 in 1891, $144,861 in 1892, and $151,344 in 1893. To the executive officers, these damage cases hurt revenue and set precedents for later verdicts. The Atlanta & Charlotte Air Line Railway president lamented large verdicts for the plaintiffs in one case: "What will our two accidents cost us based on the estimate put on Smith's life, virtually taken by his own hand!!!" One wreck involving numerous injured and dead employees and passengers might cost a railroad company large amounts in settlement costs. The 1894 Manteno wreck in Illinois on the Illinois Central produced $43,561 in claims paid out in settling cases to prevent their going to court. In the four years from 1890 to 1894 the Illinois Central paid steadily increasing personal injury claims totaling $64,328.13 in 1890, $141,363 in 1891, $191,237 in 1892, $229,614 in 1893, and $337,824 in 1894.[25]

24. Albert D. Kirwan, *Revolt of the Rednecks: Mississippi Politics, 1876–1925* (Lexington, Ky.: University of Kentucky Press, 1951), 55; John H. Reagan to James S. Hogg, 6 April 1889, quoted in Robert C. Cotner, *James Stephen Hogg: A Biography* (Austin: University of Texas Press, 1959), 167.

25. Norfolk & Western Railroad Company Records, vol. 3, p. 157, Baker Library, Harvard Business School; President Hiram W. Sibley to G. J. Foreacre, 6 January 1881, At-

Concerned about these rising legal costs, Illinois Central president Stuyvesant Fish tried to "minimize if we cannot eliminate this awful waste." The rising cost of personal injury litigation became an issue before the board of directors in 1893. The Committee on Law reviewed general solicitor James Fentress's report on these cases. Fish assured Fentress, though, that neither he nor others on the committee were "disposed to criticize your conduct of the Law Department." "They understand," Fish pointed out, "just as well as you or I that the important thing to do is, as has been done, to call the attention of the Operating Department to the increased number of accidents to persons. I have done this in such a way as to secure results, and will keep after them until I do."[26]

Rising personal injury litigation led several southern railroads to reexamine their practices and to seek ways to counteract these suits. On the Illinois Central's southern roads, the increase in litigation led James Fentress to compile an explanation for the executive officers. Fentress listed the causes of the increase in order of significance: more trains run over the lines; insufficient maintenance, with crews unable to keep up repairs; old engines pulling excessive loads; train crews overworked and "not having the necessary rest"; and finally, the distance of the personal injury agent based in Chicago from the southern states. Fentress notably did not blame the increased personal injury litigation on biased juries or personal injury lawyers; instead, he focused on tangible causes within the operational reach of the company.[27]

lanta & Charlotte Air Line Railway Company Records, VPI. Sibley later wrote Foreacre concerning the settlement strategy after the loss of these cases. He concurred with Baltimore attorney and A&C director Skipwith Wilmer, and remarked: "Wilmer is, like myself, very much out of concert with our Georgia counsel and while he agrees with me that in the face of the late decision in the Smith case we must endeavor to compromise all claims arising out of our late accidents, he is not inclined to trust the advice of our local counsel." Sibley to Foreacre, 8 January 1881, Atlanta & Charlotte Railroad Company Records, VPI. Fish Out Letters, vol. 15, pp. 294–95, ICRR-NL; Stuyvesant Fish to J. C. Welling, 17 September 1894, Fish Out Letters, vol. 17, p. 740, ICRR-NL.

26. Stuyvesant Fish to J. C. Welling, 17 September 1894, Fish Out Letters, vol. 17, p. 740, ICRR-NL; Stuyvesant Fish to James Fentress, 15 November 1893, Fish Out Letters, vol. 13, p. 673, ibid. Fish ordered the Illinois Central's Operating Department "a very radical diminution in the number of persons killed and injured on the railway" and commented that he "need not enlarge to you upon the necessity of our doing this on economic grounds let alone those of humanity." Fish to J. T. Harahan, 15 November 1893, Fish Out Letters, vol. 13, p. 674, ibid.

27. James Fentress to A. G. Hackstaff, 28 January 1890, ibid.

In the 1890s, railroad attorneys petitioned their executive officers to allow their departments to hire an agent or a full-time reporter for personal injury work. Georgia Pacific counsel James T. Weatherly's reorganization effort in 1889 marked an early effort by a major southern line to hire a personal injury agent. Litigation on the Georgia Pacific in the 1880s grew at a disturbing pace. The Georgia Pacific developed into one of the most dangerous railroads in the South, and personal injury litigation proved to be a serious threat to the stability of the company's operations. Several large wrecks in the late 1880s, one of which killed Weatherly's predecessor as general counsel, contributed to a growing litigation problem for the company. Weatherly recommended employing an agent to assist the general counsel in preparing to litigate cases. He did not want an attorney for this position but a "professional man." Weatherly defined the agent's duties: "To collect all the evidence relating to deaths, personal injuries, and all matters out of which litigation against the company might arise, while the evidence is fresh; to prevent litigation as much as possible by ingratiating himself with the people along the line, and taking their complaints in hand *early* before the lawyers have been interviewed; to attend the courts when practicable, inform himself thoroughly about the enemy's movements, about the character and complexion of juries, and tales which opposing witnesses may have to tell." For this position Weatherly sought a "man of the world, a popular man, a just, active, intelligent, and honest man." He did not, however, want a young lawyer, who is "apt to be too bookish, while the man needed in this position should be all business."[28]

The personal injury agent became an integral part of the legal department for business reasons. Increasingly costly and difficult litigation prompted the need for such a position. The division of the bar and the consequent rise of a specialized personal injury bar contributed to this development. Railroad legal departments across the South after 1890 echoed Weatherly's request for an agent to monitor jurors, gather information, and follow up on witnesses. One Illinois Central local attorney explained his need for an agent in 1893: "Upon report being made to him of an accident it should be his paramount duty to go at once and see the injured party and tell him not to employ an attorney, and to advise him that we would take the matter up with him in a day or two."[29]

28. James Weatherly to Jonathan W. Johnston, 22 September 1888, Box 4, GPRR-VPI.
29. Sidney F. Andrews to James Fentress, 10 August 1893, Fish Out Letters, vol. 13, p. 382, ICRR-NL.

When railroads needed information, sometimes they turned to local citizens with connections to them to help with a case. Railroad lawyers understood that personal injury cases often took place not just in local courts but in local circumstances. When a railroad killed a local citizen in a southern town or county, the case brought into focus social relations and considerations otherwise unrelated. Railroads retained their local attorneys to navigate them through this complicated geography. For example, in 1895 a Birmingham, Sheffield & Tennessee River train killed Cal Armstrong on the tracks. The local attorney, T. W. Cantrell, received several letters from a local citizen who gathered information on the circumstances surrounding Armstrong's death. This informer suggested that Armstrong was completely drunk and that "Bob Silpot, who is a negro of as much 'backbone' as I ever saw, will make you a good witness." The informant helped prevent a suit against the railroad. It turned out that the man's brother owned interests "considerably identified with those of the company" and gave him a free pass on the railroad. These circumstances conspired to make a recovery for Armstrong's heirs unlikely.[30]

By the 1890s the opposition lawyers of the personal injury bar had gained experience and organization, and railroad attorneys reacted to this challenge with new techniques to preserve their upper hand in personal injury suits. The Illinois Central local attorney, for example, pushed for greater enforcement of the company rule requiring prompt filing of accident reports. Compliance with this rule, he argued, allowed the attorneys either to settle or "refuse to settle the claim before it would get into the hands of an attorney." As this attorney explained to James Fentress, "There are, as you know, a number of attorneys in the city who employ agents to hurry to injured persons and secure their case. We have to meet this." In response to his local attorney's request, Fentress forwarded the correspondence to the president. Fentress attached his approval for hiring an agent but made clear his desire for the "least expense." Stuyvesant Fish gave his final approval for a personal injury agent several months later.[31]

In these same years company doctors joined agents in some railroad

---

30. R. S. Blanton to T. W. Cantrell, 19 January 1895, Birmingham, Sheffield & Tennessee River Railroad Company Records, Miscellaneous Files, VPI.

31. Andrews to Fentress, 10 August 1893, Fish Out Letters, vol. 13, p. 382, ICRR-NL; James Fentress to Stuyvesant Fish, 11 August 1893, Fish Out Letters, vol. 13, p. 380, ibid.; Stuyvesant Fish to James Fentress, 11 December 1893, Fish Out Letters, vol. 14, p. 47, ibid.

legal departments, as attorneys made efforts to rein in personal injury litigation. Company surgeons, as they were called, provided expert testimony on the severity of injuries, helped the lawyers judge the strength of their defense, and often used their contacts with injured employees to prevent the evolution of a lawsuit. When the Southern Railway reorganized the Richmond & Danville in 1894, a company doctor suggested formalized responsibilities for his colleagues. "My idea was," he wrote the Southern's officials, "that in the reorganization of your new system you would need a supervising surgeon at this point, whose duties would be to receive and compile reports from local surgeons along the various lines, watch the medico-legal aspects of cases of damages suits for personal injuries." Surgeons, like agents, evolved in the nineties into legal department attendants.[32]

Railroad attorneys increasingly used non-company medical doctors to avert possible personal injury suits. One local railroad attorney reported on a claims case to his general counsel. The case involved a man whose arm was cut off after he tried to hop a ride and the conductor hit him in the face, knocking him off the train onto the tracks. The attorney immediately put the victim "under the control of Dr. Peebles, my personal friend." In sum, the local attorney reported: "I got him [Dr. Peebles] to extort from the young man a promise . . . that no lawyer would be employed, that he, Dr. Peebles, would see that justice was done without that expense. I got him to do this that the claims for damages, which will surely be made, might be arranged on better terms than if a lawyer should be employed, provided you should believe the company liable and should direct a settlement." Similarly, when a lump of coal fractured a Seaboard Air Line Railway Company employee's skull and left him mentally incompetent, the road's attorney argued, "If Dr. Nuckols is right in his diagnosis of the case, it is to the interest of the S.A.L. Ry. to have the man properly cared for, rather than let him fall into the hands of some lawyer who may bring suit for damages on a contingent fee."[33]

In the 1890s, companies sporadically brought doctors into court as ex-

32. Dr. C. D. Hurt to W. H. Baldwin, 27 August 1894, Vice-President's Correspondence, Box 1, Folder 5, SRy-VPI.

33. John I. Hall to Alexander R. Lawton, 3 June 1881, Alexander R. Lawton Family Papers, SHC-UNC; Talcott to L. A. Boyd, 23 May 1901, John Skelton Williams Papers, Box 99, p. 178, UVA.

pert witnesses. Able to intervene in cases of injured passengers and workers before personal injury lawyers took a case and able to give expert testimony at trials, railroad doctors supplied critical information for the attorneys. In 1894, for example, the Illinois Central general solicitor received a bill from a company doctor "for medico-legal services . . . testifying outside of Chicago as an expert." In approving the allocation of resources for this kind of payment, company president Stuyvesant Fish remarked that this service was "very rare" and that he would only authorize payment if the general solicitor obtained a written understanding with the local attorneys: they were not to use the doctor's services unless absolutely necessary and only "where his services will be of greater value than the price the company pays for them."[34]

The use of company agents and doctors gave the railroad legal departments significant advantages in the resolution of claims with individuals. Doctors were expensive, even for the railroad. For individual plaintiffs the cost of expert medical testimony was often prohibitive. Railroad attorneys, though, accumulated other, less noticeable advantages. The photographic camera, for example, gave railroad attorneys a technological edge over many of their less fortunate opponents. Railroad attorneys found the use of photographs at the time of a wreck or an injury especially useful in the courtroom as evidence, and they began requesting their company's budgetary approval to acquire the expensive equipment. Often strapped for cash, contingency-fee personal injury specialists could not afford the expensive new technology and surrendered another advantage to their opposition.[35]

Almost every railroad in the South experienced a large wreck; many witnessed them regularly. A single bad accident posed significant legal challenges for railroads. On the Georgia Pacific on 14 December 1885, for example, a wreck at the 17 Mile Tank killed the road's general counsel, Bernard Peyton. Dozens of personal injury suits emerged out of this wreck, totaling hundreds of thousands of dollars claimed in damages. The

---

34. Stuyvesant Fish to James Fentress, 11 June 1894, Fish Out Letters, vol. 16, p. 714, ICRR-NL.

35. Stuyvesant Fish to James Fentress on the Illinois Central's approval to acquire a camera for its personal injury department in Chicago, 18 July 1895, Fish Out Letters, vol. 22, p. 17, ibid. For the uses of the camera by personal injury defendants and plaintiffs, see *Law Notes*, editorial "Photographs in Evidence," October 1898, p. 121.

railroad chose to settle as many as possible in the following year and was able in most cases to reduce the amount paid to 5 percent of the original claim. The Illinois Central Railroad too experienced its share of collisions and derailments: Company legal department reports showed a total of 145 wrecks between 1890 and 1894. The company paid out $389,885 in settlements for personal injuries. On average, then, the railroad's attorneys settled these cases for $2,689 each. Although some derailments led to settlements under $100, the Manteno wreck on 18 September 1893 cost the Illinois Central over $100,000 in settlements.[36]

The concern for liability and large claims led railroads to seek reasonable settlement quickly in these cases and to construct legal defenses for the inevitable lawsuits. The Southern Railway lost a freight train at Saluda Mountain, South Carolina, at 3:45 A.M. on 9 October 1894, killing the crew and derailing 13 cars of coal, 1 car of merchandise, 1 car of livestock, and 2 cars of meat. The owner of the livestock agreed to make a "reasonable claim," and the coal was the Southern's. The threat of personal injury litigation, though, posed the most dangerous claims against the Southern. In his report on the wreck, the general manager surmised foul play. "Information was received," he explained, "of a plot to wreck a train about two weeks ago and all the train men were notified to be on the lookout for the switches at Saluda and Melrose, and it has been intimated that the track had been greased. Special Agent is now at work on this clew [sic]."[37] Executive officers, though, didn't believe these rumors. They knew that "the wreckers did it" excuse had worn thin and most citizens blamed these wrecks on the railroads. Concerned about the "gossip . . . that [the] night was foggy and wet . . . and [that] it is generally supposed it was not safe to send out this train," one official informed the assistant general counsel of his preference: "This whole case raises a question which I should very much prefer to see settled out of the courts."[38]

Ownership of the facts resulted in a distinct advantage to railroads in

36. See James T. Weatherly, Annual Report, 8 December 1886, Box 3, GPRR-VPI; "Injuries to Persons" Reports of the Legal Department, Board Supporting Documents, 1890–1894, ICRR-NL.

37. W. H. Green to W. H. Baldwin, 13 October 1894, Vice-President's Correspondence, Box 2, Folder 65, SRy-VPI.

38. W. W. Finley to W. H. Green, general manager, 22 October 1894, W. W. Finley to Leslie Ryan, assistant general counsel, 14 March 1895, Vice-President's Correspondence, Box 1, Folder 30, ibid.

these cases. Wrecks often occurred at night or in places not easily accessible. As a result, railroad employees, including railroad agents and doctors, usually arrived at the scene first. Their initial reports and actions gave railroad lawyers the critical information necessary for their decisions about the wisdom of settlement and about the strength of their cases. Their expert knowledge as engineers and railroad men gave their testimony great weight in court and in settlement. In most personal injury trials, railroad lawyers built their defense around the facts, material over which they had considerable control.

When an L&N train fell into the Cahaba River in Alabama in December 1896, the L&N lawyers orchestrated the company's defense against personal injury litigation with careful manipulation of the factual evidence. The legal ramifications of the wreck extended beyond the L&N and added greater significance to the lawyers' decisions: The Cahaba River bridge over which the L&N train was running was owned, operated, and maintained by the Southern Railway; the structural beams for the bridge had been forged by the Carnegie Steel Company; and the bridge itself had been built only a few years before (in 1889–1890) by the Keystone Bridge Company, a subsidiary of Carnegie. With the liability of four companies at stake, the Cahaba Bridge wreck represented a delicate problem for the L&N's lawyers and officers.

The initial report, based mostly on rumor from the scene, was that someone had wrecked the train, but L&N chief engineer R. Montfort and his team of experts found little evidence to support the claim. Montfort searched for cross ties with wheel marks as evidence of a derailed, probably wrecked train. He found a few ties with marks and sent them to Birmingham where "if thought advisable, [they could be] used by our Law Department in making settlements on the supposition that the train had been maliciously derailed."[39]

After his initial inspection, though, Montfort "was unable to form any plausible theory as to why the bridge should fail." Despite the marked ties, he quickly ruled out wrecking, finding "no evidence . . . that any wheel left the track prior to the collapse of the bridge." For further emphasis, Montfort reported that "there is nothing that I could find in the situation that in any way justifies or supports the theory that the accident was the cause of wreckers."

39. R. Montfort to J. G. Metcalfe, general manager, 11 January 1897, LANDB.N8, Box 52, Folders 10 and 11, L&NRR-UL.

Montfort began to suspect the bridge's structural integrity. The bridge engineer for the Southern Railway was on the scene, and Montfort quietly went about his business of inspection, reserving his opinion on the matter. "I did not deem it expedient to in any way attack his bridge," Montfort wrote, "particularly as I had no definite information with regard to the manner in which the different members of the bridge were attached to each other prior to the wreck." He took extensive photographs of the wreck before moving anything at the scene. From these and the testimony of the two surviving trainmen, he determined that the L&N train had not derailed but that the Cahaba Bridge had collapsed.

Montfort set out to investigate the cause of the bridge's failure. After requesting the original strain sheets—the graphing tables that would show how much pressure the steel could take—for the Cahaba Bridge steel girders from the Carnegie Steel Company, he received only the original blueprints and a visit from a Carnegie engineer, the general superintendent of the Keystone Company. The Keystone executive spent two days at the site of the wreck, then testified before the Alabama State Railroad Commission that the bridge "would not have failed if it were not that the train had been derailed or obstructed by train wreckers." Both the Keystone's and the Southern Railway's representatives disagreed with Montfort's account of the wreck, and, though they admitted some weak features to the bridge, maintained that only a purposeful derailment could have caused its collapse.[40]

In response to this situation, Montfort tried to mollify the other companies and work around the important issues. He told one of the other companies' experts that he was "just the man we [the L&N] were looking for, and we would probably call upon him to appear for us in the law suits and testify that the accident could only have occurred by train wreckers having caused the derailment." Testing the depth of these experts' testimony, though, Montfort remarked with surprise that a mere derailment and application of brakes would knock down a bridge made by the Carnegie Steel Company. The experts admitted deficiencies, but defended the bridge on the grounds that the railroad engineers approved it and signed off on the blueprints—the Southern Railway engineer "wanted a cheap bridge, and they gave it to him."[41]

40. Montfort to Metcalfe, 14 January 1897, ibid.
41. Ibid.

According to Montfort, the atmosphere around the investigation grew increasingly tense. The stakes were high, as dozens of personal injury claims hung in the balance. The Keystone superintendent, Montfort reported to his superiors,

> stated that his mission was to see whether the Louisville & Nashville Railroad Company intended to make any claim against the Carnegie Steel Company for erecting a defective bridge; to this I replied that I was unable to say what the Louisville and Nashville Railroad Co. would do about it, that I had made my report to you and that it was all in your hands now, but that I believed we would be very glad indeed if he could convince everyone that the accident was due to wreckers: This he said he would endeavor to do, and would, if we wished, appear in any damage cases we might have.[42]

Unwilling to wait any longer for Carnegie's original strain sheets on the bridge, Montfort calculated the strength factors of the steel from the blueprints. The results shocked him. "I have no doubt," he wrote the L&N officers, "there was an error in calculations made in the draughting room of the Keystone Bridge Co., but I presume that the Carnegie Steel Co. will claim that they are not responsible." When he finally received the Carnegie original strain sheets, they only confirmed Montfort's calculations. On critical "center counter-rods" it appeared that the Keystone draftsman "mistook this 1-15/16 [inches] for 1-5/16 [inches]."[43] According to Montfort, "this error alone reduced the strength of the entire structure by over fifty per cent." Furthermore, he pointed out, cost had little to do with the deficiency, as "half of this sum [$37,000 original cost] was literally thrown away if we look at the strength of the cross-rods alone." Montfort concluded his report with the implications of his factual evidence: "The publication of this inexcusable blunder, together with the detail drawings would, in my opinion, amount to utter ruination of the reputation of the bridge building department of the Carnegie Steel Co."[44]

42. Ibid.
43. Montfort to Metcalfe, 20 January 1897, LANDB.N8, Box 52, Folders 10 and 11, L&NRR-UL.
44. Ibid.

With these startling and damning engineering reports in hand, the L&N legal department reviewed the facts and opinions. H. W. Bruce, chief attorney for the L&N, concluded that the road stood little chance of success in pursuit of a claim against either the Southern Railway, the Carnegie Steel Company, or Keystone Bridge Company. Under a contract with the Southern Railway for joint use of the bridge, the L&N effectively became an accomplice to the deficiencies. The road voiced opposition but did not object formally to the original blueprints and through long use of the bridge assented to the bridge's structural integrity. Bruce observed, "The attempt to establish such a claim would aid in fixing liability on us to our passengers and train men, and the representatives of those who were killed."[45]

Bruce advised not only avoiding a claim against the other companies but conspiring with them to orchestrate a coherent set of facts in defense of all of the companies. The lawyers took Montfort's report and shelved it. Bruce summarized his view of how the case should proceed:

> As I am now advised, I think, we should not attempt to establish a claim against the Southern Ry. Co. On the contrary, I think, we should invoke the aid of that company and the Carnegie Steel Co. in an effort to show that the bridge was properly constructed of proper material in a proper manner by skillful workmen, and was a safe structure for the purposes for which it was erected, intended and built; and we should further prove if we can, that it has since its erection been regularly and sufficiently inspected by competent inspectors as to its sufficiency and safety, and that it has all the time been properly maintained, and kept in the opinion of competent judges, a safe bridge for the purpose for which it was erected, intended and used, and was, in such opinions, safe for such purpose at the time of the wreck. If we can establish those facts, in my opinion, they ought to be successfully pleaded in bar of any action brought against us for any injury to person, or loss of life caused by the

45. H. W. Bruce to Milton H. Smith, 21 January 1897, LANDB.N8, Box 52, Folders 10 and 11, L&NRR-UL.

wreck: this somewhat upon the principle which excuses a
person from liability for injury caused by latent defects in
materials, machinery & c.[46]

Because chief engineer Montfort's expert account of the wreck jeopardized all of the companies, Bruce did not hesitate to find other expert opinion. "The opinions given by Mr. Bonscaren and Mr. Montfort are such as
to preclude our calling on them as witnesses," Bruce noted. "Their theories as to the cause of the wreck are plausible, if not probable; but it seems
to me, by no means conclusive. They are speculative and conjectural."[47]

Acting in concert with other large, national corporations—Carnegie
Steel and the Southern Railway—the L&N lawyers knowingly obscured
the facts of the Cahaba Bridge wreck of 1896. They buried their engineer's
report in an effort to limit their liability in the subsequent personal injury
cases and enhance their bargaining position in the settlements. If the
bridge was built with weak materials, the L&N lawyers were not going to
sue the bridge builder or the steel company and open themselves up to any
suggestion that they were also responsible. They would find other, more
reliable experts if they needed to. The lawyers used their company's ownership of the facts to their advantage. In the civil suits that followed, photographs, expert testimony, pieces of evidence, the strain sheets for the
bridge, the wrecked bridge itself, all in the possession of the railroad,
served only to reduce the probability of a company loss at court. It is not
clear from the L&N records or the newspapers how much the railroad paid
in settlement claims. As in any big wreck the railroad paid claims, but in
this case they manipulated the evidence to give the company a large advantage in negotiating with claimants.

Although railroad companies benefited from significant advantages, they
often faced difficult opposition at law when local interests challenged the
railroad. Unlike the big wrecks, where the railroads could take control of
the facts, bring in expert testimony to support their cases, and force plaintiffs to settle, some local issues remained just beyond the railroads' reach.

46. Ibid.
47. Ibid.

Railroad attorneys used their economic development argument to gain favor with influential elements of a locality and tried not to offend widely held social customs. Deeply committed to protecting their companies' interests, railroad lawyers and officials remained reluctant to alienate local opinion. Often, though, the two conflicted. In 1887, for example, Illinois Central general solicitor James Fentress was appalled to discover his road's blatant disregard for Louisiana sabbatarian statutes. In a hot dispute with the L&N over a New Orleans wharf property, the Illinois Central "attempted on *Sunday morning* to rush into putting down track [and was] stopped by city authorities." Fentress deemed the blunder a "great mistake" and pointed out that the Illinois Central "is too honest and respectable to take short cuts." This kind of incident and the resulting litigation, Fentress understood, threatened to generate opposition beyond the aggrieved shipper or injured worker.[48]

As railroads penetrated the rural South, their trains ran over thousands of cattle, sheep, and hogs each year. Livestock claims clogged the law departments of every road. The frequency with which trains killed livestock often led locals to consider whether the railroad in their county was worth the trouble. In deciding whether to support railroad expansion, residents of Banks County, Georgia, for example, tried "to make up their minds what sort of thing a Rail Road is, and how many . . . Cows . . . Horses . . . and Hogs will be killed." Across much of the South in the 1880s, by local tradition and law, livestock wandered free in the countryside while crops required fencing. Of course, railroads posed a distinct threat to this local practice, and rail companies supported stock-laws to fence in livestock. Railroad management opposed bills to require the railroads to fence in their tracks, preferring to place the burden of responsibility and expense on livestock owners instead. Railroads not only paid out thousands of dollars in livestock damage claims each year but also faced slowdowns and disruptions in traffic whenever a train smashed into livestock on the tracks.[49]

48. James Fentress to E. T. Jeffery, 8 July 1887, Fentress Out Letters, ICRR-NL.

49. *Athens Southern Banner*, 21 May 1869, quoted in Steven Hahn, *The Roots of Southern Populism: Yeoman Farmers and the Transformation of the Georgia Upcountry, 1850–1890* (New York: Oxford University Press, 1983), 144. For an account of the stock-law issue in the Georgia Upcountry, see Hahn, *Roots of Southern Populism*, 239–68; see also J. Morgan Kousser and Shawn Everett Kantor, "Common Sense or Commonwealth? The Fence Law and Institutional Change in the Postbellum South," and Steven Hahn, "A Response: Common Cents of Historical Sense," *Journal of Southern History* 59 (May 1993): 201–66.

Most roads adopted a policy like the Georgia Pacific's in the 1880s: "It has been the policy of the company to pay for all stock killed on the Road, except where the killing was clearly not due to any negligence on its part, and if a fair valuation could be agreed on; but it is occasionally necessary to stand suit, either because there is no liability or because an excessive price is demanded by the owner. The actions are cheaply defended and a judicious resistance, with an occasional victory, prevents many improper claims."[50]

Claimants would shop for attorneys to represent them until they found a lawyer willing to take the case. In Lexington, Virginia, the Norfolk & Western ran over a cow and a horse belonging to a local resident, who hired Frank T. Glasgow as an attorney to pursue a claim against the railroad. When Glasgow heard from the railroad about the facts of the case, he advised his client not to try it. The railroad for its part was relieved, because the "damage to our property and the overtime that had to be paid the crews due to the delays by this wreck, were far more than the amount [claimed]." But nearly a year later the railroad received notice that the claimant had retained Letcher & Letcher as attorneys to try the claim. The railroad officials wrote to the newly retained attorneys, suggesting that the facts of the case had persuaded Frank Glasgow to drop the case and enclosing their correspondence with him.[51]

The Illinois Central discovered in the late nineties that it greatest stock damage claims originated on its southern lines, undoubtedly on account of the open range practices in the region. On the system as a whole, the company paid out $51,602 on 3,068 miles of road; on only 807 miles of southern track, though, the company paid out $31,383 in stock damage claims. After a report by general counsel James Fentress, president Stuy-

---

50. On the Illinois Central, for example, in 1889, out of a total 127 cases handled in the law department on the southern lines, 34 (27 percent) were stock claims, the second most prevalent suits behind personal injuries (36 cases, or 28 percent) Bernard Peyton to Jonathan W. Johnson, 1 October 1885, Box 3, GPRR-VPI. For a recent examination of stock laws in the South and the conflict between railroads and farmers over them, see James L. Hunt, "Legislatures, Courts, and Nineteenth Century Negligence: Political and Constitutional Conflict over Standards of Liability," paper presented at the American Society of Legal Historians conference, Minneapolis, October 1997.

51. Div. Sup. Norfolk & Western to Frank T. Glasgow, 18 March 1893, Div. Sup. Norfolk & Western to Letcher & Letcher, 9 February 1894, Rockbridge Historical Society Manuscripts, Norfolk & Western Railway Co. Records, Leyburn Library, Washington and Lee University.

vesant Fish concluded that the huge volume of stock damage cases "engender[s] bad feeling" among local citizens. In 1899 the company's chief engineer determined that "if the line were fenced it would pay for itself in a little more than two years time." More than stock claims concerned the Illinois Central officials: "While this expense will be large . . . we would save more money by avoiding accidents and doing away with litigation than would be expended in the work."[52]

The experience of the L&N seemed to indicate less predictable results. According to Milton H. Smith, "the policy pursued by the management up to this time relative to fencing the right of way, has been to postpone fencing wherever it can be done, until the loss and damage resulting from the killing of stock seems to justify the expenditure." A compilation of these cases showed that the L&N spent $189,654 on claims in 1890–1891 and $175,240 in 1904–1905. Although this decline appeared to constitute very little progress, traffic over the tracks nearly doubled in the period. The L&N had spent $68,068 on fencing by 1890, but in the next decade spent another $255,912. By 1904 it had spent a total of $440,798. The investment appeared to produce a saving of $128,644, or 29 percent of the amount spent on fencing. Some divisions, such as the New Orleans & Mobile and the Memphis Line, elicited doubt about the efficacy of fencing expenditures: "Expenditures for stock killed on this division have shown heavy and persistent increases during the past three years, and have now reached such a figure as to make it appear that the large amount expended for fencing has done no good whatever." Despite these irregularities, Smith and other railroad presidents concluded in the nineties that fencing the track cut down on stock claims, accident litigation, and bad feelings.[53]

52. Stuyvesant Fish to J T. Harahan, 17 December 1896, Fish Out Letters, vol. 27, p. 361, ICRR-NL. "Now that we are still further increasing the speed of our trains, this constant killing of stock introduces a new element of danger." For reasons surrounding the South's large number of stock-damage cases, see Steven Hahn, *Roots of Southern Populism*, 239–68, on the fence, or stock, law controversy. Fish to Harahan, 27 July 1899, Fish Out Letters, vol. 41, p. 81, ICRR-NL; David Sloan to J. F. Wallace, 2 October 1899, Fish to Board of Directors, Board Supporting Documents, 4 November 1899, ICRR-NL: "The sooner we get the Road fenced the safer we will be. All of our trains, both passenger and freight, are being run at a greater rate of speed, and their weight is increasing constantly, and, quite apart from tending to prevent injuries to stock, a well fenced railroad insures safety to trains."

53. M H. Smith to H. Walters, 23 October 1905, Chairman's Correspondence, Box 19, Folder 669, L&NRR-UL.

As with stock claims, a whole body of case law established railroad negligence in the case of fires caused by engine sparks, and railroad companies regularly paid out claims for fire damage in the 1880s. Fraudulent claims, though, presented difficult problems for railroad companies. In these cases a small group of local citizens sometimes banded together to set a fire near the tracks, then pursue a claim against the railroad company. In Terry, Mississippi, the Illinois Central confronted thirty-three fire-damage suits totaling $65,343 in 1893. According to the road's district attorneys, Mayes & Harris, the outlook was grim: "The case must go to the jury and in our view this means that we will lose. . . . The great swarm of suitors and their friends makes the case an almost impossible one for us before a jury. . . . John [a railroad witness] has so many relatives who are railroad men that his testimony will be weakened." The Mississippi lawyers recommended settlement, even in the face of possible fraud. "We are being robbed," they conceded, "but as we can't prevent the robbery we should save what we can."[54]

The Illinois Central president agreed with his Mississippi attorneys and recommended securing the best possible settlement. He cautioned, though, against the recognition of such claims and wanted the citizens of Terry to comprehend the ramifications of their actions:

> One of the most provoking features of this whole case is that while conscious of being grossly swindled by citizens of Terry we cannot strike back at them effectively without doing our own business a serious injury. I should, however, think that Messrs. Mays [*sic*] and Harris, or perhaps better still the Local Attorney, would be able to impress upon the more intelligent class of citizens that human nature is so constituted that if they defraud us out of any considerable sum of money the whole personnel of the railroad will have to change before they can expect the feeling of the management to be the same toward Terry as toward the neighboring towns. While I do not want to make any threat of discrimination, it is pretty certain that

54. Mayes & Harris to James Fentress, 13 December 1893, Fish Out Letters, vol 14, p. 335, ICRR-NL.

128

the town as such, will lose a great deal more than the individual citizens can possibly make.[55]

At numerous times railroads in the New South found themselves in the unenviable position of the Illinois Central—powerless in a locality, left to try cajolery and threat. On no set of issues did railroads experience this more directly than segregation. For business reasons railroads did not want to segregate their cars, depots, or facilities, nor did they wish to police such social conflicts, but white public pressure left them in the minority on these issues. Railroads nevertheless ignored some segregation laws, delayed compliance with others, and always tried to follow their own business interests over those of the state or the public on this issue.

When segregation legislation swept through the South in the 1890s, the interstate railroad companies opposed them. Historians have long known that the railroads opposed segregation, and they have pointed out that the railroads objected to segregation's cost. Cost was part of the explanation, but so was order, efficiency, and autonomy. Railroads across the South resisted any encroachment on their business operations. Segregation became for many railroads an issue of who would run the company, the public or the railroad, local preferences or interstate demand. For the railroads it was a struggle over business prerogatives, not black rights. Railroads became ruthlessly progressive—they valued order and efficiency. Where segregation promoted order, they seemed to value it; where it was inefficient, they wanted to avoid it.[56]

Strict segregation seemed to offer order but threatened efficiency. Plainly it was inefficient to run extra cars for black passengers if there was no demand to fill them. There is no question that railroads in the South delayed complying with segregation statutes as long as possible. An 1890 editorial in a Texas newspaper called that state's segregation statute a

---

55. Stuyvesant Fish to James Fentress, 2 January 1894, Fish Out Letters, vol. 14, p. 404, ibid. Other railroads faced fraudulent fire-damage claims. The Santa Fe's Texas counsel, William Pitt Ballinger, busted a ring of arsonists making claims on the railroad: see John Moretta, "William Pitt Ballinger" (draft manuscript), 1071.

56. See also John W. Cell, *The Highest Stage of White Supremacy: The Origins of Segregation in South Africa and the American South* (Cambridge, Eng.: Cambridge University Press, 1982), esp. 14–18, 134.

"dead letter." "With the exception of the Southern Pacific road," the editor pointed out, "where the company was compelled by the indignant protests of white citizens of Luling to furnish separate coaches, the law is not observed by a single railroad in the state." As Texas railroads quietly failed to comply with the letter of the segregation law, the editor called for a tougher segregation statute.[57]

Under any circumstances the job of managing passengers was not easy, and sometimes it was downright dangerous. The Texas Brenham *Daily Banner* reported, for example, an unsettling incident on a Texas train in 1890: "A gentleman dressed in a white flannel suit strolled into the ladies coach with a cigar, and was told by a brakeman that he must either get out or put out his cigar. He refused to do either . . . gave the brakeman some pretty lurid 'sass,' and drew . . . a six shooter." Nothing resulted from this dangerous confrontation. But in another incident in Georgia, a conductor literally shot a passenger out of the train.[58]

More thoughtful conductors made difficult decisions as they weighed company rules and state regulations against unofficial rules and even the mood of passengers on their train. In one Texas case a St. Louis, Arkansas & Texas conductor expelled a well-to-do white man and his family from the first-class car despite his insistence on buying a first-class ticket from the agent who had issued him a lesser one. The man sued the railroad and won; the railroad appealed. The Texas Supreme Court upheld the decision, finding that the conductor put the family "under circumstances calculated to humiliate and mortify the feelings of the appellee and his wife, who, from the record, appear to have been people of refinement and intelligence." The court, moreover, agreed with the plaintiff that the railroad's second-class cars caused great harm to his wife and family. "It is alleged," said the court, "that the second-class coaches in which the appellee and his family were compelled to travel from Athens, Texas, to Nashville, Tennessee, were uncomfortable, foul, with smoke, dirt, and filth, and filled with Negroes and coarse whites who smoked tobacco, drank whisky, and

---

57. *Brenham Daily Banner*, 13 March 1890.

58. Ibid., 19 June 1890; *Peavy v. Georgia Railroad Company*, Georgia Supreme Court, 3 December 1888. The number of cases concerning excessive force used by conductors in ejecting passengers is large: see, for example, *Louisville & Nashville Railroad Co. v. Bizzell*, 30 So. Rep. 777; *Raynor v. Wilmington & South Carolina Railroad Co.*, 39 S.E. Rep. 821; *Atkinson v. Southern Railway Co.*, 39 S.E. Rep. 888.

used violent, profane, and obscene language in the presence of appellee and his family, in consequence of which . . . [the family was] greatly humiliated and injured." The justices concluded that the railroads through their conductors have a responsibility to police passenger behavior. "These things carriers of passengers ought not to permit in vehicles in which they undertake to transport decent men; much less, refined and delicate women."[59]

In the 1880s black passengers began demanding equal treatment in southern railroad cars and facilities. Before *Plessy v. Ferguson*, interstate railroads found vague statutes and different state laws cumbersome and litigious. An 1887 incident revealed the difficulties conductors faced on southern trains, the arbitrariness of state lines and statutes, and the vigilante violence associated with these issues:

> A well-dressed Negro man, asked by the conductor [on the Western & Atlantic] to leave the ladies' car after the train crossed the Georgia line from Chattanooga, refused to do so. When three young white men ordered him to move, he again refused and they jumped on him. The conductor returned to get tickets, and the Negro begged for protection. The conductor then told the whites to leave the Negro alone, and ordered him to the smoking car. The Negro's face was covered with blood. His silk hat was smashed and he was scared. Without further argument, he went to the smoking car and he got off the train at the next station although he had a ticket to Atlanta.[60]

Conductors were given wide authority to eject passengers from certain cars and from the train for disorderly conduct or violating company rules; in many states they had police power. But conductors had the difficult responsibility of reconciling state segregation statutes with official company rules and unofficial company policy. With segregation statutes proliferat-

---

59. *St. Louis, Arkansas & Texas Railway Company v. Mackie*, Texas Supreme Court, 19 October 1888.

60. *Atlanta Constitution*, 9 April 1887. I wish to thank Edward L. Ayers for passing this piece of evidence on to me.

ing in the nineties, the states left the railroads to police these social tensions. Conflict came over the rights of first-class black passengers, as they asserted limited but visible wealth in the New South. Railroads did not want to lose these customers but feared offending a large segment of the white population if too closely identified with black rights.[61]

Interstate railroads found it difficult to impose their views on social and racial matters in southern localities if they ran counter to the white public conventions. Even their attorneys stuck with the locals on this issue. In 1898 the Illinois Central discovered the limits of its local power when a mob of angry whites in Rives, Tennessee, lynched a black employee. Joseph Mitchell, a brakeman, apparently threw a white tramp off the train. Later, the tramp, whose legs were cut off as he fell under the train's wheels, lived long enough to tell locals a black brakeman threw him off. Upon arriving at the next station, Mitchell found a lynch mob waiting for him, the train's only black employee.

An outraged Illinois Central president Stuyvesant Fish demanded his general counsel take some action. "The fact that this particular man Mitchell happened to be a Negro does not count in my mind for or against," he wrote one of the officers. "He was in the employ of the Company, and it is just as much bound to protect him . . . as you or me . . . and we cannot carry on the business unless every man, down to the lowest, knows that the Company will protect him. . . . You will not spare any effort or any money to secure the apprehension and conviction of the perpetrators of this crime, regardless of their social position." To his general solicitor, Fish equated the deed with train wrecking, warning that if such crimes went unpunished, they would grow rampant. He then reiterated his desire to protect company men—"whether black, white, or yellow."[62]

General solicitor James Fentress, a southerner, advised against antagonizing the "low class whites" in Rives, Tennessee, but Fish demanded he

---

61. For example, wealth and power combined in a small but growing class of black attorneys in the South. Cornelius C. Fitzgerald, "Attorney and Counselor at Law," wrote the Southern's president, Samuel Spencer, after he was "forcibly ejected" from a first-class car and compelled to ride in the "coach for colored passengers." Samuel Spencer to W. A. Henderson, 18 April 1894, Box 4, Folder 03305, SRy-VPI. In 1898 one black woman tried a new tactic to prevent legal segregation when she sued a Kentucky railroad company for allowing a white man to ride in the black car. See *Law Notes*, December 1898 editorial.

62. Stuyvesant Fish to James Fentress, 24 May 1898, Fish Out Letters, vol. 35, p. 905, ICRR-NL.

put the matter before the state district attorney. When Fentress consulted his local attorneys in Tennessee on the advisability of this action, he received a lukewarm reply. "If it appears," the railroad's local attorneys counseled, "that the railroad company is taking extra efforts . . . in prosecuting the mob it would create a feeling of hostility in that locality which we might regret; on the other hand if we can accomplish our purpose by having the state attorney ferret out the murders and punish them without any active participation by the railroad company, it would be much better." Predictably, the state district attorney's prosecution failed to convict anyone; moreover, the railroad was left to defend a personal injury suit filed by the tramp's administrator.[63]

On some other issues as well railroads found that their power was limited. For example, in 1900 the L&N Railroad Company sued the Guarantee Company of North America to recover claims for the shortage of a bonded cashier in Birmingham, Alabama. Railroad companies used insurers, such as Guarantee, to bond accountants. They paid a yearly premium to guarantee these employees' accuracy, that is to insure their responsibility for handling freight charges on thousands of cars a day. Between 1881 and 1901 the L&N paid $77,000 in premiums to Guarantee Company and claimed on losses only $47,000. In most years the amount of losses paid to the L&N fell well short of the annual premiums, which averaged $4,000.

The L&N sought to recover $18,377 for the shortage of the Guarantee-insured Birmingham cashier R. M. Brown. When Guarantee offered $5,600 in settlement of the case, the L&N attorneys balked. The insurance company attorneys requested another conference, and the L&N's general solicitor, Edward W. Hines, expected a higher settlement offer. Instead, Guarantee proposed a lower settlement. An indignant Hines considered the behavior "as trifling with this Company": "We will therefore proceed with our effort," Hines warned his opposition, "to collect our claim through the courts, and do not desire to have any further negotia-

---

63. Fentress & Cooper to James Fentress, 30 May 1898, Fish Out Letters, vol. 36, p. 41, ibid. On the Santa Fe in 1906, attacks on black construction workers led general counsel J. W. Terry to try for federal intervention when the local sheriff was unwilling to defend railroad property and labor. The Santa Fe counsel used its Washington, D.C., law firm connections to urge the attorney general to demand a report from the local Justice Department attorney. See correspondence in Box 20, Folder 3, SFRR-HMRC.

tions with your company looking to compromise of the case. We will also refer your letter to the executive officers of this Company to note in order that they may know what treatment we may expect from your Company in future, and may govern themselves accordingly."[64]

Hines's show of power, though, did not advance the railroad's case. "It is usually easy to get a judgement against an Insurance Company," L&N trial attorney W. I. Grubb reminded Hines, "but the defendant in this case off-sets this by making Mr. Brown prominent in this litigation on the theory that he is the party ultimately responsible and that he is being made a scapegoat by higher officials of the Company, who, in order to get traffic, consented or acquiesced in the course of delivery until disaster came from it, and then protect themselves by shifting responsibility upon Mr. Brown."[65] Not only did the facts show Brown followed "the Company's invariable custom," but the jury panel, on which several of his friends served, favored him as well. Unable to secure a verdict, Grubb recommended settlement rather than pursuit of further litigation. Hines concurred and in a letter to Milton Smith cited the "strong sentiment in the community in favor of Brown" as the reason for settlement. After one trial and four years of litigation, the railroad settled for $6,000, only $400 more than Guarantee's original offer.[66]

The power of local juries and their community connections paled in import with that of local judges to affect a railroad company's ability to manipulate the legal process to its advantage. Minority stockholder suits offered all parties, including a local judge, the opportunity for private gain. The L&N, for example, struggled to gain possession of the South & North Alabama Railroad Company. Already the majority stockholder and bearer of bonds on floating debt, the L&N faced a minority stockholder suit that threatened to upset its efforts to secure clear title. Having removed the case to federal court, L&N attorneys debated the merits of further delay of the case. First vice-president and former chief attorney Walker D. Hines proposed a separate suit to recover judgment for the South & North's huge floating debt to protect the L&N from "claims of the minority stockholders whose stock is intrinsically worthless and valuable only

64. Edward W. Hines to J. Frank Yawger, 3 December 1903, Chairman's Correspondence, Box 11, Folder 410, L&NRR-UL.

65. W. I. Grubb to Edward W. Hines, 22 July 1904, ibid.

66. Edward W. Hines to M. H. Smith, 7 January 1905, ibid.

for blackmailing purposes." When the L&N's general counsel suggested settling the stockholder suit and buying out the remaining South & North owners, Hines replied, "we have too many people to deal with and any transaction with a part will embolden others to continue the litigation."[67]

Some of the other railroad executives betrayed less concern for these lawsuits than Hines. "The main thing," the president of the Atlantic Coast Line wrote his chairman, "is to get the title to the property of the South & North in the L&N and after that the L&N will be in a very much better position to stand a fight than it is today." The ACL president dismissed the lawyers' concerns and, pointing to his experience with the Alabama Midland Railway consolidation, reminded the chairman that against counsel's advice "we took the bull by the horns and went ahead."[68]

When the L&N finally settled the stockholder suit, local events in Alabama confirmed Hines's worst fears. The L&N's district attorney reported that the judge was "giving out information concerning the terms of settlement." If other minority stockholders discovered the terms of the settlement, they demanded a greater value for their stock and the judge received a kickback. "I have always regarded him," the L&N's district attorney warned his general counsel, "as quite a trickster, and more or less unscrupulous, and I have no doubt that he will attempt to profit by the information he has, in some way." Moreover, local speculators in Montgomery who had "figured . . . in several blackmailing suits against corporations" were trying to secure options on South & North stock. The district attorney recommended the L&N's quiet shadow-purchasing of the outstanding shares, so as not to inflate the value. Consolidations brought out speculators, even at the local level. Minority stockholders, local interests, and even judges used whatever leverage they could muster in a fight over title to railroad properties.[69]

Railroad-corporation attorneys developed a set of litigation and lobbying tactics in the 1890s that alienated many southerners. The largest class of lawsuits, personal injury cases, remained an area of distinct advantage for railroads, largely because railroad lawyers developed new techniques,

67. Walker D. Hines to Charles N. Burch, 20 March, 23 April 1903, Chairman's Correspondence, Box 8, Folder 310, vol. 2A, L&NRR-UL.

68. R. G. Erwin to H. Walters, 2 July 1903, ibid.

69. George W. Jones to Charles N. Burch, 7 January 1904, Chairman's Correspondence, Box 8, Folder 310, vol. 2B, L&NRR-UL.

especially the use of expert doctors and agents, to offset the growing expertise of the personal injury bar. In big cases, such as the Cahaba Bridge wreck, corporate attorneys twisted the facts to shield their companies from expensive lawsuits. In small cases, they might remove the case to federal court or use expert testimony to weaken the plaintiff's case. In both they held the advantage of power over the legal process and in some cases the facts themselves. When the lobbyists changed a vote or defeated a fellow-servant bill, they only reinforced what many southerners already knew from their daily dealings with the interstate railroad companies: only monopoly power could explain these deals.

William A. Anderson. Anderson and his partner, John K. Edmundson, went into the law business in Lexington, Virginia, in the 1880s. Their early practice with railroads never turned into the lucrative work they envisioned.
Courtesy Special Collections, James Graham Leyburn Library, Washington and Lee University

Anderson's partner, John K. Edmundson
Courtesy Special Collections, James Graham Leyburn Library,
Washington and Lee University

The Cahaba bridge wreck, Alabama, 1896. A big wreck like this one left hundreds
of lawsuits in its wake. Such accidents occurred with alarming frequency in the South.
*Courtesy Louisville & Nashville Railroad Company Records, University of Louisville
Archives and Records Center*

Cahaba bridge wreck (close-up). The L&N used photography to maintain a record of the wreck and help in the company's defense against claims. Photographs such as this one were used to analyze the way the bridge collapsed and thus demonstrate to a jury the cause of the wreck. The L&N, not surprisingly, blamed this accident on wreckers. *Courtesy Louisville & Nashville Railroad Company Records, University of Louisville Archives and Records Center*

Cahaba bridge wreck (close-up). The L&N attorneys buried their own engineers' report revealing that the bridge's structural steel was flawed and unable to carry the load of the bridge. This photograph documented the width of the steel. The report indicated gross negligence on the part of the L&N. A jury never heard this evidence or saw this photograph.

Courtesy Louisville & Nashville Railroad Company Records, University of Louisville Archives and Records Center

Wreck on the Norfolk & Western, two views.
Courtesy Special Collections, James Graham Leyburn Library, Washington and Lee University

Child on platform, c. 1900. Personal-injury and wrongful-death cases involving children were often the most difficult for the railroads. Damages in these cases sometimes reached as high as $25,000, and juries sympathized with the children and their families. Railroad attorneys settled these cases whenever possible.
Courtesy Louisville & Nashville Railroad Company Records, University of Louisville Archives and Records Center

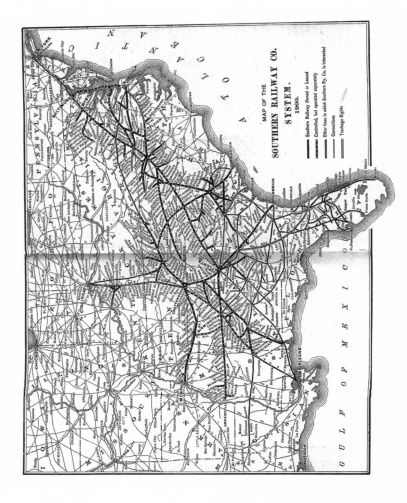

MAP OF THE
SOUTHERN RAILWAY CO.
SYSTEM.
1900.

Southern Railway Owned or Leased
Controlled, but operated separately
Other lines in which Southern Ry. Co. is interested
Connection
Trackage Rights

The Southern Railway system, 1900 (Henry Varnum Poor, *Poor's Manual of Railroads*, 1900, pp. 385–86

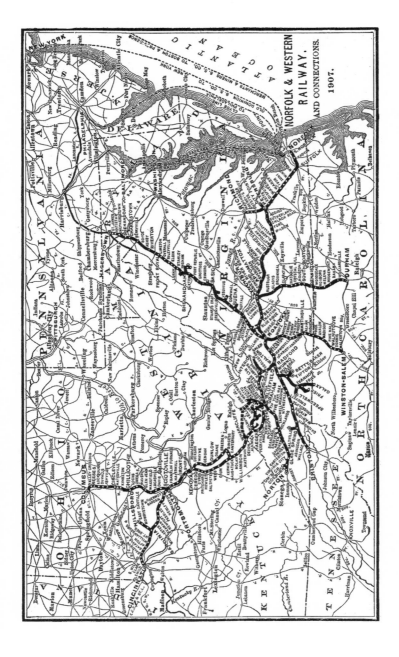

The Norfolk & Western Railway, 1907 (Henry Varnum Poor, *Poor's Manual of Railroads*, 1907, p. 595)

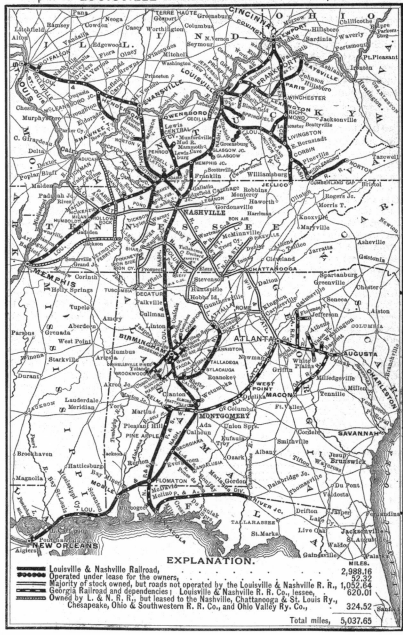

Map of the LOUISVILLE & NASHVILLE R. R. and Dependencies.

EXPLANATION.

	MILES.
Louisville & Nashville Railroad,	2,988.16
Operated under lease for the owners,	52.32
Majority of stock owned, but roads not operated by the Louisville & Nashville R. R.,	1,052.64
Georgia Railroad and dependencies; Louisville & Nashville R. R. Co., lessee,	620.01
Owned by L. & N. R. R., but leased to the Nashville, Chattanooga & St. Louis Ry., Chesapeake, Ohio & Southwestern R. R. Co., and Ohio Valley Ry. Co.,	324.52
Total miles,	5,037.65

The Louisville & Nashville Railroad, 1900 (Henry Varnum Poor, *Poor's Manual of Railroads,* 1900, pp. 417–18)

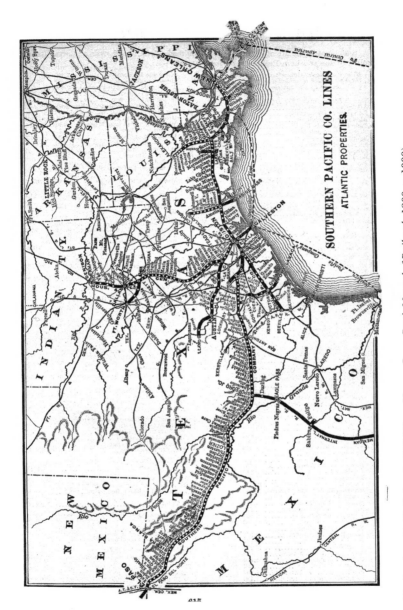

The Southern Pacific Railroad, 1900 (Henry Varnum Poor, *Poor's Manual of Railroads*, 1900, p. 1000)

FIVE

Personal Injuries and Corporate Defenses

By 1900 the professional landscape for railroad attorneys contained definite features. At the center stood the railroad companies' successful efforts in the 1880s and 1890s to divide the bar into those serving and those opposing railroad corporations. The rise of a specialized personal injury bar resulted as much from railroad policies as from the success of contingency fees or the weakening of tort law's bias toward corporations. In the localized, late-nineteenth-century South, lawyers facing a divided bar found themselves on one side or the other. On both they struggled to make a living and hold on to their professional autonomy.

Consolidation and reorganization of southern roads in the 1890s led to a highly structured professional environment on the corporate side of the bar, one that threatened the independence of the attorneys. As part of larger corporate systems, many railroad lawyers considered their professional independence at risk. Many state and local attorneys took other corporate clients, but the railroads' business demanded steadily increasing amounts of their time and attention. The balance for lawyers between increased business and loss of professional autonomy often produced beneficial results for the railroad corporations. At the same time, it perpetuated an inherent tension within the profession, and indeed the region, over the nature and consequences of dependence on the interstate corporations.

Three of the large systems in the South used a legal department hierarchy tailored to the federal demands of the many states through which they operated. The Illinois Central, Southern Railway, and Louisville & Nashville each developed a three-tiered legal department. In-house general counsel, such as James Fentress and Henry L. Stone, monitored the entire system's legal department, rarely trying cases, often advising the road's executive officers on legal issues. Below the general counsel and his assistants in the chain of command, "district attorneys" for each state hired local attorneys, tried important cases, closely monitored local attorneys, appeared before the state railroad commissions, and lobbied before the legislatures. The district attorneys performed all of these duties with varying degrees of autonomy. The district attorneys received a salary and remained free to do outside business. Most specialized in railroad legal work, though, as the litigation demands of their railroad clients left little time for other business.[1]

By 1900 district attorneys emerged as the most important link in the legal department chain of command, a result no doubt of the growing relevance of state issues to the railroads' legal business. The division system of the Richmond & Danville, under general counsel James Worthington, served as a fleeting transition between the organizational pattern of local-oriented roads and the organizational pattern of the great systems that extended over several states. When the R&D was taken over by the Southern Railway, its division system gave way to an organizational structure more sensitive to federalism, in which state or district attorneys played the principal role.

Not all southern railroads followed this three-tiered structure. Roads traversing only two or three states, as well as wholly intrastate lines, did not use district attorneys. These companies retained numerous local attorneys to handle litigation in counties and cities through which their lines ran, while their general counsel's office coordinated the legal department and managed the larger cases. The Norfolk & Western Railroad, for example, operated principally in Virginia and West Virginia, and to a lesser extent Ohio. Spur lines and short connecting branches constituted the

---

1. On the L&N after 1900, law department circulars announced a change of attorneys and indicated their jurisdictions. For the most part jurisdictions for district attorneys conformed to states, though there were some minor exceptions, probably a result of peculiar litigation patterns or minimal mileage in a state or area. "Effective this date, Messrs. King, Spalding & Little, Atlanta, Ga., are appointed District Attorneys for the State of Georgia and Cherokee County, North Carolina. . . . Local Attorneys in Georgia and for Cherokee County, North Carolina, will address their reports and communications to the District Attorneys in Atlanta." Box 16, Folder 553, L&NRR-UL.

N&W's minimal mileage in Kentucky, Maryland, and North Carolina. Thus the N&W legal department did not retain any district attorneys and instead used local attorneys in their place. Lobbying, a principal duty of district attorneys in other companies, fell to one of the strong local attorney firms. In Virginia, local attorney Horace Graham Buchanan of Richmond and in North Carolina Guthrie & Guthrie of Durham lobbied for the N&W. Unlike the larger systems that operated significant mileage in as many as ten or more states, such as the Southern, the Illinois Central, and the L&N, the Norfolk & Western did not feel the pressure of federalism in its legal department.[2]

Although the major southern roads used a three-tiered system in which the district attorneys played the pivotal role, in Texas a four-tiered system evolved out of that state's peculiar legal circumstances. Because the 1876 Texas constitution forbade Texas railroads' consolidation with "foreign" corporations, large systems retained the corporate identity of their constituent railroads. When railroad magnate Jay Gould wanted to consolidate some Texas lines into his emerging national system in 1879 and confronted the prohibitions of the Granger state constitution, he commented that he needed "the best legal advice I can obtain on how to get around this ridiculous idea." The solution, worked out by Texas railroad lawyer William Pitt Ballinger, left Texas railroads intact as they came under control of larger systems. As a result, a given system, such as the Southern Pacific, might control two or three previously independent lines in Texas, such as the Galveston, Harrisburg, & San Antonio and the Houston & Texas Central. These lines retained their corporate identity. In the case of the Southern Pacific, Baker & Botts served as "general attorneys" for both lines and, as a result, as the general counsel in Texas for the Southern Pacific system. William Pitt Ballinger and his successor Jonathan W. Terry served in a similar capacity for the Gulf, Colorado, & Santa Fe. Under these attorneys, district attorneys and local attorneys represented the company along its line. As "general attorneys" for the Southern Pacific lines, Baker & Botts coordinated the legal affairs of the several roads in the system. Texas' overwhelming size required Baker & Botts to retain district attorneys at key points in Texas and make them responsible for the casework in several counties.[3]

2. See file #2657, N&W-VPI, *Virginia Bar Association Proceedings* (1925), 155–57.
3. 1876 Texas Constitution, Article X, section 6, Sayles's Revised Civil Statutes, 1889,

In every legal department hierarchy, local attorneys tried cases in justice of the peace and sometimes general district courts as they represented the railroad on the local level. These were important duties for the southern companies. The railroads tried to secure the leading lawyers at the county level to represent their interests. When S. R. Prince succeeded E. L. Russell as general counsel of the Mobile & Ohio in 1911, he looked to hire some new attorneys in the department. Prince hired Stevens & Lyons as local counsel at Mobile for a $300 per year retainer. They brought the railroad "good lawyers" with "high standing in the community"; in addition, Stevens represented Mobile County in the state senate. The Norfolk & Western retained, among other influential local attorneys, William Hodges Mann in Prince Edward County, who ran successfully for governor of Virginia in 1909. In 1908, moreover, the N&W retained as a local attorney in Richmond W. D. Cardwell, Speaker of the Virginia House of Delegates. Other southern railroads retained similarly well-connected local attorneys, who negotiated the railroads' interests in localities across the South.[4]

Assistants and associates in the general counsel's office also brought expertise and influence to a railroad legal department hierarchy. To replace the lackluster F. J. Yerger as the M&O's assistant general counsel, S. R. Prince turned to Carl Fox, whom he lured out of the Mississippi attorney general's office. Prince hired the Mississippi attorney "because of the large amount of business we have in that state and the necessity for increasing at all times our influence in the state."[5]

The tiered hierarchy that came to characterize southern railroad legal departments in this period did not include the work of "special counsel" Ed Baxter. Baxter as special counsel represented almost all of the southern railroads, mostly before the U.S. Supreme Court and the ICC on matters affecting interstate commerce. Indeed, some historians hold him responsible for single-handedly disabling the Interstate Commerce Act. Baxter at

p. 4247. See also Alwyn Barr, *Reconstruction to Reform: Texas Politics, 1876–1906* (Austin: University of Texas Press, 1971), for an analysis of the politics surrounding the Grange-influenced constitution and for its other provisions. See Kenneth Lipartito and Joseph Pratt, *Baker & Botts in the Development of Modern Houston* (Austin: University of Texas Press, 1991), 25–27, for a description of this tiered system in Texas. Gould, quoted in John Moretta, "William Pitt Ballinger," (draft manuscript), 1081.

4. R. V. Taylor to W. W. Finley, 6 November 1911, Vice-President's File, SRy-VPI.

5. S. R. Prince to W. W. Finley, 23 December 1911, ibid.

one time represented twenty-five railroads, including all of the southern lines except the Chesapeake & Ohio.[6]

Baxter gained his prominence in southern railroad circles when railroads began to cooperate in the face of serious legal challenges. Baxter moved from district attorney for the L&N to special counsel in 1887. Milton H. Smith, president of the L&N, "detailed" Baxter "to devote practically his entire time to litigation" anticipated in the wake of the Interstate Commerce Act. Although he appeared in numerous suits involving other southern railroads to establish a line of precedents, he did so informally. In 1896 Baxter became by contract "special counsel" to nearly all the southern roads. With a five-year contract of $15,000 per year plus expenses, Baxter's contract came up for a second renewal in 1906. Baxter sought a seven-year, $20,000 contract and permission to hire "assistants."[7]

The presidents of the Illinois Central, Southern Railway, Atlantic Coast Line, and Louisville & Nashville met in New York with Baxter to hammer out his new contract. According to Milton H. Smith, Southern Railway Company president Samuel Spencer approved Baxter's requests without question. Smith, for his part, expressed dissatisfaction with the special counsel. "For many years past," he wrote in a file memo, "I have never called upon Mr. Baxter to give me certain information, or render certain services, which is covered by the terms of his employment, that he has not invariably explained it was not possible for him to render the desired service because his time was already full." Baxter wanted to hire assistants, and, according to Smith's memo, build a legal department to represent all the roads in these important cases.[8]

Smith resisted the proposal, and claimed that each company's legal department was best equipped to handle the increased litigation. The other presidents, though, approved Baxter's requests. When Baxter hired Sidney F. Andrews, former Illinois Central attorney, as an assistant, Smith com-

---

6. According to one historian, Baxter "may not have originated the arguments that destroyed the act's effectiveness, but insured that every one was presented to the many judges before whom he appeared. . . . Certainly, if any single man could be credited with the destruction of the ICC in the courts, it was Baxter." John H. Churchman, "Federal Regulation of Railroad Rates, 1880–1898" (Ph.D. diss., University of Wisconsin, 1976), 317–18.

7. Milton H. Smith to H. Walters, 8 September 1906, Chairman's Correspondence, Box 7, Folder 253, L&NRR-UL.

8. Milton H. Smith, "memo for file," 4 May 1906, ibid.

plained to his board chairman that, according to the L&N general counsel, Andrews "is not a man of capacity." Smith concluded that "it is another instance of Mr. Stuyvesant Fish's schemes to unload dead-wood onto others."[9] Smith urged other presidents to oppose Baxter's accumulation of authority.

> I feel sure that the various corporations interested can better protect their interests by utilizing their respective legal organizations, and I am also sure that this must necessarily be done to a very large extent, no matter how many assistants Mr. Baxter may employ. . . . I, for one, am not willing to rely upon Mr. Baxter and his assistants to protect the interests of the L&N RR Co. against the numerous attacks that have been, and which I anticipate will be, made upon it under the numerous laws enacted by the States, and the Act to Regulate Commerce.[10]

Baxter's 1906 contract gained approval from the major southern roads, and he continued to represent them in matters originating out of the ICC. The dispute over Baxter's employment demonstrated the difficulties of coordinated legal efforts and industry-wide representation before the courts.

The change from the loosely managed legal services of the localistic roads of the early 1880s to the tightly organized legal departments of large systems brought conflict and tension between the attorneys of various levels. Most often, the attorneys quarreled over fees and duties. In both areas railroad lawyers experienced the pinching pressure of declining independence.

When Jacob M. Dickinson became general solicitor for the Illinois Central, he discovered the Illinois Central allowed its legal department supervision over its operating line only; the legal affairs of sections under construction remained outside the legal department's authority. In early 1900, though, the chief engineer sent a bill for the legal services of the Ellis & Ellis law firm for right-of-way and condemnation proceedings on an extension. The Illinois Central district attorney to whom the chief engineer first presented the bill returned it with a note that he had nothing to

9. Milton H. Smith to H. Walters, 8 September 1906, ibid.
10. Ibid.

do with the retention of the firm. The bill landed in Dickinson's office, and he immediately tried to establish clear lines of purview for the legal department in this area. "This has arisen," he wrote company president Stuyvesant Fish, "from the fact that in some matters Attorneys are selected and report directly to the Operating Department, such as obtaining right of way etc."[11]

Dickinson recommended that the district attorney be authorized to handle these matters and that the arbitrary division between operating and construction made little sense for legal issues. "We pay him [the district attorney] a salary and he is expected to attend to all legal business in his jurisdiction; the Local Attorneys, except in a few instances, rendering him needful assistance in consideration of annual passes received by them. I see no reason why [the district attorney] could not have attended to this work." According to Dickinson, the legal department should have authority over "all legal work of whatever character." Although he argued that such authority would prevent payment of excessive fees authorized by those not in a position properly to judge legal results, Dickinson undoubtedly harbored some bureaucratic, budgetary protectiveness. Without any input or control, he did not want to pay the bills of another department through his budget.

Beyond these concerns, leading counsel voiced discomfort over their positions of authority. Many of these attorneys, trained in the law under a judge, gained a reputation at the bar for forceful argument and persuasion in the courtroom. Their roles changed, though, in the new hierarchy, as they accrued more responsibility for supervision of attorneys under them. "I agree with you," Stuyvesant Fish consoled his general counsel, "that it is beyond any human capacity to keep touch with and control over, the Local Attorneys scattered over ten States, and at the same time prepare and argue cases." Leading counsel for the large railroad systems increasingly found themselves in conference rooms, not courtrooms. A large portion of their work entailed supervision and review of the action taking place at a lower level.[12]

11. J. M. Dickinson to Stuyvesant Fish, 5 January 1900, Fish Out Letters, ICRR-NL.

12. Stuyvesant Fish to James Fentress, 14 November 1891, Fish Out Letters, vol. 9, p. 56, ibid. Cravath firm historian Robert T. Swaine points out that "the great corporate lawyers of the day drew their reputations more from their abilities in the conference room and facility in drafting documents than from their persuasiveness before the courts." Robert T. Swaine, *The Cravath Firm and Its Predecessors, 1819–1947* (New York: Ad Press, 1946),

As general solicitor for the Illinois Central in 1901, Jacob M. Dickinson spent considerable time compiling the district attorneys' reports into an annual report of the railroad's legal work. For each district he broke down the numbers of cases tried, won, and lost and the cost of litigation, and compared them with previous years and other districts. Dickinson used these comparative and raw data to develop a systematic understanding of the Illinois Central's legal business. He also used them to monitor his subordinates' efforts. For example, after completion of his 1901 annual report, Dickinson sent each district attorney a long letter detailing his performance for the year. For the Mississippi district attorneys, Mayes & Harris, the results augured bad news: "For the year . . . $20,282 more was paid out in your district than for the preceding year. This is an increase of nearly fifty per cent, and is in excess of the proportionate increase of business as represented by the increase in the amount of cases disposed of. In your district with a mileage of 497, 283 cases were disposed of as against 281 disposed of in Duncombe's, Knight's, Steven's, Barge's and Drennan's districts comprising a mileage of 2,496."[13] Five pages of comparative data drew a bleak picture for the Mississippi district attorneys. "This is a bad showing for Mississippi," Dickinson pointed out, "for which we must find some remedy if possible." Dickinson did not blame his district attorneys, though, for the poor numbers; instead, he explained, "much of the litigation there is due to the litigious character of the people and the character of the lawyers with whom we have to contend."

In addition to this annual report and performance review, Dickinson compiled and circulated a breakdown of expenditures for the law department by district, including payments for injuries to persons, loss of and damage to freight, livestock damage, court costs, fees for local attorneys, and miscellaneous expenses. Dickinson also reported monthly expenses for "law books and publications," tools of the trade in an increasingly specialized and highly information-driven profession.[14]

1: 371. Marc Galanter and Thomas M. Palay, *Tournament of Lawyers: The Transformation of the Big Law Firm* (Chicago: University of Chicago Press, 1991), 6, note that others date the transition earlier. Gerard Gawalt marks the shift in the 1880s—see Gerard W. Gawalt, ed., *The New High Priests: Lawyers in Post–Civil War America* (Westport, Conn.: Greenwood Press, 1984), 59. Railroad district attorneys undoubtedly began to experience this change of roles in the 1880s.

13. Jacob M. Dickinson to Mayes & Harris, 13 August 1901, Board Supporting Documents, ICRR-NL.

14. Ibid. On the increased use of technology and information in the development of the

State or district counsel managed dozens of lower-level attorneys in the hierarchy. As litigation demands changed, state counsel adjusted their retainers. After 1900 all state and district attorneys received clear directives from railroad officials to minimize their department costs. The leaders of newly reorganized large systems, such as the Southern Railway, trimmed fixed costs and watched variable operating costs carefully. In the economic depression of 1907, officials further scrutinized operating costs. When one Santa Fe district attorney suggested hiring more local attorneys, state counsel Jonathan W. Terry flatly rejected the request. "We have approximately 100 miles of road in your territory," Terry observed. "If we should have a local attorney at every point suggested by you, we would have one for about every fifteen miles of main line. . . . It is not our practice to have more than one local attorney in each county, regardless of the number of justice courts." Increased litigation pressure conspired with slow economic conditions and company concern for costs to produce tension within the hierarchy. In this environment attorneys at each rung struggled to serve the company's interest without sacrificing their own professional identity.[15]

Leading railroad lawyers experienced a clear division of authority separating them from leading railroad managers. Although railroad management allowed some lawyers considerable voice in corporate decisions, only a few railroad lawyers attained a position of authority over corporate policy. For example, Walker D. Hines joined the law department of the L&N in 1890 as a legal secretary. He left to attend law school at the University of Virginia, from which he graduated in 1892 after one year of furious course-work. He rejoined the L&N law department in 1894 as a district attorney but ascended to assistant chief attorney within three years. In 1901 Hines, promoted to first vice-president of the L&N, joined the road's management.[16]

corporate law practice, see Galanter and Palay, *Tournament of Lawyers*, 8. Report of the General Solicitor, Board Supporting Documents, ICRR-NL.

15. Jonathan W. Terry to S. T. Bledsoe, 30 November 1907, Box 31, Folder 14, SFRR-HMRC.

16. For example, Robert S. Lovett of Baker & Botts rose to Southern Pacific general counsel and eventually became a member of the board of directors. See Lipartito and Pratt, *Baker & Botts*. Victor Morawetz too gained a legal reputation that opened management and board doors for him. At a lower level, district attorneys, such as Jefferson M. Falkner for the L&N, served as vice-President and on the board of directors of the South & North Alabama Railroad. William L. Grubbs, "The Most Brilliant Career of Any Louisville Lawyer" (draft manuscript, 1972), L&NRR-UL. Hines eventually returned to law practice in 1904 in Lou-

Although Hines maintained a deep interest in the legal affairs of the L&
N, he drew a clear line between the legal department and the executive
officers. In 1903 the L&N legal department grappled with the intricacies
of a minority-stockholders suit on the South & North Alabama Railroad
Company subsidiary. Hines directed Charles Burch, L&N general solicitor, to render a legal opinion on the best course of action in the case.
"Please understand," he demanded, "that I want your definite advice as
to the course to be pursued in the litigation and as to the reasons therefore
from the standpoint of law and legal practice. If you should reach the conclusion that a policy of delay is best in order to insure ultimate success it
will then be for the management to decide whether the considerations in
favor of expeditious action, if that is possible, outweigh the legal reasons
in favor of delay."[17]

What Hines and other railroad managers demanded of their attorneys
was exactly what the attorneys were selling—expertise in railroad law.
These attorneys derived their considerable power before courts, legislative
committees, state and federal commissions, and in business conferences
from their ability to use the law and the legal process. Nevertheless, experienced railroad attorneys, such as the Santa Fe's Texas counsel Jonathan
Terry, offered more than just legal acumen; they served as the railroads'
legal institutional memory. In an appearance before the Texas railroad
commission in 1905, for example, Terry delivered a convincing refutation
of a proposed rate increase. "While I may not be the senior in age," Terry
reminded the commission, "I am senior in period of practice before this
body, among the railroad attorneys, and therefore think that possibly I
may be able to throw some light on the general situation." No doubt the
commissioners listened carefully to the railroad attorney who probably
knew more about railroad law than they. Indeed, Terry probably knew
more about the course of the Texas railroad commission's decisions over
twenty years than did anyone on the commission.[18]

Similarly, the Norfolk & Western's local attorney in Richmond, Horace

---

isville. Two years later he became general counsel of the Atchison, Topeka, & Santa Fe system. A year later, in 1907, he joined the Cravath firm in New York, continuing his work as
general counsel for the Santa Fe system.

17. Walker D. Hines to Charles N. Burch, 23 April 1903, Chairman's Correspondence,
Box 8, Folder 310, vol. 2A, L&NRR-UL.

18. J. W. Terry testimony, 30 March 1905, Box 20, Folder 4, SFRR-HMRC.

Graham Buchanan, cited his value to the company in 1916 in terms of institutional memory. Buchanan lobbied for the railroad for many years before the legislative committees and the state commissions, and he wanted a permanent position with the company's legal department. Buchanan pointed out that his firm office held several thousand documents on file concerning the legislature, the railroad business, and the Norfolk & Western. "These files are invaluable," he observed, "and they are the property of our company [law firm]." Buchanan implied that not only the files but also the institutional memory he carried would become the property of the Norfolk & Western if he were hired on a permanent basis.[19]

At N&W, both local attorneys, such as Horace Graham Buchanan, and general solicitors, such as Theodore W. Reath, assumed responsibility for managing their company's business legal environment. Theodore W. Reath became N&W general solicitor in 1907, replacing Joseph I. Doran, who rose to general counsel. As general solicitor, Reath's main responsibility concerned overseeing ongoing litigation, while Doran advised the company's officers on an array of legal questions. Reath understood, though, the broad features of the business legal environment: "With the large increase of business . . . there has also come increased litigation, and as the business of the company grows so will grow litigation, and we will also be confronted with many questions pertaining to legislation, both Federal and State; work before the I.C.C.; work before the Commissions of the various States and, in some degree, political matters."[20] The Norfolk & Western, like other Southern railroads, searched for attorneys capable of managing successfully a complex and changing business legal environment.

In Texas the Southern Pacific felt it had found attorneys with the necessary experience, skills, and connections to represent the company in any court of law. The road retained Baker & Botts and relied on the expertise of Edwin B. Parker to advise them. In 1900 the Texas Bar Association heard Parker present a paper on personal injury litigation in Texas. Parker believed that Texas had become a "a hot bed for anti-railroad personal injury litigation." According to Parker, anti-railroad litigation exploded in the mid-nineties. Parker determined that between 1881 and 1899 the re-

19. Horace Graham Buchanan to W. S. Battle, 15 March 1916, Subject Files, N&W-VPI.

20. Theodore W. Reath to L. E. Johnson, 1 April 1907, ibid.

ports of Texas' supreme and appellate courts recorded 1,283 personal injury suits brought against railroads, and that of these cases only 154 were appealed by the plaintiffs, while 1,129 were appealed by the railroad defendants. This difference represented a stunning number of losses for the railroads at the trial court. Parker found that over the same period, railroad cases constituted the vast majority of all personal injury suits in Texas.[21]

In addition, Parker uncovered evidence "of the peculiar hardships suffered by Texas railroads." He compared the personal injury litigation suits of Texas lines in 1899 with those in western states (see table). Parker used a miles operated to number of suits ratio to illuminate the difference between Texas lines and their regional brethren: for non-Texas western lines the ratio was 1 suit to 49 miles operated, for Texas lines 1:14. Even more startling, the miles-to-amount-claimed ratio stood at $180.00 per mile for non-Texas lines but at $1,208.00 per mile for the Texas roads.

Parker tried to explain the origins of this discrepancy. He dismissed any difference in policies adopted by the roads or in their physical conditions—neither factor varied enough to assign it as the cause for such a wide divergence in data. Parker also checked the ICC report for 1898 to determine whether Texas lines registered more accidents, but he found little difference in the number of accidents between Texas lines and those in the western region.

Parker considered whether the Texas railroads were "responsible for the extraordinary warfare waged against them through the courts." Railroad companies in the seventies and early eighties adopted a no-settlement policy with regard to personal injury suits and, as a consequence, forced plaintiffs into the courtroom; by the nineties, though, most companies found settlement the more attractive option. Heavy verdicts and rampant prejudice resulted from the railroads' early intransigence, he suggested, and set the precedent for later claims. As a result, railroads' increased desires for

---

21. Edwin B. Parker, "Anti-Railroad Personal Injury Litigation in Texas," *Texas Bar Association Proceedings* (1900): 166–67. In his study of New York City personal injury litigation, Randolph Bergstrom finds a "tort explosion" in personal injury suits at the turn of the century. Despite this increase, he found that plaintiffs achieved success less often and recovered lower damages over the period 1870–1910. After thorough examination of the causes for the dramatic increase in suits, Bergstrom concludes that "a change of mind" best explained the "tort explosion." The public, he argues, came to view these injuries as not accidental but the responsibility of another. Randolph E. Bergstrom, *Courting Danger: Injury and Law in New York City, 1870–1910* (Ithaca, N.Y.: Cornell University Press, 1992), 168.

PERSONAL INJURY SUITS AGAINST RAILROADS IN 1899

Company*	Miles Operated	No. of Suits	Amt. Claimed ($)	Amt. Paid ($)	Amt. Paid per Mile ($)
Western States					
A.T.&S.F.	5,831	71	753,560	24,421	4.49
Wabash	2,336	75	350,890	31,007	43.27
C.R.I.&P.	1,305	55	704,099	8,377	6.12
U.P.	2,848	44	466,860	44,235	15.53
M.P.	5,380	130	—	51,912	9.65
M.K.&T.	1,221	16	178,004	24,089	19.73
St.L.S.W.	598	12	91,900	1,375	2.30
Texas					
St.L.S.W.	667	29	412,590	4,991	7.48
M.K.&T.	841	137	2,595,007	183,050	217.66
G.C.&S.F.	1,277	100	1,414,824	47,632	26.83
I.&G.N.	825	32	542,777	49,277	59.73
S.P.	1,067	53	1,279,460	102,082	95.67
H.&T.C.	569	56	863,450	58,054	102.03
S.A.&A.P.	687	42	226,671	48,287	70.29
H.E.&W.T.	192	10	97,250	9,719	50.62

Source: Edwin Parker, "Anti-Railroad Personal Injury Litigation in Texas," 169.

*Abbreviations are as follows:

A.T.&S.F.	Atchison, Topeka & Santa Fe
C.R.I.&P.	Chicago, Rock Island & Pacific
G.C.&S.F.	Gulf, Colorado & Sante Fe
H.&T.C.	Houston & Texas Central
H.E.&W.T.	Houston, East & West Texas
I.&G.N.	International and Great Northern
M.K.&T.	Missouri, Kansas & Texas
M.P.	Missouri Pacific
S.A.&A.P.	San Antonio & Arkansas Pass
S.P.	Southern Pacific
St.L.S.W.	St. Louis Southwestern
U.P.	Union Pacific

out-of-court settlements met with scorn on the part of a general public able to secure large verdicts through the court system. Neither this scenario nor this sentiment was peculiar to Texas, however, and did not explain for Parker his state's lone, unenviable record in personal injury suits.[22]

According to Parker, statutory changes bore much of the responsibility for the situation in Texas. In 1891 the Texas legislature removed the common law fellow-servant rule as it applied to railroad companies. The rule's abrogation, he contended, "has tended to very materially increase the personal injury litigation against railroad companies."[23] The statute opened up a whole new field for previously doomed litigation. Parker considered the act "unjust" discrimination against railroad corporations, for only railroad corporations were subject to it. Other corporations with equally dangerous workplaces retained the fellow-servant defense under common law. Moreover, statutory changes concerning the transfer of causes of action and the survival of causes of action for personal injuries multiplied to "encourage 'the traffic of merchandising in quarrels, of mixing in litigious discord.' " Parker observed, "that as soon as an accident on a railroad occurs the injured parties are besieged by 'strikers' or 'runners' for some personal injury damage lawyer, with the view of securing a 'contract' with the injured person by which an interest, usually one-half, in the cause of action is transferred to such lawyer, with exclusive power to collect the damages by suit or otherwise." Parker conceded that "many honorable gentlemen and able lawyers with high professional standards" tried personal injury cases for plaintiffs, but he pointed out that these lawyers did not engage in the aggressive tactics of those "who make a specialty of anti-corporation personal injury litigation."[24]

Parker saw a stark division of the legal community over personal injury litigation. He considered the introduction of the contingency fee responsible in part for the increase in the number of personal injury suits and the reluctance on the part of plaintiffs to settle out of court. Parker cited several cases from personal experience in which railroad companies offered high settlements for wrongful death ($3,000 to $5,000) to an employee's family when the companies did not consider themselves liable. Under the

22. Parker, "Anti-Railroad," 171.
23. Ibid., 173.
24. Ibid., 175, 176.

influence of contingency-fee lawyers, the families took the companies to court only to lose and receive nothing. Parker considered these practices so common "that the methods here referred to are openly and unblushingly followed by a very large per cent of the 'attorneys at law' who make a specialty of anti-corporation personal injury litigation." "Gambling" and "speculation" were how Parker described the practices of these lawyers.

The jury system also had to take some blame for Texas' anti-railroad litigation, according to Parker. Weak-kneed trial judges were unwilling to remove a case on evidence, and they failed to instruct juries properly. More significant, the jury-selection process compromised the whole enterprise. Jury commissioners appointed by the judge selected Texas' juries. Because the judge often handed these appointments to political operatives, Parker asserted, the commissioners "frequently select professional jurors who actually importune them to be placed on the jury list." Parker suggested further that in cases against railroad companies the minds of these jurors are often made up before they enter the jury box: "Many of them have themselves had claims against, or have lost positions with, railroad companies, and their prejudices are as deeply rooted as their intelligence is dwarfed."[25]

Parker accounted for the general prejudice of juries against railroads in other ways as well. He cited the common misconception that "the juror feels that he is not treading on the toes of any of his neighbors, but is indirectly drawing money from abroad and putting it into local circulation."[26] In addition, he recounted the politically charged atmosphere in Texas against railroads, "about the only available combination of capital on a large scale to denounce and assail."

Finally, Parker held the railroads themselves partly responsible. The rail-

25. Ibid., 186.
26. Ibid., 189. Edward Purcell maintains, however, that local prejudice, though prevalent, remains too amorphous to quantify. He argues that local prejudice was not the driving force behind corporate defendants' removal to federal court, nor was it as widespread as some historians assume. Moreover, Purcell maintains that local prejudice worked both ways. Purcell quotes one Norfolk & Western attorney who in 1911 congressional testimony remarked on local juries' fair treatment of his road. Edward A. Purcell, *Litigation and Inequality: Federal Diversity Jurisdiction in Industrial America, 1870–1948* (New York: Oxford University Press, 1992), 138. Although correct in his assessment of local prejudice's role in removal, Purcell's depiction remains static. The testimony of railroad lawyers across the South document the power of local prejudice and the widening of it in the late nineteenth century, though both they and I admit it is difficult to quantify.

road companies' public relations suffered from an image problem. As railroad managers busied themselves with the affairs of the company and left little time for public relations, "the attacks of the agitator, made from the stump, or through the public prints, remain unanswered." Railroad companies, Parker contended, did little to combat public sentiment against them and by remaining indifferent or unresponsive contributed to their negative image.[27]

All of these conditions, however, beset railroad lawyers in nearly every southern state. Other features of Texas law led Parker to conclude that the legal environment encouraged what he called "speculative" personal injury suits. Plaintiffs in Texas needed to file no deposit or security for costs in these suits if they swore an affidavit of inability to pay these costs. As a result, according to Parker, "suits are filed which are without any real merit." Parker further suggested that most such affidavits were false and that plaintiffs often were able to pay the costs. In addition, Parker pointed to Texas' weak rules of pleading and practice and observed: "The merest tyro can prepare a petition in an action for damages." Because Texas law allowed plaintiffs to sue a railroad company in any county through which the line ran, personal injury lawyers, Parker contended, selected counties most favorable to them for such suits, "counties where the greatest prejudice exists against railroad companies, where the largest verdicts can be procured with the greatest felicity."[28]

This flexibility of venue in Texas conspired with the Texas railroad consolidation act to stack the odds in favor of plaintiffs. In his paper, Parker did not address Texas' consolidation act as an explanation for high personal injury verdicts, but more than any statute this one stacked the odds against railroads in these cases. The act required that in any consolidation of railroad companies the constituent companies remain intact and domiciled in Texas. For example, each major system, such as the Southern Pacific, included several independent Texas railway corporations in its holding company. For personal injury litigation, the implications of the consolidation act included the inability of Texas railroad corporations to remove a suit into federal court under federal diversity of citizenship law. Domiciled in Texas under the consolidation act, Texas railroads could not claim diversity of citizenship when sued for personal injuries in Texas.

27. Parker, "Anti-Railroad," 189.
28. Ibid., 179–81.

Texas railroads, then, could not avail themselves of one of the most effective tactics for defeating personal injury suits.[29]

Parker was at the top of the Southern Pacific's legal hierarchy in Texas. He had tried many cases for the Southern Pacific, and he knew all of the judges, trail lawyers, and insurance companies in the state. Parker's depiction of the personal injury environment was undoubtedly biased and designed to encourage the Texas bar to press for legislative relief. But it revealed the depth of some railroad attorneys' conviction that the tide had turned and the plaintiff now had the advantages in the state courts. The most prominent features of this new litigation landscape included both a sharply divided bar with competent, aggressive, and successful personal injury specialists, and statutory, procedural, and judicial changes that diminished railroad advantages in these cases. Unable to remove cases, Texas railroads faced a difficult litigation environment, one in which local power and prejudice remained unchecked.[30]

Railroad defendants across the South witnessed the change in personal injury litigation around 1900 that Edwin Parker documented for Texas. Their success in court, both at the trial and appellate court levels, deteriorated in the face of increasing challenges from plaintiffs seeking personal injury claims. The change in the personal injury legal environment prompted in reaction a series of defensive tactics on the part of railroad companies.

One court docket study of three West Virginia counties demonstrated the adversities railroad defendants experienced at the turn of the century. According to this study, the litigation rate—that is the number of suits relative to the population—in these counties from 1870 to 1940 rose against railroad companies in the eighties and early nineties, sharply declined during the nineties' depression, and rose again steeply from 1900 to 1908, when the Federal Employers' Liability Act (FELA) passed. At the state su-

---

29. See Purcell, *Litigation and Inequality*, for the importance of removal to federal court as a tactic to defeat personal injury suits against railroad corporations.

30. Edward Purcell also emphasizes the importance of the rise of the personal injury bar around 1900: "By altering the balance of inequality, especially in the huge and murky informal legal process, personal injury specialists steadily drove up the total costs that accidents imposed on corporations. Further, by raising the specter of perjury, dishonest claims, and unethical tactics—which, regardless of their frequency, corporate attorneys seemed to fear deeply—they raised the threat of persistent and unfairly imposed liabilities." Purcell, *Litigation and Inequality*, 162.

preme court, railroad defendants found their success rate against employees fall from 80 percent in the 1890s to 44 percent in the 1900s, and against non-employees from 59 percent to 39 percent. At the trial court level, railroads regularly settled close to 70 percent of the cases. Of the remaining cases that went to trial, plaintiffs won on average only 43.3 percent between 1881 and 1895, but they succeeded on average in 66.15 percent of the trials between 1896 and 1916. Although over the whole period only 15 percent of employee suits went to trial and employees won nearly all of these, non-employee plaintiffs took railroads to trial more frequently and achieved greater success beginning around 1900.[31]

Railroad legal departments documented these changes in their annual reports to their boards of directors. On the Illinois Central, for example, the company paid out $26,902 in settling 411 employee personal injury claims in 1898. The following year the company paid $52,564 in 1,833 cases. The statutory dismantling of Mississippi's fellow-servant rule and increased prejudice against railroad corporations, some historians allege, explain this increase. In 1900 fully half of the Illinois Central's personal injury litigation originated in Mississippi. The Illinois Central district attorneys in Mississippi blamed the rise in personal injury litigation in their state on "the general shortage of pasturage for lawyers in any other field of litigation."[32]

Most railroad lawyers recognized that changes in personal injury litigation depended on an array of related causes. Precisely what all those causes

31. Frank Munger, "Social Change and Tort Litigation: Industrialization, Accidents, and Trial Courts in Southern West Virginia, 1872–1940," *Buffalo Law Review* 36 (1987): 85, 97, 100. Munger points out that when broken down in five-year periods, these success rates fail to conform to changes in the litigation rates. In other words, according to Munger, "the peak litigation rate reached in the early 1890s accompanied a relatively low success rate, and followed a period of equally low success. The rising rate between 1906 and 1910 was accompanied by a relatively low success rate and followed a period of moderately high success for plaintiffs." He concludes that "neither rules of law nor trends in circuit court outcomes can explain the decline in tort litigation against railroads." Non-employee cases going to trial jumped from 57 percent of the total between 1890 and 1899 to 85 percent between 1900 and 1909. Their success rate rose from 40 to 60 percent in the same period.

32. David L. Lightner, *Labor on the Illinois Central Railroad, 1852–1900: The Evolution of an Industrial Environment* (New York: Arno Press, 1977), 372–73; Mayes & Harris to Jacob M. Dickinson, 7 November 1901, quoted in Robert L. Brandfon, *Cotton Kingdom in the New South: A History of the Yazoo Mississippi Delta from Reconstruction to the Twentieth Century* (Cambridge, Mass.: Harvard University Press, 1967), 170.

were was something these attorneys speculated about in their reports. The number of accidents directly and proportionately affected the number of personal injury cases, and railroad lawyers and officers pushed their operating departments to reduce accidents by improving safety. Other causes included the amount of traffic or business on the line, the number of employees working for the road, and the number of passengers traveling on the trains. In the nineties depression years, for example, less traffic and business resulted in fewer employees working, fewer passengers traveling, and fewer accidents. The personal injury litigation rate dropped considerably in these years for most southern railroads and picked up again as the region emerged from the depression in the late nineties. Railroad attorneys often blamed other causes, though, for increases in personal injury litigation. Sharp personal injury lawyers and their tactics received universal attention from railroad lawyers. The success rate of plaintiffs in court, as well as statutory weakening of railroad defenses, also drew comment—when potential plaintiffs saw others win in court, they were encouraged and filed suit themselves.

The plaintiffs' attorneys even initiated new uses of old legal doctrines to secure judgments against railroads. The legal concept of wantonness referred to careless neglect but differed from simple negligence. It required a conscious act of neglect or omission of a duty—a reckless disregard. At the turn of the century the standard legal treatises and manuals on railway law neither deeply examined the subject nor indexed it. The concept was a rarity in the courts; it appeared to be the equivalent of gross negligence. According to an Alabama lawyer, personal injury specialists succeeded in using the concept to override the contributory negligence defense around the turn of the century:

> It is difficult to define, difficult for the plaintiff to prove, and yet more difficult for defendant's counsel in a damage suit to keep out of the case, as civilization seems to have progressed to that stage where wantonness can at least be "boldly asserted," if not "plausibly maintained," in every case where damages are claimed from railroad corporations in suits for personal injuries.
>
> Formerly the battle was waged and the case won or lost on the issues of simple negligence and contributory negligence. They still occupy an important place in this

character of litigation, and yet they have been more or
less forced into the background by this doctrine, which,
if old, is yet constantly bobbing up in some new garb or
trapping.[33]

For the railroad attorneys, the resurrection of the wantonness doctrine
threatened to render nugatory the contributory negligence defense in
many cases. Its use in the Alabama courts remained haphazard, and judges
had charted no clear interpretation for its application. Nevertheless, it
proved effective in some Alabama cases, enough to prompt a bar association paper on the subject.[34]

From the perspective of the railroad attorney, all of these developments
conspired to turn a favorable personal injury legal environment into an adverse one. Asked to explain the "increase in litigation" on the Santa Fe in
1908, the general claim agent reported to state counsel Jonathan W. Terry
that he had settled two hundred to three hundred personal injury claims
per month in the year. Several serious accidents monopolized his time and,
as a result, "less serious claims reached the hands of attorneys, resulting in
suits." Furthermore, he reminded Terry of the changing litigation environment: "You are aware during the past few years there has been a great
deal of adverse legislation, as well as adverse opinions to railroad companies, and by reason thereof many claims which a few years ago were easily
defended have now become dangerous." Rumors of high settlement offers
by the railroad spread quickly through the saloons, this agent reported,
and compounded his difficulties. "The lawyers and their 'strikers' and
'booters,' " he observed, "are thoroughly organized, in my judgment;
and the fact that jurors are not placed under the rule by the Court permits
them to hear at least a part of what is being narrated." According to this

33. Paul Speake, "Wantonness in Personal Injury Cases," *Alabama Bar Association Proceedings* (1903), 134.

34. "In pleading, wantonness has caused much tribulation to lawyers and much work for
the courts. The lawyers seem to have difficulties in various directions—sometimes stating
facts constituting simple negligence and styling them 'wanton'; sometimes coupling the
words 'negligently and carelessly' with 'wantonly.' . . . It is worth questioning . . . why a
more general allegation of negligence or of wantonness is sufficient on the part of the plaintiff
in charging the wrong-doing, while a defendant, pleading contributory negligence, is required to state specifically and in detail the facts constituting it." Speake, "Wantonness,"
148.

agent, the jurors voted for high damages, thinking that the railroad offered as much in settlement.[35]

In these circumstances railroad attorneys turned in defense to more informal legal processes. They hinged their efforts on company doctors, personal injury agents, tactical delays, removal to federal court, and the use of expert testimony. Railroads experimented with all of these defensive tactics in the nineties. Around the turn of the century, though, their attorneys formalized, expanded, and routinized them as they became more necessary than ever to deal with the rising litigation.

By 1900 large southern railroads retained a host of company doctors in addition to attorneys. When Jacob M. Dickinson replaced James Fentress as Illinois Central general solicitor in 1899, he brought the company's doctors under the aegis of the law department. "It seems to me," he suggested to Stuyvesant Fish, "that the Chief Surgeon ought to make reports to the Legal Department, of which he is really an adjunct. . . . On the L&N, the surgeons, while not under the control of the Law Department, reported in writing on every case of personal injury, immediately after examination. Such reports were necessary, in order to know the gravity of the injury, and the advisability of compromising."[36]

In 1901 Charles M. Blackford, an attorney for the Southern Railway in Virginia, addressed that company's medical department on the intersections between law and medicine in the company's affairs. Concerned about the company's continued ability to prevail in court against personal injury claims, Blackford contended that "the outside world should know little about" the communication between his and the medical departments. The revelation of such communication, Blackford was concerned, would be "fatal before a jury." Blackford then turned to the surgeons' reports, which recorded for the railroad's files in explicit detail the injuries to a potential plaintiff:

> Reports you must make . . . but any counsel for the company of much experience knows to his sorrow that if . . . one of your pea-green reports . . . gets before the court,

35. W. L. Alexander to Jonathan W. Terry, 7 February 1908, Box 31, Folder 20, SFRR-HMRC.

36. J. M. Dickinson to Stuyvesant Fish, 20 December 1899, Board Supporting Documents, ICRR-NL.

> we have a hard time. . . . The counsel for the plaintiff in
> cross-examining the surgeon always calls for it. . . . I
> shudder when I think how often I have denied having it,
> though it was at the time in my green bag at the hotel,
> where I always leave it to enable me to tell the truth. . . .
> If one of you gentlemen knew what it was to be subjected
> to the torture of having a sharp opponent hold up one
> of these pea-green reports and comment upon it before a
> country jury, you would resign rather than sign one.

Despite his jaundiced regard of juries, Blackford maintained that the role of the company's surgeons was vital to his work. Truthfulness on the part of the medical department allowed the attorneys to assess the proper strategy for the company: "an opinion equally clear that the injury is serious should, if the company is to blame, induce it to avoid a losing suit."[37]

Similarly, Blackford counseled against partisan testimony, which he characterized as "one of the greatest troubles the law department has to overcome." Because he had to face the jury and the opposing attorney, Blackford understood that "whitewashing reports" only ruined the company's case in court. Juries and especially personal injury attorneys recognized the difference between the truth and the company line. Moreover, Blackford contended that departmental bias in an effort to avoid blame for a wreck or accident only worsened his position: "The intense partisanship of the commentators and the desire of each department to free its own skirts from blame produces this state of affairs. I had been defending railroad companies for at least a decade before I believed that a railroad man could do a wrong or make a mistake. I put all the blame on the juries and the communistic state of public sentiment. The juries and public sentiment are very bad, but if official comment and official action could be a little more tempered . . . the litigation would be clearly reduced."[38] Blackford recognized the juries' biases; as a railroad attorney he hoped to reduce their significance in the courtroom. That these biases prevailed throughout the South in personal injury suits against railroads Blackford did not question; his concern centered on how best to mitigate them.

Baker & Botts initiated efforts in Texas along the Southern Pacific lines

37. Charles M. Blackford, "The Relation Between the Medical and Law Departments of a Railway Company," *Virginia Law Register* 7 (February 1902): 680, 685.
38. Ibid., 686.

to foil the anti-railroad prejudice they saw in juries across the state. After victory in a 1906 San Antonio case, W. B. Garrett explained to Edwin B. Parker: "This verdict [for the Southern Pacific defendant] was quite a surprise to a number who heard the case. We succeeded in getting four *good* men on the jury who were friends of our friend who helped me." Railroad attorneys, especially in Texas, where railroads could not remove cases to another state, considered jury selection an important element in their defense, and they took great measures to ensure favorable jury panels whenever possible.[39]

Railroads employed full-time personal injury agents as well as claim agents to prevent cases from going to court, to watch juries, and to help establish the best possible defense if the plaintiff sued for damages. Sometimes young lawyers just starting practice with the company or else young men without legal training, these agents sifted out the meritorious claims from the fraudulent and recommended to the railroad the best course of action in each case. Most railroad attorneys considered their role essential. Jonathan W. Terry, for example, promised to back his road's general claim agent "in any application for authority for an increase in your force. We take the liberty of making the suggestion, owing to the fact that the success of the Law Department is largely dependent upon the work of the Claim Department." As if voicing a mantra, railroad attorneys recited the benefits of good claim work:

> We believe that a prompt adjustment of meritorious claims against the company is much to be desired, and that the company has all to gain by following this policy. As soon as the public in general begins to have evidence of the fact, and acknowledge the fact that the railroad is willing to be reasonable at all times in the settlement of claims which are just and meritorious, the sooner in our judgment the railroad will receive the hearty cooperation of the public, its sympathy and good will, in combatting claims which are not bona fide and which are fraudulent in their character.[40]

39. W. B. Garrett to Edwin B. Parker, 23 June 1906, Box 11L, Folder "Austin DA," BBHC-RU.

40. Jonathan W. Terry to W. L. Alexander, 9 January 1908, Box 38, Folder 17, SFRR-HMRC; Beall, Kemp & Ward to Baker & Botts, 25 April 1910, Box 11L, Folder "El Paso DA," BBHC-RU.

In carrying out their duties, claim agents could act with more latitude than railroad attorneys. Rules of professional conduct, monitored by area bar associations, governed railroad attorneys' actions, but company claim agents subscribed to no comparable professional code. In personal injury cases the lawyers' professional conduct rules demanded that railroad attorneys deal directly with claimants' attorneys. A claim agent, though, was free to deal with injured persons directly. When the attorneys of claimants proved unreasonable and refused settlement, according to the Illinois Central general solicitor James Fentress, "it would be unprofessional in the Legal Department to deal with the client over the head of his attorney." The company's agents, "under no such restriction," stepped in to make an offer of settlement directly to the claimant. "These matters sometimes become quite delicate," Fentress conceded, "but the purpose has been to handle them for the interests of the Company, and at the same time without lowering the professional standard."[41]

Sometimes agents voiced unease over their law departments' directives. An employee's injury on the Big Sandy & Cumberland Railroad in 1905 prompted the company's attorneys to seek a statement releasing its liability. The agent, though, questioned the propriety of seeking release from a "loyal employee of the company . . . [who] said he would not bring suit under any circumstances, and he felt rather hurt that the company did not have that confidence in him." The general counsel followed procedure, though, and he needed a statement. He reported to the road's executive officers that the statement was not "a release, but it is a statement which makes such admission as would exonerate the company in case of litigation." The general counsel urged the road's officers to compensate the loyal employee in some way.[42]

Agents provided the attorneys with other important services. In El Paso, Texas, railroads found increasingly hostile local sentiment after 1900. In reviewing the severity of the situation with Baker & Botts, the district counsel for the El Paso & Southwestern System explained how his line tried to meet this threat:

41. James Fentress to Stuyvesant Fish, 4 August 1899, Board Supporting Documents, ICRR-NL.

42. J. J. Divine to James L. Hamill, 15 November 1905, James L. Hamill to J. Mortimer, 22 November 1905, N&W-VPI.

It was suggested some time ago that an agent be employed by the railroad companies to keep track of the jurors and ascertain all he could with reference to all of them. Some years ago we had such an agent, whom we paid, and it was his particular business to find out and keep a written record of how every juror voted in every personal injury case that came before the court, and also to gather all data that he could with reference to the panel when we had cases likely to be tried before it. We found this of very great assistance to us and it was finally suggested that the roads combine and have one agent.

In addition, these attorneys pointed out that successful resolution of claims depended not only on the quick work of the agent but also on that of the local attorneys. "We are convinced," they suggested to Baker & Botts, "that the situation here could be greatly improved if the local attorneys and claim agents were both given full and absolute authority to settle any litigation or claim for damages without having to consult with the superior officers of the company. The delay . . . very frequently prevents a settlement that would be extremely beneficial to the company."[43]

The advantage of court delays to railroads in the eighties and nineties dissipated across the South as states opened new courts after 1900 in an effort to speed up the litigation process. The backlog of district court cases had long made expeditious resolution of personal injury cases through settlement more attractive to many plaintiffs than the two- or three-year or longer process of litigation on a crowded docket. "The establishment of the new District Court here eighteen months ago," Baker & Botts's district attorney in El Paso reported, "resulted in giving the personal injury lawyers a chance to have their cases called for trial almost as soon as filed, and curtailed our chances for settlement."[44]

43. Hawkins & Franklin to Baker & Botts, 16 May 1910, Box 11L, Folder "El Paso DA," BBHC-RU. Also see Fentress to Fish, 4 August 1899, Board Supporting Documents, ICRR-NL: "Many of the personal injuries are settled immediately upon their happening and for small sums, by the Operating Department, through Mr. Losey, Chief Claim Agent. Indeed, I have urged Mr. Losey, since his appointment, to get there as soon as an accident happens and close up all we can, upon small payments, where there is manifest injury, before the parties have gotten sore and talked to lawyers."

44. Maury Kemp to Baker & Botts, 13 August 1914, Box 11L, Folder "El Paso DA," BBHC-RU.

The notorious delays in state courts—delays so favorable to the railroad defendants—prompted citizens, politicians, and some lawyers to call for reform. Railroads, on the other hand, denounced such changes as unnecessary and counterproductive. When the Texas Bar Association, for example, recommended changes in civil procedure to expedite the litigation process, Santa Fe general counsel Jonathan W. Terry objected. "I am of the opinion," Terry explained, "that undue haste in bringing on the trial of cases will cause more injustice than the delays that are complained of. Fraud, mistake or other weakness in the case of the prosecution or of the plaintiff is quite often developed by a few months delay." Fearing the loss of his defendants' power, Terry warned of populist results to such reform: "It has occurred to me that the whole tendency of the plan recommended by the Committee of the Bar Association, including the nine jurors verdict proposition, is in the nature of a return to ancient Athens, where the trials were had by popular vote."[45]

Not all legislated reform, however, was viewed by the railroads as unwelcome. For example, one southern railroad appreciated the uniformity brought about by federal Safety Act, passed in 1893. The Illinois Central's president thought it was in "the interest of the Railroad Companies that Congress should control as many of these questions as possible for the reason that we then have one uniform law." He was concerned that since the Illinois Central "running through ten States would be obliged to keep all of its cars up to the most rigorous standard exacted by any one State."[46]

And the value of safety itself was gradually borne upon the managers of southern railroads: as they tightened operating costs after 1900, they grew more frugal on claims and more concerned for the costs of accidents. They pressed the law departments to cut costs, settle when necessary, and find solutions for expensive cases. The attorneys in turn pushed management to reduce the number of accidents and improve safety as a means to lower litigation costs. In Temple, Texas, for example, the Santa Fe attorneys noticed the prevalence of accidents in the switching yard in 1907. As an example of the connection between safety and the law, they pointed out to

45. J. W. Terry to Ed. J. Hamner, 18 July 1908, Box 38, Folder 2, SFRR-HMRC.
46. Stuyvesant Fish to J. T. Harahan, 4 March 1893, Fish Out Letters, vol. 11, p. 940, ICRR-NL; Harahan to Fish, 12 February 1894, ICRR-NL. See Kurt Wetzel, "Railroad Management's Response to Operating Employees' Accidents, 1890–1913," *Labor History* 21 (1980): 351–68.

the superintendent the case of a switchman who was killed in the yard. The attorneys settled the case for a large amount. But if the case had gone to trial, the attorneys knew the plaintiff would argue "that this man probably stepped in a hole which caused him to lose his footing." Even though the railroad attorneys did not believe this, they reported "there was sufficient evidence to warrant plaintiff to go to the jury on that issue. . . . It is probably true that much of the timber lying loose in these yards are placed there by the switchmen themselves using the same as chock blocks and leaving it where the last man had occasion to use it . . . even if . . . true, it would not relieve us of liability for an accident." Finally, the railroad's attorneys turned to the safety issue: "Had these yards been perfectly clear there would have been no occasion for us to expend any money whatever in settlement of the Doeckle claim." Within the month, the Santa Fe general manager ordered the general superintendent to put all yards "in first-class condition."[47]

47. A. H. Culwell to K. S. Hull, 10 December 1907, F. G. Pettibone to W. E. Maxon, 31 December 1907, Box 31, Folder 11, SFRR-HMRC.

SIX

Progressive Reform and the Railroads

Around the turn of the century, southern railroad companies consolidated and merged into a handful of enormous rail systems, traversing the entire region, each servicing ten or more states and hundreds of thousands of people. Their consolidation came on the heels of a major depression in the 1890s and was part of a larger national pattern of merger in the rail industry. The depression beginning in 1893 eventually dragged one-quarter of the nation's railroads into receivership. The depression was particularly hard on the South and on southern railroads. From 1894 to 1898, dividends on southern railroads floated at only one-fifth to one-third the national rate, and of the 128 major lines in receivership in the nineties, 33 were southern. The weakness of these railroads spurred outside capital to consolidate them. Through the heart of the South, the Southern Railway Company emerged out of the collapsed Richmond & West Point Terminal Company in 1894. J. P. Morgan's Southern system combined over 7,000 miles of railroad. In the Deep South states, the Illinois Central continued to control the vital north-south axis along the Mississippi River. Along the coastal plain, the Atlantic Coast Line, itself a 1,676-mile conglomeration of over one hundred formerly independent lines, swallowed the Plant system in 1902, adding 2,000 miles of fourteen railroad companies to its system. In the same year the Atlantic Coast Line gained a controlling interest in the Louisville & Nashville, while J. P. Morgan secured similar control over the Atlantic Coast Line. These consolidations culminated in 1903, when it appeared that the Morgan financiers owned and controlled three of the five largest rail systems in the South.[1]

Only one large system along the coastal plain remained free of northern control. The Seaboard Air Line, formed in 1900, consolidated eighteen corporations into one continuous system of 2,600 miles. John Skelton Williams, a Richmond banker, served as the Seaboard Air Line's first president, and he actively promoted the growth of southern industries and development. Northern stockholders financed the Seaboard Air Line, and seven of nine directors lived in New York City, but New York financiers did not control the company—Williams and his regional partners did.

Under the pressure of non-local ownership, though, even Williams's vision for regional development fell victim to outside interests. New York banker Thomas Fortune Ryan financed the Seaboard Air Line through bonds. He subsequently maneuvered to devalue the stock with demands for bond repayment and then to buy out stockholders in order to gain controlling interest in the railroad company. Williams and other southern stockholders sued for an injunction to prevent Ryan's moves and enlisted Allen Caperton Braxton, Virginia's progressive lawyer responsible for its new corporation commission, to draft the brief. Braxton and Williams alleged that the Seaboard Air Line represented the South's hope for independent development. They were "hoping that this new and extended railroad system could be utilized for the development of the South Atlantic states, and maintained as an independent and peculiarly Southern system, exclusively in the ownership or control of Southern interests." The South, he argued, was in a tributary relationship to the big railroad companies. The argument failed to prevent Ryan's takeover, and the Seaboard Air Line too depended on northern financiers after 1904.[2]

The language of Braxton's brief and his call for local or at least regional control of large transportation systems appealed to many southerners, who during and after the great consolidation movement had trouble discrimi-

---

1. John F. Stover, *The Railroads of the South, 1865–1900: A Study in Finance and Control* (Chapel Hill: University of North Carolina Press, 1955), 256–57, 263, 275. By 1900 five great systems—the Southern Railway, the Illinois Central, the Seaboard Air Line, the Atlantic Coast Line, and the Louisville & Nashville—controlled three-fifths of the rail mileage in the South. The other major lines included the Norfolk & Western, the Chesapeake & Ohio, the Mobile & Ohio, and the Texas lines—the Santa Fe, the Missouri, Kansas & Texas, the Cotton Belt, and the Missouri Pacific.

2. Memorandum, Box 62, John Skelton Williams Papers, UVA.

nating between developmental companies and trusts. The former they appeared to welcome, the latter they distrusted. Progressive reformers in the South called for an end to the tributary status of the region and to the monopolization of the railroad industry. The great national corporations, especially the railroads, Progressives warned, retarded growth and fostered dependency, as well as abused the public trust and mulcted the average southerner in countless ways.

For the railroads' attorneys, describing the distinction between developmental companies and monopolies grew especially troublesome. William A. Wimbash, a Georgia railroad attorney, expressed this difficulty in a 1906 bar association address. Wimbash suggested that "unless subjected to some wholesome restraint the monopolistic character of railroads will inevitably develop those selfish qualities which are incompatible with the public interest." At the same time, Wimbash pointed out, "It is not to be forgotten . . . that the railways have contributed enormously to the development of the country, and are essential to its continued prosperity." Wimbash, moreover, considered the role of the railroad attorneys to be that of the negotiator: "It is the true relation between common carriers and the public that we [the bar] should seek to discover and preserve." State railroad commissioners, state legislators, railroad attorneys, newspaper editors and shippers, farmers, and businessmen all spoke up not just for their interests but for the proper means to reconcile the place of these large interstate corporations in southern politics and economy.[3]

Many southerners, the depression of the 1890s fresh in their minds, came to view the railroads not as promoting but as retarding economic development. The railroads, meanwhile, emerged out of the depression reorganized and consolidated, bigger than ever. Sometimes it seemed to southerners that railroads actively discouraged any development that did not directly benefit the railroad. For example, one railroad president confided his efforts to squelch a local effort to build a road. "I have succeeded so far," the Knoxville & Augusta Railroad president reported to W. W. Finley of the Southern in 1900, "preventing it [the wagon road along the line] being macadamized in Blount County and hope still to fight it off, and consequently can charge higher freight rates when the roads are bad than when they are good."[4]

3. William A. Wimbash, "Judicial Review of the Rates of Carriers," *Georgia Bar Association Proceedings* (1906), 410.

4. W. P. Hood to W. W. Finley, 28 May 1901, Vice-President's Files, SRy-VPI. I am indebted to Edward L. Ayers for finding and passing on this quotation to me.

Aberdeen, Mississippi, for example, felt flush in 1898 as the Illinois Central planned to extend its line into the Alabama coalfields through the fledgling town. Expectations among the town's leading citizens soared. They collapsed quickly on the rumor that the Illinois Central's officials planned to bypass Aberdeen. The prospect of being "bypassed and spurred" encouraged few in the town, and citizens felt as if promises were made and not kept. "We are seemingly powerless to prevent it," the town's judge explained to James Fentress, "and will have to rely on the officials' keeping good faith with our people." Aberdeen, according to Fentress, had always favored the Illinois Central and eagerly sought the road's main line business. When presented with the judge's plea for "good faith," however, president Stuyvesant Fish revealed the realities of post-depression railroad building: "The line, in order to deliver coal economically, must be built on the shortest and cheapest route. We have no option whatever in the matter. We can, of course, refrain from building, but if we build at all to the Alabama coal fields, we must select the cheapest route, regardless of how it will affect other people. I have written this plainly . . . so that you can explain the matter fully to our friends in Aberdeen."[5]

Many southerners were convinced of railroad overcapitalization, and saw railroad rates as arbitrarily excessive, railroad taxes as suspiciously low, and railroad practices as arrogantly unfair. Railroad leaders faced the difficult task of proving their companies did not hinder economic growth with unfair business practices. In general, southerners grew impatient with the railroads' economic development posturing, and politicians fueled their impatience with anti-railroad rhetoric. A group of reformers in every southern state took up the cause of Progressive change, and their first target became the interstate railroads. Most Progressives did not consider themselves enemies of business, but instead as reformers who believed that adjustments needed to be made, systems checked, and excesses contained. Allen Caperton Braxton, in charge of the committee to develop a state corporation commission in Virginia, found that he was called "little short of a wild-eyed anarchist" because he "advocate[d] even the serious consideration of applying to corporations rules and regulations of laws like all other people have to submit to." Braxton, and other Progressive reformers, wanted fairness in the business economy, not radical reform. They of-

5. E. O. Sykes to James Fentress, 21 October 1898, Fish Out Letters, vol. 38, p. 245, ICRR-NL; Stuyvesant Fish to James Fentress, 24 October 1898, Fish Out Letters, vol. 38, pp. 243–44, ibid.

fered a pragmatic approach, seeing themselves as mediators between extremes. Progressives tackled issues as diverse as child labor, workmen's compensation, health and safety issues, school reform, and prohibition.[6]

As the South's economy picked up in the late 1890s, Progressive reformers turned more of their attention on the powerful and seemingly arrogant railroad corporations. They strengthened the railroad commissions in nearly every state and began a decade of legislative activity that could not fail to impress the railroad officials and attorneys with its scope, detail, and careful construction. Progressive reformers achieved their greatest political success in Alabama, Georgia, North Carolina, Florida, and Texas. Even in states with weaker reform movements, though, such as Virginia, Kentucky, Tennessee, and Louisiana, the railroads faced numerous adverse measures. For large interstate corporations with operations in nearly every southern state, weak reform states provided little comfort when over half of the states through which their lines ran embarked on significant change.[7]

Anti-railroad agitation peaked in the years 1906–1907 for southern legislatures; railroad attorneys around the South had of course for years before this sensed the changing atmosphere. They formalized the lobbying functions of their local and district attorneys, cooperated with one another on legislative matters in a more regularized fashion, and avoided local political skirmishes. In these years, 1900 to 1914, southern legislatures pre-

6. For a thorough account of the Progressive concern with economic development, see Dewey W. Grantham, *Southern Progressivism: The Reconciliation of Progress and Tradition* (Knoxville: University of Tennessee Press, 1983), 147–56. For the standard railroad case for economic development and against regulatory reform, see Jefferson M. Falkner, "Some Comments as to the War upon the Railroad Interests Now Being Waged by a Few Wholesale Merchants in Birmingham and Elsewhere," Chairman's Correspondence, Box 13A, Folder 472, L&NRR-UL. Allen Caperton Braxton to John W. Todd, 20 January 1902, Allen Caperton Braxton Papers, UVA, quoted in Edward L. Ayers, *The Promise of the New South: Life After Reconstruction* (Oxford: Oxford University Press, 1992), 413. For the history of the social and educational reform movements in the South, see also William A. Link, *The Paradox of Southern Progressivism, 1880–1930* (Chapel Hill: University of North Carolina Press, 1992).

7. For a detailed account of the strengthening of state commissions, see Maxwell Ferguson, *State Regulation of Railroads in the South* (New York: Columbia University Press, 1916). Both Ferguson and Dewey Grantham considered Progressive regulatory legislation of poor quality, though high volume. Grantham, *Southern Progressivism*, 156. My point here is that compared to earlier efforts, Progressives drafted better legislation.

sented the railroad attorneys with a dizzying volume of lobbying work, and the lawyers responded with a variety of strategies for protection of their companies' interests.

After 1900 nearly all the southern railroads retained some of their attorneys as lobbyists. In this new business environment their job changed from entrepreneurial lobbying for their company exclusively to associational lobbying for the railroad industry, as well as for their company. It required less electioneering and more committee appearances, less influence peddling and more legal and political strategy. As politicians across the South responded to Progressive calls for railroad regulation, railroads discovered the impotence of their election tactics. No longer able to secure friendly legislatures with decisive campaign contributions, railroads resorted to defensive strategies aimed at minimizing the damage of proposed legislation. These efforts increasingly brought railroad lawyers before legislative committees to testify on the effects of proposed legislation. Lawyers became the purveyors of expert information on the railroad industry and on the effects of any proposed statutory changes.[8]

Although lobbyists for the railroads skillfully worked the legislative halls, they also took advantage of changes in other arenas, especially the judiciary, to use the entire legal system to protect their clients' interests. The *Munn v. Illinois* decision in 1877 prompted all watchful railroads to protect their property in the legislative lobbies. All of the railroads were warned of the improbability of judicial review of the reasonableness of rates. So, the railroads followed state legislative matters closely, using all of their considerable power and persuasion to prevent legislative meddling in their business.

Railroad attorneys, however, did not abandon entirely the judicial arena

---

8. Edgar Lane, *Lobbying and the Law* (Berkeley: University of California Press, 1964), 6. Lane first observed the distinction between associational, common interest pressure groups and entrepreneurial, one-time special interest parties (seeking a charter, for example). Lane, however, gives no indication of when, how, and why associational lobbying became more prevelant. As early as 1897 the associational lobby concept hit southern railroads. Ed Baxter suggested to James Fentress "that the law department (of Southern roads) impress upon the managements of their respective companies the importance of an efficient organization of some kind to prevent unjust legislation." 9 December 1897, Fish Out Letters, vol. 33, p. 675, ICRR-NL. See also Robert H. Weibe, *The Search for Order* (New York: W. W. Norton, 1968), 183 on the changes in lobbying around 1900. See, for example, Horace Graham Buchanan to L. E. Johnson, 20 March 1916, Subject Files, N&W-VPI.

for protection of their property. They recognized that legislatures behaved in response to public demands and that despite considerable expense and effort railroads could never call a legislature completely reliable. Courts, on the other hand, valued precedent and followed principles. Railroad attorneys undoubtedly favored the judicial forum and at the first opportunity maneuvered to overturn the *Munn* holding.

The Supreme Court gave its first indication of weakening *Munn* in the Minnesota rate cases of 1890, and railroad lawyers initiated a series of challenges in the 1890s that culminated with a reversal of the *Munn* ruling at the end of the decade. The Court ruled in favor of the railroads in the Minnesota rate cases and held that the judiciary possessed the authority to determine the reasonableness of rate regulation. In the same year, Texas politics erupted in Populist fervor, and railroads in that state faced increased regulation under reformist governor James Stephen Hogg. Hogg's ascendancy led the state legislature to enact a series of railroad-regulation measures, one of which created a strong railroad commission with the power to regulate rates. Texas railroad attorneys contested that authority in the Supreme Court. In 1894 the high court ruled in *Reagan v. Farmer's Loan & Trust Company* that the Texas commission could not enforce unreasonable rates. Finally, in 1898 the court elaborated on its earlier decisions in *Smyth v. Ames*, when it affirmed judicial review of reasonableness of rates and mandated that the test of reasonableness include a "fair return" on the value of railroad property. *Smyth v. Ames* doctrine instituted a gross earnings formula to separate interstate and intrastate business. Holding that states could not set unreasonable intrastate rates, the Court tried to separate intrastate from interstate business. In doing so it relied on an easily manipulated, highly complex, and judicially unwise formula that the railroad attorneys used to hide the earnings from each side of the business. The effect of the decision was to allow railroads to contest every downward revision of state rates as "confiscatory."[9]

By 1898, then, the railroad attorneys had engineered a remarkable re-

---

9. Richard C. Cortner, *The Iron Horse and the Constitution: The Railroads and the Transformation of the Fourteenth Amendment* (Westport, Conn.: Greenwood Press, 1993), 129. See Robert C. Cotner, *James Stephen Hogg: A Biography* (Austin: University of Texas Press, 1959), for an account of the battle over railroad regulation in Texas. See James F. Doster, *Railroads in Alabama Politics, 1875–1914* (Tuscaloosa, Ala.: University of Alabama Press, 1957), 85, for an excellent example of the absurdity of the formula.

versal. The federal courts, able and willing to rule on the reasonableness of state rate regulations, became a safe haven in the strategic thinking of railroad attorneys. Most often in future struggles, railroad attorneys sought injunctions from federal courts to restrain state authorities from enforcing unreasonable rates. With *Munn* fatally weakened and the confusing *Smyth v. Ames* doctrines in its place, railroad attorneys exploited the situation to develop a mixture of lobbying and litigation tactics, all designed to protect the railroads' interests in the face of the Progressive challenge.[10]

Railroad lobbyists had good reason to seek refuge in the courts. The legislatures across the South emerged from the long depression of the 1890s suspect of railroad claims of economic development and convinced that the five major reorganized and consolidated systems required regulation. The southern states showed no sign of concern about the Supreme Court's decisions. They continued to interpret them as favoring state regulation. The question was not whether states could regulate railroads but what degree of regulation was reasonable. Since the federal government did not act strongly to regulate railroad practices, southern states stepped up and began enacting all sorts of regulatory measures. The editor of *Law Notes*, a national legal affairs monthly, commented on the changing legislative climate. He allowed that railroad corporations compiled a record of "wickedness or oppression" in their litigation and that they "employed the best legal talent, who resorted to every shift and device to defeat the most righteous claims." These abuses, the editor pointed out, slowed as railroads, out of either altruism, fear, or more probably self-interest, reformed their practices, recognizing that "people have rights." Despite this change, the editor lamented, state legislatures showed evidence of harsh reprisals. "In many of the states it is evident that the repentance of railroad companies cannot possibly allay the resentment of the people for past iniquities." He then observed that "the legislatures are not to be appeased until the companies are laid prostrate. . . . Enactments hostile to railroad companies have increased in virulence."[11] In the face of this change, the editor praised the railroad legal departments for their increasing reliance

10. See Doster, *Railroads in Alabama Politics*, 185–231. In Alabama the federal judge, Thomas G. Jones, had served as the L&N's counsel before his appointment to the bench. Braxton Bragg Comer considered him "railroad environed," because Jones granted the railroads' requests for injunctions.

11. *Law Notes* (April 1898).

on the Fourteenth Amendment's due process clause and on the judiciary branch as the proper means and forum to protect their companies' interests.

At the turn of the century, legal observers regularly complained about what they called "the flood of legislation" or "overlegislation" in the states. In the South both the large number of proposed bills in a given session and the character of them threatened railroad corporations. Eighty-three anti-railroad bills came before the Texas legislature in 1907, and other state legislatures delivered similar numbers of bills. Of most pressing concern for railroads was that the southern legislatures after 1900 strengthened their states' railroad commissions, set maximum freight and passenger rates, and increased railroad taxes.[12]

In addition, though, they enacted a host of general legislation designed to weaken the railroads' overwhelming advantages in the courts, the legislatures, and the workplace. For example, nearly every southern state considered employers' liability acts. These were more sweeping than earlier legislation to limit the fellow-servant defense through the vice-principle definition. These state employers' liability statutes effectively eliminated the fellow-servant doctrine and weakened both contributory negligence and assumption-of-risk defenses. Commenting on a Virginia bill, one Virginia railroad president lamented, "public opinion is demanding that loss of life caused by railroads should be lessened and I am looking to see in the future harsher laws against railroads." Most states passed fresh requirements on railroads to meet safety standards or, in some cases, to adopt specific safety devices. Some states, particularly the southwestern states of Texas, Oklahoma, and Mississippi, required railroads to employ larger crews on their trains and provide shelters for their workers on the line. Some limited the number of hours railroad employees could work. Many outlawed the free railroad passes to state officials, and most extended prohibition legislation into railroad coaches and depots. Arkansas generated pages of general legislation, requiring certain roads to maintain a depot, keep an agent, stop for passengers, build a station depot, and other actions in specified towns or counties.[13]

12. Ibid. (October 1899), on Senator Charles Frederick Manderson's concerns before the American Bar Association; Grantham, *Southern Progressivism*, 147.

13. See Virginia, which had rejected limitation of the fellow-servant defense on four occasions in the 1890s, Statutes, 1901–1902, p. 335, and 1912, p. 583; Texas Statutes, 1909, pp. 64, 279; North Carolina Statutes, 1911, p. 343; Georgia Statutes, 1909, p. 160; Missis-

The legislative situation had so completely reversed itself that railroad lawyer-lobbyists sometimes looked to the state commissions and courts for more favorable hearings. They fought hard in the legislatures to prevent the passage of adverse legislation and achieved some success, but they all recognized that their control of the region's legislatures slipped away after 1900. Even special acts of the legislature, which had flowed with ease out of the southern legislatures in the 1880s, required careful finesse. When the Santa Fe Railroad president sought acquisition of another Texas line in 1908, for example, the general counsel warned that it would "bring about the necessity of another consolidation bill, and give the political bushwackers another opportunity to talk about railroad absorption."[14]

After 1900 railroad officials demanded and expected from their lobbyists regular reports on the state legislatures, detailing each bill, how it affected the company, its chance for success, and its ultimate fate. Throughout the South the railroad lobbyists after 1900 clamored in chorus against the "reactionary tendency" of the legislatures. Lobbyists in most southern states relied on the state senate to curb potentially harmful legislation, but in the Progressive period even the upper house failed to resist the pressure for reform. "The most we can hope for," summarized one railroad lobbyist, "is to modify the character [of legislation], and perhaps defeat some of the worst bills." Despite the adverse political atmosphere, railroad lobbyists compiled an admirable record of success. The L&N's Georgia lobbyists deemed the 1904 legislative session potentially the most hostile in many years. But they reported to the L&N general counsel "that we succeeded with the assistance of other interests affected

sippi Statutes, 1908, p. 204; and Arkansas Statutes, 1911, p. 55. Mississippi Statutes, 1912, p. 161, and 1913, p. 218; Texas Statutes, 1909, p. 179, and 1910, p. 123. W. E. Mingea to L. E. Johnson, 8 February 1904, Subject Files, N&W-VPI. Some of the most popular reforms included requiring suitable caboose cars, Virginia Statutes, 1910, p. 392; requiring derailing devices on tracks, Texas Statutes, 1913, p. 334; requiring electric headlights on locomotives, Texas Statutes, 1907, p. 54; requiring ash pans that could be cleaned without an employee's going under the locomotive, Texas Statutes, 1909, p. 67; requiring use of cinder deflectors, South Carolina Statutes, 1912, p. 777. Georgia first enacted this legislation in 1890–91 limiting the number of hours for trainmen to thirteen. Georgia Acts, 1890–91, p. 186; Texas Statutes, 1909, p. 180 and 1907, p. 222; North Carolina Statutes, 1907, p. 665. On free pass legislation, see South Carolina Statutes, 1903–1905, p. 900; Texas Statutes, 1907, p. 93; Arkansas Code of Statutes, 1905 and 1907.

14. Jonathan W. Terry to E. P. Ripley, 10 August 1908, Box 38, Folder 3, SFRR-HMRC.

in defeating in one way or another every legislative proposition—and there were a great many of them—inimical to railroad interest."[15]

After 1900 southern railroad companies' attorneys increasingly shared information and cooperated more formally in their efforts to defeat certain bills. Railroad attorneys, overloaded with cases, commission work, and legislative matters, voiced concern that the sheer volume of proposed legislation might overwhelm their efforts. The L&N's Kentucky district attorney thought he could defeat a bill to give telephone companies the right to condemn the right-of-way of railroad companies. "At the same time, however," he reported to the company's executive officers, "there are so many bills now pending in the Kentucky legislature against railroad interests . . . I am apprehensive that some of the inimical bills may slip through." The summary report from the Tennessee district attorney confirmed a similar deluge of proposed legislation. Although the state failed to muster a significant regulatory coalition, its representatives generated plenty of work for the L&N lobbyist. He characterized the session as "ninety days of as hard and constant struggle as any I ever care to participate in." Reporting on the most serious bills, this lobbyist listed eighteen important legislative fights. As for the L&N's own poposals, their Tennessee lobbyist confessed that he waited long into the session before presenting any bills. "It was necessary to have the least opposition as possible in the defensive fights we were making," he explained. "In other words, we did not want any of the committees to meet that we could help." Even in Tennessee, where Progressives never generated extensive railroad reform, railroads found themselves on the defensive so much so that their proactive legislation lost its priority.[16]

15. King & Spalding to Walker D. Hines, 5 December 1902, Chairman's Correspondence, Box 3, Folder 75, L&NRR-UL; H. Walters to Milton H. Smith, 16 March 1903, Miscellaneous President's Office, Box 102, Folder 75014, ibid.; King & Spalding to Walker D. Hines, 5 December 1902, Chairman's Correspondence, Box 3, Folder 75, ibid.; King, Spalding & Little to Charles N. Burch, 13 August 1904, Chairman's Correspondence, Box 9A, Folder 349, ibid.

16. For the effects of "overlegislation" on the legal profession's thought, see Barbara C. Steidle, "Conservative Progressives: A Study of the Attitudes and Role of Bar and Bench, 1905–1912" (Ph.D. diss., Rutgers University, 1969), 33, 41. Steidle points to the annual summaries of the presidents of state bar associations for evidence of the dramatic increase in legislation. By the late 1900s many state bar presidents abandoned the attempt to summarize their states' legislation—it had grown so voluminous. In addition, bar associations debated what one speaker called "the congestion of law." T. B. Harrison to W.L.M., 13 February

In Kentucky, as in other states, railroad lobbyists confronted a diverse set of hostile general bills. The L&N district attorney for Kentucky lobbied the 1906 legislature, sidetracking over thirty-two anti-railroad House measures. Some, such as House Bill No. 130, which compelled railroad companies to provide depots every four miles on their lines, represented the desires of specific local interests, and the railroad lobbyists killed most of these. In his final report the L&N's Kentucky lobbyist confessed that some favorable bills failed "from lack of time and on account of trying to defeat so many inimical bills." As in Tennessee, railroad lobbyists in Kentucky, where Progressive reformers managed only a weak reform effort, put aside their legislation in the heated contest to defend their companies against proposed legislation.

Railroad attorneys across the South did not contest every measure in the both the legislature and the courts. Some measures they let go and complied with the law. After the passage of a 1909 Texas statute requiring railroads to build sheds to cover their repair yards, for example, one railroad attorney complained about the measure. "This looks like a bare effort to impose duties upon certain persons because they are railroad companies for the benefit of other persons because they are railroad employees." He urged the general attorneys of Texas railroads to contest the legislation's constitutionality in court. Others counseled compliance, however. Baker & Botts, Texas counsel for the Southern Pacific lines, conceded that the measure probably was unconstitutional but advocated a course of obedience. "The expense will not be great," they pointed out, "and as a question of policy . . . it is best to erect the sheds." In the calculus of operating costs and safety measures, this legislation balanced in the company's long-term favor. If the repair sheds promoted a safer workplace, they might quickly recoup their installation costs through a lower number of personal injury suits.[17]

Other measures failed to meet this test of cost and benefit. Another Texas proposal in 1909 threatened to prohibit a railroad's removal of shops from anyplace where they had been for five years. The Santa Fe's Texas attorney briefly encapsulated his railroad's objections to the mea-

1906, Chairman's Correspondence, Box 19, Folder 689, L&NRR-UL; John B. Keeble to Henry L. Stone, 16 April 1907, Chairman's Correspondence, Box 22, Folder 722, ibid.

17. A.H.M. to James Hagerman, 30 June 1909, Box 36, Folder 9, SFRR-HMRC; Baker & Botts to "All General Attorneys," 6 July 1909, Box 40, Folder 10, ibid.

sure: "The public should not undertake to act as general manager of a railroad." Railroads feared this kind of legislation more than any other. It threatened their autonomy and questioned their expertise, and it revealed local priorities in legislation and widespread distrust of large corporations. Its purpose, moreover, was to guarantee continued employment opportunity for railroad communities, as railroads cut operating costs to meet the demands of a slow economy.[18]

Cooperation among the interstate railroad companies to defeat this kind of legislation produced burdens that fell unevenly, and, as a result, sometimes caused as much friction and resentment among the railroads as it did coordination and success. In 1906 the Virginia legislature considered two bills that most railroads considered adverse. For some reason the Atlantic Coast Line withdrew its opposition to the measures in the middle of the session. "This 'breaking of the ranks' practically makes a successful fight impossible," reported the N&W lobbyist to Joseph I. Doran. In a similar situation, the Santa Fe's Texas counsel, Jonathan W. Terry, expressed his and other's dissatisfaction with some other major Texas lines' failure to cooperate. "During the present session of the legislature," Terry explained to the attorneys of the offending lines, "we have not received the usual assistance of the Missouri, Kansas & Topeka and the Gould lines." Terry found their absence particularly bothersome, since "most of the hostile bills that seem to have the best chance of passage, seem to have originated on the line of the M.K.&T."[19]

In part, southern railroads gained closer cooperative relationships from common ownership, especially after the consolidations of the late nineties. The Atlantic Coast Line, for example, under the influence of Morgan banking interests acquired the L&N in 1903 and, as a result, brought it into the same financial banking family as its competitor, the Southern Railway. The implications of this consolidation showed in the L&N's effort to lease or buy the Western & Atlantic Railroad in 1903–1904. The Georgia legislature in these years was increasingly characterized as a place where "the feeling . . . seems to be somewhat bitter against the railroads." A year later, though, Milton Smith wrote Atlantic Coast Line chairman H. Walters to secure his help in acquiring the Western & Atlantic: "I have, for

18. Jonathan W. Terry to N. A. Stedman, 12 February 1909, Box 38, Folder 27, ibid.
19. Jonathan W. Terry to Coke, Miller & Coke, 15 February 1909, Box 39, Folder 10, ibid.

some time, been trying in an indirect and covert way, to induce agitation on the subject of selling the road . . . if you can come to an understanding with Mr. Samuel Spencer, you may, through your representatives and friends, quietly add to the agitation throughout the State. . . . I am inclined to think there would be little or no opposition unless it is sustained or fomented, either directly or indirectly, by the Southern Railway interests." Enlisting the cooperation of the Southern Railway through common board members, Smith prevented opposition from the only other major railroad system in the state.[20]

At the national level a railroad industry lobby developed in the years after 1900, as Congress increasingly took up railroad regulatory measures. As an outgrowth of the Railroad Attorneys' Conference in 1906, a committee of railroad lawyers appeared before congressional committees to oppose passage of the 1908 version of the Federal Employers' Liability Act. One member concluded that the railroad attorneys needed a permanent organization to lobby Congress on matters affecting the industry. "In these times of fanaticism," he stated, "when in so many cases legislative power has arrayed itself against the railroad interests of the country . . . we ought to strive together in every proper and legitimate way to prevent the enactment of these various laws, not only by Congress, but also by the States." This attorney suggested cooperating with "business men of prominence, who are opposed to all drastic and fanatical legislation, but as a rule they are not asked to express an opinion." The railroad industry's attorneys, he warned, "have heretofore let it [lobbying] go too much by default."[21]

At the national level, Ed Baxter, in his position as special counsel for nearly all southern railroads, did more than any railroad attorney to dismantle the ICC's power in cases before the Supreme Court. In 1897, after he engineered a major victory for the railroads in the Alabama Midland cases, he suggested to Southern Railway attorneys and others that the railroads should look "to perfecting an organization to prevent unjust legislation by Congress."[22]

20. H. Walters to Milton H. Smith, 16 March 1903, Milton H. Smith to H. Walters, 9 May 1904, Chairman's Correspondence, Box 2, Folder 21, vol. 1, L&NRR-UL.

21. Alexander G. Cochran, quoted in *PRAC* (1908), 293.

22. William Shaw to W. W. Finley, 6 December 1897, Vice-President's Files, Box 1, Folder 53, SRy-VPI.

Some of the southern roads took Baxter seriously, but only in 1906, when the threat of the Federal Employers' Liability Act loomed large did the railroads organize a joint federal lobbying effort. In 1906 and 1907, the railroads, led by the southern lines, retained ex–U.S. senator Charles J. Faulkner at a yearly salary of $15,000 and a monthly expense account of $600. Alfred P. Thom, general counsel for the Southern Railway, urged all railroads to contribute to the lobbying effort on a percentage-of-industry-earnings basis. According to Thom, Faulkner "has . . . the entire confidence of" the congressmen. Many railroads responded to Thom's request, and Faulkner's duties involved coordinating railroad attorneys' testimony before legislative committees and developing the arguments they deployed before the committees.[23]

No lobbying tool was more effective and more reviled than the railway free pass. Just as lawyers wanted to shake the image of the lobbyist as corrupt, railroad companies wanted to legitimize the use of free passes. The free pass system, already spiraling out of control for most railroads, frustrated the legal departments charged with monitoring it as much as it did the traffic managers concerned with recouping lost operating costs. Southern Railway president Samuel Spencer testified before the Interstate Commerce Commission that he desperately wanted to end the practice of issuing free passes. Meanwhile, North Carolina State Supreme Court justice William Clark, in whose state the Southern operated significant railroad mileage, summarized the extent of the free pass problem before the National Convention of Railroad Commissioners: "The evils of the free-pass system and the immoral purposes to which it has been put have met wide public condemnation. . . . In [North Carolina] the railroads absolutely ignored the statute, so much so that I find that the chairman of the North Carolina Railroad Commission stated . . . that 100,000 free passes were issued annually in that State."[24]

The free pass became a symbol of railroad corporations' unfair advantage, a rallying point around which Progressives built reform coalitions to check railroad power. In Virginia, reformer lawyer Allen Caperton Braxton headed the 1901–1902 Constitutional Convention's committee on cor-

23. Alfred Thom to Joseph I. Doran, 22 May 1907, Subject File #3402, N&W-VPI. For an example of fraudulent billing, see Subject File #1323, ibid.

24. *Law Notes* (November 1899), (October 1899).

porations. One sympathizer with Braxton's efforts to secure a strong corporation commission advised Braxton on the weakness of his allies and the strength of his opposition, especially the railroads: "You will have a disorganized mob at your back, with a thoroughly organized and subsidized body of corporation attorneys in your face." He further revealed his fears for Braxton's measures: "If you can exclude Railway and Corporation counsel and attorneys from the General Assembly, we would have no difficulty in passing the requisite Legislation. . . . I fear free passes to all officials and railway attorneys in the General Assembly . . . are the source of all our troubles and kill those two things and you will have fair [hearing]."[25]

In 1906 the anti–free pass agitation culminated in an amended Interstate Commerce Act, which limited the issuance of interstate railroad passes. When the amended act passed, southern railroads scrambled to assess its impact. The amendment outlawed free transportation to those not employed full-time by the railroad company. As a result, the use of the free pass to retain local attorneys became illegal, as did distributing passes to legislators or judges and others not on the company's payroll. The general counsel of the L&N, Henry L. Stone, queried his local attorneys for opinions concerning intrastate free passes over which the Interstate Commerce Commission had no constitutional authority. The district attorneys for Kentucky wrote Stone explicitly advocating the continuation of free passes for intrastate travel:

> In fact, we do not believe that the company can afford, consistent with its interests, to decline to issue these passes. The company or its representatives are continually asking favors of persons, and influencing those persons to favor it by the issue of this complimentary transportation; and in case it should not issue this transportation to persons who have favored it, or are in a position to favor it,

25. R. V. Gaines to Allen Caperton Braxton, 2 January 1901, Braxton Papers, UVA. Progressive candidate George Berge ran for governor in 1904 in Nebraska and campaigned against the free pass system. Before a legislative committee considering an anti–free pass bill, he summarized the issue: "I find that they [free pass holders] generally admit that the railroads, when they issue free passes, expect some service in return." George W. Berge, *The Free Pass Bribery System* . . . (1904; reprint, New York: Ayer Co., Arno Press, 1974), 165.

it would soon find, in our opinion, that it would have very few, if any, friends. As a railroad pass is the only weapon with which a railroad company may protect itself, and so long as the company can avoid hostile legislation or acts inimical to the company's interests by favoring those in authority with free transportation without making itself amenable to the law, we see no good and sufficient reason why the company should relinquish this valuable privilege. We think the company gets a larger return for the free transportation it gives than any other expenditure it makes.[26]

Stone's own views mirrored those of his district attorneys. He advocated strict adherence to the law with regard to interstate passes but continuing the liberal distribution of intrastate passes. Stone felt that the railroad pass problem had grown to "enormous and burdensome proportions, particularly in the states of Kentucky, Tennessee, and Alabama." But he was not willing to give up the practice, since "there is no denying the fact that now-a-days a railroad carrier has practically nothing else to defend itself with against hostile legislation and oppressive assessments for taxation, or to obtain necessary grants of privileges by State, county, or municipal action, except the issuance of free transportation." Stone felt the free pass was "the only means left it to protect [the railroads'] interests."[27]

These attorneys hated the entitlement nature of the free pass system, but they also respected the value of the practice for their work. In the 1880s the free pass emerged as the best vehicle for insurance against anti-railroad measures. It was not an outright cash bribe, and so the free pass masked the railroads' power relationship with people of influence. In fact, doubters in the railroad legal departments questioned the real effect of the practice. By the turn of the century, pressure mounted for reform, as the free pass became a symbol of railroad bribery and public opinion turned against it. Some southern states enacted anti–free pass provisions in their constitutions, but these measures failed to curb the practice.[28]

26. T. B. Harrison and B. D. Warfield to Henry L. Stone, 6 September 1906, Chairman's Correspondence, Box 4, File 131, L&NRR-UL.

27. Henry L. Stone to W. L. Mapother, 7 September 1906, ibid.

28. For example, Arkansas, Mississippi, Florida, Kentucky, and Alabama prohibited the distribution of free passes to state officials, including legislators, in their respective constitu-

For all the headaches, railroad companies were loath to give up the free pass, and that determined resistance might be the best testament to the power that the free pass generated for the railroad corporations. The L&N attorneys even admitted to violating "the letter and spirit" of the revised Kentucky state constitution by issuing free passes to state officials. They did so because the state legislature had not yet passed an enabling act, and "it was deemed disadvantageous to the interests of our company to abandon this custom, at least, before positive legislation had been enacted." There were very few practices for which railroad attorneys would violate the letter and spirit of the law—the pass was one of them. It bestowed upon them a decided advantage in the courts, in the legislative lobbies, and before the railroad commissions. The railroad free pass symbolized the dilemma railroads faced in the entire political arena in these years. As the railroad business legal environment changed, railroad officials remained reluctant to change their methods of wielding power and influence. In this case the free pass, symbol of the 1880s excesses, undermined railroad power both because of the public outrage and revenue losses accompanying its use. As the free pass' effectiveness dwindled, railroads turned to their lawyers as lobbyists for protection of their interests.[29]

As the political atmosphere after 1900 grew increasingly hostile to railroad corporations, some railroads ventured into the political maelstrom, while others distanced themselves from direct involvement. The L&N, notably, waged public, large-scale political efforts in Kentucky against William Goebel and in Alabama against Braxton Bragg Comer. In each case the L&N relied on old and familiar tactics, when it heavily financed opposition candidates and loudly denounced the reformers through railroad-controlled press.[30]

Other railroads considered the L&N's public displays of political involvement ill-advised. The Illinois Central, though not a significant presence in Kentucky, weighed the alternatives to political intervention in the

tions, but only Mississippi and Arkansas passed enabling acts to give this prohibition the force of law. See *Interstate Commerce Commission, Railways in the United States in 1902*, Part IV, Table X.

29. Henry L. Stone to W. L. Mapother, 7 September 1906, Chairman's Correspondence, Box 4, Folder 131, L&NRR-UL.

30. See Maury Klein, *A History of the Louisville & Nashville Railroad* (New York: Macmillan, 1972), 380–94. See Doster, *Railroads in Alabama Politics*, 138–39, for an account of Comer's campaign for the railroad commission presidency.

Goebel candidacy. Its district attorney and lobbyist in the state wondered "if the Illinois Central could be separated from the other railroads in the state." If so, they considered "it very likely that we should have a fair showing with the legislature." But they thought it unlikely. "We are so allied, from the nature of our business, with the L&N Railroad, that the legislation will be influenced by the antagonism to that road which has become a strong factor in the politics of Kentucky." In the increasingly volatile political environment, the Illinois Central found it could not separate itself from the animosity toward the L&N's behavior. Already lumped in with the L&N in the public mind, the only alternative for the Illinois Central and other railroads was greater associational cooperation. The district attorneys recommended following the L&N's lead and backing the Republican nominee opposed to Goebel's reforms, but they advised doing so quietly. [31]

Even the L&N exhibited a divided mind over the wisdom of interfering with local politics after 1900. In 1903 the L&N became part of the Atlantic Coast Line system, and the new chairman of the board articulated a less political role for the L&N, one similar to that of the ACL. The occasion was the chairman's receipt of a letter from a Kentucky attorney questioning the L&N's interference in the 1903 circuit court judge elections. The letter writer alleged that the L&N had allowed its candidate to canvass the shops and yards in Louisville but had barred the incumbent from similar access. The attorney understood from previous meetings with the ACL chairman that he "would not allow the L&N Railroad as such, either directly or indirectly to interfere with political or judicial matters in Kentucky." In his response to the attorney, the chairman contested this statement and pointed out that "there have, in fact, arisen in other states questions which have threatened the very life of this corporation, and, as the millennium has not yet come, we may expect vital questions of this kind to arise again." He would not forswear the L&N's interest in political matters, but he agreed that the general policy was "to avoid taking active steps in local politics." After this exchange, the chairman instructed L&N president Milton H. Smith either to open the shop doors to all candidates or, preferably, to none. From observation the ACL chairman concluded

31. Pirtle & Trabue to James Fentress, 6 July 1899, Fish Out Letters, vol 41, p. 815, ICRR-NL.

that railroad interference in local politics engendered a long-term bitterness that was not offset by temporary partisan advantage.[32]

Smith's replies to the ACL chairman's meddling demonstrated his continued desire to shape local politics and illuminated the fundamental difference in perspective between him and the chairman. Although Smith did not directly challenge the chairman's observations and suggestions, his reply questioned the wisdom of them by implication. Smith pointed out that "the relations of Col. Bennett H. Young [the attorney] to the Louisville & Nashville Railroad Company and to corporate interests generally have been so extended, and the story of the relations of Judge Shackelford Miller to the L&N R.R. Co. (he was formerly, by reason of partnership, an attorney of the company), covers so long a period and so many incidents, that I hesitate to explain by letter." Smith's history lesson implied that on the ground level the L&N needed to interfere in politics. Much later, after the judge won reelection, Smith reported to the chairman that "Judge Shackelford Miller is the Judge that has decided, I believe, every case that comes before him relating to the L&N R'd Co., against the company regardless of law, facts, or decisions of the higher courts."[33]

Milton Smith involved the L&N actively in local politics because he viewed certain judges and politicians as threats to the interests of the company. After 1900, though, Smith's interference militated against the company's interests, sparked opposition, and won few lasting friends. Moreover, the L&N and other railroads found at this time that the animosity they generated in local political economies widened to larger regional or state political economies. This realization did not necessarily mean that companies were willing to withdraw completely as independent actors in the political arena; pressures such as the adverse decisions of a judge tended to make railroads nervous. Railroad companies were thus left to face a difficult dilemma: how to protect their interests in a hostile political environment without getting involved in the political process.

The answer some companies came up with was a muted participation. One such company was the Norfolk & Western, which maintained a con-

32. Bennett H. Young to Henry Walters, 17 October 1903, Henry Walters to Bennett H. Young, 24 October 1903, Chairman's Correspondence, Box 3, Folder 101, L&NRR-UL.

33. Milton H. Smith to H. Walters, 26 October 1903, 9 May 1904, Chairman's Correspondence, Box 3, Folder 101, L&NRR-UL.

siderable interest in Virginia electoral politics. Of course, the company retained numerous active and retired public officials in its legal department, but it also exerted some pressure in state elections to protect its interests. When U.S. Senator Thomas S. Martin's Democratic machine geared up for his reelection in 1905, the N&W refused to get on board. In 1893 large amounts of railroad money had helped elect Martin, an old C&O local attorney, over the popular former governor Fitzhugh Lee. From his powerful position Martin constructed a state-wide Democratic Party machine that only the Progressive independent governor Andrew J. Montague disrupted in 1901. Montague's success led Martin and the Democratic machine to envelop the Progressive movement, adopt some of its language, and support some of its limited reforms. Martin began to distance himself from the railroad corporations and supported the Federal Employers' Liability Act. The N&W did not appreciate his Progressive leanings on the FELA nor his stand on labor matters.[34]

Once the N&W's president and the general solicitor decided to oppose Martin, the N&W attempted to organize other railroads in the state against the senator. "So far as you can consistently do so," N&W president L. E. Johnson instructed Joseph I. Doran, "our local attorneys should be impressed with the fact that we are not supporting Mr. Martin." Doran replied that he would inform the local attorneys personally with discretion and "take opportunity from time to time of sowing the seed as you wish." For the N&W, quiet political involvement seemed an important way to protect its interests in a rapidly changing business environment.[35]

In Alabama the legislature turned against the railroad interests after 1900. After great parliamentary maneuvering, the legislature strengthened the state railroad commission in 1903 by making its members elective and giving them the power to regulate rates. Once unleashed, the anti-railroad sentiment in Alabama gathered force behind the leadership of Braxton Bragg Comer, who in 1904 ran for the presidency of the newly empowered railroad commission on a platform of rate reduction, better service, and equitable settlement of claims. Comer won the office but quickly discovered its impotence in the face of the railroad attorneys' stratagems. He

34. See Raymond H. Pulley, *Old Virginia Restored: An Interpretation of the Progressive Impulse, 1870–1930* (Charlottesville: University Press of Virginia, 1968).

35. L. E. Johnson to Joseph I. Doran, 6 March 1905, Joseph I. Doran to L. E. Johnson, 7 March 1905, Subject File #3620, N&W-VPI.

held extensive hearings on the rate issue, but the railroad attorneys gave all the right answers, giving Comer a lesson on the legalities of rate, tax, valuation, and other issues. Outgunned and outmaneuvered, Comer realized that only the office of governor possessed the power to challenge the railroads, and he announced his candidacy in the fall of 1905.[36]

Comer's candidacy introduced a lightning rod for anti-corporation feelings in the public. After Comer was elected, he considered calling a special session of the legislature to deal with the dismal performance of the state's bonds, L&N attorneys grew worried that Comer's men might turn the session into an anti-railroad festival. The L&N retained a special lobbyist, John V. Smith, who met with the governor and watched the legislature. A former railroad-friendly president of the Alabama State Railroad Commission, Smith lost the 1904 commission presidency election to Comer. A year later, the L&N put him on the payroll for special legislative work. In his meeting with the governor, Smith urged him not to call the special legislature: "It would be a grave injustice to the railroads at this time, in the present state of the public mind, to make any such recommendations." Smith was most concerned "that many members of the Legislature would be candidates for political office, every one of whom would endeavor to make political capital for himself by making war upon the railroads."[37]

Even railroad attorneys in the Alabama legislature left their post to join the Comer forces. George Jones explained to Milton H. Smith the powerful pull of Comer's cause on the once-reliable attorney-legislators. He surmised that the House Speaker, Alfred M. Tunstall, attorney for the Southern Railway, "did not strongly oppose the extra session in his talk with the Governor." Remarking that Tunstall was "more of a politician than . . . a railroad man," Jones summed up the situation: "In other words, Col. [Jefferson M.] Falkner and I have long since reached the conclusion that Tunstall and a number of other railroad attorneys in this State are constantly looking out for their own political fences rather than for the interests of their clients—the railroads." Milton Smith agreed with this assessment, pointing out that Tunstall's political positioning not only jeop-

---

36. Doster, *Railroads in Alabama Politics*, 133, 144. See also Sheldon Hackney, *Populism to Progressivism in Alabama* (Princeton: Princeton University Press, 1969).

37. John V. Smith to Henry L. Stone, 19 September 1905, Chairman's Correspondence, Box 18, Folder 642, L&NRR-UL.

ardized his clients but even his father, who as one of the associate railroad commissioners drew Comer's ire for defending the railroads.[38]

Moreover, at the state Democratic convention, the railroads witnessed wholesale conversion of their "attorneys." One railroad attorney could hardly believe the display of political whim: "This majority for Comer was caused largely by Division Counsel and Local Counsel of the railroads in Alabama." He described many of the convention's railroad attorneys as overtly pro-regulation: "In looking over the convention, you could find several delegations that had in it a Local Counsel or Division Counsel of some railroad, wildly cheering at the wildest demands of Comer's leaders." "What are we to expect from our opponents," he asked, "when our own attorneys are fighting us?" The very pillars of the "friendly" legislature crumbled under the weight of a changed political environment. The people, it turned out, grew sour on railroad visions of economic development and followed Comer's calls for reform of the monopolies. In true testament to the power of this movement, the railroad lawyer-legislators followed too.[39]

The 1907 legislature, elected on Comer's platform, embraced railroad reform openly, and the railroad lobbyists used all their means to subvert its acts. The L&N's lobbyists proposed strengthening their ranks with personnel and resources. State counsel Smith and Jones both believed that "with our conservative friends in the Senate, and the employment of some first class attorneys in addition to such of our regular attorneys as might be selected . . . we could defeat most of the adverse measures proposed in Comer's platform." They suggested that "if $25,000 or $30,000 is raised by the interested companies, and spent in legitimate ways in an open fight against hostile legislation, we can defeat it, or so modify it that it will not hurt us."[40] In this the L&N lobbyists received wholehearted support from Milton H. Smith, whose opposition to Comer and his platform hardened into obstinacy.

Comer's campaign to lower railroad rates stemmed from his belief that

38. George W. Jones to Milton H. Smith, 10 September 1905, ibid. See Hackney, *Populism to Progressivism*, 16, for an account of the Turnstall family's railroad political power. George W. Jones to Milton H. Smith, 10 September 1905, Milton H. Smith to H. Walters, 12 September 1905, Chairman's Correspondence, Box 18, Folder 642, L&NRR-UL.

39. R. E. Steiner to Charles A. Wickersham, 11 September 1906, Chairman's Correspondence, Box 21, Folder 750, L&NRR-UL.

40. Henry L. Stone to Milton H. Smith, 9 January 1907, ibid.

the railroads' watered stock and overcapitalized properties kept rates falsely high and that the railroads engaged in deceptive accounting to drive their valuation down for tax purposes. In fact, railroad companies regularly charged capital improvements to operating expenses, lowering their net return, and, as a consequence, their taxes. Comer contended that the railroads through their artificially high rates strangled business development in the state. Railroad attorneys countered that if the state pushed rates down further and forced the railroads into receivership, the business development of the state would suffer, capital would become scarce, and the people would pay for these losses.[41]

At the center of southern railroads' defensive strategies was the interstate nature of the railroads' business and the due process protections of the Fourteenth Amendment. These two pieces of the legal landscape allowed attorneys latitude in the face of Progressive legislation. Federal control of interstate commerce put rate controversies into federal courts, where constitutional guarantees of due process and protection of property gave railroads needed defenses. In the Progressive political atmosphere after 1900, the rate issue assumed great significance in the battle between reformers and the railroads (and since in the historical literature), but it was not the only issue that generated heated contests. An equally explosive issue—reform of corporation tax laws—threatened the railroads' earnings and power. Many southern railroads accumulated special tax exemptions and privileges upon charter in the 1850s and 1870s, and lines that consolidated or swallowed up other roads carefully preserved the original charters' tax provisions. Different forms of tax exemption were scattered across the states, but the standard outlines included a thirty-year exemption for railroads to construct their roads, a provision for loss of exemption once a railroad company paid a dividend of 8 percent, and an exemption for a certain number of years after completion of the originally chartered line. Railroads with such tax exemptions available to them, then, commonly dragged out construction of the chartered route and through tricky accounting procedures avoided claiming a dividend over 8 percent. Often railroads acquired dormant charters to lines not built for the sole benefit of their tax exemptions. The same Progressive reform forces that battled against unfair and discriminatory rates also examined these jealously guarded loopholes. Whole political campaigns turned on these potent is-

41. Doster, *Railroads in Alabama Politics,* 144, 155–56.

sues of railroad taxation, and the railroad attorneys turned from lobbying the legislatures to appealing to more sympathetic federal courts.

Many southern states inaugurated the post-depression years with efforts to raise privilege taxes, remove exemptions, regularize tax valuation and assessment, and discourage stock-watering through tax reform. Reformers considered railroads grossly overcapitalized through stock-watering and, as a result, charging inflated rates. For tax purposes, though, they thought railroads vastly undervalued, and, as a result, not contributing their fair share. In Mississippi, for example, the 1890 constitution limited tax exemptions to five years. The state revenue agent, Wirt Adams, initiated a long-term campaign to invalidate the Illinois Central's tax exemption, which had been gained through the charter of its subsidiary, the Louisville, New Orleans, & Texas Railroad Company. In 1898, moreover, the state's revenue act left the privilege tax rates in place, but imposed "on each railroad claiming exemptions under maximum and minimum provisions in their charter an additional privilege tax per mile of $10.00." Corporate lawyers in Mississippi defended the corporate tax exemptions; against the backdrop of the resurging white supremacist movement, W. D. Gibbs, an attorney for the Illinois Central, called them "the most potent factors in the battle of white civilization against African barbarism" and scoffed at "the mere 'political agriculturalist' who raises his crop in town and in lawyer's office 'by putting hay-seed in his hair' and shouting 'down with corporations!' "[42]

Tax exemptions inflamed passions against the railroad corporations in the two decades before 1900, but their opponents failed in these years to muster the political and legal forces necessary overturn them. In the late 1880s, for example, the Georgia Pacific's Mississippi tax exemption came under fire in the legislature. The road's president reported to the new general counsel: "Various threats and efforts have been made to tar us, but we have succeeded so far in defeating or crying down all claims of this nature [repealing tax exemption]." The Georgia Pacific's success derived in large measure from the power of economic development in the legal and political atmosphere of those years.[43]

---

42. For a detailed account of this campaign, see Robert L. Brandfon, *Cotton Kingdom in the New South: A History of the Yazoo Mississippi Delta from Reconstruction to the Twentieth Century* (Cambridge, Mass.: Harvard University Press, 1967), Chapter 8; *Interstate Commerce Commission, Railways in the United States in 1902*, Part V, State Taxation of Railways; *Jackson Clarion-Ledger*, 23 February 1888.

43. Jonathan W. Johnston to James T. Worthington, 26 June 1889, Box 1, R&DRR-VPI.

In Tennessee, the Mobile & Ohio successfully protected its chartered tax exemptions against a protracted state suit to recover back taxes. The attorney general, George W. Pickle, brought the suit in 1891, challenging the validity of a tax exemption derived whenever the company declared a dividend of less than 8 percent. At stake were $88,197 in taxes between 1885 and 1889. After several lower court decisions upheld the state's claim, the Supreme Court of the United States reversed those decisions in favor of the Mobile & Ohio in an 1895 decision.[44]

As prosperity returned to the South, with it came the political will to curb railroad-corporation tax breaks. In the face of growing Progressive challenges, railroads relied on their attorneys to deflect encroachment on their interests. Two clear preferences emerged as a response to the Progressive challenge in Tennessee: use federal law and courts to settle the case if possible without losing any legal entitlements and cooperate with other interested parties to repeal the offensive law.

In 1901, Tennessee's revenue act, following an earlier 1899 provision, took aim at consolidated railroad companies with suspected watered stock. Section 10 of the act levied a one-tenth of 1 percent transfer tax on the capital stock of consolidated railroad companies. The Southern Railway, having recently consolidated the Mobile & Ohio into its system, appeared to be one of the main targets of the legislation. Progressives in Tennessee saw interstate corporation power as increasingly monopolistic, the kind of power that the conglomerated Southern represented as it swept up formerly local- and state-owned lines into its giant system. In 1901 the Southern's attorneys scrambled to respond to the new legislation and the secretary of state's announced determination to collect the transfer tax.

Upon notification by letter of the state's determination to collect this tax, F. P. Poston, division counsel for the Southern, drafted a hurried internal opinion. Poston considered the 1901 act not relevant to either the Mobile & Ohio or the Southern Railway because it became law after the two lines consolidated and was not retroactive. A similar 1899 act, however, threatened both companies. At issue stood the precise relationship between the Mobile & Ohio and the Southern. Poston considered the relationship one that fell under the broad outline of the act. Yet despite the act's relevance to both companies, according to Poston, it remained inapplicable for several reasons. Most important, Poston cited the Mobile & Ohio's 1847 charter, which provided "that the capital stock . . . shall be

---

44. *Mobile & Ohio Railroad Co v. State of Tennessee*, 153 U.S. 486.

forever exempt from taxation, and the road, . . . shall be exempt from taxation for the period twenty-five years from the completion of the road, and no tax shall ever be laid on said road, or its fixtures, which will reduce the dividends below eight per cent."[45]

While Poston's opinion traveled by mail to M&O general counsel E. L. Russell, Russell drafted an opinion for Samuel Spencer, president of the M&O and the Southern Railway. Russell, too, concluded that only the 1899 act was relevant, and similarly concluded that it was inapplicable, though its inapplicability arose for different reasons. For one thing, Russell asked what right the state of Tennessee had to issue a tax on all of the M&O capital stock, which represented the value of assets running through four states. Such a tax, he pointed out, "would inevitably lead to confiscation."[46]

Russell's opinion also diverged from Poston's in regard to whether the relationship of the M&O and the Southern was such as fell within the law's scope. He argued that no sale, transfer, or consolidation had taken place between the two companies and that the Southern in no way controlled the business of the M&O. Russell conceded, "It is true that the Mobile & Ohio Railroad Company and the Southern Railway Company have the same President and the same Vice Presidents. . . . It is also true that the Southern Railway Company has purchased and owns a majority of the capital stock of the Mobile & Ohio Railroad Company, but it does not attempt to, nor does it control, the business of the Mobile and Ohio. . . . [It] is operated as a distinct and independent railroad and as a distinct and independent corporation." When Russell received the Southern's division counsel's opinion, he bluntly wrote the M&O vice-president, "It is manifest . . . that Mr. Poston has failed to grasp the facts connected with the transaction under discussion." For Russell, the M&O's relationship with the Southern fell outside of the act's purview. Russell undoubtedly manufactured a fine distinction, for the Southern de facto controlled the M&O. It was a technicality, but one on which important legal questions turned.[47]

All of the division and general counsel's correspondence and opinions

45. F. P. Poston to E. L. Russell, 30 May 1901, President's Correspondence, Box 1, Folder 0923, SRy-VPI.
46. E. L. Russell to Samuel Spencer, 31 May 1901, ibid.
47. E. L. Russell to Samuel Spencer, 31 May 1901, E. L. Russell to Col. A. B. Andrews, 1 June 1901, President's Correspondence, Box 1, Folder 0923, SRy-VPI.

landed quickly in New York at the law offices of Francis Lynde Stetson. Stetson specialized in railroad corporation law and represented the Southern's interests in the financial capital. He was a polished, experienced, and successful corporate attorney with the kind of authority that corporate boards appreciated. Like Russell, Stetson viewed the relationship between the M&O and the Southern beyond the scope of Tennessee's 1899 revenue act. Stetson, moreover, recommended taking the offensive in federal court against the Tennessee secretary of state to seek to enjoin him from collecting the tax. Calling Russell's attention to *Smyth v. Ames* and *Fitts v. McGhee*, Stetson directed him to produce an opinion on the viability of the Southern's removing to federal court.[48]

Russell produced two opinions that detailed the viability of removal for the two railroad companies and explored new areas of legal strategy for the attorneys. Russell concluded that the Southern might have difficulty sustaining a removal suit. Reviewing *Smyth v. Ames* (169 U.S., 466), *Fitts v. McGhee* (172 U.S., 516), and *In Re Ayers* (123 U.S., 443), Russell considered such a suit in possible violation of the Eleventh Amendment. Even if the suit named the state officers, not the state itself, Russell pointed out the difficulties *"if the Southern Railway* files a bill in the Federal Court, not claiming any violation of any contract." In summary, Russell said "that there is no ground or room for any allegation to the effect that the two acts in question are unconstitutional, unless it can be alleged and shown that the acts attempt to impose an unconstitutional tax." In order to satisfy the Eleventh Amendment, as interpreted in these cases by the Supreme Court, the suit needed to assert the act's unconstitutionality, a criterion Russell considered unlikely. Fearing the use of distress warrants to seize the road's property to enforce the act, Russell examined by what process the state authorities might proceed under the law. The secretary of state, Russell decided, would have to either bring suit against each company to collect the taxes or file a bill in chancery. Given these circumstances, Russell concluded that the best course of action for the companies included securing an injunction in federal court and taking their chances in that more favorable environment.[49]

48. Francis L. Stetson to E. L. Russell, 4 June 1901, President's Correspondence, Box 3, Folder 23245, ibid.

49. E. L. Russell to Francis L. Stetson, 10 June 1901, President's Correspondence, ibid. For a full examination of the Eleventh Amendment and these relevant cases, see Cortner, *The Iron Horse and the Constitution*, 130–48. See also John V. Orth, *The Judicial Power of the*

Division attorney Poston, though, recognized the exact nature of the dilemma for the two companies. At the heart of the issue stood the question of the relationship between the M&O and the Southern and the continuation of tax exemptions for the M&O. If the two companies admitted consolidation and the validity of the tax, all the M&O's tax exemptions might be lost forever. If they fought the transfer tax, they might awaken the Tennessee authorities to the possibilities of removing the M&O's tax-exempt status. The transfer tax, the attorneys finally concluded, represented a one-time levy on consolidation, not an annual assessment on the capital stock. As such, the Tennessee authorities sought $5,300 from the M&O and $180,000 from the Southern.

Poston concluded that the merger or consolidation did not qualify as a merger by law. "While this is my opinion," he wrote Russell, "from an examination of the authorities, I think the question is one fraught with grave danger." Poston revealed the delicate extent of the road's dilemma: "I believe that the officials of the State of Tennessee have not, as yet, discovered that there may be this question involved in this transaction, and the probabilities are that they will not discover it unless the exemption on the tax claimed by the Secretary of State is agitated in the courts." If they did discover it, Poston thought the railroads "may have trouble, and, in the event of an adverse decision, the effect would be much more disastrous than payment of the $5,300 in question." Poston recommended compromise and settlement.[50]

Meanwhile, Russell drafted a letter of protest to the Tennessee secretary of state outlining the companies' reasons for failure to pay the transfer tax. He, of course, denied that the companies had in fact consolidated and strenuously upheld the M&O tax exemption. Concerned about the possibility of future litigation, Southern counsel Francis L. Stetson instructed Russell that "it is undesirable to write to Tennessee officials any letter not absolutely necessary." Stetson further ordered Russell to "adjust [the] entire claim . . . upon satisfactory assurances of finality [from Tennessee officials]." He left the decisions to Russell, who, as the attorney on the scene, might be able to interpret the Tennessee officials' maneuvering. Stetson,

United States: The Eleventh Amendment in American History (New York: Oxford University Press, 1987).

50. F. P. Poston to E. L. Russell, 29 June 1901, President's Correspondence, Box 3, Folder 23245, SRy-VPI.

though, made it clear to Russell that he should guard the tax exemption and the divorced relationship of the companies: "I trust you may be able to preserve our legal position . . . but I leave to your good judgment the adoption of the best practical method of securing this result."[51]

Russell met personally with Tennessee attorney general George W. Pickle to discuss the tax dispute. The attorney general considered the distinction between the two companies contrived and artificial and, according to Russell's report, "insisted that we were attempting to consolidate indirectly, so as not to bear the burdens of consolidation." After considerable jousting, both sides agreed to delay action on the matter, the attorney general willing to let the matter rest for several weeks. In the meantime, F. P. Poston set about to construct another opinion. After dismissing most of the attorney general's arguments, Poston feared "that an effort may be made to get the Legislature to pass an Act revoking the authority of the Southern Railway Company to do business in the State."[52]

Long before the state authorities in Tennessee—or for that matter in the region—realized their power to revoke charters, the Southern legal department fleshed out the ramifications of this kind of action. Alabama eventually followed just such a policy in 1907 to bring the Southern into conformity with its rate changes, and North Carolina governor Robert B. Glenn used similar tactics, eventually arresting the Southern Railway president, W. W. Finley, to enforce the 1907 passenger rate reduction. In 1901 in Tennessee such drastic action had yet to materialize. Neither the political nor the economic circumstances warranted extreme measures. In the meantime railroad lawyers from various lines cooperated in lobbying for the 1901 revenue act's repeal at the next session of the Tennessee legislature, in 1903. They successfully amended the revenue act to protect their roads' tax exemptions and clarify the applicability of the transfer tax.[53]

---

51. E. L. Russell to John W. Morton, draft letter, 5 July 1901, Francis L. Stetson to E. L. Russell, 9 July 1901, ibid.

52. E. L. Russell to Col. A. B. Andrews, 28 August 1901, F. P. Poston to E. L. Russell, 7 September 1901, ibid.

53. For an analysis of the North Carolina struggle's place in the legal fight over state and federal authority, see Cortner, *The Iron Horse and the Constitution*, 146–47. Cortner emphasizes a similar struggle in Minnesota that produced the landmark rate case in Minnesota in 1913. W. G. Elliot to H. Walters, 2 February 1903, Chairman's Correspondence, Box 1, Folder 8, L&NRR-UL; Tennessee Statutes, 1903, p. 1141 (Chapter 398). The new revenue act applied to out-of-state corporations merging with Tennessee corporations and stated that

Although some legislative measures, such as privilege taxes, barely affected day-to-day railroad operations, others in the 1900s seriously threatened the railroad companies' autonomy. For example, the 1907 Texas legislature considered an "Act to protect the lives and property of the travelling public and the employees of the railroads." The "full-crew bill," as it came to be called, regulated the duties of the various trainmen and required railroads to operate their trains with a larger crew than was usually their practice. In Oklahoma a similar measure came before the legislature. The railroads objected to the bill because it would raise their operating expenses, and though they compiled careful data to document this contention, the railroad attorneys remained circumspect about using it to make a fight. The Santa Fe general manager bluntly stated to his counsel, "This is the most dangerous, and I believe would be the most costly, railroad measure that has been introduced in the Oklahoma legislature." If the railroad lobbyists could not engineer a defeat of the bill, they could at least modify it in such a way as to make it unconstitutional. "I do not believe any of the general managers would object seriously to a joker being introduced which would have a tendency to cripple its constitutionality," the Santa Fe manager pointed out.[54]

Issues of race and employment were at stake in the full-crew bill, according to the Santa Fe management. The bill redefined specific duties for trainmen and in so doing mandated a new position of employment on trains. "This is inserted for the purpose of undertaking to have porters on our trains or releasing the brakemen from doing porter's work, which, of course, is objectionable in the extreme," the Santa Fe managers insisted, "because . . . a colored man acting as porter and brakeman on short passenger trains is very much better than an exclusively white brakeman, as that individual will not keep the cars clean. The colored man can do the necessary flagging and is not above cleaning up the train." From the railroad's perspective, the legislature threatened to impose another set of society's racial preferences on their business. Segregation of railway coaches and depots presented similar burdens, but the full-crew bill posed a greater danger. The legislature responded not only to societal pressure for white

the new company "shall by virtue of such lease, purchase, consolidation, or merger, exercise such franchise." The rights of franchise included tax-exempt privileges derived from charter.

54. F. G. Pettibone to Jonathan W. Terry, 13 April 1908, Box 23, Folder 7, SFRR-HMRC.

porters, but, more significantly for the railroads, to labor pressure for additional white jobs on trains. In the economic downturn of 1907–1908, the railroads fought to lower operating costs, but the full-crew bill mandated higher operating costs and set a worrisome precedent for legislative management of railway business practices.[55]

The Santa Fe's lobbyist in Oklahoma, J. R. Cottingham, reported the struggle to the lines' general solicitor, Gardiner Lathrop. "After a fight which almost became historic," Cottingham recounted, "our friends" eliminated the provision for the "extra-brakeman, termed a flagman." To defang this bill required effective lobbying. Cottingham summarized his effort: "In this fight we enlisted every friend we could get. We had no inducement to offer except that the provisions of the bill were unfair, unreasonable and unjust, represented demands made by pretended labor agitators in excess of any right they could reasonably insist on." The Oklahoma measure died from lobbyist persuasion. In Texas' 1908 legislature, the Santa Fe's lobbyist had a more difficult time: "if our own employees had let us alone, there would have been practically no legislation concerning railroads in Texas this year."[56]

After the Texas Supreme Court declared the full-crew bill unconstitutional in 1908, the railroads succeeded in closeting another, similar effort until 1913. A new full-crew bill came before the Texas legislature in that year, and the railroad attorneys orchestrated an opposition similar to that in the 1908 Oklahoma battle, but with one twist. The railroad attorneys enlisted the support of the farmers' lobby to help defeat the bill. The farmers, Terry and other railroad lobbyists contended, would bear the brunt of the full-crew cost, since the cost would be passed on to them. With some careful persuasion they convinced the farm bloc that the legislation represented the interests of labor against the interests of business and the "wealth producers," the farmers. The farm lobby weighed in heavily for the railroads on the issue, sending representatives to Austin to lobby.[57]

In addition, Terry addressed all the Santa Fe local attorneys with a request that they put together effective opposition in their localities. He cited the expensive efforts of the line to repair its roadway and the need to

55. Ibid.

56. J. R. Cottingham to Gardiner Lathrop, 15 April 1908, Box 23, Folder 7, SFRR-HMRC; Jonathan W. Terry to E. P. Ripley, 9 April 1908, Box 40, Folder 12, ibid.

57. Hiram Glass to Jonathan W. Terry, 17 January 1913, Box 23, Folder 7, ibid.

lower the cost of transportation, and he pointed out to them, "This bill is a counter-move, the purpose of which is to increase the cost of transportation. The claim that it will prevent accidents to any material extent is a pretense, the real object of the bill being to increase the number of jobs." He urged his cohorts to "have petitions and remonstrances against this bill sent to the members of the Senate and House." Other state railroad counsel issued similar circulars to their local attorneys, and if the Santa Fe was typical, these attorneys used their local influence and connections to flood the legislature with objections to the bill. Needless to say, the concerted pressure killed the bill on the floor of the House, and railroad attorneys concurred that "the farmers and stockraisers are responsible for defeating the measure, and entitled to the credit as well." The politics of Progressivism culminated in Texas, once a Populist stronghold, with farmers and railroads cooperating to defeat labor's demands.[58]

Progressives brought new challenges to the railroad political economy in the South. They were concerned with laying down the line between monopolies or trusts and developmental companies. They targeted specific railroad abuses and built reform coalitions around them. Historian Sheldon Hackney considers the railroad regulatory issue central to the transition from Populist agrarian revolt in the 1890s to Progressive reform after 1900. In his study of Alabama politics, Hackney shows that the railroad reform issue combined with humanitarian and clean politics reform movements to form a new coalition, "an alternative method of combating plutocratic corporations without rending the fabric of society." Comer's campaigns against "railroad bossism," Hackney points out, came up against the scare tactics of the railroad attorneys who threatened lost prosperity and timid capital. When Comer's reformers finally secured control of the state Democratic convention in 1906, they proudly boasted that they had wrenched "the political control of this state from the domination of foreign railroads." Alabama Progressivism, according to Hackney, was "realistically concerned with the problems of an urbanizing and industrializing society."[59] Far from nostalgic, these reformers targeted specific reforms to make their society less dependent on large corporations.

The railroads faced a new kind of opposition after 1900. In Alabama,

58. Jonathan W. Terry to "All Local Attorneys," 10 February 1913, Hiram Glass to "All General Attorneys," 13 February 1913, ibid.

59. Hackney, *Populism to Progressivism*, 285, 331.

Georgia, North Carolina, Texas, and elsewhere across the South, railroad opponents posted successes where in the past they floundered in failure. Even in Kentucky, Tennessee, and Virginia, proposed Progressive legislation threatened railroad corporation power. Reformers benefited in these years from better organization, more determined adherents, and more cagey strategies for success. In Alabama, for example, the 1907 legislature lowered the passenger fare to two and one-half cents per mile, declared freight rates on intrastate traffic as of January 1 the maximum rates, provided a state board of assessment to value the railroads' properties for tax purposes, outlawed the free pass to non-employees, passed elaborate legislation designed to prevent railroads from seeking redress in the federal courts, and even funded the state's attorney general's office to defeat railroad injunction suits.[60]

The new Progressive reformers were led by a new group of lawyers. The personal injury lawyer, the trial attorney, and the progressive reformers were all united in their opposition to the monopoly power of the interstate railroad corporations. The split in the bar between corporation attorneys and personal injury attorneys carried into the political arena. Reformers, such as Wilk Call, James Stephen Hogg, and Frank S. White, represented a new opposition to the conservative Democratic pro-railroad men. Their roots lay in the division of the bar across the South in the 1880s, when the interstate railroad companies demanded total allegiance from their counsel.

60. Doster, *Railroads in Alabama Politics,* 160–61.

SEVEN

The Road to Uniform Regulation

At the Virginia Constitutional Convention of 1901–1902, delegates debated one of the major issues facing the convention—the establishment of a state corporation commission. At the turn of the century most railroads fought any form of regulation with every weapon at their disposal. In Virginia the proposed State Corporation Commission would have authority to impose regulation on the railroads. Reformers, mostly Progressives, considered regulation of railroads imperative. They were led by Allen Caperton Braxton, the chairman of the convention's committee on corporations, who stated emphatically in the face of daily newspaper criticism that the convention needed to decide whether "the people or the railroads would control the government of the commonwealth." The debates covered all of the major issues that the growth of interstate railroad corporations presented in the South, from federal removal to tax valuation, rate regulation, the rights of out-of-state railroad companies, and employers' liability. Several of the delegates were railroad-corporation attorneys, and many were lawyers who had done some work for the railroads. He felt that many of the delegates who were also railroad attorneys were "acting in the interest of the big corporations rather than in the interest of the State." Braxton privately called the corporations' behavior "grasping, selfish, tyrannical, overbearing, [and] relentless." William A. Anderson, onetime railroad attorney in the 1880s, now attorney general of Virginia and fellow delegate to the convention, was not so sure, though he supported Braxton every step of the way. Anderson claimed to "have no clients here except the people of Virginia" and believed "the same is true of other gentlemen who have discussed this question, whether they may be so fortunate or unfortunate, some of them, as to be railroad attorneys."[1]

Anderson represented a community that was bypassed by the great interstate systems, and he called for federal regulation to limit what he thought was the monopolistic power of the railroads. "There were nine or ten independent railroad companies operating in the State," Anderson pointed out. "Now there is practically but one . . . a little coterie in New York, or Philadelphia or Chicago, yes, and a still smaller coterie in the city of New York, practically and ultimately directs the policy and controls the operations of every railroad system in Virginia." Anderson called for federal regulation because only one-tenth of these railroads' business was intrastate and was therefore under the purview of the proposed state regulatory commission.[2]

One of the most contentious issues for the committee turned out to be the rights of "foreign" corporations operating within Virginia, whether they had to have a Virginia charter to operate, and whether the state could control them. Rufus A. Ayers, president of the Big Stone Gap & Powell's Valley Railway Company and a director of the Interstate Railroad Company, defended the right of the L&N to operate and build branches without acquiring a Virginia charter, and exercise the right of eminent domain in the state. Ayers argued that no railroad would want to acquire state charter just to operate five or eight miles of coal line along the border of the state with Tennessee or Kentucky. He pushed for the committee to grandfather in all corporations operating in the state, requiring all future railroads to have a domestic charter. Berryman Green, railroad attorney for the Danville & Western Railroad, recalled a case in which a non-Virginia corporation that was operating lines in the state used the protection of federal court to get out from under Virginia's law. Green went further, attacking the L&N as "the most infamously unjust and oppressive railroad that has ever afflicted the world . . . a grasping monopoly of the worst kind."[3]

1. Allen W. Moger, *Virginia: From Bourbonism to Byrd, 1870–1925* (Charlottesville: University Press of Virginia Press, 1968), 234–35; *Proceedings and Debates of the Constitutional Convention of Virginia*, 2395; Braxton, quoted in Edward L. Ayers, *The Promise of the New South: Life After Reconstruction* (Oxford: Oxford University Press, 1992), 414.
2. *Proceedings and Debates of the Constitutional Convention of Virginia*, 2400.
3. Ibid., 2813.

Green and Ayers argued over where to draw the line between promoting healthy growth and encouraging grasping monopoly, between fostering a developmental trust and allowing an oppressive one. Ayers argued that "the good faith of Virginia requires that this company [L&N] shall be left with the power [of eminent domain], without holding it up as a highwayman and saying, 'Yes, you can build, but . . . only upon the terms of becoming a Virginia corporation.' " Ayers lost the debate on the floor, as the delegates followed the lead of the chairman. Allen Caperton Braxton considered the right of eminent domain too important, "a high prerogative of sovereignty," to be lightly offered, arguing that "it should be surrendered only to a private corporation of the State itself which can control it absolutely." To Braxton the objective of requiring a domestic charter for foreign corporations was "to prevent their hauling citizens . . . into the United States courts for matters which they wish to litigate." He suggested that "this is no new idea," and he pointed to several southern states, South Carolina and Mississippi among them, that required domestic charters for interstate companies in their constitutions.[4]

When the debate turned to the employers' liability provisions and the delegates began discussing limitations on the powerful railroad defenses of fellow-servant liability and contributory negligence, the railroad attorneys at the convention moved to adopt language that would protect the contributory negligence defense for the railroad companies. One of these amendments to the employers' liability section of the constitution read "knowledge by any such employee injured of the defective or unsafe character or condition of any machinery . . . shall not of itself bar a recovery for an injury caused thereby. Nothing in this section shall impair the doctrine of contributory negligence." J. C. Wysor, a lawyer and telephone company director though an enthusiastic supporter of establishing a corporation commission, introduced the amendment, and other corporation attorneys, such as W. Gordon Robertson and Alfred P. Thom, supported him in the ensuing debate.[5]

Other delegates were not convinced that the companies needed such protection. Charles V. Meredith, the former city attorney of Richmond, considered the amendment another in a long line of unjust corporation defenses. "At every session," Meredith argued, "we have been met by the

---

4. Ibid., 2831, 2827.
5. Ibid., 2836.

attorneys for the railroads insisting that these people should not be protected in their lives and limbs; holding that the property of the railroad should be protected in preference to the lives and limbs of our fellow citizens. . . . You may use soft language. You may undertake to express it so as to give some salve for your own consciences, but the question is a question of life and limb on one side and property on the other." Another delegate pointed to the high accident rate on the railroads in Virginia and concluded, "if this thing keeps on, they will kill or hurt one next year for every mile [of rail in the state]." The amendment failed to pass, so Gordon Robertson, the N&W's attorney in Roanoke, introduced another amendment to embarrass the proponents of the employers' liability section. His language would have specifically referenced the Mississippi case that the section's proponents kept relying on for support in their argument. This amendment also failed to pass, and the railroad attorneys were foiled.[6]

At the Virginia convention those in favor of a powerful, constitutionally mandated state corporation commission met opposition from the group of railroad attorneys that made up a minority of the delegates. These opponents suggested that the legislature should retain the power to form and oversee the corporation commission and that the constitutional convention was no place to be deciding such weighty matters. Alfred Thom, general counsel for the Southern Railway, W. Gordon Robertson, counsel for the N&W, Alexander Hamilton, general counsel for the ACL, and Eppa Hunton, corporation attorney and former senator, formed the main opposition to the constitutional convention's forming a corporation commission. They were powerful attorneys in the state and heavily connected to the state's major interstate railroad corporations.

Despite their ties to the railroad corporations, these delegates insisted that they were not biased, at least no more so than any of the other delegates. Robertson had "heard a great deal in private talk" about how "the railroad attorneys will, as a matter of course, defend the railroads." He discounted this, pointing out that shippers and farmers too were likely to defend their own interests. Mostly he conjured up the fear that the commission would be vulnerable to railroad influence. "If these railroad companies are the monsters they are represented to be," Robertson argued, "is there not a danger, I say, of these giant railroad combinations . . . getting hold of the commission? Is it not much easier to get three men

6. Ibid., 2839, 2847.

than it is to control a majority in the Senate and in the House of Delegates?"[7]

The commission's proponents were not easily swayed by such protestations. To most of them the railroads were not like any other group, farmers or shippers, but instead far more grasping and powerful. When Alfred Thom suggested to one commission advocate that the committee seemed to be putting the corporations in "straightjackets," the delegate responded, "No, we want to put a good suit of clothes upon them, so that they may be able to appear on all occasions in respectable society." As to the minority report opposing the proposed commission, one delegate called it a "marvellous, funny, opera bouffe." As to Robertson's claims that there were no complaints about railroads from the public, J. C. Wysor said he heard loud and clear the call, "'Take the horrid beak of corporate greed from out our hearts.'" As to the suggestion that the legislature should handle regulating the railroads, Wysor laughed, "The Legislature indeed! You cannot get the Legislature to fix the finger on Henry Clay's statue, at the foot of Capitol Hill." As to the fear that the railroads might control the commission, Wysor scoffed at the idea: "I do not know whether he [Robertson] is speaking for the corporations he represents."[8]

Once a southern state developed a railroad commission, it often turned out that the commission relied on the railroad attorneys for advice and information in its decision making. It was not that the railroads "bought" or "controlled" the commissions, as so many of the Virginia delegates feared, but that the railroad attorneys and officials became the primary source of expertise on transportation issues. One Virginia delegate, a lawyer and onetime member of the House of Delegates and State Senate, pointed out the difficulty with railroad regulation. "The classification in railroads is such a difficult and abstruse matter," he said, "that it is practically impossible for an outsider to get a correct statement of rates that he can rely upon unless he has an expert to make the examination for him."[9]

Railroad attorneys around the South testified before state regulatory commissions, becoming the experts on rates, valuation, and other regulatory issues. When the commissions needed to decide these complicated matters, they listened carefully to what the railroad attorneys had to say.

7. Ibid., 2246.
8. Ibid., 2321, 2278, 2323, 2325, 2327.
9. Ibid., 2274.

The attorneys' long courtroom and legislative experience gave weight to their views before the commissions. Most of the commissioners were not trained attorneys, and some were only marginal experts on railway rates or accounting. C. C. McChord, Kentucky's leading railroad commissioner and president of the National Association of Railway Commissioners in 1908, called attention to this state of affairs in his address to the association. He considered "the average state commission" to be "in the most hopeless and helpless condition imaginable" when "trying to cope with the trained experts of the railroads." The commissioners were at a disadvantage without "sufficient clerical force and expert assistance," especially when ruling on rates and valuation. So many of them listened to the railroad attorneys, for after all their arguments on these issues were coherent and forceful, backed by legal precedent and judicial opinion.[10]

The state of state and federal regulation was shifting as the railroad attorneys challenged rate regulation at every opportunity. In an 1897 landmark decision, the *Alabama Midland Railroad* case, the United States Supreme Court restricted the Interstate Commerce Commission's power of federal railroad regulation. At issue were the differing rates that railroads charged at different points for hauling similar goods. Cities whose rates were higher felt discriminated against, as if the railroads were conspiring to favor others and choke them. The decision denied the commission the power to alter railroad rates when conditions at different points were "substantially" different. More important, the Court reversed the ruling that the commission's factual findings were conclusive. Since district courts could review railroad appeals of ICC decisions, the ruling meant that railroads could wait to introduce damning evidence until their case reached the comfortable surroundings of a federal district court. The decision, most historians agree, emasculated the commission and left southern railroads able to continue charging discriminatory rates.[11]

The decision did little to solve the thorny problem of rate regulation and discrimination across the South. The Troy Board of Trade, which brought the original case against the Alabama Midland Railroad Company

10. *National Association of Railroad Commissioners: Proceedings of the Twentieth Annual Convention* (Washington, D.C., 1908), 11.

11. See Kenneth R. Johnson, "The Troy Case: A Fight Against Discriminatory Freight Rates," *Alabama Review* 22 (July 1969): 175–87, and Maury Klein, *A History of the Louisville & Nashville Railroad* (New York: Macmillan, 1972), 357.

before the ICC in 1892, mirrored the concerns of small-town business-men, merchants, and shippers across the South in the early nineties. As railroads slipped out of local control into larger systems, railroad managers imposed rate schedules that revealed steep inequities between competitive, market points and non-competitive, small localities. Popularly known as long-and-short-haul discrimination, these rate differences often depended on the relative competitive environment at each place. Such discrimination had been always been part of the railroad business and certainly preceded the arrival of interstate railroads in the South. But the interstate companies added a new and disturbing twist to the issue—because they controlled the rates across such vast distances, they had the power to make or break a city. As rates at competitive points fell, railroads relied on their monopoly over local, small-town rates to create their margin of profit on the whole system. Businessmen in small towns, such as Troy, focused intently on their own competitive environment, where they argued that the railroad discriminated in favor of other commercial centers, such as Montgomery, Alabama, or Columbus, Georgia.[12]

After the depression of the nineties, railroad officials resisted state and federal commission interference with their rate structures. Newly reorga-nized, large systems pressed not only to cut costs but also to boost reve-nues. Even the president of the Illinois Central, whose southern lines were regular revenue producers, lamented the poor revenues his railroad earned and what he considered the ICC's inaccurate revenue reports. He directed his general solicitor to "bring the facts to the knowledge of our District Attorneys, so that, through them, the Local Attorneys, the people, and particularly the Courts, Congress, and Legislatures, shall be made to ap-preciate that the reports published by the Federal Government deliberately and persistently misstate and overstate the amount of money actually earned by the Railroads."[13]

Small-town wholesalers, shippers, and other businessmen found Illinois Central president Stuyvesant Fish's complaint ridiculous. From their per-spective the railroads could not help but make money. Railroad auditors,

---

12. For an excellent explanation of the competition-regulation dilemma for railroads, see Maury Klein, "Competition and Regulation: The Railroad Model," *Business History Review* 64 (summer 1990): 311–25.

13. Stuyvesant Fish to James Fentress, 19 April 1897, Fish Out Letters, vol. 29, p. 740, ICRR-NL.

they surmised, routinely manipulated the company books to show low earnings and to hide illegal rebates. They had good reason to be suspicious. In a letter marked "personal," for example, the Southern Pacific's auditor, E. M. Underhill, threatened to reveal his privileged information. Underhill explained to the first vice-president that the company officers reduced his salary and assigned his duties to others in an effort to freeze him out of his position. Underhill could determine no good reason for this. "From 1880 to date, I have become the recipient and custodian of much confidential information regarding the Cos. Affairs," Underhill allowed, "my possession of which, though it has been carefully and faithfully guarded by me, is considered by some as a dangerous possession, to be overcome or neutralised, by forcing me out of the Cos employment." Underhill listed the company's offenses that he was either party to or witnessed in his years with the Southern Pacific: "the persistent and flagrant violation of the I.S.C. [Interstate Commerce] Law, and the law of the State of Texas, by which illegal rebates and refunds aggregating hundreds of thousands of dollars have been made and charged out, and that, in such a flagrant manner, that Mr. Stubbs [company attorney] wrote that in so making them, our people were evidently 'devoid of all fear of God or the Law.' "[14]

Underhill, moreover, claimed to possess "the evidence of these refunds" which the company entrusted to him so that "they might not be available to the I.S.C. Commission in case of an enquiry." Company officials, he pointed out, made clear that they planned to hold him accountable for the refund coupons. "I am advised that their surrender, and possible subsequent loss or destruction on the part of the Co., might render me personally liable, in their absence, for the charges made on the books." Underhill went on to accuse his auditing department of cooperating in "repeated and constant violation of the Gould-Huntington agreement," accounting tricks to give the Galveston, Harrisburg & San Antonio a "fictitious earning capacity . . . possibly unduly influencing the sale of its bonds," many of which the Southern Pacific held, and the intentional lowering of the company's Louisiana roads' earnings to provide an argument against the establishment of a railroad commission. Underhill reminded the company officials that he possessed "written proof" of these

14. E. M. Underhill to Charles F. Crocker, 22 November 1896, Box 2:0, Folder 6-5873, BBHC-RU.

secret violations of the law; indeed, they asked him to return the rebate "vouchers," the hard evidence. "I have considered all of the above matters confidential," he wrote the first vice-president, "and have kept them inviolate, but I am naturally sore, and very indignant at the treatment I have received, and am in no mood to tamely submit."[15]

Underhill's threat was not lost on company officials, who quickly forwarded his letter to Southern Pacific general counsel and former Baker & Botts partner Robert S. Lovett. One company officer warned Lovett that Underhill's letter "shows conclusively his animus in the matter as well as his object—and I hope it may be of service to you." Apparently, Underhill's attempt to retain his Southern Pacific job failed. In 1898 he, like so many other disgruntled former railroad officials, went to work for one of the regulatory agencies—in this case, the Interstate Commerce Commission in its investigation of Texas railroads. That year Baker & Botts requested from the head office in San Francisco all information and letters on Underhill, but it seemed he only wrote one. It is not clear from the railroad records whether Underhill ever deployed his written proof, but both Underhill and the railroad recognized the value of such inside information.[16]

Almost every southern state produced its band of aggrieved, small-town businessmen who brought complaints of discrimination before state commissions and the ICC. They accused the railroads of the same underhanded, illegal maneuvering to which Underhill alluded. More than any other railroad practice, rebates symbolized discrimination for these critics. But even while many southern businessmen attacked the railroads' monopoly power over their community, they too stood ready to accept a rebate or special favoritism from the railroad.

In Griffin, Georgia, M. H. Brewer, "wholesale dealers in grain and provisions," emerged to challenge the Southern Railway's local rates in 1897. Brewer, like many such businessmen, sympathized with the railroads' arguments demanding a fair rate of return. After reading Southern vice-president W. W. Finley's defense of the Southern's rates in the local newspaper, Brewer wrote Finley to explain his opposition. "I agree with you,"

15. A. Hutchinson to Robert S. Lovett, 29 March 1897, E. M. Underhill to Charles F. Crocker, 22 November 1896, ibid.

16. A. Hutchinson to Robert S. Lovett, 29 March 1897, William Mahl to Baker & Botts, 25 August 1898, ibid.

he conceded, "in the position you take in reference to railroads' being entitled to receive a profit upon the improvements they make upon their property." Brewer, though, refused to allow the railroad to make a profit on his town or his business. "I do not agree with the policy of the roads in obtaining revenue," he wrote Finley. "They should comply with the law giving all their patron[s] an equal show to do business and build up the communities in which they live. I am not fighting railroads I am fighting their policy. I do not believe it right to make my city pay a high rate for the purpose of protecting the trade of other cities."[17]

The Southern Railway, though, considered the local business in Griffin only a small part of its total volume. As he prepared for the ICC case against Brewer in 1896, the Southern's counsel outlined the basic argument. "Taking into account all that the company has been able to realize, either from its local, or competitive business, or both," he wrote, "[i]t has not been able to earn a sufficient amount to pay interest and dividends upon the present capitalization of the road from Atlanta, via McDonnough to Columbus, and, in fact, has not been able to earn a fair interest upon the present value of that portion of the road."[18]

The railroad articulated a macroeconomic view of rates and returns on the whole system, while Brewer argued from a microeconomic position, suggesting that regardless of the system's whole, its parts were discriminatory. Brewer's micro perspective was a product in part of the intense localism alive throughout southern counties and towns. Like other businessmen who protested against high local railroad rates, Brewer was not interested in dismantling the whole railroad system. "I am not an enemy but a friend to railroads," he insisted. "Their managers with few exceptions are broad minded and liberal but from long custom are in a rut and do not know exactly how to get out of it."[19]

Southern Railway officials took Brewer seriously. He informed them that he planned "to wait a short time before filing a bill to enjoin your line and the Central against further or continued discrimination against Griffin and other places." But he warned that, "unless the matter is settled soon"

17. M. H. Brewer to W. W. Finley, 24 May 1897, Vice-President's File, Box 2, Folder 40, SRy-VPI.

18. Ed. Baxter to W. W. Finley, 14 November 1896, Vice-President's File, Box 1, Folder 15, ibid.

19. Ibid. See Johnson, "The Troy Case," for a similar localism in Alabama.

he would get "every station between Atlanta and Macon on the Central and every one between Atlanta and Columbus on your line to file a bill against you."[20] Brewer, though, ended his letter to vice-president Finley with a postscript designed to catch his attention. He asked Finley to consider his friend, a town doctor, for the railroad's local surgeon position. "If you can have him appointed to the position," Brewer suggested, "I will accept it as a personal favor to myself."

Later, Finley discovered more about Brewer's motivations. In June 1897, Brewer informed the Central of Georgia, a Southern subsidiary, that he had developed a new case for the commission, one that he said "would stick." As a gesture of explanation and conciliation, the Central gave Brewer a personal tour of the shops, yards, and offices of the railroad to give him "some idea of what a Railway consisted of . . . to let him see the number of persons who were employed in the Railway service, and who were dependent on the Railways for their daily support."[21]

Brewer, though impressed, continued to use his vehement opposition before state and federal commissions as a bludgeon to extract personal favors from the Southern Railway. "Although he did not tell me positively," the Central's tour guide and vice-president reported to Finley, "I inferred from what he said that he had been obtaining concessions from [the railroad] before the Southern Railway took possession."[22] Brewer desired more personal concessions from the Southern similar to the ones he had gained from its predecessor. When the railroad refused, Brewer stated his intention to run for the state legislature and if elected work for a higher tax on railroads. The Central's officers discovered that Brewer had in fact received Columbus rates from the predecessor road: "His firm was the only one favored in that respect, and consequently it must have been in an illegal way." They dispatched their local attorneys to find out more about Brewer's past dealings as possible leverage on him. Later, even as he presented a case in Atlanta before the ICC against railroads, Brewer milked concessions from them, convincing the Southern Railway Company to treat him to supper, the theater, and his room.[23]

20. Ed. Baxter to W. W. Finley, 14 November 1896, Vice-President's File, Box 1, Folder 15, SRy-VPI.
21. John M. Egan to W. W. Finley, 7 June 1897, Vice-President's File, Box 2, Folder 22 marked "Central of Georgia Railway Company," ibid.
22. Ibid.
23. John M. Egan to W. W. Finley, 4 April 1897, John M. Egan to W. W. Finley, 2 April 1897, Vice-President's File, Box 2, Folder 22 marked "Central of Georgia Railway Company," SRy-VPI.

Brewer, it turned out, was party to the dirty work of illegal rebates before the Southern's consolidation with the Central of Georgia. He represented a difficult challenge for the railroad and its attorneys. The political
atmosphere allowed insiders like Brewer to manipulate popular opposition
to railroad abuses in an effort to secure either favorable concessions for
himself or his town, whichever came first. Without question, railroad
abuses in the eighties and nineties fueled growing public opposition, but
after consolidation railroad companies found their choices in places like
Griffin, Georgia, limited and unattractive. They could hold the line and
refuse to give the town or Brewer rebate privileges, and face federal and
state lawsuits and other local restrictions on their business. Or they could
pay off Brewer, lose money, and face federal and state lawsuits and other
local restrictions on their business.

Businessmen such as M. H. Brewer, both individually and collectively
in their associations, acquired significant power to extract concessions
from railroads. When in 1898 the Southern, for example, decided to abolish differential rates on half-full carloads, the wholesale grocers took action. "A movement is on foot looking for cooperation among wholesale
grocers," one Southern official reported. The consequences for the railroad were clear to this official. "It seems to me desirable to prevent these
people from invoking the assistance of the ICC and the U.S. Court in this
matter," he suggested, "and to take some action which will pacify them
and keep them from using their grievances to incite the public against railroad corporations, especially at this time when a marked improvement in
this respect is noticeable within this state." Faced with the ugly prospect
of legal proceedings and negative public opinion, the railroad restored the
differentials. Railroads depended on shippers and businessmen for the majority of their traffic and, as a result, for their profits. Even in communities
where the railroad held a monopoly, it depended on the development of
traffic there, especially as its interstate business at competitive points faced
tighter margins of profit.[24]

Railroad officials realized that their cause required similar unity of pur-

24. William Shaw to W. W. Finley, 17 February, 24 February 1898, Vice-President's
Correspondence, Box 1, Folder 53, SRy-VPI. Railroad spokesman, especially attorneys, consistently maintained that railroads held a greater stake and interest in these communities than
did other businessmen, because the railroads' livelihood depended on the growth of traffic
in the region. See, for example, Walker D. Hines's testimony before the Senate Committee
on Interstate Commerce, 23 May 1902, copy in Walker D. Hines Papers, Barriger Collection, St. Louis Mercantile Library.

pose. Southern railroads, at least all but the Chesapeake & Ohio, retained Edward Baxter in 1896 as "special counsel" for all cases before the ICC and U.S. courts involving matters of interstate commerce. Baxter tried to impose unity on the twenty-five roads he represented. He was not always successful. Railroad officials put associational interests above their companies' only when the latter remained secure. In 1898 one road threatened to drop its appeal in a joint case and Baxter urged the Southern Railway's officials: "If that Company shall insist upon having the appeal dismissed as to it, it will be unfortunate for the other appellants. It will indicate a want of harmony in our own ranks, and it will be equivalent to an endorsement of Judge Severens' decision by one of the parties whom I assume to represent." Baxter understood that in this particular case the rate adjustment did not affect some roads, including the one that wanted to drop the appeal. "It ought to be remembered," he warned, "that this is but one of the many cases involving the long and short haul clause; and if each company is to act as it may deem most to its own interest, without regarding the interests of the southern railroads generally, it will interfere very materially in the defense of such cases."[25]

After the 1897 Supreme Court decisions limiting ICC authority, the commission engaged in a concerted lobbying effort to strengthen its powers. It beseeched Congress every year beginning in 1898 to enact legislation legalizing pooling and bestowing rate-making authority on the commission. The commissioners loudly denounced the Supreme Court's decisions in the late nineties, claiming that they violated the intent of the original Interstate Commerce Act and that they stripped all power from the agency. The newly reorganized railroads under the New York financiers, the commissioners argued, had the freedom and the inclination to raise rates indiscriminately. Fanning fears of a few greedy New York financiers' exclusive ability to control rates across the country, the commissioners enlisted the support of shippers, wholesalers, and national business associations. Many railroads eagerly sought passage of the pooling provision, but most remained suspicious of the ICC's motives.[26]

25. Ed. Baxter to W. W. Finley, 17 March 1898, Vice-President's File, Box 1, Folder 15, SRy-VPI.

26. *ICC v. Cincinnati, New Orleans & Texas Pacific Railway Company*, 167 U.S. 479. Gabriel Kolko argues that interstate railroads supported greater federal regulation from the inception of the ICC in 1887. He notes the federalized regulatory environment and the states' increased pressure on railroads after 1900 as the primary motivation among railroad

The L&N took the lead among southern railroads in the effort to prevent further legislation empowering the ICC. As assistant chief attorney, chief attorney, then first vice-president for the L&N, Walker D. Hines formulated the road's legal arguments and coordinated its public and private opposition to the ICC. He appeared regularly before the U.S. Senate Committee on Interstate Commerce to present the railroads' response to the commissioners. In a circular letter to southern railroad officials, Hines outlined his opposition to further legislation empowering the ICC. He warned his counterparts, "it seems to be the idea to keep these matters to which the railroads do not object prominent, with the apparent hope of getting the railroads in the attitude of urging action, and then the friends of the Commission will see to it that no bill can be brought forward which does not, as the price of these amendments supposed to be desired by the railroads, concede all the powers which the Commission would like to exercise."[27]

The commission, according to Hines, gravitated away from its original, broad-minded understanding of the long-and-short-haul provision under chairman Thomas Cooley. The commission seemed to be headed toward the "narrow and impossible" view "that all interstate rates may be substantially fixed on a mileage basis." He foresaw that if given the authority, the commission would fix rates with "utter disregard of commercial conditions, perhaps reducing local rates to the basis of low competitive rates." In the South and the rest of the country, coming out from years of depression, rates between competitive points stood at historic lows, and railroads' profit margins depended on the higher local rates more than ever. Hines emphatically called for cooperation in an effort to defeat any em-

executives for greater federal control. Kolko, though, overplays the railroads' control over the ICC and the coordination of the industry's "capture" of the regulatory process. See Gabriel Kolko, *Railroads and Regulation, 1877–1916* (New York: W. W. Norton, 1965), 231–39. For an opposing view, see Albro Martin, *Enterprise Denied: The Origins of the Decline of American Railroads, 1897–1917* (New York: Columbia University Press, 1971); see also Herbert Hovenkamp, *Enterprise and American Law, 1836–1937* (Cambridge, Mass.: Harvard University Press, 1991).

27. See Bernard Axelrod, "Railroad Regulation in Transition, 1897–1905: Walker D. Hines of the Railroads Versus Charles A. Prouty of the Interstate Commerce Commission" (Ph.D. diss., Washington University, 1975). Milton H. Smith to "Sir," 27 November 1897, Vice-President's File, Box 2, Folder 37, SRy-VPI. Signed by Smith, this circular letter was undoubtedly prepared for Smith by Hines.

powering legislation: "It is almost impossible . . . to exaggerate the importance of railroad companies taking the proper steps to prevent any such vicious legislation."[28]

Hines kept up a running public and private campaign to prevent congressional legislation extending the commission's power. For each ICC annual report after 1898 demanding such legislation, Hines published an opposition pamphlet, distributed to newspapers, other railroads, and legislators. In one such piece Hines placed his faith in the power of localities to negotiate their rates with the railroads: "It is far safer to leave these communities to fight their own battles—aided as they will be by their respective railroad lines, since each line is, of course, identified in interest with the welfare of the places on its own line as against all other places on other lines—than it would be to commit the entire commercial fate of every section of the country to any human tribunal." Of course, for most southern communities, this appeal rang hollow, as consolidations stripped localities of any competitive advantage. Most localities did not consider themselves on equal footing with the powerful corporations, and did not look to them for "aid."[29]

According to Hines, the commission's demands for its own empowerment showed that the agency had been swayed by shippers and business associations. He knew that the ICC considered its mandate to be more railroad rate control, especially after the Progressive reforms of 1906. Hines went on the offensive. He loudly accused the commission of creating and fostering the public's appetite for anti-railroad legislation. When the commission's annual report championed the support of a national trade association conference, Hines pointed out that the report "omits to say that conference was also attended, and actively advised, by one or more members and officers of the Commission."[30]

In 1904 Ed Baxter reiterated Hines's assertions. The ICC's quiescence in long-and-short-haul cases led Baxter to conclude "that the real motive

28. Milton H. Smith to "Sir," 27 November 1897, Vice-President's File, Box 2, Folder 37, SRy-VPI. For a thorough examination of the early ICC and Thomas Cooley's fair-minded leadership of it, see Ari Hoogenboom and Olive Hoogenboom, *A History of the ICC: From Panacea to Palliative* (New York: W. W. Norton, 1976), 21–32.

29. Walker D. Hines, "Interstate Commerce Commission: Its Twelfth Annual Report Considered," Barriger Collection, St. Louis Mercantile Library.

30. Ibid. See also Walker D. Hines, "The Proposals of the Interstate Commerce Commission," *The Forum* (March 1902): 3–14, Barriger Collection, St. Louis Mercantile Library.

in voluntarily dismissing said appeals is to induce Congress to amend the Act." Baxter too pointed out the powerful groups allied against the railroads: the cattle raisers' associations from Canada to the Gulf, he observed, passed formal resolutions "to aid the Interstate Commerce Commission in having the act amended." According to Baxter, the "Lumber Men of the South and the Fruit Growers Association of the Southeast" backed the commission's bid for greater regulatory power.[31]

Hines's remarks before Congress drew attention from state railway commissioners, who were constantly wrestling with the problems of railroad valuation and rates. At the National Association of Railway Commissioners meeting in 1905, R. Hudson Burr, a commissioner from Florida, criticized Hines for his testimony to Congress. He suggested that Hines and the L&N gave three different valuations for their line in Florida, the Pensacola and Atlantic, all in his official capacity as attorney for the L&N. Valuation became a vital issue for railroads and commissions. It determined rate structures and taxes. It was the key factor in nearly every court decision about rates and ability to control them. "Every controversy that gets into court over the action of a commission runs right into the question as to what the property is worth, what it is earning—what it is producing for the investors," one state commissioner said at the National Association meeting. "What ought it, in good conscience, to produce for the investors?" Some commissioners argued that valuation of railroad property depended on many factors, including the price of steel, and that valuation could fluctuate dramatically from day to day. There was little agreement, but much indignation among state commissioners about the accuracy of Hines's testimony.[32]

Some railroad attorneys began to think that the fight was not worth the trouble, that valuation, rates, and taxes were best left to one agency and that that agency might be the ICC. The whirlwind of the Progressive legislative challenge along with all of the other adverse changes in the railroad business environment led some railroad attorneys to search for new ways to escape the chaotic nature of state regulation. The L&N fought regula-

---

31. Ed. Baxter to Milton H. Smith, 28 September 1904, Chairman's Correspondence, Box 14, Folder 494, L&NRR-UL.

32. *National Association of Railroad Commissioners: Proceedings of the Twentieth Annual Convention*, 180; *National Association of Railroad Commissioners: Proceedings of the Seventeenth Annual Convention* (Washington D.C., 1905), 69.

tion prominently and forcefully in Alabama and elsewhere, but Henry L. Stone, the road's general counsel, questioned the wisdom of knee-jerk reactions against federal regulation. Prompted by a letter from Farrar, Jonas & Kruttschnitt, railroad attorneys in New Orleans, to President Theodore Roosevelt in 1907 advocating greater national regulation of railroads, Stone broached the concept with L&N president Milton H. Smith. "In my opinion," Stone explained, "rather than have the constant annoyance, trouble and expense resulting to interstate railroad carriers by reason of hostile orders from State railroad commissions and drastic legislation by State legislatures, it would be far better for such carriers to be brought under one comprehensive act of Congress, thus bringing about the unity of control and regulation."[33]

Stone's perspective demonstrated his experience in the trenches fighting Governor Comer in Alabama. "Divided control over the matter of rates, rules and regulations," Stone warned his superior, would result in "financial embarrassment." At the heart of the problem, according to the general counsel, stood the political atmosphere for railroads: "The members of State rail road commissions, as a rule, are politicians who use their official positions to reduce the intra-state rates or to impose other restrictions upon the carriers within their jurisdiction, in order to gain popularity and promotion in office without due regard to the interests of the railroad companies affected. Again, members of the Legislature in framing legislation hostile to railroad interests, in a majority of cases, do so with the same motives that actuate most of the members of the railroad commissions." Stone preferred to empower the Interstate Commerce Commission, members of which, he thought, were "more conservative in their rulings, and, coming from different sections of the country . . . not likely to use their official positions to subserve any private ends."[34]

Smith, for his part, considered his general counsel a victim of trench warfare, beset with a bunker mentality, unable to discern the greater threats in the world at large. "I am impressed with the idea," Smith wrote his company's chairman, "that Col. Stone has been, and is now being, so harassed with State legislation that he unconsciously underrates the danger from national legislation." As for the states, Smith confidently pointed out

33. Henry L. Stone to Milton H. Smith, 10 April 1907, Chairman's Correspondence, Box 22, Folder 773, L&NRR-UL.
34. Ibid.

that except for Alabama, "we have also, during the last twenty-five or thirty years, been quite successful in preventing unjust or injurious legislation in Kentucky, [and] Tennessee." Smith eventually showed that he understood his attorney's dilemma. He concluded his assessment of the relative dangers of state and federal railroad regulation with remarkable indecisiveness: "Altogether, I am at a loss to decide as to the better course." This startling, private confession came from the railroad president most associated with unwavering protection of laissez-faire principles from encroachment by state and federal regulation.[35]

Smith had good reason to be unsure. Some of the state commissions worked hard to limit railroad power and control rates for their state's businesses. The Texas commission, for example, was one of the most powerful in the South and exercised its authority over intrastate rates increasingly after 1900. The long depression kept interstate rates at historic lows in the mid-nineties, but railroads initiated rate increases as traffic picked up at the turn of the century. The Texas commission proposed, among other measures, a rate decrease on cotton in 1905. Santa Fe counsel Jonathan Terry appeared before the commission to present the railroads' argument against the proposal. He tried to clarify the roads' position. "If we had some way to present some matters more clearly to the Commission," one Santa Fe officer recommended to Terry, "they would not look upon railroads with the evident distrust that they seem to have at this time." The Santa Fe contended that significant capital improvements so necessary to handle the increased traffic and tonnage explained the railroad's large expenses; a rate decrease would hurt the railroad's ability to finance the capital outlay. The commission, though, remained suspicious; they considered high expenses a function of overcapitalization. To prove beyond doubt the necessity of these capital improvements, the Santa Fe legal department took some of the commissioners on a ride to show them the new capital outlays and explain their costs. Despite Terry's efforts at show and tell, the commission approved the rate decrease.[36]

Struggles over rates across the South turned on questions of railroad valuation and the conditions of railroad property. After the nineties de-

---

35. Milton H. Smith to H. Walters, 11 April 1907, Chairman's Correspondence, Box 22, Folder 773, L&NRR-UL.

36. W. C. Nixon to Jonathan W. Terry, 15 March 1905, Box 20, Folder 4, SFRR-HMRC.

pression nearly every major railroad in the region required significant capital improvements to its tracks, engines, and yards in order to carry the increased tonnage and heavier traffic. Without these improvements, railroads argued, deterioration would bring on disaster. Rate increases, or at the very least rate stability, were necessary to make these capital improvements. Opponents, though, questioned the railroads' statistics, suggesting that proper valuation of railroad property showed bloated capital accounts. They pushed for lower rates and independent valuation of railroad property. They felt assured that any independent accounting would justify their position.

Railroad attorneys tried all sorts of arguments to convince the public that they were not overcapitalized, that rate decreases would prevent capital improvements, and that their valuations were honest and correct. In 1905 Jonathan W. Terry testified before the Texas Railroad Commission on valuation and rate of return. Terry contested the commission's assumption of the power to define a fair rate of return for railroad companies, and even questioned the authority of the commission to regulate in the area of rates and valuation. He explained the reasons for the high cost of construction in the 1870s and 1880s, dismissed the value of the "scrip" for unsurveyed lands donated to the roads, and suggested that railroads spent huge sums on capital improvements without issuing stocks or bonds. Moreover, Terry defended the rights of stockholders against railroad commission rate tampering:

> I say that the 8 million dollars we lost during the period we were waiting for the country to develop, is just as much a legitimate part of the cost of the road as the money that went into the dumps. Any business man, engaging in a business that might not begin to pay him for the first few years, would expect to earn that money back when the prosperous years did come, but it seems to be suggested that the people that invested their money in these railroads, should not only sustain that loss, but that they should have their property depreciated by time and should be brought down to what, years after the road has built, it might be rebuilt for.[37]

37. Jonathan W. Terry testimony, ibid.

The railroad attorneys in Texas considered rate decreases little more than political posturing. Faced with a proposed sugar rate reduction by the Texas commission, Santa Fe officers suggested deflating the commission's political ambitions with delay or postponement. "It has just occurred to me," the road's general freight agent wrote Jonathan Terry, "that it might be a good scheme to, shortly before the hearing date, make an appeal to the Commission for a postponement of the hearing. If we could get it set over to a date after the political conventions, it might remove one of the principal motives for the proposed reduction."[38]

The attorneys, though, met these reductions in Texas with legal arguments as well. They contended that many of the Texas commission's intrastate rate adjustments carried interstate ramifications. Indeed, they argued that the commission purposefully worked to adjust interstate rates through the device of manipulating intrastate rates. "If our surmise is correct," one Santa Fe officer wrote Jonathan Terry, "that the proposed reduction is for the purpose of influencing or changing the rates from New Orleans to Texas points, it is certainly a most unwarrantable interference with interstate rates . . . and ought to be opposed as vigorously as possible."[39]

The threat of state-commission regulation did not always promote unity among the railroads. In Texas, for example, the commission's cotton rate reduction in 1909 stung several lines, and their attorneys recommended a railroad response. The railroads' lobbyist in Austin, N. A. Stedman, warned "all interested attorneys" that the proposed cotton rate reduction, a Farmers' Union threat to seek remedy in the legislature barring commission action, and a proposed lower passenger fare all conspired to demonstrate "the necessity for organized action on the part of the railroad companies." After a meeting of the Texas roads' general managers, the lines decided to make a stand in opposition: "I think under no circumstances should we acquiesce in any of these measures whether pending before the Legislature, Railroad Commission or elsewhere, which will in any

38. J. S. Hershey to Jonathan W. Terry, 4 May 1906, Box 15, Folder 7, SFRR-HMRC.
39. Ibid. See also Jonathan W. Terry to Gardiner Lathrop, 26 May 1908, Box 36, Folder 8, SFRR-HMRC. See Hiram Glass, "Railroads—National Versus State Control," *Texas Bar Association Proceedings* (1908): 196, for another argument supporting the contention that Texas' commission purposely worked to affect interstate rates through intrastate rate changes.

way reduce our present earnings." The Texas lines, the attorneys suggested, should jointly file suit to enjoin the enforcement of the commission's new rate. When the Missouri, Kansas & Texas and the Cotton Belt railroads did not join in the action, the Santa Fe general counsel lamented those attorneys' cowardice; in his opinion, they were "too ready to take fright at small clouds on the political horizon."[40]

In neighboring Oklahoma, Santa Fe attorneys feared an equally authoritative railroad commission. In 1908 one Santa Fe attorney reported that "the present commissioners were elected upon the theory that it was their duty to reduce railroad rates. . . . In my judgment the question of rate regulations is by far the most serious question that railroads of the new state will have to contend with." As Oklahoma's commission caught the regulatory spirit, lines such as the Santa Fe confronted a new challenge. Oklahoma followed other southern states, such as North Carolina and Alabama, and ordered in 1908 a two-cent-per-mile passenger fare. Jonathan Terry recommended that the road contest it outright. "We are now laboring under the embarrassment," he pointed out to his Chicago superiors, "of defending the three-cent rate in Texas, while we are apparently submitting to the two-cent rate in Oklahoma." Terry, though, received notice from general counsel in Chicago to concede the rates. "Conditions are so inflamed," they explained, "in that state [Oklahoma] at the present time that we feel constrained to submit to the two-cent rate for the time being, and perhaps, until the legislature adjourns . . . it seems to us the lesser of two evils not to attack the Oklahoma rate."[41]

As state railroad commissions across the South grew more powerful and authoritative, they concentrated mostly on issues of money, such as rates and valuation of railroad property. The increased vigilance of the commissions, however, did not prevent the railroads from ignoring some statutes or regulations. In contests over power between commissions and corporations, the real test of strength rested on enforcement and compliance. Indeed, railroad companies frustrated state commissions with the same

40. N. A. Stedman to "Interested Attorneys," 12 January 1909, N. A. Stedman to Terry, Gavin & Mills, 16 January 1909, Box 20, Folder 4, SFRR-HMRC; Jonathan W. Terry to E. P. Ripley, 22 September 1910, Box 2, Folder 4, ibid.

41. S. T. Bledsoe to Jonathan W. Terry, 13 January 1908, Jonathan W. Terry to Robert Dunlap, 27 January 1908, Gardiner Lathrop to Jonathan W. Terry, 3 February 1908, Box 31, Folder 14, ibid.

tactics of non-compliance they used so effectively on the ICC. Railroads, upon the advice of their attorneys, chose which state statutes or state-commission directives to comply with and which to ignore, evade, or procrastinate over. Railroad commissioners tried to make their decisions more binding. At the National Association of Railway Commissioners, a committee met to develop recommendations. "In some instances," the committee's chair from South Carolina reported, "these delays [in compliance] have amounted to such proportions as to paralyze the usefulness of the commission and even to threaten its existence."[42]

On the issue of segregation, railroads delayed compliance as long as they could. Railroad attorneys used the interstate nature of their business to avoid state legislative interference. When Maryland's 1904 separate coach act was tested in the courts, Norfolk & Western general counsel Joseph I. Doran watched with interest. The case, *Hart v. State*, went to the Maryland Court of Appeals, where the court held that the statute did not apply to interstate passengers, but only to those passengers traveling within the state. Doran reminded the Norfolk & Western president that "this decision does not conflict, but on the contrary sustains the advice I gave you some years ago in regard to compliance with the Virginia act. You will recall that on trains running from Bluefield, West Virginia, through portions of Virginia . . . our company disregards the Act of Virginia and does not separate the races."[43]

Several southern state courts began to construe their laws as applicable only to intrastate passengers, as railroad attorneys argued that states could not regulate interstate commerce. Their arguments rested on several significant Supreme Court decisions. In an 1877 case regarding violation of

---

42. *National Association of Railroad Commissioners: Proceedings of the Twentieth Annual Convention*, 217. See John H. Churchman, "Federal Regulation of Railroad Rates, 1880–1898" (Ph.D. diss., University of Wisconsin, 1976), 286. Churchman describes the railroads' refusal in the late nineties to either settle or comply with the ICC's directives. The Southern Railway ignored five orders, which Churchman considers "symptomatic of the decision of several roads, particularly those in the South, to test the authority of the Commission in the courts" (287).

43. Joseph I. Doran to L. E. Johnson, 4 April 1905, Subject File #1530, N&W-VPI; *Hart v. State*, 60 Atl. Rep. 457. For an analysis of the interstate commerce clause and segregation, see W. G. Thomas, "Railroad Attorneys and the Issue of Segregation Before and After *Plessy*" (paper presented at the *Plessy v. Ferguson* Revisited Conference, Howard University, Washington, D.C., November 15, 1996).

Reconstruction civil rights statutes, *Hall v. De Cuir*, a black plaintiff sued over separate compartments on steamboats plying the interstate waters of the Mississippi. The Court found that the state law outlawing segregated facilities interfered with interstate business and that interstate companies were "at liberty to adopt such reasonable rules and regulations . . . as seemed . . . most for the interest of all concerned." Later, in 1910 the Court handed down another significant ruling, in the case of *Chiles v. Chesapeake & Ohio Railway Company*. The Court ruled that in the absence of any federal law on the issue, interstate companies may follow the dictates of business and reasonableness and either comply with or ignore state segregation statutes that interfered with interstate business.[44]

Unpredictable trial court decisions added weight to the growing recognition among railroad attorneys that their companies' non-compliance with Jim Crow, no matter how constitutionally sound, was politically damaging. Railroad general counsels could not believe some of the high verdicts coming out of southern juries. For example, a 1911 case, *Alabama & Vicksburg Railway Company v. Morris*, before the Mississippi Supreme Court demonstrated how much railroads stood to lose on segregation issues. Pearl Morris sued the railroad company because it failed to segregate its first-class cars. When she discovered that three black men were also riding in the only first-class car with her, she requested that either the three men or she be assigned new seats. The railroad refused or ignored her request and she claimed to have suffered "distress of mind and spirit" on her trip. A jury of all white men at the trial court found in her favor and determined that the railroad pay in damages $15,000, a stupendous sum for a case in which the plaintiff was not injured at all but suffered "distress."

The railroad appealed to the Supreme Court on the grounds that the separate-car law was not applicable to first-class cars, that the damages were excessive in any case, and that the law violated the interstate commerce clause of the Constitution. The Mississippi court ruled against the railroad, though it lowered the damages to $2,000. The court determined that the law applied to first-class cars: "It was the purpose of the Legisla-

44. *Hall v. De Cuir* (95 US 485); *Chiles v. Chesapeake & Ohio Railway Company* (30 Sup. Ct. 667); *McCabe et al. v. Atchison, Topeka & Santa Fe Railway Company et al.* (186 Fed. Rep. 966). For another review of this issue, see Joseph R. Palmore, "The Not-So-Strange Career of Interstate Jim Crow: Race, Transportation, and the Dormant Commerce Clause, 1878–1946," *Virginia Law Review* 83 (November 1997): 1773–1817.

ture to separate the races, for entirely obvious reasons." Moreover, the court held that the law applied to all intrastate commerce and that this case did not involve interstate travel.

The Mississippi court went further, though, in its opinion. It staked out the state's rights in the area of race relations and segregation, regardless of interstate commerce protections. It argued that the legislature did not intend to limit the law to intrastate travel. "Enforced intermingling would be distasteful to both races," the court pointed out. The court admitted that the segregation laws burdened railroad corporations: "True the application of the statute to interstate trains necessarily imposes additional expense upon the carrier." These laws, the court said, were accepted by both races, by all Mississippi citizens. Finally, for the court, peculiar state conditions override a theory of interstate commerce. "We therefore decline to limit the application of the statute to intrastate commerce. Possessing the knowledge of local conditions common to all residents of our section." In a final jab at the powerful railroad attorneys, the court offered the following: "that a law found to be necessary in our state should be assailed by a corporation created by the state may account for the amount of the verdict in this case."[45]

Some states' attorneys aggressively prosecuted railroad companies that failed to follow segregation statutes. Commonwealth attorneys in localities in Kentucky, for example, indicted both the Chesapeake & Ohio and the L&N in 1905 for failure to comply fully with the state's segregation statute. The C&O ran one passenger train without separate coaches because the black coaches failed to make it to the station for switching in time for departure. The case revolved on whether the fact that the C&O normally ran separate coaches, that the incident marked the first and only time the black coach failed to arrive in time for the switch, and that no black passengers were traveling on the train all provided adequate excuse for the railroad's failure to comply with the statute. For the Shelby County commonwealth attorney, apparently these considerations did not justify non-compliance; the railroads, it was suggested, should keep idle extra coaches for black passengers in emergency situations.[46]

45. *Alabama & Vicksburg Railway Company v. Morris* (60 Sou. Rep. 11), *American and English Railroad Cases*, n.s., 68, p. 112. See also *Louisville, New Orleans & Texas Railway Company v. State* (66 Miss. 662).

46. *Chesapeake & Ohio v. Commonwealth of Kentucky*, 84 S.W. Rep. 566. See also *Commonwealth v. Louisville & Nashville*, 87 S.W. Rep. 262, for a case in which the L&N was indicted for "willfully failing to furnish sufficient coaches or cars." Lacking sufficient white-

By 1911 some railroads, such as the L&N, exercised the power that the Supreme Court outlined in *Chiles v. Chesapeake & Ohio* and wrote company rulebooks that complied with the various southern state segregation laws. To assert their privileges under the interstate commerce clause on the segregation issue—to in a sense use the protection of the interstate commerce clause to defy local law—meant to risk the kind of high verdicts that Pearl Morris won in *Alabama & Vicksburg v. Morris*. Interstate railroads could have used their prerogative under *Chiles* the other way, to refuse to segregate on interstate routes for interstate passengers. The Court had left them the opening, and the state courts, with the exception of Mississippi and Tennessee, had ceded the ground, following the Supreme Court rulings. Railroads, though, were responsible to the public and to public pressures. Most of the large roads decided in the years around 1910 to abandon the interstate commerce defense of segregation and to follow the local rules of the states in which they did business.[47]

In the legislatures across the South, railroad attorneys tried to obfuscate or derail further segregation efforts. The most important segregation bills for the railroads were the separate depot measures in the early 1900s. Interstate railroads resisted erecting separate depots and waiting rooms because of the expense. The Norfolk & Western, for example, opposed a 1904 bill in Virginia to segregate waiting rooms by race in towns with populations over five hundred persons. The company's local attorney and lobbyist, Horace Graham Buchanan, reported during the session that "at the present time there does not appear to be any public demand for the passage of the Bill or an attempt to crystalize public sentiment behind it." The company, though, put together an estimate of the expense necessary to comply with the separate-waiting-room bill. Their engineer's report estimated an "extremely heavy expense" and recommended that "every effort possible should be made to prevent its passage." His estimate was $24,000 to renovate the stations along the line, not including the largest and newest ones in Norfolk, Petersburg, Farmville, Lynchburg, Buena Vista, and Pulaski, all of which would need complete restructuring.[48]

only cars on its run from Greensburg to Lebanon, Kentucky, the L&N forced some white passengers to ride with black passengers.

47. Catherine A. Barnes, *Journey from Jim Crow: The Desegregation of Southern Transit* (New York: Columbia University Press, 1983), 12; Patricia Hagley Minter, "The Codification of Jim Crow" (Ph.D. diss., University of Virginia, 1994).

48. Horace Graham Buchanan to Joseph I. Doran, 26 February 1904, C. Underhill to N. D. Maher, 2 March 1904, Subject Files, N&W-VPI. See also Joseph I. Doran to L. E. Johnson 18 March 1904.

When Texas passed a law requiring separate depot facilities by race in 1909, Santa Fe Railroad attorneys considered the best ways to evade the strict requirements of the law. The railroad did not want the expense of erecting barriers or separate facilities in its many depots. The attorneys considered strict enforcement of the law unlikely and unreasonable. After all, many small, western Texas depots witnessed so few blacks that special facilities for them would go practically unused.

Texas railroad lawyers had long contested the railroad commission's assumption of the power to regulate depots. Around 1900, though, the commission rested its right to regulate in this area on the issue of railroad disregard for public convenience. In particular, the commission targeted the railroads' inconsistent efforts to provide heating and lighting in their depots. On this basic issue of the public's safety and convenience, the commission successfully penetrated a previously closed area of regulation. In 1910 the Texas Supreme Court upheld the commission's power to regulate depots. Santa Fe counsel Jonathan Terry summed up his views on the matter to the road's general superintendent: "In any event, we think that it is necessary for the railroad commission . . . to make some order, and it is probable that the commission will not require the maintenance of separate waiting rooms at places where the same is not reasonably necessary." The Santa Fe, under advice from its general counsel, simply carried on with business as usual, its depots presumably segregated only in the large, urban centers where the public demanded and expected it. Along the vast expanses of its lines, though, in small towns and hamlets, the Santa Fe paid little attention to the separate-depot requirement, convinced that no reasonable interpretation would demand strict compliance and basing that position on a flimsy reading of the act's second section.[49]

Only in 1923 did a citizen complaint force the Santa Fe to rectify its loose interpretation of the statute. A traveling insurance salesman from Dallas issued a formal complaint to the Texas Railroad Commission. As he sat in the men's section of the Santa Fe Railroad depot at Slaton, Texas, he drafted his grievance: "There are now in this room 17 negroes, 14 white persons, 6 Mexicans. In the Ladies Department there is a conglomeration of negroes, whites and Mexicans. A Beautiful Sight."[50]

49. Robert Lewis Patterson, "State Regulation of Railroads in Texas, 1836–1920" (Ph.D. diss., University of Texas, 1960), 303–10; Jonathan W. Terry to W. E. Maxson, 16 August 1909, Box 41, Folder 5, SFRR-HMRC.
50. J. E. Eaves to Railroad Commission of Texas, 15 April 1923, Box 41, Folder 5, SFRR-HMRC.

The Texas commission investigated and forced the railroad to explain its non-compliance. The Santa Fe attorneys rested their hopes on their loose interpretation of the statute, worked out twelve years earlier, which allowed for reasonableness. They balked at the expense necessary to create and maintain separate facilities in places where blacks rarely traveled or lived. Other railroads, they were quick to point out, followed the Santa Fe's line of reasoning. "If the law were rigidly enforced," one railroad official wrote Terry before the commission's hearing, "it would mean a heavy expense to this company, as, with one or two exceptions, none of our depots on the Panhandle & Santa Fe Railway are provided with separate waiting rooms for negroes. There is a similar condition on other lines in this section: in fact, at Amarillo there are no separate waiting rooms in the depots of either the Rock Island, the Fort Worth & Denver City, or the Santa Fe." It seemed that in Texas, where the depot segregation law had been in effect for fourteen years, most railroads ignored the statute and did not even provide separate depot waiting rooms.[51]

With a total population of four thousand people and only approximately thirty black families in Slaton, Texas, the railroads "have received no complaint from the citizens of Slaton or from the travelling public due to not having separate waiting rooms for negroes." At the hearing the railroad tried to produce citizens to "testify . . . that separate waiting rooms are not necessary." According to the Santa Fe division attorneys, "The Slaton witnesses were not much enthused over the hearing and admitted on cross-examination that the depot facilities had been reasonably sufficient and satisfactory. . . . there were some loose expressions of opinion to the effect that at times there were promiscuous interminglings of white and negro passengers at the depot." The commission's response sealed the issue—it ordered the company to comply with the law. The attorneys consoled themselves with the supposition that as more cotton farms moved into remote reaches of Texas, more blacks would follow, and the railroad would be forced to do something about the facilities anyway.[52]

As late as 1916, the Santa Fe still had no separate water closets by race in its Louisiana facilities, despite statutes requiring such segregation. A citizen complaint led to an investigation into this discrepancy by the Louisi-

51. F. A. Lehman to Jonathan W. Terry, 25 April 1923, ibid.
52. Lehman to Terry, 7 June 1923, Terry to Lehman, 25 June 1923, Madden, Trulove, Ryburn & Pipken to Terry, 6 July 1923, ibid.

ana Board of Health. "We have separate water closets at all of our stations in Louisiana for men and women, but they are not separated as to color," one local Santa Fe official confirmed for Jonathan Terry. Though states across the South passed segregation statutes at the turn of the century, lax enforcement and compliance followed. The Texas railroads could get away with ignoring state segregation laws for fourteen years, but they were forced to pay immediate attention to the railroad commission's rate decisions. Railroad attorneys and officials witnessed in these years repeated attempts by state commissions to set intrastate rates. Railroad officials found that they were juggling numerous regulatory contests in various states through which their lines ran. Many railroad attorneys recognized the need for a more uniform resolution of the federalized system of regulation.[53]

53. W. E. Maxson to Terry, 16 June 1916, Box 13, Folder 9, SFRR-HMRC.

EIGHT

Liability and Federal Regulation

In personal injury litigation, and segregation statutes and rate regulation as well, railroad lawyers began to wonder if a more uniform system of regulation might lessen their companies' overall costs and minimize their exposure to damaging lawsuits. The passage of the initial Federal Employers' Liability Act (FELA) in 1906 restructured the legal landscape for personal injury litigation. It offered more stable, federal regulation, but railroad attorneys were slow to see this as a benefit. They spent several years fighting the measure. The FELA prompted the first "railroad attorneys' conference" in Louisville, Kentucky. Southern railroad lawyers in particular attended this L&N-organized event. The conferees shared arguments, ideas, and briefs about every aspect of the FELA, all in an effort to render it ineffective.

The 1906 FELA, Congress' first effort at tort reform, evolved out of the growing concern within the Interstate Commerce Commission for railroad safety and out of the contests between railroad employees and company officials. The act generally protected workers from the fellow-servant rule by abolishing it for interstate railroads. The FELA abrogated the fellow-servant rule as a defense against personal injury suits in federal courts, weakened the use of the contributory negligence defense, and barred the assumption-of-risk and contributory negligence defenses when defendant railroad companies violated any federal safety act. The act benefited from railway labor-organization lobbying efforts. The railroads tried to persuade Congress to leave the bulk of the fellow-servant rule in effect.

But after the railroad labor lobby worked over the Congress, the FELA passed, undiluted.[1]

The FELA emerged in large part out of the ICC's experience with the Safety Appliance Act of 1893. Section 8 of the Safety Appliance Act (SAA) barred the assumption-of-risk defense when defendants violated the provisions of the act. Charged with the responsibility of enforcing the SAA, the ICC found that the safety measures only marginally improved the conditions of railroad workers and provided little amelioration of the inequities of the legal process. In subsequent court cases, the ICC discovered the limitations of the SAA and the extent of the common law defenses facing injured railroad workers. With little of the fractious debate surrounding the passage of the SAA in 1893, Congress passed the FELA.[2]

At the 1906 railroad attorneys' conference, the lawyers argued about whether the FELA was constitutional or not. Some participants considered the FELA merely a limited constitutional extension of the SAA. John I. Hall, a Georgia attorney, and Alexander P. Humphrey, general counsel of the Southern Railway, led those who considered the act constitutional. Hall considered the act dependent on the SAA: "I believe Congress had the power to pass this act. . . . I think therefore, that to the extent that this act applies to injuries to persons which is the result of a failure to observe the Safety Appliance Act, the courts would hold it was constitutional." According to Hall, "if an employe is injured by a collision of trains, this act does not cover it, unless the collision was the direct result of a violation of an act of Congress with reference to safety appliances."[3]

1. Walter Licht, *Working for the Railroad: The Organization of Work in the Nineteenth Century* (Princeton: Princeton University Press, 1983), 188–90, argues that workers spearheaded the movement for safety legislation. Gabriel Kolko, *Railroads and Regulation, 1877–1916* (New York: W. W. Norton, 1965), argues that railroad-corporation interests constituted the most influential group in support of uniform federal regulation.

2. *Johnson v. Southern Pacific Company*, 117 Fed. Rep. 462, 196 U.S. 1, and *Schlemmer v. The Buffalo, Rochester & Pittsburgh Railway Company*, 11 Pa. Dist. Ct. 679. Lower courts decided both cases in favor of the defendant railroad companies, as they narrowly construed the SAA. In 1904 the Supreme Court overturned *Johnson*, and in 1907 *Schlemmer*. For a detailed examination of these cases, the SAA, and the origins of the FELA in the ICC, see Viva Rivers Moffat, "The Origins of Federal Tort Reform: Administrative Activism and a Common Law Solution" (master's thesis, University of Virginia, 1993).

3. John I. Hall, quoted in *Proceedings of the Railroad Attorneys' Conference: Employers' Liability Act* (Louisville, Ky.: Westerfield-Bonte Co. Press, 1906), 35–36—hereafter *PRAC* with year of publication—in John W. Barringer III Railroad Collection, St. Louis Mercantile

Others, though, considered the act unconstitutional; to view it otherwise, in their opinion, jeopardized future contests. L&N district attorney John B. Keeble, the leading figure opposed to Hall's position, denied that Congress had the power to enact the FELA and hoped that the railroad attorneys would agree to test the measure before the Supreme Court. "I believe whenever we undertake to say that this act does not mean what it expressly says on its face it does mean," Keeble pointed out, "it will be a concession of weakness before the court." For emphasis Keeble elaborated on his views by noting that "this act has a positive and distinct personality, and it undertakes to declare that there is a right under this act whenever an employe is injured from the negligence of an employe." Should the attorneys follow Hall and Humphrey's position, Keeble warned, "it would merely temporize the matter. . . . we would just have a series of acts following up this act, if we admit the principle."[4]

In the 1906 conference railroad attorneys focused entirely on the threat of federal regulation under the FELA, ignoring the potential uses of the FELA to escape state regulation. John Hall conceded in his argument that "the practice and the rule of liability are so variant in the different States" that he could not "suggest a course to be pursued by railway attorneys in all cases."[5] But Hall focused his attack on the FELA, not the diverse state rules. Many wanted to get away from the interstate nature of their business as a matter of law, and in this way they hoped to hide from federal regulation. Edward W. Hines's brief, as presented to the conference members, for example, argued: "If Congress has jurisdiction, that jurisdiction is exclusive when Congress has once acted, and it is unreasonable to suppose that it was contemplated by the framers of the Constitution that Congress

Library. Conferees proposed different interpretations of two important recent decisions. The first, *Johnson v. Southern Pacific Company* (196 U.S. 1) in 1904, upheld the constitutionality of the Safety Appliance Act. The other, *Peirce v. Van Dusen* (78 Fed. Rep. 693), was decided in the Sixth District Circuit Court of Appeals by Justice John Marshall Harlan and Judge William Howard Taft, who, as one brief pointed out, "seems to be spokesman for the present administration, and who will likely be a member of the United States Supreme Court, which will pass upon the constitutionality" of the FELA. In that case the court said: "Undoubtedly the whole subject of the liability of interstate railroad companies for the negligence of those in their service may be governed by National legislation, enacted by Congress under its power to regulate commerce among the States." Those who considered the FELA unconstitutional argued this quote was an obiter dictum. See *PRAC* (1906), 254–63.

4. *PRAC* (1906), 55.
5. John I. Hall to H. L. Stone, 16 October 1906, ibid., 306.

should have power to take from a State the right to regulate the liability of employers to employes performing duties wholly within the State merely because some part of the business of the employer might be interstate commerce, or even because some duty of the employe might incidentally relate to interstate commerce."[6] The majority of attorneys, it seems, gave their attention to avoiding or dismantling the FELA without regard for the act's possible benefits in the face of conflicting state statutes limiting railroad defenses. Their determination revealed the importance they assigned to federal removal as a tactic to defeat personal injury suits. In federal court, railroad defendants accrued tremendous advantages over plaintiffs, and any limitation of their power in this arena drew sharp protest from these railroad attorneys.

The 1906 FELA, railroad attorneys quickly pointed out, covered a wide range of employees, even many not engaged in interstate commerce. In cases taken to the Supreme Court, railroad lawyers challenged the breadth of the act. Their strategy succeeded, and in 1908 the Supreme Court declared the 1906 FELA unconstitutional. It overstepped Congress' power to regulate interstate commerce by including under its provisions employees engaged strictly in intrastate business.[7]

Congress moved quickly to enact another FELA with proper limitations. The 1908 FELA's swift passage inspired a similar conference, one that demonstrated the complexities of the federal-state regulatory dilemma for the railroad attorneys, particularly those in the South. Like its predecessor, the new act abolished the fellow-servant rule in federal courts, substituted comparative negligence for contributory negligence, and abrogated assumption-of-risk and contributory negligence defenses when defendants violated a federal safety act. Moreover, the FELA outlawed contracts that in any way limited liability on the part of employers. Its constitutional strength and the changed political atmosphere in the southern states combined to reverse most southern railroad attorneys' position on both the constitutionality and potential utility of the act.[8]

In the 1890s a number of southern states limited employers' defenses by statute, but those few early efforts did little to change the overwhelm-

---

6. Edward W. Hines, quoted ibid., 222.

7. The Employers' Liability Cases, 207 U.S. 463.

8. See Edward A. Purcell, *Litigation and Inequality: Federal Diversity Jurisdiction in Industrial America, 1870–1948* (New York: Oxford University Press, 1992), 165.

ing supremacy of the common law as the rule in most personal injury cases. Mississippi, for example, adjusted its common law liability rules as early as its 1890 constitution. The limitations, though, amounted to an elaborate vice-principle rule to replace the harsh fellow-servant doctrine—an effort to redefine fellow servants to exclude company employees in positions of authority over the injured worker. It did not touch the concepts of contributory negligence and assumption of risk. Further revisions in 1896 and 1898, moreover, grandfathered pending personal injury suits before 1898—a legislative victory for the railroads. Around 1900, though, even the common law's doctrines weakened, as judges questioned some concepts and new doctrine entered the legal debate. In 1906 statutory limitations of the fellow-servant rule, assumption of risk, and contributory negligence tumbled out of state legislatures. Employers' liability bills, more broad and sweeping than previous vice-principle limitations, appeared in nearly every southern state legislature in 1906 and 1907.[9]

Many states tried to prevent railroads from removing their cases to federal court, where, according to state commissioners and regulators, railroads found a friendly environment. Interstate-railroad lawyers jealously protected their company's rights of removal to federal court; they offered consistent testimony to the advantages of removal in all cases. When the Kentucky legislature took up discussion in 1898 of railroad regulatory bills, including a corporate domiciliation bill, the Illinois Central's district attorneys in that state grew worried. "It is very important to us to remove cases to the Federal Court," they explained to James Fentress, "especially when actions for damages for personal injuries are brought in the granger counties and especially in Western Kentucky. . . . The same is true where the injury is caused by the negligence of fellow servants."[10]

Railroad attorneys' use of removal to federal court offended some because it smacked of special privilege. One angry North Carolina attorney,

9. Mississippi Constitutional Amendment, 1890, sec. 193 (codified 1892, sec. 3559); Mississippi Acts, 1896, p. 96, and 1898, p. 82. For other vice-principle limitations, see Alabama Code 1897, secs. 1749–50 (1885); Texas Acts, 1891, p. 25—compare with Texas Acts, 1909, p. 279, for an employers' liability act. Only Georgia abrogated the fellow-servant rule entirely before 1900—see Georgia Code, 1895, secs. 2297, 2323, (1856)—but its statute was weak, and it passed an employers' liability act in 1909 (Acts, 1909, p. 160). See Lawrence Friedman, *A History of American Law* (New York: Simon & Schuster, 1973), 480–84.

10. Pirtle & Trabue to James Fentress, 24 January 1898, Fish Out Letters, vol 34, p. 152, ICRR-NL.

for example, delivered his opinion on the Southern Railway's use of the federal court: "I have long known that this giant octopus which is now in the toils of the law, stood in open defiance of the laws of this free state, and that the aid of the inferior federal judiciary could be invoked at its bidding to protect it in its bold resistance of the law."[11]

The 1908 railroad attorneys' conference met in Atlantic City, New Jersey, in mid-July. It attracted more conferees than the 1906 meeting, but it remained an L&N Railroad Company–inspired and southern-dominated event. L&N general counsel Henry L. Stone again served as chair of the conference. The sessions again revolved around L&N prepared questions concerning the FELA. Conference members spoke openly about the ramifications of the new law. In these detailed discussions, the southern conferees revealed just how much the legal environment of their states had shifted. One attorney contested the new act's constitutionality on the basis that it failed to distinguish between hazardous and non-hazardous employment, therefore promoting an "unreasonable classification." He explained: "I am fully aware that all the uncertainties, and all the odds are against us, not the least of which is that courts reflect the public idea and the public sentiment; and we are no longer discussing an evolution of the common law or an evolution of the civil law on the question of master and servant, but we are face to face with a widespread demand that something along this line be done."[12] Most participants agreed that the Supreme Court, having struck down the first FELA, would hold the new act constitutional. Most of the southern attorneys agreed that the public was against them.

The attorneys' initial and adversarial impulse to defeat the FELA, so apparent in 1906, dissolved into ways to use the federal law to escape more onerous state regulations. After some initial discussion among the conferees on the nature of interstate commerce, Birmingham & Atlantic Railroad attorney L. Z. Rosser cast the FELA's utility in stark terms:

> I hope the United States courts will open a refuge to which I can escape. We have been undertaking to flee from the United States court as an evil, whereas it ought to be a refuge. . . . Theoretically, the United States regu-

11. R. B. McLaughlin to Benjamin F. Long, 19 July 1907, Benjamin F. Long Papers, SHC-UNC.

12. *PRAC* (1908), 100.

lates interstate traffic, while the State is potential in the matter of intrastate traffic. Practically, however, because in interstate traffic the power of Congress is supreme and exclusive, a train carrying interstate and intrastate traffic must abide Federal regulation. . . . In view of the recent trend of State legislation, now almost always antagonistic to railroads, the established validity of this Act will work only one substantial change: Federal jurisdiction will be enlarged to take in suits of employes when damages are sought for personal injuries. . . . If this Act will enable us to try actions for personal injuries to employes in the Federal courts, then I welcome, rather than regret, its speedy operation.[13]

Rosser, then, hoped to use the federal courts to "escape from local prejudice and influence."

While some New York and New England railroad attorneys feared the onset of socialism in Rosser's suggestions, southern attorneys generally applauded his opportunistic view of the FELA. As general solicitor for the Chesapeake & Ohio, Henry T. Wickham expected the conferees to attack the constitutionality of the new act and "was very much surprised" to find "the consensus of opinion" against such a course. Wickham, though, confessed to his concern with the grasping power of Virginia's State Corporation Commission over intrastate commerce and his efforts to escape it with claims of interstate business. "We have them, at our homes," Wickham dramatized, "very much closer to us and very much more vigorous at times than the Interstate Commerce Commission, including daily association, which is exceedingly unpleasant at times." After an investigation of C&O traffic, Wickham told the conference, his office discovered that 85 percent of it was interstate and only 15 percent intrastate. Although the ratio applied to most large systems, Wickham was surprised to find that on his road 85 percent of its customers engaged in intrastate business, while only 15 percent carried on interstate commerce. For Wickham these inverse ratios

13. L. Z. Rosser, quoted ibid., 119. Some southern attorneys continued in the opening conference session to focus on the 1906 venue of attack on the FELA. Expecting to "prepare for war" with the FELA, John B. Keeble, the 1906 session's outspoken advocate of resistance to the FELA, was disappointed with the turn toward accepting this regulation.

characterized the nature of the regulatory dilemma for most railroads: the vast majority of the railroads' traffic was interstate commerce while the vast majority of their customers' business was intrastate. As for the FELA, Wickham suggested "that we should contend, as far as we consistently can . . . that the Interstate Commerce Commission, the Interstate Commerce Act and the power of Congress are supreme and paramount and exclusive."[14]

Since many of the participants considered the act a possible venue for escaping the vagaries of state practices, the focus of the meeting turned to procedural questions under its provisions. Most railroad attorneys thought the FELA exclusive "and that actions thereunder can be maintained only in the Federal courts." Based on these conclusions, one Kentucky district attorney for the L&N suggested removal to federal courts as the wisest procedure:

> I think it is obvious that it is to the interest of the carriers that cases arising under the Act shall be tried in the Federal courts, rather than in the State courts, not only because of the manner of instructing the juries by Federal judges, in contrast with the manner of instructing juries by State judges . . . but also by reason of the fact that the juries in the Federal courts are drawn from a wider area and are likely not to be affected by local prejudices, as they are when drawn in the home county of the plaintiff.[15]

The Kentucky state counsel for the Chicago, New Orleans & Texas Pacific agreed with his L&N counterpart but considered the plaintiffs' attorney the real threat in the state courts. "Very frequently the lawyer who brings these cases runs the court," he pointed out. "He is the little political boss in his neighborhood, and almost invariably that same fellow has a greater fear and dread of the United States court than any other thing that you can present to him." According to this attorney, the greater expertise

14. Henry T. Wickham, quoted ibid., 140–45 Edward D. Robbins, New York counsel for the New Haven & Hartford Railroad, worried that "if you once vest the whole power over the railroads of this country in the hands of one centralized government, a national party may be got up that will sweep us into New Zealandism." Ibid., 120.

15. *PRAC* (1908), 234–35.

of the federal judges combined with the greater stakes in federal courts to eliminate the local plaintiffs' attorneys' advantages, to make witnesses testify truthfully, and to secure a fairer trial for the railroads. Procedural rules added to the railroads' preference for federal courts; in Kentucky, for example, only nine of twelve jurors rendered a verdict, but the federal courts required unanimity.[16]

Not all southern conferees found it necessary to flee the state courts; indeed, some considered them as fair and equitable as the federal courts. Gregory L. Smith, L&N district attorney in Mississippi and Mobile County, Alabama, found state judges favorable to railroad attorneys. Moreover, he suggested, "The lawyers who represent damage suits have not, as a general rule, the same confidence of the juries that the lawyers who represent the railroad companies have. They have not . . . the same professional standing in their communities, and they do not have as much influence, in spite of the fact that there is a prejudice against corporations." Smith's boss, Henry L. Stone, chairman of the conference and L&N general counsel, interrupted his discourse to disagree: "While that may be true [for the district], I do not think his statement will apply to all the counties in the State of Alabama." Smith conceded, though, the intimidating power of the federal courts and judges on personal injury lawyers, witnesses, and jurors, adding that the damage lawyers avoided federal court with damage claims just under the $2,000 floor: "So that if we kill a man we practically have a limitation upon the amount of our liability."[17]

The irony of southern attorneys denying states' rights and seeking refuge in the federal courts was not lost on chairman Stone. One Mississippi attorney summed up his remarks with a call for a consistent procedure for local attorneys' removal of damage cases to federal court: "I believe it is to be to the interest of the public service corporations in this country to have their affairs administered as completely as they possibly can, in the matter of control, by the Federal Government." In response to this statement, Stone quipped, "And you come from Mississippi?" The Mississip-

---

16. John Galvin, quoted ibid., 235.

17. Gregory L. Smith, quoted ibid., 248–49. Smith's testimony received support from another Mississippi attorney, James H. Neville, general counsel for the Gulf & Ship Island Railroad, which ran wholly within the state. He had "little cause of complaint against juries of my State . . . but I know I have brethren representing corporations who have had a widely different experience" (253). Despite this agreement, he concurred that the federal courts inspired fear and gave more fair verdicts: "[I] know that I have seen, much better results in the Federal court" (254).

pian blamed the politicized state railroad commission's onerous regulations for turning him into a federal booster.[18]

As the conference wrapped up its discussions, a fragile consensus emerged in favor of using the FELA to the advantage of the railroads. Even those who considered the FELA unconstitutional and advocated a direct challenge to it welcomed some federal regulation in this area. "I would rather have one boss than forty-odd bosses," the L&N's George W. Jones confessed. "I shall welcome the day when the Federal Government shall wipe out every vestige of State rights in connection with the regulation of interstate carriers." Considering the likelihood of state legislatures' completely dismantling railroad defenses, James P. Helm, general counsel for the Henderson & St. Louis Railway, motioned that the attorneys' committee consider whether "we are fighting for something for which we ought not to fight." "In other words," Helm clarified, "do we want to fight against the Federal jurisdiction, and fight to save the State courts' jurisdiction, or as much of it as we can, or should we welcome the chance to seek the Federal forum?" L. Z. Rosser, who first raised the issue, seconded the motion, stating simply: "I have a profound conviction that the learned lawyer who aids in declaring this Act unconstitutional is an enemy of every railroad in the United States."[19]

Railroad attorneys quickly dissected the FELA after the July conference. Word spread of its impact on personal injury suits and the best strategies for turning it to their advantage. Baker & Botts directed all division and local attorneys of Texas railroads to remove any damage suit to federal court under the FELA. "Under this procedure," they advised, "all questions of law will go up to the Supreme Court of the United States on writ of error and we will interpose another obstacle in the way of the damage litigant." The attorneys turned the FELA to their advantage. "With the knowledge that these cases can be taken to the Supreme Court of the United States," a Santa Fe attorney with smug assuredness reminded his agent, "the tendency will be to induce more voluntary and advantageous settlements. Assuredly so when these gentlemen find that they cannot litigate by a pauper's affidavit or on a credit in the Supreme Court of the United States."[20]

18. *PRAC* (1908), 257.

19. Ibid., 285, 303–304.

20. Baker & Botts to "All Division and Local Attorneys," 17 July 1908, Box 38, Folder 17, SFRR-HMRC; A. H. Culwell to W. L. Alexander, 15 April 1909, Box 36, Folder 9, ibid.

When states began passing employers' liability acts, railroad attorneys explored the ramifications of the changes in the legal environment. For the most part, they sought means to evade the burdens of this legislation. Relying on removal to federal court to wear down their opposition, the lawyers looked for means to differentiate between inter- and intrastate business. Some jobs in the railroad business appeared more directly connected to interstate commerce than others. "We are inclined to think," a Santa Fe attorney explained, "that the better reasoning is that if a car repairer is actually repairing a car that is engaged in interstate commerce which loaded with a shipment destined from one point in this state to a point in another state and while so engaged is hurt, we may take advantage of the federal act." These attorneys even considered whether section laborers' cases might be removable under the logic that interstate things travel over the tracks on which they work. They concluded that these cases might not qualify for removal, remarking that "fortunately, it is not very often the case that an accident to one of these employees is very serious."[21]

On advice from their legal departments, railroad managers issued new directives to modify policy: "It has been concluded that it is highly desirable to prosecute as many of these cases as possible in and through the Federal Courts, and to do this, it is necessary for a federal question to be raised somewhere in the proceedings, and for that reason it is desired to ascertain in case of injury, to one of our employees as to whether or not the injured party was engaged in handling interstate business, regardless of whether the party is out on line between stations or doing switching in the yard." The new policy called for prompt reports on the type of commerce involved in each injury. In other words, in a switching yard coupling accident, the railroad attorneys sought and gained removal if they could document that the contents of the cars being coupled by the injured workman were bound for another state. In this situation railroads possessed even greater advantages, which derived from their ownership of the facts. According to one Texas attorney, "we want to make this Texas [employers' liability] act so obnoxious as that howling mob, to-wit: legislature labor committee that caused its passage, will ask to have it repealed at the next session."[22]

Not all situations favored removal to federal court under the FELA for

21. A H. Culwell to W. L. Alexander, 26 April 1909, Box 36, Folder 9, ibid.
22. F T. Pettibone, general manager, to W. E. Maxson, general superintendent, 6 May 1909, A. H. Culwell to Madden & Trulove, 30 April 1909, ibid.

railroads. Texas railroads labored under that state's consolidation act, which prevented removal to another state. In El Paso, Texas, for example, several high verdicts in personal injury cases came out of the federal court in 1910. Baker & Botts's district attorneys there evinced little surprise:

> The history of litigation at this place in the federal court bears out the statement that the largest verdicts that have been rendered here have been rendered in the federal court. The jurors in that court are almost without exception summoned from the eastern end of the district, from small cattle towns, many of whom have had claims against the various companies for shipment of cattle, freight, etc. . . . Many of these juries in the federal court are composed of men none of whom reside in either the city or county of El Paso, and as a rule are composed of the ignorant class which will likely go to extremes whenever the opportunity presents itself.[23]

Other attorneys confirmed this assessment. The Texas & Pacific Railway's attorney, for example, counseled against removal in El Paso, "as the class of jurors which is drawn from the out-laying counties, are in the main, an indifferent lot, as compared to the class of jurors they get in the city of El Paso." The Santa Fe attorneys concurred, concluding that "we will keep out of the Federal Court unless forced there by original suit; in which event, under the present status of the FELA, we will be forced to remain there and try the case."[24]

In 1910 an amendment to the FELA shut down the railroad attorneys' avenues for removal. Under this modification once an FELA case came before any court, federal or state, it remained in that jurisdiction. Railroad attorneys, of course, challenged the anti-removal amendment directly and looked for ways around it, filing removal petitions when there was diversity of citizenship. The Supreme Court, though, backed up several lower fed-

23. Beall, Kemp & Ward to Baker & Botts, 25 April 1910, Box 11L, Folder "El Paso DA," BBHC-RU. According to these attorneys, the plaintiff's lawyer in one case was "a man who recently came here named Johnson, who, we understand, was a former railway engineer and who lost his arm in an accident, and subsequently took up the study and practice of law."

24. W. L. Hall to Baker & Botts, 21 May 1910, W. W. Turney to Baker & Botts, not dated, Box 11L, BBHC-RU.

eral court decisions and construed the amendment to mean that no cases under the FELA could be removed.[25]

After 1910 personal injury cases under the FELA evolved into what one historian has called "another high stakes litigation form." Employees chose state courts as their preferred forum for FELA cases. To qualify for FELA provisions, though, injured employees needed to prove that they were engaged in interstate commerce. As state worker's compensation laws developed across the South after 1911, injured employees found a more secure avenue for marginal claims. Under the FELA, unlike workers' compensation statutes, plaintiffs sued for unlimited damages but had little further recourse against an adverse decision. As a result, according to legal scholar and historian Edward Purcell,

> plaintiffs with strong cases on the merits stretched for an interstate commerce allegation to avoid a small workmen's compensation award; those with weak claims denied that they were working in interstate commerce, preferring the certainty of workmen's compensation to the unacceptably high risks of an unpromising lawsuit. Employers followed the converse strategy. Pushing a weak claim within the ambit of interstate commerce could force a plaintiff to settle cheaply or abandon his suit, whereas establishing that a meritorious claim arose in intrastate commerce could push liability onto the state's workmen's compensation system, reduce the worker's recovery drastically, and save the employer many thousands of dollars.[26]

Southern states enacted workmen's compensation laws slowly beginning in 1913. By 1925 all but six states—Arkansas, Florida, Mississippi, Missouri, North Carolina, and South Carolina—had enacted some form of workmen's compensation. In these holdout states injured railroad workers chose either a state claim or action under the FELA. Both venues were risky and expensive for workers and neither ensured the relatively predictable results of workmen's compensation. Louisiana, Oklahoma, Texas, West Virginia, and Kentucky passed workmen's compensation laws before

---

25. See Purcell, *Litigation and Inequality*, 166.
26. Ibid., 168–69.

World War I, while Alabama, Georgia, Tennessee, and Virginia followed immediately after the war. Because these statutes did not apply to employees engaged in interstate commerce, the courts drew the line between inter- and intrastate activities. In determining this line, railroads as ever held the advantage in their control of the facts.[27]

In the lottery that personal injury litigation had become, railroad attorneys continued to rely on the informal legal process for advantages over employees. Faced at the turn of the century with increasing litigation and a specialized personal injury bar, they turned with increased regularity to company doctors, claim agents, tactical delays, removal to federal court, and the use of expert testimony. When the first FELA passed, railroad attorneys fought it as unconstitutional. After the southern states enacted broad Progressive reform in 1906 and 1907, railroad attorneys viewed the 1908 FELA with greater appreciation for its utility and began to use it to keep their cases in federal court.

"Regulation has run riot," T. M. Cunningham told the Georgia Bar Association in 1908. Cunningham, general counsel for the Central of Georgia, estimated that the Congress and the state legislatures passed over 15,000 laws annually. He deemed this a "legislative debauch." Interstate railroads, in particular, faced dizzying regulation, so much that Cunningham considered compliance a herculean task.[28]

The complications of overlapping state and federal regulation led some railroad attorneys to call for greater federal control over the industry. A maze of state regulations and commissions bedeviled these attorneys, and by 1908 many considered the national oversight of the ICC preferable to the status quo. Hiram Glass, for example, presented a paper to the Texas Bar Association in 1908 advocating a stronger, more effective ICC. A prominent railroad attorney from Texarkana, Glass became Texas attorney

27. For each state's workmen's compensation statute, see William R Schneider, *Workmen's Compensation Law* (St. Louis: Thomas Book Co., 1922); also, for an overview, see Gustav F. Michelbacher and Thomas M. Nial, *Workmen's Compensation Insurance* (New York: McGraw-Hill Book Co., 1925).

28. T. M. Cunningham, "The Use of Injunctions by Federal Courts as to State Laws," *Georgia Bar Association Proceedings* (1908): 157–58.

and lobbyist for the principal railways in Austin in 1910. In his opinion, the question of the day no longer centered on whether or not commissions should control railroad rates, but which commissions.

Glass lamented the confusion created under the federalized regulatory system. As an example, he examined the newly passed Federal Employers' Liability Act and compared actions under it with those under Texas common and statutory law. In an important distinction, Texas law allowed the surviving wife, children, and parents to recover damages, while the FELA limited recovery to the wife and children. In another example, Glass pointed out, federal law mandated a maximum sixteen-hour continuous workday for trainmen, while Texas law limited the hours of consecutive service to fourteen. Comparing other statutes, Glass concluded: "It is not difficult to imagine what a labyrinth and maze of inequalities might be encountered if it should be attempted to carry the comparison through all the States. . . . That the railroads of the country have been seriously handicapped in the operation of their roads, and put to much expense in endeavoring to comply with the various and conflicting laws of Congress and the different States, can not be denied."[29]

What Glass objected to was not regulation but conflicting and overlapping regulation. "Laws on the subject should be uniform," Glass averred, "and the railroads should not be compelled to attempt compliance with conflicting laws, or be subject to conflicting jurisdictions." As an example, Glass examined the fate of the Kansas City Southern Railway, which with its Texas line, the Texarkana & Fort Smith Railway, owned a continuous line from Kansas City to Port Arthur, Texas. The line, though, ran through six different states; moreover, it entered and exited three of these states a total of six separate times. Similar to most roads, the Kansas City Southern carried and classified only 15 percent of its traffic as intrastate, but the road faced regulation from six state commissions. To comply with the various commissions in each state, it compiled separate reports and maintained separate accounts on its minimal intrastate traffic. Worst of all, Glass pointed out, the public bore the cost of these conflicting and overlapping regulations through higher rates. No state would give up its powers to regulate this commerce, Glass warned, but only Congress and the ICC could enact uniform regulation for what had become an obviously national, interstate business.

29. Hiram Glass, "Railroads—National Versus State Control," *Texas Bar Association Proceedings* (1908): 193.

When Congress passed the Mann-Elkins Act in 1910, it intended to resolve the tension between state rate regulation and interstate business. After its passage, the railroad attorneys met in another L&N–inspired associational conference to discuss the most important federal regulatory act since 1887. As they had in 1906 and 1908 on the FELA, the attorneys debated the constitutionality and the meaning of the act for their companies. The Mann-Elkins Act, like the Hepburn Act of 1906, fell short of full empowerment for the commission; instead, it burdened the commission with lukewarm authority and pressed the railroads into continued competition. Under the act, pooling remained prohibited, as did long-and-short-haul discrimination. The act gave the commission authority to determine whether rates were "just and reasonable" without setting any guidelines for determining those decisions and created a special Commerce Court to hear appeals of commission decisions. In its final form the Mann-Elkins Act reflected the fundamental division within Congress over the legislature's power to oversee railroad regulation. Though both Presidents Roosevelt and Taft worked for a balance of power between railroads and shippers in the administrative process, neither successfully prevented the eventual imbalance favoring the shippers.[30]

Some attorneys considered the act an unconstitutional delegation of legislative power to the ICC. "It seems to me," remarked Henry T. Wickham, general solicitor for the C&O, "to be an unconstitutional power. . . . we are presented here with the question as to whether we are going to submit absolutely, to lie down, or whether we have got any rights left at all under the Constitution." Others found sound constitutional basis for the act's delegation of rate review authority to the commission but feared the commission's amalgamation of power. The Southern Railway's assistant general counsel considered the commission capable of creating a schedule of maximum rates, using its limited review authority: "It can take it up piece by piece, as they are doing, and practically come to the making of a schedule of maximum rates. But under this Act, of course, they have power simply to deal with individual rates. I doubt very seriously whether that is not taking away the management of the company."[31]

---

30. See Stephen Skowronek, *Building a New American State: The Expansion of National Administrative Capacities, 1877–1920* (Cambridge, Eng.: Cambridge University Press, 1982), 263–71.

31. Henry T. Wickham, quoted in *PRAC* (1910), 42; C. B. Northrop, quoted ibid., 51.

Of particular concern to the railroad attorneys, the long-and-short-haul discrimination provision received widespread attention. The act expressly forbade such discrimination, but it provided for relief from immediate enforcement by petition to the ICC. The attorneys picked apart the language of the act in an effort to understand which discriminatory rates might be allowed to stand and under what conditions. On these matters they came to little general agreement, leaving these decisions for the advisement of each attorney to his client.[32]

On a clause embedded in the long-and-short-haul provision, southern railroad attorneys voiced grave concern for the increased power of the commission over competitive rates. The act required that for an upward change in rates a railroad needed to file an application and to clearly demonstrate changed conditions other than the elimination of water competition. "In many sections of this country . . . take it in the valleys of the rivers that make from the Atlantic coast into the interior of the South—all rail rates are made in competition, to a greater or less extent with water rates," the Southern Railway's special counsel and Washington lobbyist explained. "And so the question is one of very great—I might say almost vast—importance." He argued that unless water competition were destroyed or eliminated, a railroad need not apply to the commission to raise its rates; therefore, only when the railroad eliminated water competition in a rate war did the road need to show the commission in its application changed conditions that justified the increase.[33]

Henry L. Stone, general counsel of the L&N, disagreed, suggesting that in all cases the railroad needed to show changed conditions, even when water competition remained. According to the Southern's lobbyist, Congress intended no such construction of the act. Alabama Great Southern general counsel Edward Colston agreed: "I believe that there was a condition—a well-known condition—in this country; a condition that was made rank and notorious by conduct such as (again without intending to be offensive) was carried on by the great trusts of crushing out competition. Competition is regarded in the law as a thing of extreme value, something that is to be preserved. The people seem to think they have a vested right in the preservation of competition. And it was to preserve competition that this provision of this law, in my judgment, was enacted." The

32. See *PRAC* (1910), 211–57.
33. R. Walton Moore, quoted ibid., 285.

attorneys were unable to agree on the meaning of the section, so they deferred judgment. One attorney summed up his reasons for supporting the Southern's position: "If we adopt the other construction, that we have got to go to the Commission . . . you are going to lose thousands of dollars to your companies before you can get the rates reduced, and . . . you make a good deal more money by raising your rates . . . and taking the chances of having to pay a fine or two."[34]

Near the end of the conference, some attorneys suggested striking back at the shippers, whom they considered responsible for the new regulatory act. When the attorneys debated whether to contest a provision requiring the railroads to reveal information about shipments upon request, Edgar J. Rich of the Boston & Maine answered no: "I think here is an opportunity to make these agitators, these commercial bodies, sit up and think." Missouri Pacific general counsel James C. Jeffrey agreed: "I think nine-tenths of all our troubles we have today . . . is due to these Chambers of Commerce, and Merchants' Exchanges, and trade organizations like them. Every time the traffic man of a railroad leaves the employ of a railroad he goes to one of these bodies and tries to see what trouble he can make in the railroad business." Ed Colston, though, likened their approach to that of kicking a hornets' nest. The power of the opposing interests impressed Colston, who warned his fellow conferees: "You will find that these great commercial bodies in the United States exercise a powerful, tremendous influence with the people that make the laws. And I am not in favor of any construction of a statute whose construction is professedly based upon an effort to hit back at that class of the community, because they are a powerful and influential body of people." Colston blamed the numerous federal regulatory acts on the abuse of power by the trusts, particularly the Standard Oil and American Tobacco trusts, which "would go and bribe the agents of railroads to let them know the names of the men that were getting goods in a certain community and they would avail themselves of that information to advance their own business dealings in an improper way." Stonewalling the commission and the commercial organizations, Colston thought, would bring nothing but worse legislation.[35]

34. Edward Colston, quoted ibid., 303; E. B. Peirce, quoted ibid., 307.
35. Edgar J. Rich, quoted ibid., 516; James C. Jeffrey, quoted ibid., 516; Edward L. Colston, quoted ibid., 517–18.

The conference broke without resolution on many of the most important questions. Deferred for examination by an executive committee, these questions inspired active debate but little clear consensus. Unable to move beyond basic agreement on the fundamentals of the Mann-Elkins Act, the attorneys reserved the most important decisions for assessment within their own companies.

They had little choice. For the transportation industry the Mann-Elkins Act deepened the commitment to enforced competition among the carriers. The ICC's new mandate made no room for either rate increases or pooling. After the rate hearings of 1910, the landscape of regulation appeared even more unfriendly to carriers than before the passage of Mann-Elkins. Shipper interests, represented by Progressive attorney Louis Brandeis, fought the railroads' requested rate increases. Brandeis's argument used the scientific management principles of Frederick Winslow Taylor to expose the railroad companies as inefficient, bloated, and weak corporate structures. Presented with a clear argument from Brandeis, a coherent rationale to regulate the railroads, and a mandate to hold down rates, the newly empowered ICC denied the rate increase. Impressed with Brandeis's case, the commission retained him as special counsel after 1910, a clear indication to the railroads of the commission's policy direction. Between 1910 and 1917 the commission approved only one rate increase, despite repeated requests for relief.[36]

By 1916 railroad attorneys, such as S. T. Bledsoe of the Santa Fe, considered the "system of regulation" as one that "causes continuous conflict, controversy and litigation." Using Progressive language in their defense, railroad attorneys, such as Bledsoe, decried the inefficiency of the regulatory system: "That reasonable, just and uniform regulation of transportation companies . . . is necessary, no right-thinking man will now deny. That unreasonable, unnecessary, unjust and conflicting regulation impairs efficiency, reduces earning power and serves no useful purposes whatever, no one will gainsay. Every dollar unnecessarily expended as a result of such regulation means . . . a decrease in service efficiency or an increase in transportation rates." As states vied for commercial supremacy through railroad regulation, Bledsoe concluded that "the protection and freedom of commerce against discriminating State regulation must be found, if at all, in national authority."[37]

36. Stephen Skowronek, *Building a New American State*, 267–71.
37. S. T. Bledsoe, "The Commerce Clause of the Federal Constitution and Legislation

The regulatory commissioners, though, also recognized the importance of the railway interests in the American economy. They wanted to encourage development and were not lining up to hurt the railroad corporations. "The great railroad systems," one commissioner in 1905 pointed out, "have made mighty strides in the development of every enterprise." And he cautioned against those "who seemed to be dwelling upon the fact that there was some demarcation between the interests of the people and the interests of the railroads." Railroad commissioners also realized that they needed to balance these interests, not crusade against the railroad companies as monopolistic monsters. R. Hudson Burr addressed the 1911 National Association on the topic: "It has been long recognized that among the chief beneficiaries of the legislation establishing these bodies have been the carriers themselves."[38]

Ari and Olive Hoogenboom pointed out the lag between the movement to regulate and the reasons for regulation in the railroad industry. The Progressives, they note, led many Americans to the idea that federal or even state regulation of the industry was necessary and good. "By the time they had convinced the public that action was needed," they argued, "their solution no longer fitted the railroad situation, which differed radically from the late nineteenth century." Railroads, it turned out, were no longer overbuilt, overcapitalized behemoths, but undernourished, rickety enterprises. They needed new capital to repair and upgrade track and equipment to handle the rising tonnage of shipping after the turn of the century. Meanwhile, they faced reform efforts to lower rates and watched as the general level of freight rates dropped to a historic low in 1916.[39]

By late 1916 the failure of the Wilson administration's attempt to reexamine railroad regulation paled in comparison with the inadequacy of the national rail system to handle war preparations. As the demands of U.S. involvement in World War I required coordination in the transportation industry to carry the glut of freight loads, the Wilson administration called first for voluntary cooperation among the railroads. At the same time,

Enacted Pursuant Thereto, Applicable to Railway Transportation," *Texas Bar Association Proceedings* (1916), 302.

38. *National Association of Railroad Commissioners: Proceedings of the Seventeenth Annual Convention* (Washington. D.C.: Government Printing House, 1905), 73; *National Association of Railroad Commissioners; Proceedings of the Twenty-third Annual Convention* (Washington, D.C.: Government Printing House, 1911), 18.

39. Ari Hoogenboom and Olive Hoogenboom, *A History of the ICC: From Panacea to Palliative* (New York: W. W. Norton, 1976), 40.

however, the attorney general reminded the carriers of his intention to enforce anti-trust and anti-pooling laws. The administration's mixed signals left railroad managers unsure and indecisive. By 1917 the severity of the transportation problem induced the president to nationalize the rail industry, and in 1918 Walker D. Hines, former L&N counsel and president of the Santa Fe Railroad, replaced William McAdoo as director general of the United States Railroad Administration. Under government control, the priority shifted from appeasing small shippers with rate control to moving freight and coordinating carload shipments for the war effort.[40]

After the war, of course, the country faced a resurgence of the same long-contested issues between the railroads and their adversaries—except in 1920 the participants possessed the experience of war-time government ownership. Few, especially not the railroads, wanted long-term government control, but agreement on the shape of the railroad regulatory landscape came less easily. Small shippers in the South considered government policy in war years overly favorable to the large railroad systems and they looked for a return to the ICC's sensitivity to their concerns. Railroads, of course, welcomed a new order that would include pooling and more flexible rate structures.

A several-month-long congressional debate produced the Transportation Act of 1920, which moved away from the old emphasis on enforced competition toward a regulated cartel. The act permitted pooling and encouraged consolidation in an effort to create a small number of large, competitive systems. According to one political scientist, the act "framed a new order in the relations between state and society in industrial America. . . . Nationalism superseded localism."[41]

40. Skowronek, *Building a New American State*, 274–75; see also Walker D. Hines, *War History of American Railroads* (New Haven: Yale University Press, 1928).

41. Skowronek, *Building a New American State*, 283; see also Maury Klein, "Competition and Regulation: The Railroad Model," *Business History Review* 64 (summer 1990): 319, for an analysis of why "the 1920 act came a generation too late." Klein suggested that the act, among its other deficiencies, forced strong roads to absorb and maintain weak ones—something that all large systems after the experience of the 1880s wanted to avoid. In addition, of course, Klein documented the rise and effect of other forms of transportation, especially cars and trucks, on the railroads.

NINE

The Changed Law Business

Railroad attorneys across the South observed their clients' effect on the marketplace of the law business. The first and most prominent interstate corporations in the region, railroads fostered and perpetuated a divided bar. District attorneys for the railroads struggled with the new circumstances of their corporate retention. Often their struggles revolved around their salaries and their independence. When Baker & Botts sent its annual legal report for each Texas line in the system to the Southern Pacific's general counsel in New York, the firm argued for a salary increase for its Houston & Texas Central work. Their $6,000 retainer, they pointed out, had not changed in years; in the meantime, the roads' litigation had dramatically increased. Other systems, moreover, paid their state attorneys $8,000, furnished clerical help, and provided for an assistant. Finally, Baker & Botts faced dwindling outside business. "The fact is," they stated plainly, "that we could do very much more general practice but for the impression that our time is devoted wholly to the business of these companies. Of course, our general practice is always subordinate to our railroad practice and we give the railroad companies our first and best service."[1]

The firm knew how easily it could lose its independence and come to rely on the railroad for business. If potential clients had the impression that Baker & Botts did railroad work exclusively, they might take their business

1. Baker & Botts to General Thomas H. Hubbard, 10 March 1897, Box 11L, Folder 2, BBHC-RU.

elsewhere. Appearances were important in client development, and the firm did not want to surrender its independence entirely. The railroad companies, on the other hand, gained a form of in-house counsel by fostering such dependence. As litigation mounted, Baker & Botts and other state-level railroad attorneys tried to secure greater salary to compensate for lost outside business and the subsequent loss of autonomy.

Baker & Botts and other state attorneys found most of their time swallowed up with supervision of local attorneys. The firm described its "method" for operation of the legal department in Texas: "to . . . advise the local attorneys distinctly as to the evidence and witnesses by which it is to be established, and frequently as to the form of pleadings and as to the authorities, and then to follow the case up closely until finally disposed of." The firm prided itself on close supervision of all casework, and its increasingly corporate practice demanded it. On these grounds Baker & Botts requested $10,000 a year as retainer. The Southern Pacific general counsel relented, agreed to the raise, but demanded expense and hourly billing sheets in the future.[2]

Just as state attorneys suffered from loss of independence in their work for the railroad, other railroad attorneys, especially local attorneys, confronted similar trade-offs. When the Seaboard Air Line Railway wanted to transfer the division counsel from its attorney's firm to him individually, it wanted to do so with a change in compensation. Urging no change, attorney J. Randolph Anderson explained to the railroad's president his difficult circumstances:

> It [salary] is surely not excessive for the work and [time] involved particularly when you consider that the railroad [has] the first claim upon my time and that all other work must [be] . . . up and sacrificed to that of the company, and that the amount [of] railroad work here makes such heavy demands upon my time as [to] deprive me of the

2. Ibid.; General Thomas H. Hubbard to R. S. Lovett, 20 March 1897, Box 11L, Folder 2, BBHC-RU. Galanter and Palay point out that billable hours became the norm in the 1960s. Before then, most corporate law firms kept a loose record of time but did not itemize their bills to clients. Marc Galanter and Thomas M. Palay, *Tournament of Lawyers: The Transformation of the Big Law Firm* (Chicago: University of Chicago Press, 1991), 35. Railroads in the late 1890s were concerned strictly with expenses and variable costs. The legal department was no exception.

chance of building up much if any outside [business]. . . .
I realize fully that the represent[ation] of the company
will prevent me from doing much else or from building
up any outside business to speak of for we have lost most
of our large clients among the big shippers for that reason (as much of their business is against the road).[3]

By 1900 the railroad corporations' demands for specialized legal work
and their increasingly heavy litigation load split the bar into those serving
railroad corporations and those representing individuals or groups, the big
shippers for example, often against railroads.

In an effort to explain the rise of personal injury litigation in Texas
against railroads, Baker & Botts partner Edwin B. Parker pointed out in a
1900 bar association speech that railroads in the South bore some responsibility for the circumstances in which they found themselves. Railroad
corporations, he argued, adopted a no-settlement policy in the 1870s and
1880s with regard to personal injury suits, and, as a consequence, forced
plaintiffs into the courtroom, where railroads held innumerable doctrinal
and fiscal advantages. This no-holds-barred, bare-knuckle approach won
few friends among the citizenry. Heavy verdicts and rampant prejudice,
Parker averred, resulted from railroads' early intransigence and set the
precedent for later cases. In the face of greater claims, mounting litigation,
and changing legal doctrine, railroad corporations switched policy in the
late 1890s to search for settlement at all times. Railroads' desires for out-
of-court settlement, though, met with scorn on the part of a general public
increasingly able to secure large verdicts through the court system and to
exploit a growing, talented, and specialized personal injury bar.[4]

As railroads consolidated in the late 1890s, moreover, local attorneys
who could once play one railroad corporation's offer off another and take
advantage of the considerable business railroads brought to both sides of
the bar often found all lines in their jurisdiction controlled by the same
company. The local attorney either represented the railroad or fought it in
the courts. By 1900 the legal representation of those aligned against the

3. J. Randolph Anderson to John Skelton Williams, 7 July 1902, John Skelton Williams
Papers, UVA.
4. Edwin B. Parker, "Anti-Railroad Personal Injury Litigation in Texas," *Texas Bar Association Proceedings* (1900).

railroad reached a level of competence and size that railroad legal departments restructured their operations and practices to meet this new adversary.

At times railroad companies used questionable tactics to perpetuate a divided bar and a monopoly on legal talent. One Southern Pacific district attorney in Texas, W. B. Garrett, reported to general attorneys Baker & Botts on his efforts to derail a serious personal injury case. Garrett proposed a deal for the plaintiff's attorney: an $8,000 out-of-court settlement in exchange for the plaintiff's attorney keeping the settlement "perfectly quiet," leaving the case on the docket until the court convenes, withdrawing from representing any other cases against the railroad company, and becoming an assistant attorney for the railroad. The plaintiff's attorney agreed to the terms. Although he warned Garrett that he could not assist with one case in which he had been an active participant, this disloyal attorney promised Garrett "some important information in connection with this case." Garrett justified the $8,000 settlement expense to his superiors: "in view of the plaintiff's condition, and in view of the fact that by settlement of this case we will be able to obtain an opportunity for good results during the next court, I cannot help but feel it is a good settlement on the part of the company." For the railroad attorneys, the generous settlement to the injured plaintiff, who was, according to the railroad's surgeon, a "cripple for life," kept a case of admitted negligence out of the hands of the jury. Quiet preserved it from public knowledge and use in the jury room. The plaintiff's lawyer remained a railroad attorney until the 1960s. The railroad attorneys secured long-term victory with short-term settlement loss, a small price to pay.[5]

Railroad attorneys recognized the changes in the legal environment and met them with new organizational efforts to protect their clients' interests. Heavy litigation often led railroad attorneys to hire a claim agent, as the Georgia Pacific did as early as 1888. Railroads carefully guarded their advantages of talent and experience to maintain their supremacy, especially in personal injury litigation. When, for example, C. G. Larew threatened to leave his post as assistant claim agent for the Norfolk & Western in 1906 to practice law, general solicitor Joseph I. Doran created a position for him in the legal department. Doran offered him a position as an assistant local attorney without the usual assignment of a particular county. Doran ex-

---

5. W. B. Garrett to Baker & Botts, 24 March 1904, Box 11L, Folder 2, BBHC-RU.

plained this unusual position to the N&W president. "There is another practical reason why I should prefer to keep Mr. Larew in some way connected with the company and on the staff," Doran wrote confidentially. "The reason is that a man so thoroughly versed and experienced in the avenues of information and methods of investigation of the Claims Department as Mr. Larew could be a most troublesome and dangerous opponent. He would know exactly how to reach the witnesses and learn which of them are adverse to the company in any matter."[6]

The arrival of interstate railroad corporations brought divisive changes to the bar across the local economies of the rural South. In Texas the Santa Fe Railroad searched for an agent to cover affairs in rural Johnson County. State counsel Jonathan Terry's assistant attorney explained, "In a small place like Cleburne where there is not a great deal of litigation outside of suing corporations, you will understand that very naturally all of the bar who are not arrayed with the railroad companies, have a common interest in being allied against it. . . . They [the town lawyers] have really not yet fully appreciated the possibility of railroad claims. . . . Of course, what we want to do is to prevent if possible the development of this appreciation."[7]

Terry's assistant offered the position to a man who, it turned out, wanted to run for sheriff and thought it politically unwise to do such work for a railroad corporation. In testament to the power of the sheriff in small communities, especially the power to pick jurors, the railroad attorneys thought "it is probably more to the company's interest for him to be elected sheriff than it is to be in our service." Several months later, Terry's assistant attorney reported that the opposition attorneys grew more militant and threatened to give the railroad real problems at the bar. Once again, the Santa Fe lawyers sought a claim agent for this hot spot on the line. They considered turning to the sheriff-candidate again but received intelligence from a local source that the man had faked a claim against the road and sued the company five years earlier. As if this were not enough to condemn him, he was related to the county judge and "under his control." In a small, rural county, such choices often grew problematic, and railroads found it a challenge to secure and maintain power in these localities.[8]

6. Joseph I. Doran to L. E. Johnson, 19 February 1906, Subject Files, N&W-VPI.

7. C. K. Lee to Jonathan W. Terry, 16 April 1906, Box 15, Folder 15, SFRR-HMRC.

8. C. K. Lee to Jonathan W. Terry, 10 May 1906, T. J. Lee to Jonathan W. Terry, 19 August 1906, ibid.

A growing anti-railroad litigation struggle faced Baker & Botts in El Paso, Texas. Their district attorneys, Beall & Kemp, expressed concern about the personal injury bar and its mounting success. To ameliorate the El Paso situation, Baker & Botts recommended hiring an agent, "someone who will spend a considerable part of his time about the courthouse; watch cases, mix with the witnesses, find out everything that is going on, thoroughly familiarize himself with the personnel of the juries, their histories, antecedents, prejudices, + c, and see that no 'jobs' are put up against you." In addition to this recommendation, the state attorneys informed their El Paso district counsel of ongoing efforts to divide the bar. Baker & Botts explained "that it will come to pass that all of the attorneys representing the railways and street railways at El Paso, will agree to accept no employment against any other company and then you will be able to cooperate in making common cause against those who bring personal injury cases."[9]

Baker & Botts and the other Texas general attorneys orchestrated an agreement in 1905 to divide further the Texas bar. In exchange for a free pass, local attorneys gave up all suits against any railroad corporation. This "El Paso agreement" demanded unswerving allegiance; railroad local attorneys long barred from taking personal injury suits faced even more stringent limitations under this rule. Texas general attorneys issued orders in 1909 to local attorneys to swear whether they ever took suits against railroads. Some local attorneys took deep offense at the requisite submission, others responded with humor. One zealous local attorney swore his fealty this way: "You bet your ———. Never so long as my head is hot will I bring suit or appear in court as attorney against a railroad over whose line I have been extended the courtesy and favor of a pass. I have never sued a railroad nor appeared in court as an attorney against a railroad on whose line I 'packed a pass.' That's the kind of pass packer I've always been, am now and will ever be."[10]

9. Baker & Botts to Wyndam Kemp, 10 October 1906, Baker & Botts to Beall & Kemp, 4 May 1906, Box 11L, Folder "Austin DA," BBHC-RU.

10. Memorandum, Baker & Botts to all attorneys, 11 August 1909, ibid. See also Joseph I. Doran to L. E. Johnson, 11 July 1904, Subject Files, N&W-VPI, on the appointment of G. A. Wingfield as assistant to local attorney in Roanoke, Virginia. Wingfield became a partner of William Gordon Robertson, longtime N&W local attorney in Roanoke, but he represented an injured brakeman with a pending suit against the company. Doran and other legal department officials debated whether Wingfield could be retained, given his status as a per-

Others, though, balked at the system. One local attorney complained that in nearly the four years he "lost on an average of not less than $750.00 per year in overflow and freight claims." He suggested that the railroads "withdraw their transportation and restore the former status of allowing their local attorneys to bring commercial suits, but not personal injury suits." This local attorney held on for many years, but in 1918 resigned, citing the railroad business as a losing proposition. "We have abided your instructions to take no suits against other railroads," he lamented, "which instructions first applied only to personal injury suits and after a few years to all character of suits for damages, notwithstanding every other firm of railroad lawyers in Dallas so far as we know have uniformly taken damage suits against roads not represented by them."[11]

In El Paso, some railroad attorneys exacerbated the difficulties. According to the "El Paso agreement," all street and steam railroad attorneys agreed, for free passes, "not to accept employment against other companies, and that all would co-operate in making common cause against the plaintiffs in personal injury cases." Baker & Botts's district attorneys reported that "the community of interests and feeling does not exist so far as the street railway is concerned." In addition, some firms failed to receive their passes and "propose to represent the plaintiffs in any suits" against other railroads. With money to be made on both sides of the bar, railroad district and state attorneys struggled to keep the line of division clear.[12]

After 1900, railroad attorneys at all levels negotiated compensation with the railroads in terms that revealed the changed litigation circumstances. Division attorneys in Texas reported that the "reputation abroad that Texas courts have for giving and sustaining large verdicts against railway[s]" generated increasing litigation in their districts. They regularly cited the railroad demands on their practice and railroad work's precluding other business. As one local attorney explained to Baker & Botts, "The railways come in contact with the people in so many ways that there exists, always more or less friction, although much of it does not develop into

sonal injury lawyer. The Norfolk & Western attorneys finally allowed him to represent the company and wrap up the case for the brakeman. W. M. Imboden to Baker & Botts, 16 August 1909, Box 11L, Folder "Rusk DA," BBHC-RU.

11. W. J. J. Smith to Baker & Botts, 15 August 1909, W. J. J. Smith to Baker & Botts, 16 April 1918, Box 11L, Folder "Dallas DA," BBHC-RU.

12. Beall, Kemp & Ward to Baker & Botts, 25 April 1910, Folder "El Paso DA," ibid.

litigation, and as any attorney who is known as a representative of a railroad company is looked upon by many people with more or less disfavor, and often loses business that would have come to him otherwise."[13]

State attorneys in Texas generally held the line on salary increases, fending off a steady stream of attorney complaints and demands. When extended, salary increases often came with an attached proviso. For its district attorney in El Paso, Baker & Botts responded that "we hope with your active cooperation and assistance to be able to materially reduce before long, the litigation." To another attorney, Baker & Botts cautioned, "This increase, therefore, is made with the understanding that if in the future the volume of litigation should decrease, you will accept a proportionate decrease in your salary." For these lower-level attorneys, such a suggestion betrayed mixed motives; the railroads' state attorneys pushed them to lower litigation and thereby reduce their volume of work.[14]

The Santa Fe's district attorney for Oklahoma admitted that he could no longer retain local attorneys for just a free pass. He predicted a continuation of increased litigation with the coming of statehood. To general counsel Jonathan W. Terry, he stated simply, "It is going to be impossible to get the best attorneys simply for transportation. . . . Some attorneys that I would prefer, stated frankly that they do not feel like they could afford to take it for transportation only." In the local economies of southern small towns, the railroad generated considerable business for both sides of the bar, and a free pass no longer carried the bargaining power it once did.[15]

In response to the growing litigation, the rise of the personal injury bar, and the adverse public sentiment, most railroad attorneys after 1900 pressed those below them in the hierarchy to employ methods to counteract these forces. In Texas Baker & Botts passed down the chain of command the directive to lessen litigation. In its retainers, such initiatives were expressly provided. The Fort Worth district attorneys' retainer contained this proviso: "Use your influence to prevent litigation, as well as defeat

---

13. Beall & Kemp to Baker & Botts, 7 May 1900, Beall & Kemp to Baker & Botts, 26 October 1900, G. G. Kelley to Baker & Botts, 4 December 1915, ibid.

14. Baker & Botts to Beall & Kemp, 5 October 1900, Baker & Botts to W. J. J. Smith, 9 January 1902, Box 11L, Folder "Dallas DA," BBHC-RU.

15. S. T. Bledsoe to Jonathan W. Terry, 20 November 1907, Box 31, Folder 14, SFRR-HMRC.

suits brought against the company. Of course, we would very much rather that through your efforts in assisting the Claim Department and otherwise, litigation should be prevented or reduced to a minimum and at the end of the year you would show a record of not having tried a single case." In addition, Baker & Botts moved after 1900 to place some local attorneys on a small salary, possibly in an effort to remove their incentives to litigate.[16]

In 1907, Texas passed a law outlawing the issuance of free passes to railroad attorneys except "to general attorneys and attorneys who appear in courts of record to try cases and receive a reasonable annual salary." This statute cut out many local attorneys and forced railroads to use salaries as retainers. In making one local attorney salaried, Baker & Botts spelled out the new directives: "This employment contemplates that you shall use your influence to prevent the company being involved in litigation as well as to protect its interests in the courts. In a word, that you should be the legal representative of the company in your county and use your best endeavors to promote and protect its interests in and out of the courts." When the local attorney requested a better offer, Baker & Botts was quick to point out the economic burdens of the new law. Two years later this local attorney quit railroad work, and the district attorneys requested that Baker & Botts authorize a replacement. Apparently, local attorneys were not salaried in every county through which the lines ran, only those where such expense seemed justified. The district attorneys appealed to Baker & Botts: "The litigation in that County as against the railway has not been very large, but owing to the increased population of the county, it is increasing, and a local attorney upon the ground may be exceedingly useful in preventing litigation as well as assisting in the trial of cases, and, of course, a damage suit is likely to be filed in which a local attorney would be in a position to more than earn his entire annual salary." Obviously, railroad attorneys considered such salaried local attorneys good buys. Baker & Botts approved the allocation and retained the local attorney to try cases and to "be active and diligent in keeping the company out of trouble and out of the courts . . . and use their influence to promote good feeling between the public and the company."[17]

16. Baker & Botts to Stanley, Spoonts & Thompson, 1 June 1903, Box 11L, Folder "Fort Worth DA," BBHC-RU.

17. Baker & Botts to W. C. Carpenter, 5 July 1907, Baker & Botts to W. C. Carpenter, 8 July 1907, Proctor, Vandenberge, Crain & Mitchell to Baker & Botts, 16 February 1909, Box 11L, Folder "Victoria DA," ibid.

When Baker & Botts placed local attorneys on salary, it faced increased requests for raises. One local attorney in Wharton County pointed to the increase in litigation in his area and desired a corresponding increase in salary. More important from his perspective, representing the railroad carried business consequences at the divided bar—it limited his client base. Although the district attorneys supported this solicitous local attorney in his request, Baker & Botts as state attorneys held the final say. Their response indicated the true needs and desires of the railroad corporation: "He is a good man and we appreciate him, but as a practical question the greatest assistance that he has rendered the G.H.&S.A. R.R. Company since his return to Wharton is to let it be known that he represents the company and has not taken any litigation against it. We do not underestimate the importance of this, but of course the railway company cannot afford to employ all of the strong and reputable lawyers on its line and pay them substantial salaries in order to keep them from accepting employment against it.[18]

Baker & Botts, as general attorneys for the Southern Pacific, accumulated extraordinary authority over the road's hierarchy of attorneys in Texas. Early on, the Houston firm fended off challenges to its authority from the Victoria district attorneys, once general counsel to several lines consolidated into the Southern Pacific system. The Houston firm's responsibility to the railroad required that it maintain high-quality representation at the district attorney level, where most serious cases were handled. In El Paso, Baker & Botts intervened in the selection of a new partner for their district attorney's firm. Normally, partner selection rested with the firm, and outside interference was intolerable. In 1909 in El Paso, though, Baker & Botts mixed tact with blunt realism to shore up a dangerously exposed area of the Southern Pacific's legal operations. The old firm of Beall & Kemp threatened to fall apart after the death of Judge Kemp. Kemp, for his part, had failed to stem the rising tide of anti-railroad litigation in the area. Baker & Botts summed up his limitations: "In his prime he was quite a strong lawyer of the old school, but . . . his training, render[ed] him un-adapted to pursuing the vigorous, aggressive course in the defense of railroad damage suits so essential under present day conditions

---

18. G. G. Kelley to Baker & Botts, 4 December 1915, Box 11L, Folder "Wharton Co. Local Atty," ibid.; Baker & Botts to Proctor, Vandenberge, 15 June 1916, Box 11L, Folder "Victoria DA," ibid.

in order to cope with the methods adopted by the lawyers who make a specialty of bringing actions of this kind." Although Kemp's son rose to partner upon his father's death, the elder Beall desired retirement.[19]

The state general counsel understood the requirements of the district attorney slot at El Paso. They searched for someone who "had experience sufficient in the railroad litigation, and especially in negligence cases to enable him to handle the El Paso situation, which . . . is a somewhat difficult one." Baker & Botts's partners agreed that the position demanded a "rough and tumble trial lawyer," and they communicated this need to the young Kemp. Baker & Botts partner Edwin Parker spent three days in El Paso assessing the situation and the members of the local bar. Parker "very frankly, but in a kindly and delicate way," told Beall & Kemp "that they could not hope to hold the G.H.&S.A. and Southern Pacific business unless they associated a strong, experienced and vigorous trial lawyer with them." As Baker & Botts set about finding and retaining an appropriate partner for the younger Kemp, they assured their superiors that "in the meantime we will endeavor to see that all pending litigation has proper attention, if necessary, sending some one from our office to participate with Messrs. Beall and Kemp in the preparation and trial of such cases." Baker & Botts, then, not only selected a partner for its El Paso district attorneys but stepped in to run its operations until the firm stabilized. Railroad attorneys, such as Beall & Kemp in El Paso, experienced a distinct loss of autonomy when they took a place in a railroad legal department hierarchy. The tiered department that characterized southern railroads by the turn of the century reflected the exigencies of federalism in the region.[20]

At the state level, railroad lawyers wanted to reverse the public perception of their activities as corrupt, especially their lobbying for railroad clients. Sometimes, this required a more dependent relationship with their clients. The Norfolk & Western's Virginia lobbyist, Horace Graham Buchanan, doubled as the road's local attorney in Richmond. Buchanan collected lobbying fees from the N&W's legal department totaling $46,500

19. See Kenneth Lipartito and Joseph Pratt, *Baker & Botts in the Development of Modern Houston* (Austin: University of Texas Press, 1991), 26–27; Baker & Botts to Wm. F. Herrin, 10 March 1909, Box 11L, Folder "El Paso DA," BBHC-RU.

20. E. B. Parker to H. M. Garwood, 9 February 1909, Box 11L, Folder "Victoria DA," ibid.

between 1904 and 1915. Averaging $4,000 per session, Buchanan's firm received fees of $5,000 in 1906, 1908, and 1910, $8,500 in 1912, $10,000 in 1914, and $7,500 in 1915. The arrangement, though undoubtedly profitable, did not suit Buchanan. "I am put in the position of charging a specific fee for purely legislative work, which, if known, would give color to the charge that I am a lobbyist," he wrote to the N&W, "I am not ambitious for the honor, especially as you and I have striven for many years past to get the public away from the impression that a lobby, as that term was used in the past, was being maintained by the railroads." Buchanan wanted to become a salaried attorney in the N&W's legal department to eliminate the appearance of his role as lobbyist. Others in the N&W legal department agreed:

> It is a fact that all the men who represent railway companies in Richmond—such as Mr. McIlwaine, Division Counsel of the Atlantic Coast Line, Mr. Berlingett of the Virginian, Mr. Wall of the C&O, etc. . . . —have specific railway standing; that is, they are all regular employes of the companies. . . .
>
> Since I have had anything to do with legislative matters, I have tried earnestly to prevent the idea that the railway companies were maintaining a lobby in the usual acceptation of that term; but rather to have it understood that we were gentlemen of character, representing as employes having knowledge of the subject.

Buchanan, this Norfolk & Western official suggested, should become a full-time representative to dispel public perception of the lobbyist as corrupt, bought and controlled purely by the political needs of the corporation.[21]

Railroad lawyers, though, proved reluctant to surrender their autonomy to the corporation. Their training, professional ethics, and sensibilities resisted a relationship of subordinate status. As a result, a negotiated independence developed in which railroad lawyers demanded significant salaries from railroads for the privilege of their priority attention. Railroad

---

21. H. G. Buchanan to L. E. Johnson, 20 March 1916, H. G. Buchanan to W. S. Battle, 15 March 1916, W. S. Battle to N. D. Maher, 17 March 1916, Subject Files, N&W-VPI.

companies in exchange for such munificence exacted a certain loss of professional autonomy. In the midst of these changes, railroad lawyers found their duties evolving as well. Leading attorneys appeared in courtrooms less often, monitoring instead the activities of lower attorneys engaged in the company's defense. Greater supervisory activities trickled down and increasingly occupied state or district attorneys. The railroad corporation expected all attorneys in the hierarchy to give its business first priority and to protect its interests constantly, whether in the courts, before the commissions, in the halls of the legislature, or in the streets of the town or city. By 1913, when Baker & Botts requested a $30,000 retainer from the Southern Pacific, the firm defined its duties with broad scope: "It will be our constant endeavor in the future as in the past to promote to the utmost of our ability and influence the interests of the properties under your jurisdiction, not only in the conduct of litigation and attention to legal matters in which they are interested, but in every other way within our power."[22]

In the late nineties some southern railroad attorneys considered cooperating formally to bring change in their clients' legal environment and soften the blow of adverse decisions and legislation. The joint retention of Ed Baxter as special counsel provided some coordination and cooperation, but Baxter's operations remained distinctly on the outside of the legal departments. As the pressures of the Populists, Progressives, and other reformers mounted, the attorneys realized the benefits of shared knowledge, of coordinated counterattacks, and of planned litigation strategy. Throwing aside the competitive, cutthroat distrust of their clients, they tried to build an associational identity in which the concerns of their industry superseded some of the parochial or entrepreneurial competitiveness that remained from the heady days of the 1880s.

In September 1906, fifty-two railroad lawyers gathered in Louisville, Kentucky, for a two-day conference on the Federal Employers' Liability Act. This extraordinary gathering, southern-inspired, -called, and -directed, seems unimaginable in the competitive atmosphere in the 1880s. Yet, at least three conferences took place between 1906 and 1910. The 1906 conference membership included thirty-seven southern railroad attorneys, the remaining fifteen representing mostly midwestern roads. More than any other line, the Louisville & Nashville took responsibility for fostering an associational response. Although the L&N's president re-

22. Baker & Botts to W. B. Scott, 22 April 1913, Box 11L, Folder 2, BBHC-RU.

mained deeply protective of his company's autonomy in the marketplace, its general counsel, Henry L. Stone, called the conference. L&N attorneys prepared a set of questions on the FELA for the members to address, and Stone served as chairman of the conference.[23]

Stone and the other L&N attorneys considered the FELA unconstitutional and hoped to use the conference as a means to shape a successful plan to overturn it. In his invitation to all attorneys, Stone explained his hopes "to exchange views and endeavor to agree upon a uniform line of action to be taken by the railroad companies in the defense of actions against them" under the FELA. In his opening remarks, moreover, Stone suggested preparing a report at the end of the conference and "establish[ing] a bureau of information in order that we may be kept informed of the cases that may arise . . . the different steps taken in them and the defenses made, the briefs of counsel and the arguments before the court." Recognizing the importance of public opinion, some conferees expressed concern over the possible publicity of their remarks. One quipped to the chair, "You know how it is with us, the newspapers get most that we say." Stone reassured him and others that the proceedings of the conference were "not intended for publication."[24]

Not all were clear, though, on the gathering's purpose beyond general discussion of the FELA or on the proper format or procedure for the event. Some considered the conference a brainstorming session, designed to generate ideas but not to mandate a certain course of action. After some discussion of the first L&N prepared question, for example, Edmund F. Trabue, Illinois Central district attorney for Kentucky, voiced discomfort over affirming or negating each question by a vote: "It seems to me it would be very impolitic for us to put ourselves on record here upon this question, because . . . it might have an effect which was never intended. What we are here for is to swap views on these important questions and to determine, if we can, what would probably be decided ultimately by the

23. See L&N district attorney Edward W. Hines's memorandum to H. L. Stone on the FELA and the strategy for discerning a test case: "It might be well to address a letter to each of our District Attorneys calling attention to the act and to our purpose to test its validity as soon as a favorable opportunity is presented, and it might also be well to communicate or confer with the general counsels of the various railroad companies of the country relative to testing the validity of this act." *PRAC* (1906), 227.

24. H. L. Stone to "all attorneys," 8 September 1906, *PRAC* (1906), 2; H. L. Stone, quoted ibid., 1; C. O. Hunter, quoted ibid., 15.

Supreme Court of the United States." L&N district attorney John B. Keeble explained his understanding of the conference's purpose: "We are here to devise ways and means to get away from this act, and what is the best way to do it is what we should consider and not yield anything."[25]

Others dissented from Keeble's strong-minded approach, and the conference came to a crossroads on the issue of voting on each question. With clear division on this important question and with significant strategic considerations at stake, members moved to submit the question to a smaller committee for resolution. One member suggested unanimity: "We will all have to agree to go in and fight on one line, and we can adopt that one line of battle to test the right of Congress to pass this legislation at all." The conference avoided a vote on this issue by setting up a special committee, but the dissension on voting continued to dog the attorneys in subsequent conferences. At a 1910 meeting, for example, a similar concern over voting led Santa Fe general counsel Gardiner Lathrop to clarify his understanding of the conferences' goals: "Of course, nobody is going to be bound, after this Conference in dealing with questions which may arise on his own line in concrete cases that may be put up." A vote on the questions, Lathrop averred, determined the group's confidence in a certain course of action: "We might feel that it [the decided vote] was safe and prudent and the proper course to pursue. . . . I know it would be helpful to me to find out what the majority of lawyers here think."[26]

Another conference on the FELA in 1908 produced similar calls for greater unity and associational action. Alexander G. Cochran, vice-president and general solicitor of the Missouri Pacific system, urged the conference to greater associational organization. "In organization there is strength," Cochran pointed out. "Only the legal departments of these companies have not been organized." Conceding "a great difference of sentiment among lawyers" on points of law, Cochran pressed his fellow railroad attorneys: "there must be greater unity; that we must stand more together. . . . We should appoint our committees and move forward as an unbroken column in defense of what we believe to be right."[27]

25. Edmund F. Trabue, quoted ibid., 47; John B. Keeble, quoted ibid., 53. When asked to clarify "get away from it," Keeble stated, "Kill it."

26. John I. Hall, quoted in *PRAC* (1906), 73; Gardiner Lathrop, quoted ibid. (1910), 59.

27. Alexander G. Cochran, quoted ibid. (1908), 290.

By 1910, when railroad attorneys met to discuss the Mann-Elkins Act, the tension among conferees between the interests of their association and those of their respective companies remained unresolved. In fact, the difficulties of the long-and-short-haul discrimination provision in the new act only exacerbated their divided loyalties. "We are confronted with this situation," advised Edgar Rich, general solicitor of the Boston & Maine, "nine people out of ten—yes ninety-nine out of a hundred—feel that there is absolutely no justification for charging more for a less service than for a greater service." Citing railroad success in New England, Rich suggested a unified "propaganda of education, not merely for the effect upon the legislatures and Congress, but for the effect it would have upon the courts . . . through the active efforts of the railroad attorneys." In addition, Rich suggested that the attorneys cooperate to keep track of forthcoming litigation so that they "could devise some means whereby the best talent of the country can be employed in defending the railroad's case when it comes before the courts."[28]

Despite Rich's and others' calls for unity and cooperation, some attorneys still put their companies' interests first. Hoping to get a vote on a thorny issue concerning the long-and-short-haul provision, Edward Colston, general counsel for the Alabama Great Southern, protested vigorously when the attorneys voted to defer answering the question. In response, E. D. Robbins, general counsel of the New Haven & Hartford, offered, "This is not a court; it is not a legislature. We are here to confer together and exchange opinions, and any action on our part is all out of place." Colston vehemently disagreed, only to have Robbins respond in defense of his company's interests: "We have no power. Our action has absolutely no weight whatever. . . . I don't want to stand up here and make a vote. It embarrasses me, because if I declare myself with others here it may get to the Interstate Commerce Commission. . . . I have got to advise a client. It would not do me the slightest good, after I got my client in jail, to say that ninety-nine out of a hundred here had a different opinion than the court."[29]

This statement revealed the limits of associational power. Within their companies attorneys drew strict limits around their duties and the legal functions they performed. Willing to discuss constitutional questions in

28. Edgar Rich, quoted ibid. (1910), 347.
29. E. D. Robbins, quoted ibid., 302.

conferences, they reserved legal advice and counsel for their clients' specific circumstances. In public bodies, such as the Interstate Commerce Commission, state legislatures, and Congress, railroad lawyers faced broad legal challenges to their companies' power and authority. As industry representatives, these attorneys agreed on some general approaches to important legal questions, but they remained skeptical of committing themselves to any specific course of action. Individual circumstances dictated each of their companies' responses to litigation and regulation.

For the lawyers, associationalism threatened to impose further limits on their professional autonomy. In addition, the corporate structure and the divided bar both constrained lawyers' choices and removed control of decisions to others. Lawyers responded to these changes with some misgivings. They could not help but feel diminished. Local attorneys expressed frustration at their place in the system, especially at the corporation's policies limiting their business. They also begrudged their loss of control over cases and strategy. State counsel too suffered under the hierarchy's limitations on their business and autonomy, but their choices remained wider than the local attorneys'. Although general counsels gained responsibility for all of their corporation's legal affairs, they spent less time in court and more managing their departments; moreover, they too operated within limits set by executive officers. Lawyers did not make policy for the railroad corporations, but they often carried the responsibility of presenting and evaluating the various policy alternatives.

The discontent over the corporations' place in the business of the law profession infected the Alabama Bar Association at its thirty-ninth annual meeting in 1916. Weeks before the meeting, association member William A. Denson petitioned Alabama's lawyers through local bar associations. Denson's letter condemned the state bar association, as well as the state judiciary, legislature and government:

> The administration of justice in Alabama is dominated by
> the corporation lawyers of the State. These men are em-
> ployed by the public service and general industrial corpo-
> rations, both foreign and domestic, of their respective
> localities, including the railroads and Alabama Power
> Company. These men, numbering less than one hundred
> all told, control absolutely the legislative, judicial, and ex-
> ecutive policy of the State of Alabama and they exercise

their control with an eye single to the interests of their powerful clientele which is in constant clash with that of the main body of citizenry of the State.[30]

Worse, according to this critic, corporation lawyers manufactured diversionary or obscurantist issues, such as prohibition, on which they could divide, while hiding their basic agreement on corporation issues.

At the state bar association meeting, Walker Percy, the elder statesman of the corporation bar in Alabama, initiated long-winded discussion over a response to Denson's letter. Percy considered the letter an attack on the association's honor, which he felt bound to defend. Percy spoke for several minutes to the association on the congeniality of the bar, the common ground uniting corporation and anti-corporation lawyers, and the dignity of the governmental branches. His autobiographical examples depicted not necessarily a united bar, but at least a civil one. He pointed to several instances when he worked either with a "damage suit lawyer" or on progressive reforms. Percy, for example, supported a personal injury lawyer for a judgeship, though only after opposing him steadily for twelve years. His support for a state workmen's compensation act united him with damage lawyers:

> No man believes that the question of fault—which after all is a question of forgetfulness—should determine the question whether a widow should be a pauper thrown upon the world, or whether she should be adequately provided for. If that act be passed, I expect that it will double the cost of personal injuries to the clients I represent. It will very largely increase the compensation that the negro workmen and their families in this State will receive; it will give compensation in many cases where it is not now recoverable. It will cost my own firm a large sum of money, Mr. Harsh and Mr. Beddow [personal injury lawyers] some money, yet did any lawyer here give that a thought to his personal interests?[31]

30. *Alabama Bar Association Proceedings* (1916), 158–59.
31. Ibid., 162–63.

By 1916 when the bar association unanimously passed a resolution in support of workmen's compensation, many corporations, particularly the Illinois Central, were searching for a reliable system of personal injury insurance. In any case, no railroad corporation attorney in 1916 could afford to cast the sole demur to a bar association resolution supporting a progressive reform. As for the standards of the legal profession, corporation lawyers, and governmental officials, Percy considered Alabama more chaste than ever:

> I have heard talk . . . about how the business man was to
> blame; about how the corporate interests were to blame,
> or somebody else was to blame. . . . I know the lawyers
> of this State; we are not as powerful as the lawyers were
> in days of old; not as potent in the community because
> the business man has become a great factor; but there
> never was a time when a more brave, more high-minded,
> more clean, more loyal men comprised the profession
> than today. There are crooked corporation lawyers of
> course, and there are crooked anti-corporation lawyers of
> course, but the world is getting better and the standards
> are getting better and higher. . . . The great corporations
> of this country have learned that a corporation has no
> place in politics.

Particularly offended by the criticism of the state's judiciary, Percy asked for a resolution to condemn the letter as "so entirely without foundation as to appear to be the absurd vaporings of a disordered mind."[32]

Not all bar association members felt as offended as Percy. Some considered Percy too sensitive, caught up with matters of honor. Others agreed with Percy's expressions of indignation but counseled against a formal response from the bar, while one member estimated that only one-third of the association represented corporations and two-thirds were "lawyers on the other side." Another member voiced the sentiments of those many attorneys whose general practice sometimes included corporation work but most often the matters of common people: "I believe that Alabama should encourage corporations to come into our State to help develop our match-

32. Ibid., 166.

less resources, but at the same time, I do not believe that Alabama should be made the spawning ground for trusts." After motions and debate on the issue, the association ignored the letter but passed a resolution expressing general support for the state's judiciary.[33]

The development of interstate railroads in the eighties brought specialization in corporate law and sharp division of the bar. For Walker Percy in Birmingham, railroad clients offered a combination of personal opportunity and regional development. But the railroad corporations contributed to tension within the profession over the bar's ideals and to disagreement over the shape of economic development. In 1916, the divisions in the bar between corporation and anti-corporation lawyers remained alive and sensitive, as did the dissonance over the corporation's place and practices in the region.

33. H. F. Reese, quoted ibid., 167; Walter S. Smith, quoted ibid., 175.

Conclusion:
Law and Power

Southerners were not alone in their difficulty discerning the line between trusts and developmental corporations, but the lagging development of the region and the region's dependence on outside capital set southerners apart in their great discomfort with new economic order. Were lawyers to blame? The 1916 bar association memorial to Alexander Hamilton, long-time general counsel for the Atlantic Coast Line, by a fellow Virginia corporation attorney recalled the poor public record of the railroads. "A sentiment of passionate misunderstanding of their [railroads'] motives and purposes had been created by designing men, in a large part of the public," Hamilton's biographer wrote. "The misdeeds of a few in railroad management had been exaggerated to such an extent as to bring the calling of a railroad official into disfavor with unthinking and undiscriminating persons, until it has not been unusual to hear that a representative of a railroad must be classed an unpatriotic citizen."[1]

This sympathetic biographer would not have included Hamilton's contemporary and fellow Virginian William Alexander Anderson in the category of designing men in railroad management. Anderson came from a family of distinguished lawyers; his father served on the Supreme Court of Appeals of Virginia. After fighting in the Civil War, Anderson attended law school at the University of Virginia before opening a practice in Lexington. An ardent Democrat, the young lawyer became counsel in the early

1. *Virginia Bar Association Proceedings* (1916), 124.

eighties for the Richmond & Allegheny Railroad and later in the decade vice-president and general counsel of the Pittsburgh & Virginia Railroad, both northern-owned and New York–financed development schemes. Disillusioned with railroad business after these railroads came under control of larger systems, Anderson successfully ran for attorney general in 1901 under the independent progressive platform of Andrew J. Montague. As attorney general, moreover, he actively prosecuted railroad corporations for violations of Corporation Commission directives.

Anderson's deep involvement in Lexington, Shenandoah Valley, and Virginia business and political affairs widened and strengthened his law practice. He retained investments in real estate, agricultural lands, and mineral properties, but his development projects fell victim to outside interests, at least according to his bar association biographer and fellow Lexingtonian: "Great projects for the development of his community, section and State, in the manner of railroads, highways, industries, mines, towns, etc., were conceived, striven for and developed by his colossal resource and energy. It is believed that had not the trusts at that time, about 1890, begun to exist and produce a deadly atmosphere of repression and failure for independent developments outside of themselves, Glasgow [Virginia] would have grown into a great city and would have been a monument to his far-sighted vision and sound judgment."[2] In such a dependent region, "independent developments" took on heroic trappings for some observers and later historians, and the lost promise of Glasgow, Virginia, glowed brightly in the minds of reformers.

All of the unfulfilled expectations about Glasgow could not diminish railroads' contribution to the phenomenal growth of other southern towns. Birmingham, Alabama, owed its existence to the railroad. The advent of the L&N Railroad in 1871 transformed the town center, once a cornfield, into an industrial hub. The city's population grew exponentially, from 3,006 inhabitants in 1880 to 38,415 twenty years later. By 1899, though, some of Birmingham's citizens regarded the city's railroads as an obstacle to further growth and a public danger. Of particular concern to businessmen and residents, railroad tracks crossed busy Birmingham streets, often blocking them for hours as the L&N, Southern, and other lines switched

2. Ibid. (1930), 187–88.

cars and delivered freight. A local newspaper reported 161 switches in one day. Not just annoying for their delay, some of these were particularly dangerous. "Flying switches" referred to an engine shoving an unconnected single boxcar to smash into the coupling of another train of cars, a practice regularly executed across busy downtown streets by Birmingham's interstate railroads.[3]

Many Birmingham residents pressed the city to require railroads to build viaducts, for either the tracks or the streets, to relieve daily congestion and danger in the city. Railroad attorneys Jefferson M. Falkner and L. Sevier defeated all such efforts, largely because of their close relationship with the city council members. The railroad lawyers seemed to have power in the councils and legislatures, even in the city Chamber of Commerce, where they headed off any proposals which could cost their companies revenue. One observer remarked, "The railroads have men on guard in the Chamber of Commerce and have had for twenty years."[4]

Railroad power and influence in Birmingham met an accomplished adversary in 1911, though, when James T. Weatherly became city commissioner. Weatherly's legal career began with the Georgia Pacific in 1886 as assistant general counsel. He quickly rose through the legal departments of the Georgia Pacific and the Southern Railway to become a prominent railroad attorney in Birmingham. Weatherly used his inside knowledge and understanding of the railroad business and legal environment to bring some Progressive change on the issue of grade crossings in the city. He threatened to enforce the city's law on franchises for all of the numerous small spurs, sidetracks, and other encroachments of the railroads. Railroads had quietly built many of these facilities without franchise rights, in clear violation of the law, the forced compliance with which, railroad attorneys warned, would bring a legal mess. Exploiting his railroad expertise, Weatherly forced the railroads to abandon their delay tactics and eventually won a small victory for the city in 1914.[5]

----

3. Carl V. Harris, *Political Power in Birmingham, 1871–1921* (Knoxville: University of Tennessee Press, 1977), 233.

4. Ibid.

5. Harris, *Political Power*, 236. The *Birmingham News* deemed it "the first big fight the city has ever won against the railroads."

Weatherly's success demonstrated the difficulties Progressive reformers faced in their contests with the railroad corporations. To succeed often required corporation attorney experience and expertise. Even with strong legal counsel, such as Weatherly in Birmingham, George W. Pickle in Tennessee, Frank S. White in Alabama, or William A. Anderson in Virginia, Progressives confronted obstruction, delay, obfuscation, and resistance from railroad legal departments. When Alabama's railroad lawyer-legislators, for example, followed public opinion in 1907 and voted Progressive, the railroads retreated to the federal court system, where they were able to find shelter for years under the eye of federal judge Thomas Goode Jones, a former L&N attorney. Even an obvious public danger in an urban center and an inefficient use of public space, such as Birmingham's flying switches and railroad street crossings, proved difficult issues for Progressive reformers when railroads stood in opposition to reform.

Railroad lawyers effectively defended their clients, though their conflation of company with regional interests satisfied few southerners. Even Progressive reforms did not resolve the dilemma of southern dependence on the large companies and the corporations' monopoly power. After rate wars, tax fights, and labor-management contests, the railroad corporations appeared to some the same powerful, insensitive conglomerates. As the first large interstate corporations in the region, railroads confronted a regional political economy colored by its dependence on outside capital. The sources and meanings of dependence generated heated controversy for both observers and later historians. No region suffered as dangerous a rail network as the South. ICC statistics broadcast the region's inferiority in grim numerical accounts of death and injury. No one seemed immune; both Bernard Peyton, the Georgia Pacific's first general counsel, and Samuel Spencer, the Southern Railway Company's first president, died in southern train wrecks. The South's place as the most dangerous regional rail network gave eerie resonance to the charge of an outside conspiracy to keep the region economically weak and dependent. When attorneys manipulated the law and the legal process to escape the consequences of these personal and regional disasters, they further aggravated the tension within southern society over the behavior of large national corporations.

The accident rate seemed symbolic of everything wrong with the South. The tragedies added up to regional backwardness, a condition defined by lack of capital, poor construction, mismanagement, and poor human capital. The sum of the parts prompted critics, reformers, and historians to view the railroads as responsible for so much of the South's problems. Accidents did not end with destroyed engines, mangled cars, torn-down trestles, broken bodies, and fractured lives. Accidents reverberated through the legal system, as claimants filed suit and lawyers engaged in tactical skirmishing. In this arena too, railroad accidents seemed to symbolize for many southerners the deep inequities of the region's political economy. The railroad lawyers' manipulation of the legal and governmental process, even at the most local levels, offended the sensibilities of many southerners. Law and government seemed to them to work only for the corporation. Both required power and influence far in excess of what most citizens were able to muster. They gradually realized that railroads, once built and operating in their communities, could control the democratic process and, if unchallenged, avoid responsibility for so much damage.[6]

In the 1880s, lawyers helped construct and maintain a business environment that promised local and regional growth but featured prominent advantages for railroads. Railroad corporations tried to monopolize legal talent in local communities across the South and accrued definite advantages of experience, skill, and expertise over weakly represented opposition. In addition, railroads cultivated friendly and solicitous state legislatures and local councils through their lawyers' active lobbying. At the same time, they financed elections, lavished free passes on influential men, and retained some legislators as local attorneys. In trial and appellate courts across the South, railroad dominance rested on advantageous legal principles, such as the fellow-servant rule. Finally, the federalized legal structure of the region and the interstate nature of the railroads gave them distinct advantages in these years, making them difficult to regulate and even more intractable in litigation.

Growth and expansion in the eighties sparked divisiveness. The opportunistic exploits of railroad financiers in the eighties led some southerners to view railroad men with skepticism and railroad lawyers with disdain.

6. Sloppy construction and engineering in the 1880s railway boom provided fodder for those who considered the accident rate indicative of a larger phenomenon in the southern economy—its colonial dependence. On the other hand, the ICC's second explanation, the quality-of-labor theory, deflected attention away from an outside conspiracy toward the region's responsibility for its human capital. *Interstate Commerce Commission: Statistics of Railways in the United States* (Washington, D.C., 1899), 108; *Interstate Commerce Commission: Statistics of Railways in the United States* (Washington, D.C., 1891), 97; see also the 1894 report, p. 75, for a reference to the "inferior" grade of labor in the South.

Watered stock, cheaply built roads, rate discrimination, free passes, corrupt lobbying, and other abuses eroded public perception of railroad corporations. The Farmers' Alliance, and eventually the Populists, capitalized on this discontent. Uncomfortable with the way railroad lawyers used the legal and governmental systems to their clients' advantage, Populists voiced the concerns of a growing number of southerners. The Populists, though, offered solutions that alienated most. Nationalization of the railroad system, their party plank, flew in the face of most southerners' calls for greater railroad competition.

Southerners in the nineties grew increasingly concerned with monopoly power. At issue was nothing less than the place of the interstate corporation in southern society. At what point did a corporation become a monopoly? When did a railroad company pass from being a positive good to a dangerous combination? For many southerners the answer was clear: when the corporation left local control, when its priorities no longer served the interests of their locality or state, when it cost locals in rates, taxes, or bond payments. These questions entered the public discourse of nearly every southern state in the 1880s and remained potent well into the twentieth century. For the most part, lawyers rested railroad-corporation power on perfectly legal foundations. The free pass, the fellow-servant rule, election support, and removal to federal court did not qualify as illegal in the late nineteenth century. The legitimate quality of these practices became the most troubling aspect of railroad power for southerners.

Between 1894 and 1903, southern railroads consolidated and merged into a handful of large systems. They came under the management of financiers such as J. P. Morgan, more interested in long-term development of their properties. Their newfound developmental focus, however, failed to convert southerners to their cause. Just as large railroad corporations changed ownership and business practices, public opinion, inflamed by both past abuses and possibilities of unsurpassed monopoly power, turned sour for railroads. The consolidation of these lines into a few powerful conglomerates only made them even more ominous to many southerners.

Progressive reformers came forward to challenge railroad power, and, like the Populists, sought to limit railroad monopolies and to make democratic governmental institutions responsive to non-railroad interests. While the Populists were distracted by the panacea of free silver, the Progressives focused their sharp attacks on monopoly power. Unlike the Populists, Progressives welded together reform coalitions at the local and state level aimed at specific railroad practices. For these reformers the consequences of railroad dominance included corruption, inefficiency, waste, fraud, and hypocrisy. They found receptive audiences for their railroad reform efforts.

Railroad lawyers discovered widespread public opposition to their manipulation of power. Progressives unified their demands, developed expert legal counsel of their own, and challenged the railroads. Responsibility for much of this animosity, many railroad lawyers conceded, rested with the arm-twisting practices of some of their brethren. The heady expansion of the eighties and early nineties led some railroad lobbyists to buy votes and wink at corruption. The harsh dictates of the fellow-servant doctrine alienated and offended accident victims and drew the skeptical attention of progressive reformers. While depression gripped the southern economy and businesses failed at alarming rates in the nineties, railroads took cover in court-sanctioned receiverships. Economic development wore thin as a justification for granting railroad leeway, and past railroad abuses in the legislature overshadowed whatever reasoned arguments their lawyers made after 1900.

The Progressive years witnessed fractious contests over railroad power and railroad practices, but these did not prevent corporation attorneys from adapting to the new circumstances. Adopting Progressive rhetoric and methods, railroad lawyers fought successfully through the courts to protect their clients' interests by portraying them as efficient engines of the economy. They worked the legislative halls, convincing elected representatives of their clients' worth to the community and region. They met regulatory challenges with long and detailed defenses of their clients before state and federal commissions. In some cases they wore the opposition down through the legal process; in others the law carried them past challenges. Between 1880 and 1916, the railroad corporations' state and local attorneys evolved into an important link between the corporation and the general public. The South's federalized political and legal geography, its strong tradition of states' rights, and its historical aversion to northern or national intervention combined to elevate the importance of state counsel for large railroads in the region. A similar set of circumstances trickled down the railroad legal department hierarchy to local attorneys. Less powerful within the corporation but equally significant, local attorneys carried the interests of the railroad corporation into virtually every community in the South.[7]

---

7. On the power of the southern locality to resist change from outside and various pro-

Lawyers continued to wield power and influence in the southern political economy after 1916. In states and localities courts and parties remained the principle arena for decisions concerning corporations and their activities. In the new regulatory and administrative councils, grafted onto the state of courts and parties in the Progressive period, lawyers also acquired significant power. Regulatory administration developed into a new arena for lawyers' specialization. Lawyering for the railroad corporations evolved into a highly specialized and exceedingly complex practice between 1880 and 1916, but the need for influence and power continued.[8]

The boom days, though, were over for the legal business that the railroad generated in the South. The turn of the century could still find southern lawyers proclaiming their ascendency over the planter: "In no State or country is the influence of lawyers more deeply felt than in the South." By 1916, Walker Percy saw the role of the lawyer as diminished: "We are not as powerful as the lawyers were in days of old." Businessmen, he suggested, surpassed the lawyer to the mantle of power. Worker's compensation, the FELA, state commissions, and the ICC all reduced the litigation load for railroads, replacing local trials with regularized systematic administrative processes. The legal business in the towns and counties across the South diminished, as railroad companies brought much litigation in-house and relied on high-level state counsel to handle the rest.[9]

The expansion of interstate railroads in the eighties and early nineties generated heated opposition in the South. For every interest railroads aided, others took offense. Railroad lawyers stood as the central target of the opposition, not just because they defended railroads but because they wielded power in the state of courts and parties. The Populist opponents in the nineties objected to the way government and law functioned, for it seemed to them that the railroad lawyers perverted the democratic system, manipulating it to favor their corporate clients. The use of the free pass and the retention of state legislators as railroad lawyers confirmed for many

gressive efforts at social change, see William A. Link, *The Paradox of Southern Progressivism, 1880–1930* (Chapel Hill: University of North Carolina Press, 1992).

8. George H. Gilliam's forthcoming work on Virginia's regulatory environment in the late nineteenth and early twentieth centuries should begin to address the question of the degree to which lawyers helped managed the state corporation commission.

9. Fabius H. Busbee, "Duty of Southern Lawyers Toward Negro Question," *Alabama Bar Association Proceedings* (1904), 107; *Alabama Bar Association Proceedings* (1916), 162–63.

the steep inequities of railroad power. When the Southern Pacific Railroad left hundreds of men in Coxey's Army in 1894 stranded on an uncoupled train in the middle of the Texas desert, it demonstrated to many southerners the arrogance and cruelty of railroad corporations' political monopolism.[10]

A new round of railroad-company consolidation brought fresh forces to the reform effort in the South. Progressive reformers, unlike the Populists, directed their efforts at specific railroad abuses and employed regulatory methods to correct them. This strategy proved more successful than the Populists' attempts at wholesale economic restructuring and nationalization of the railroad system. Indeed, Progressive reformers put railroads on the defensive in many southern states, and railroad lawyers faced a new challenge—not just how to defend their railroad clients but how to persuade the general public that the business practices of the newly consolidated systems bore little resemblance to the past abuses of their predecessors.

Southern railroad lawyers tried to adapt to the Progressive challenge. When Progressives successfully empowered state commissions and proceeded to regulate intrastate commerce, railroad attorneys recognized the efficacy of national regulation. Their calls for national uniformity for interstate commerce even adopted the Progressive language of efficiency, economy, and scientific regulation. Similarly, after fighting the 1906 Federal Employers' Liability Act as unconstitutional, southern railroad attorneys recognized the viability of the 1908 FELA as a shelter in which to escape onerous state statutory provisions. When progressive reformers turned to state and federal regulatory commissions, railroad lawyers developed into experts in administrative law. Adapting to this new arena, they went before commissions with data, legal arguments, precedent, and expert witnesses. The effort to build limited associational identity, moreover, sprung from the unified challenge of southern business groups. In Texas, another example, the Progressive initiatives on behalf of labor—the full-crew bill— failed when railroad attorneys united their own coalition of interests, including farmers and consumers. Central to their argument against the bill, Progressive goals of efficiency and economy provided railroad attorneys with an effective language of opposition.

10. Robert C. Cotner, *James Stephen Hogg: A Biography* (Austin: University of Texas Press, 1959), 425. The superintendent of Frisco responded to calls for aid for the Army, "There is no power on earth to compel us to operate our road if we do not want to" (426).

The Progressive challenge to railroad power in the South must be judged a mixed success. Railroad lawyers succeeded in delaying, sidetracking, and sometimes stopping reforms. Their skillful use of the court system, legislative lobbying, and public discourse guaranteed that victories for Progressive reformers were hard-won. James Weatherly's efforts in Birmingham took years and brought about only minimal change in the railroads' switching practices. And although Congress successfully passed the employers' liability act in 1908, railroad lawyers succeeded in manipulating the new act to their advantage until 1914. In addition, railroad lawyers helped prevent for years the adoption of workmen's compensation legislation in many southern states.

For the lawyers the dilemma of their dependence on corporate practice became a self-fulfilling prophecy of amorality. They became sly practitioners of making a virtue out of a necessity. They turned nearly every piece of their work for the railroads into a kind of civic duty, championing the growth and benefits that their clients promised. Lawyers were small businessmen at heart, even the ones who developed into state general counsel for the big interstate railroads. They never lost that sensibility, worrying about their retainers and where the next client was coming from. Yet they portrayed themselves as something more, as civic-oriented, broad-minded, and duty-bound, called to a higher order. The bar associations across the South rang with the rhetoric of their professional role, namely, that justice and truth in precedent and law would come only if the lawyers did their duty.[11]

Doing their duty meant defending the corporate interests with full force. Lawyers cultivated amorality in their work as a part of their professional ethic. Their role was not to judge the actions of their clients, but to defend them, and to do so vigorously so that the legal process could work. The railroad lawyers could twist almost any situation into one that demanded their civic-minded approach. When Illinois Central president Stuyvesant Fish wanted to prosecute the white mob that had lynched a black employee in Tennessee, general solicitor James Fentress intervened and stopped the action. He was looking out for his client in a practical way.

---

11. I would like to thank Linda Przybyszewski for her thoughtful comments about lawyers' professional amoralism that she offered on my paper "Railroad Attorneys and the Issue of Segregation Before and After *Plessy*," presented at *Plessy v. Ferguson* Revisited Conference (November 1996).

The moral issues of lynching, mob violence, and the company's duty to protect its employees were in the very front of Fish's mind, but Fentress swept them away without consideration. Instead, he groped for a response that did not raise opposition from the local white community. Besides, he suggested, such prosecution was the duty of others in the legal system, and the Illinois Central should leave that job to them. Fentress saw no need to take a moral stand on these issues in this case.

In other areas the lawyers used their carefully honed professional amoralism. When their clients faced personal injury and wrongful death suits, they used every legal tactic to help their clients avoid any responsibility. It seemed in these cases that when the moral issues were most apparent, when the moral choices most significant, the lawyers stood more than ever behind their professional ethic. The death of a child, for example, presented the most compelling cases. Sometimes, the railroad lawyers determined that the company was guilty of negligence in these cases. Then, especially when they found they were negligent, the case became more "dangerous" and they used every tactic to defeat the case. The same was true for employees injured in the line of work. The companies blamed the employees, never the equipment or practices. Even when equipment malfunctioned and the company was liable, the attorneys pushed the plaintiffs to the wall, outspending and outlasting them. The Cahaba Bridge wreck in Alabama showed the ease with which the railroad attorneys dismissed their own chief engineer's report and denied that their company had any responsibility for the disaster.

The legal system in the New South had steep inequities. For plaintiffs the walls were almost too high to scale. The idea of professional amoralism depended on a fair field, on the notion that plaintiffs and defendants would have equally able counsel and that legal doctrine would not dramatically undermine either of their positions. The railroad corporations wielded tremendous power through the law, and their attorneys used the advantages of corporate size, wealth, and power. The rise of a vigorous, well-financed, and determined personal injury bar began to level the field some, as did the repeal of some offensive doctrines, such as the fellow-servant rule. But these challenges to the railroads did not spring up like mushrooms in the dark. Instead, they took years to develop and were fought at every point by the railroad lawyers.

With the advantages of the law, doctrine, and corporate size on their side, lawyers could carry railroad corporations untouched through the gauntlet of reformers, litigants, legislators, and competitors. They could escape, for the most part, public blame, professional condemnation, and self-censure. Some, however, such as David Schenck, grew disquieted with the inequality in the law and the way many railroad lawyers exploited it. He would not defend his employers' wrongs and ultimately lost his job because of it. Few railroad lawyers made such moral choices, though. Instead, most of them viewed the matter very differently from Schenck—that it was their professional duty to defend the railroad corporations' wrongs. They believed that their public behavior was necessary, even good, for their community, and this made up for any private misgivings. Free of moral responsibility, lawyers could gain a comfortable living through collusion with railroad corporations in manipulating a region desperate for a measure of prosperity.

Selected Bibliography

NOTE ON MANUSCRIPT SOURCES

Railroad company records provided the majority of primary sources I consulted for this book. My focus on the lawyers and their activities meant that I needed to look beyond the board of directors' minute books and executive officers' letter books. I wanted to find the records of the legal departments of the railroads: reports, letters, case files, subject files, any documents that the legal departments generated. My first research trips were to Virginia Polytechnic Institute to look at the huge Norfolk and Southern Railroad Collection, which holds the records of the Norfolk & Western Railroad and the Southern Railway and all of their subsidiaries. I found significant legal department records in the Norfolk & Western, Southern, and Georgia Pacific papers, as well as legal correspondence in the papers of many other smaller railroads. The annual reports of the railroads' general counsels were particularly valuable. They summarized each case, giving the main issues involved, the strategy used to win the case, and the final disposition of it. Often, the annual report included commentary from the general counsel on the state of the legal department's efforts and the cases themselves. The Norfolk and Southern collection is probably the best railroad collection for southern railroads, covering more than a hundred railroad companies and spanning from the 1850s to the mid–twentieth century.

The Illinois Central Railroad Company records at the Newberry Library present the most complete set of records for a single company that I encountered in my research. The correspondence of the executive officers, both incoming and outgoing, is in bound volumes of letter books, over fifty huge volumes in all. In addition, the collection includes large trunks full of "miscellaneous" material. I found dozens of complete legal department reports in these trunks, as well as significant correspondence between state counsel and the company's officers. The collection includes annual reports from general and state counsel to match those I had found in the Norfolk and Southern collection.

The University of Virginia Library's Special Collections include the letter books of John Skelton Williams, president of the Seaboard Air Line, and represent one of the only collections of Seaboard material that I was able to find. The L&N Collection at the University of Louisville also contains a large number of records, emphasizing the correspondence of the executive officers. I did not find many legal department records or annual reports in the collection, but the correspondence of Milton H. Smith included significant legal materials. The records of the Gulf, Colorado & Santa Fe at the Houston Metropolitan Research Center offered me one of those rare and unexpected research gold mines. I was in Houston to research the Baker & Botts History Collection at Rice University and on a whim went to the Houston public library's special collections to see what it might have. The archive held the papers of William Pitt Ballinger, a prominent railroad attorney in Texas. In addition, though, the archive had the Santa Fe's records, including over three hundred boxes of material, nearly all of it legal department records and correspondence. These records combined with the Baker & Botts law firm records constitute some of the best late-nineteenth-century and twentieth-century legal records and offer an unparalleled view into the legal culture of the Southwest, especially Texas. Finally, I wanted to find material from law firms in the South. The large collection of material donated to Rice University by Baker & Botts of Houston is a tremendous resource for historians. I found other manuscript collections of railroad lawyers at the Southern Historical Collection at the University of North Carolina–Chapel Hill and the University of Virginia.

Nearly every southern library and historical society has railroad material, most of it relatively minor and incomplete. Nevertheless, this material was very useful when pooled with that in the larger collections. For example, several libraries I consulted have accident books, such as the Filson Club's Nashville, St. Louis & Chattanooga Railway Company accident records. Other libraries, such as the Baker Library at Harvard and the Leyburn Library at Washington and Lee University, have small holdings of material on southern railroads. The Rosenberg Library in Galveston has a tremendous collection of material on Walter Gresham, once a prominent railroad attorney and legislator in Texas, and on several Texas railroads, including the Gulf, Colorado & Santa Fe and the Galveston & Western Railway. I found some Central of Georgia records in the Norfolk & Southern Collection at Virginia Tech and in the Alexander R. Lawton papers at the Southern Historical Collection at UNC–Chapel Hill. Though not consulted for this study, a set of records for the Central of Georgia Railroad is also held at the Georgia Historical Society.

Not all of the large railroads or law firms have donated their records to libraries, and some are still in the company archives. For example, I contacted CSX Transportation, Inc., to inquire about the records of the Seaboard Air Line, the Atlantic Coast Line, and the Plant system. I received some indications that these records might be at the corporate offices in Tallahassee, Florida; but after further correspondence it appeared that CSX did not have any nineteenth-century records at all. My guess is that the company does have some records but could not find them, and it is possible that one day they will be available for historians to use.

Law firms offer a difficult problem for researchers, since most of their records are confidential. Many of the large law firms, such as King & Spalding in Atlanta or Hunton, Williams in Richmond, represented railroads in the late nineteenth century and have files of records on these clients. Some firms are reluctant to let researchers use these records since there is no termination date to the obligation of confidentiality for clients. My hope is that more law firms will follow the lead of Baker & Botts and donate their records to public institutions.

PRIMARY SOURCES

Railroad Company Records
Baker Library, Harvard Business School, Cambridge, Mass.
  Norfolk & Western Railroad Records
Filson Club, Louisville, Ky.
  Nashville, St. Louis & Chattanooga Railway Company Accident Records
Houston Metropolitan Research Center, Houston, Texas
  Gulf, Colorado & Santa Fe Railroad Company Records
Leyburn Library, Washington and Lee University, Lexington, Va.
  Norfolk & Western Railroad Company Records
  Richmond & Allegheny Railroad Company Records
Newberry Library, Chicago, Ill.
  Illinois Central Railroad Company Records
Rosenberg Library, Galveston, Texas
  Galveston & Western Railway Company Records
  Gulf, Colorado & Santa Fe Company Records
St. Louis Mercantile Library, St. Louis, Mo., John W. Barriger III National Railroad Collection
  Gulf, Mobile & Ohio Railroad Company Records
  Proceedings of the Railroad Attorneys' Conference: Employers' Liability Act.
    Louisville, Ky.: Westerfield-Bonte, 1906, 1908.
  Proceedings of the Railroad Attorneys' Conference: Questions Arising Under the Mann-Elkins Bill. Louisville, Ky.: Westerfield-Bonte, 1910.

University of Alabama Library, Tuscaloosa, Ala.
  Memphis & Charleston Railroad Company Collection
University of Louisville Archives and Records Center, Louisville, Ky.
  Louisville & Nashville Railroad Company Records
Virginia Historical Society, Richmond, Va.
  Richmond, Fredericksburg & Potomac Railroad Company Records
Virginia Polytechnic Institute, Blacksburg, Va.
  Alabama Great Southern Railroad Company Records
  Atlanta & Charlotte Air-Line Railway Company Records
  Augusta Southern Railroad Company Records
  Big Sandy & Cumberland Railroad Company Records
  Birmingham, Sheffield & Tennessee River Railway Company Records
  Cape Fear & Yadkin Valley Railway Company Records
  Charlotte, Columbia & Augusta Railroad Company Records
  Cincinnati, New Orleans & Texas Pacific Railway Company Records
  East Tennessee, Virginia & Georgia Railroad Company Records
  East Tennessee, Virginia & Georgia Railway Company Records
  Georgia Company Records
  Georgia Pacific Railway Company Records
  Illinois & St. Louis Railroad & Coal Company Records
  Louisville, Evansville & St. Louis Consolidated Railroad Company Records
  Memphis & Charleston Railroad Company Records
  Middlesborough Mineral Railroad Company Records
  Norfolk & Western Railroad Company Records
  Norfolk & Western Railway Company Records
  Pocahontas Coal Company Records
  Richmond & Danville Extension Company Records
  Richmond & Danville Railroad Company Records
  Roanoke & Southern Railway Company Records
  Shenandoah Valley Railroad Company Records
  South Carolina & Georgia Railroad Company Records
  South Carolina Railway Company Records
  Southern Improvement Company Records
  Southern Railway Company Records
  Virginia Midland Railway Company Records
  Western North Carolina Railroad Company Records

Manuscripts
Houston Metropolitan Research Center, Houston, Texas
  William Pitt Ballinger Papers
Rice University Library, Houston, Texas

Baker & Botts History Collection
Rosenberg Library, Galveston, Texas
    Walter Gresham Papers
Southern Historical Collection, University of North Carolina, Chapel Hill, N.C.
    Alexander Boyd Andrews Papers
    William Carson Ervin Papers
    Alexander R. Lawton Family Papers
    Benjamin F. Long Papers
    David Schenck Diary
    Samuel Spencer Papers
    William Thomas Sutherlin Papers
    Samuel McDowell Tate Papers
    Robert Watson Winston Papers
St. Louis Mercantile Library, St. Louis, Mo., John W. Barriger III National Railroad Collection
    Walker D. Hines Papers
University of Kentucky Library, Lexington, Ky.
    Samuel Wilson Papers
University of Virginia Library, Charlottesville, Va.
    William Alexander Anderson Family Papers
    Allen Caperton Braxton Papers
    Rosser Family Papers
    Thornton Family Papers
    John Skelton Williams Papers
Virginia Historical Society, Richmond, Va.
    Williams C. Wickham Family Papers

Published Sources

Bailey, William F. *The Law of Personal Injuries Relating to Master and Servant.* Chicago: Callaghan, 1897.

————. *The Law of the Master's Liability for Injuries to Servant.* St. Paul, Minn.: West Publishing, 1894.

Berge, George W. *The Free Pass Bribery System: Showing How the Railroads, Through the Free Pass Bribery System, Procure the Government Away from the People.* 1904. Reprint, New York: Ayer Co., Arno Press, Politics and People Series, 1974.

Blackford, Charles M. "The Relation Between the Medical and Law Departments of a Railway Company," *Virginia Law Register* 7 (February 1902), 679–90.

Bledsoe, S. T. "The Commerce Clause of the Federal Constitution and Legislation Enacted Pursuant Thereto, Applicable to Railway Transportation." *Texas Bar Association Proceedings* (1916), 266–304.

Blount, William A. "The Past, Present and Future Status of Employers and Employees." *Alabama Bar Association Proceedings* (1908), 185–203.

Breckinridge, William C. P. "The Lawyer: His Influence in Creating Public Opinion." *Virginia Bar Association Proceedings* (1891), 153–71.

Brown, Armistead. "Alabama's New Corporation Law." *Alabama Bar Association Proceedings* (1905), 154–80.

Brown, Julius L. *Reply of Julius L. Brown, Attorney Cincinnati and Georgia Railroad Company, to Speech of Major Joseph B. Cumming, Attorney Georgia Railroad Company.* Atlanta: Constitution Publishing, 1881.

Bryan, Shepard. "Defects in the Law of Georgia Regulating Corporations." *Georgia Bar Association Proceedings* (1901), 176–82.

Busbee, Fabius H. "Duty of Southern Lawyers Toward Negro Question." *Alabama Bar Association Proceedings* (1904), 105–30.

Clark, Champ. "The Country Lawyer in Public Affairs." *Georgia Bar Association Proceedings* (1907), 70–75.

Cleveland, Frederick, and Fred Powell. *Railroad Finance.* New York: Longmans, Green, 1912.

———. *Railroad Promotion and Capitalization in the United States.* New York: Longmans, Green, 1909.

Cooper, Lawrence. "Our Railroad Commission as a Political Factor." *Alabama Bar Association Proceedings* (1905), 140–53.

———. "Stop! Look and Listen! As Applied to Popular Agitation." *Alabama Bar Association Proceedings* (1912).

Cumming, Joseph B. "Lawyers, the Trustees of Public Opinion." *Georgia Bar Association Proceedings* (1886), 88–97.

Cunningham, T. M. "The Use of Injunctions by Federal Courts as to State Laws." *Georgia Bar Association Proceedings* (1908), 143–71.

Davis, Richard B. "Liability of Employer to Employee for Damages Resulting from Negligence of Co-Employees." *Virginia Bar Association Proceedings* (1890), 113–30.

Dresser, Frank F. *The Employers' Liability Acts and the Assumption of Risks in New York, Massachusetts, Indiana, Alabama, Colorado, and England.* St. Paul, Minn: Keefe-Davidson, 1903.

Falkner, Jefferson M. "Some Comments as to the War upon the Railroad Interests Now Being Waged by a Few WholeSale Merchants in Birmingham." Printed Speech. Montgomery: 26 July 1902.

Glass, Hiram. "Railroads—National Versus State Control." *Texas Bar Association Proceedings* (1908), 184–202.

Haney, Lewis Henry. *A Congressional History of Railways in the United States, 1850–1888.* Madison, Wisc., 1910.

Harrison, Fairfax. *A History of the Legal Development of the Railroad System of the Southern Railway Company.* Washington, D.C., 1901.

Hines, Walker D. "The Proposals of the Interstate Commerce Commission." *The Forum* (March 1902), 3–14.

———. "Railroad Regulation and Politics." *Engineering Magazine* 34 (December 1901), 511–12.

———. *War History of American Railroads.* New Haven: Yale University Press, 1928.

Hopkins, John L. "The Lawyer in Government." *Georgia Bar Association Proceedings* (1906), 125–35.

Jerome, William Travers. "Public Opinion, Its Power, Some of Its Evils, and Injustices, and Our Duty as Lawyers to It." *Georgia Bar Association Proceedings* (1906), 197–207.

Jones, George W. *Summary of Statutes of Alabama Affecting Railroad Corporations.* Montgomery, 1908.

McGregor, T. H. "Employers' Liability Act." *Texas Bar Association Proceedings* (1917), 180–90.

McKinney, William M. *A Treatise on the Law of Fellow-Servants.* Northport, N.Y.: Edward Thompson, 1890.

Parker, Edwin B. "Anti-Railroad Personal Injury Litigation in Texas." *Texas Bar Association Proceedings* (1900), 166–90.

Parrish, Robert L. "Master and Servant." *Virginia Bar Association Proceedings* (1892), 131–50.

Patterson, Christopher S. *Railway Accident Law: The Liability of Railways for Injuries to the Person.* Philadelphia: T. & J. W. Johnson, 1886.

Persons, A. P. "Public Opinion of the Law and of Lawyers." *Georgia Bar Association Proceedings* (1901), 271–81.

Prentis, Robert B. "Some Observations About Government Control of Railways and the Virginia Case." *Virginia Bar Association Proceedings* (1909), 205–55.

Poor, Henry Varnum. *Manual of the Railroads.* New York: H. V. and H. W. Poor, 1880–94.

———. *Poor's Manual of the Railroads of the United States.* New York: H. V. and H. W. Poor, 1895–1916.

Ray, Eugene. "Young Lawyers and Some of the Obstacles They Encounter." *Georgia Bar Association Proceedings* (1904), 164–73.

Schenck, David. *North Carolina Railroad Decisions, 1837–1883.* Richmond: William Ellis Jones, Book and Job Printer, 1883.

Speake, Paul. "Wantonness in Personal Injury Cases." *Alabama Bar Association Proceedings* (1903), 134–56.

Street, Robert G. "Report of the Committee on Jurisprudence and Law Reform." *Texas Bar Association Proceedings* (1889), 59–64.

Thomas, Henry Walter. *Digest of the Railroad Laws of Georgia.* Atlanta: Franklin Printing and Publishing, 1895.

Thomas, William H. "A Recent Industrial Decision." *Alabama Bar Association Proceedings* (1912), 323–30.

Thornton, William W. *The Law of Railroad Fences and Private Crossings: Including Injuries to Animals on Right of Way Caused by Negligence*. Indianapolis: Bowen-Merrill, 1892.

Weatherly, James T. "Judicial Delay in Alabama." *Alabama Bar Association Proceedings* (1884), 47–50.

White, Frank S. "Annual Address by the President." *Alabama Bar Association Proceedings* (1913), 57–65.

Wimbash, William A. "Judicial Review of the Rates of Carriers." *Georgia Bar Association Proceedings* (1906), 409–26.

Winston, Robert Watson. *It's a Far Cry*. New York: Holt, 1937.

———. *Talks About the Law*. Raleigh: Edwards & Broughton, 1894.

Wood, Clement R. "Progressive Ideals for the Lawyer." *Alabama Bar Association Proceedings* (1912), 210–24.

SECONDARY SOURCES

Books

Armes, Ethel M. *The Story of Coal and Iron in Alabama*. 1910. Reprint, New York: Arno Press, 1973.

Auerbach, Jerold S. *Unequal Justice: Lawyers and Social Change in Modern America*. New York: Oxford University Press, 1976.

Ayers, Edward L. *The Promise of the New South: Life After Reconstruction*. Oxford: Oxford University Press, 1992.

———. *Vengeance and Justice: Crime and Punishment in the Nineteenth-Century American South*. Oxford: Oxford University Press, 1984.

Ayers, Edward L., and John C. Willis, eds. *The Edges of the South*. Charlottesville: University Press of Virginia, 1990.

Baker, George P. *The Formation of the New England Railroad System: A Study of Railroad Combination in the Nineteenth Century*. Cambridge, Mass.: Harvard University Press, 1949.

Baker, Lewis. *The Percys of Mississippi: Politics and Literature in the New South*. Baton Rouge: Louisiana State University Press, 1983.

Barr, Alwyn. *Reconstruction to Reform: Texas Politics, 1876–1906*. Austin: University of Texas Press, 1971.

Benson, Lee. *Merchants, Farmers, and Railroads: Railroad Regulation and New York Politics, 1850–1887*. New York: Russell & Russell, 1969.

Bergstrom, Randolph E. *Courting Danger: Injury and Law in New York City, 1870–1910*. Ithaca: Cornell University Press, 1992.

Berk, Gerald. *Alternative Tracks: The Constitution of American Industrial Order, 1865–1917.* Baltimore: Johns Hopkins University Press, 1994.

Blake, Nelson M. *William Mahone of Virginia.* Richmond: Garrett & Massie, 1935.

Bloomfield, Maxwell. *American Lawyers in a Changing Society, 1776–1876.* Cambridge, Mass.: Harvard University Press, 1976.

Bodenhamer, David J., and James W. Ely Jr., eds. *Ambivalent Legacy: A Legal History of the South.* Jackson: University Press of Mississippi, 1984.

Brandfon, Robert L. *Cotton Kingdom in the New South: A History of the Yazoo Mississippi Delta from Reconstruction to the Twentieth Century.* Cambridge, Mass.: Harvard University Press, 1967.

Brock, William. *Investigation and Responsibility: Public Responsibility in the United States, 1865–1900.* New York: Cambridge University Press, 1984.

Campbell, E. G. *The Reorganization of the American Railroad System, 1893–1900.* New York: Columbia University Press, 1938.

Carlton, David. *Mill and Town in South Carolina, 1880–1920.* Baton Rouge: Louisiana State University Press, 1982.

Cash, Wilbur J. *The Mind of the South.* New York: Knopf, 1941.

Chandler, Alfred D., Jr. *The Visible Hand: The Managerial Revolution in American Business.* Cambridge, Mass.: Belknap Press of Harvard University Press, 1977.

———, ed. *The Railroads: The Nation's First Big Business.* New York: Harcourt, Brace, World, 1965.

Chesson, Michael B. *Richmond After the War, 1865–1890.* Richmond: Virginia State Library, 1981.

Clarke, Malcolm. *The First Quarter Century of the Richmond and Danville, 1847–1871.* Washington, D.C., 1959.

Coatsworth, John H. *Growth Against Development: The Economic Impact of Railroads in Porfirian Mexico.* DeKalb: Northern Illinois University Press, 1981.

Cobb, James C. *Industrialization and Southern Society, 1877–1984.* Lexington: University Press of Kentucky, 1984.

Cochran, Thomas C. *Railroad Leaders, 1845–1890: The Business Mind in Action.* 1953. Reissued, New York: Russell & Russell, 1966.

Cortner, Richard C. *The Iron Horse and the Constitution: The Railroads and the Transformation of the Fourteenth Amendment.* Westport, Conn.: Greenwood Press, 1993.

Cotner, Robert C. *James Stephen Hogg: A Biography.* Austin: University of Texas Press, 1959.

Cumming, Mary. *The Georgia Railroad and Banking Company, 1833–1945.* Augusta, Ga., 1945.

Dabney, Virginius. *Virginia, the New Dominion: A History from 1607 to the Present.* Charlottesville: University Press of Virginia, 1983.

Dew, Lee A. *The JLC & E: The History of an Arkansas Road.* State University: Arkansas State University, 1968.

Dewey, Donald. *Monopoly in Economics and Law.* Chicago: Rand McNally, 1959.

Dewey, Ralph L. *The Long and Short Haul Principle of Rate Regulation.* Columbus: Ohio State University Press, 1935.

Doster, James F. *Railroads in Alabama Politics, 1875–1914.* Tuscaloosa, Ala.: University of Alabama Press, 1957.

Dozier, Howard D. *A History of the Atlantic Coast Line Railroad.* Boston: Houghton, Mifflin, 1920.

Dykstra, Robert. *The Cattle Towns.* New York: Knopf, 1968.

Eller, Ronald D. *Miners, Millhands, and Mountaineers: Industrialization of the Appalachian South, 1880–1930.* Knoxville: University of Tennessee Press, 1982.

Fels, Rendigs. *Wages, Earnings, and Employment—Nashville, Chattanooga & St. Louis Railway, 1866–1896.* Nashville: Vanderbilt University Press, 1953.

Ferguson, Maxwell. *State Regulation of Railroads in the South.* New York: Columbia University Press, 1916.

Fishlow, Albert. *American Railroads and the Transformation of the Ante-Bellum Economy.* Cambridge, Mass.: Harvard University Press, 1965.

Fogel, Robert William. *Railroads and American Economic Growth: Essays in Econometric History.* Baltimore: Johns Hopkins Press, 1964.

Forbath, William E. *Law and the Shaping of the American Labor Movement.* Cambridge, Mass.: Harvard University Press, 1991.

Freyer, Tony. *Forums of Order: The Federal Courts and Business in American History.* Greenwich, Conn.: Jai Press, 1979.

Friedman, Lawrence M. *A History of American Law.* New York: Simon & Schuster, 1973.

Galanter, Marc, and Thomas M. Palay. *Tournament of Lawyers: The Transformation of the Big Law Firm.* Chicago: University of Chicago Press, 1991.

Gaston, Paul M. *The New South Creed: A Study in Southern Mythmaking.* New York: Knopf, 1970.

Gawalt, Gerard W., ed. *The New High Priests: Lawyers in Post–Civil War America.* Westport, Conn.: Greenwood Press, 1984.

Goldfield, David R. *Cotton Fields and Skyscrapers: Southern City and Region, 1607–1980.* Baton Rouge: Louisiana State University Press, 1982.

Graebner, William. *Coal Mining Safety in the Progressive Era: The Political Economy of Reform.* Lexington, Ky.: University Press of Kentucky, 1976.

Grantham, Dewey W. *Southern Progressivism: The Reconciliation of Progress and Tradition.* Knoxville: University of Tennessee Press, 1983.

Grodinsky, Julius. *Transcontinental Railway Strategy, 1869–1893: A Study of Businessmen.* Philadelphia: University of Pennsylvania Press, 1962.

Hackney, Sheldon. *Populism to Progressivism in Alabama*. Princeton: Princeton University Press, 1969.

Hahn, Steven. *The Roots of Southern Populism: Yeoman Farmers and the Transformation of the Georgia Upcountry, 1850–1890*. New York: Oxford University Press, 1983.

Hall, Kermit L., ed. *Main Themes in United States Constitutional and Legal History*. New York: Garland Publishing, 1987.

Harris, Carl V. *Political Power in Birmingham, 1871–1921*. Knoxville: University of Tennessee Press, 1977.

Hobson, Wayne. *The American Legal Profession and the Organizational Society, 1890–1930*. New York: Garland Publishing, 1986.

Horwitz, Morton. *The Transformation of American Law, 1780–1860*. Cambridge, Mass.: Harvard University Press, 1977.

Hovenkamp, Herbert. *Enterprise and American Law, 1836–1937*. Cambridge, Mass.: Harvard University Press, 1991.

Hunt, Robert S. *Law and Locomotives: The Impact of the Railroad on Wisconsin Law in the Nineteenth Century*. Madison: State Historical Society of Wisconsin, 1958.

Hurst, James Willard. *The Growth of American Law: The Law Makers*. Boston: Little, Brown, 1950.

———. *Law and Social Order in the United States*. Ithaca: Cornell University Press, 1977.

———. *The Legitimacy of the Business Corporation in the Law of the United States, 1780–1970*. Charlottesville: University Press of Virginia, 1970.

Johnson, Arthur M., and Barry E. Supple. *Boston Capitalists and Western Railroads: A Study in Nineteenth Century Railroad Investment Process*. Cambridge, Mass.: Harvard University Press, 1967.

Joubert, William H. *Southern Freight Rates in Transition*. Gainesville: University of Florida Press, 1949.

Kalven, Harry, and Hans Zeisel. *The American Jury*. Chicago: University of Chicago Press, 1971.

Keller, Morton. *Affairs of State: Public Life in Late Nineteenth Century America*. Cambridge, Mass.: Belknap Press of Harvard University Press, 1977.

Kirkland, Edward C. *Industry Comes of Age: Business, Labor, and Public Policy, 1860–1897*. New York: Holt, Rinehart, 1961.

———. *Men, Cities, and Transportation: A Study in New England History*. 2 vols. Cambridge, Mass.: Harvard University Press, 1948.

Kirwan, Albert D. *Revolt of the Rednecks: Mississippi Politics, 1876–1925*. Lexington, Ky.: University of Kentucky Press, 1951.

Klein, Maury. *The Great Richmond Terminal: A Study in Businessmen and Business Strategy*. Charlottesville: University Press of Virginia, 1970.

————. *A History of the Louisville & Nashville Railroad.* New York: Macmillan, 1972.

Kolko, Gabriel. *Railroads and Regulation, 1877–1916.* New York: W. W. Norton, 1965.

Kostal, R. W. *Law and English Railway Capitalism, 1825–1875.* Oxford: Clarendon Press, 1994.

Kousser, J. Morgan. *The Shaping of Southern Politics: Suffrage Restriction and the Establishment of the One-Party South, 1880–1910.* New Haven: Yale University Press, 1974.

Lambie, Joseph T. *From Mine to Market: The History of Coal Transportation on the Norfolk & Western Railway.* New York: New York University Press, 1954.

Lane, Edgar. *Lobbying and the Law.* Berkeley: University of California Press, 1964.

Letwin, William. *Law and Economic Policy in America: The Evolution of the Sherman Antitrust Act.* New York: Random House, 1965.

Licht, Walter. *Working for the Railroad: The Organization of Work in the Nineteenth Century.* Princeton: Princeton University Press, 1983.

Lightner, David L. *Labor on the Illinois Central Railroad, 1852–1900: The Evolution of an Industrial Environment.* New York: Ayer Co., Arno Press, 1977.

Link, William A. *The Paradox of Southern Progressivism, 1880–1930.* Chapel Hill: University of North Carolina Press, 1992.

Lipartito, Kenneth, and Joseph Pratt. *Baker & Botts in the Development of Modern Houston.* Austin: University of Texas Press, 1991.

MacAvoy, Paul W. *The Economic Effects of Regulation: The Trunk-Line Railroad Cartels and the Interstate Commerce Commission Before 1900.* Cambridge, Mass.: MIT Press, 1965.

McIntosh, Wayne. *The Appeal of Civil Law: A Political-Economic Analysis of Litigation.* Urbana: University of Illinois Press, 1990.

Maddex, Jack P., Jr. *The Virginia Conservatives, 1867–1879.* Chapel Hill: University of North Carolina Press, 1970.

Martin, Albro. *Railroads Triumphant: The Growth, Rejection, and Rebirth of a Vital American Force.* Oxford: Oxford University Press, 1992.

Michelbacher, Gustav F., and Thomas M. Nial. *Workmen's Compensation Insurance.* New York: McGraw-Hill Book Co., 1925.

Miller, George Hall. *Railroads and the Granger Laws.* Madison: University of Wisconsin Press, 1971.

Moger, Allen W. *Virginia: From Bourbonism to Byrd, 1870–1925.* Charlottesville: University of Virginia Press, 1968.

O'Brien, Gail Williams. *The Legal Fraternity and the Making of a New South Community, 1848–1882.* Athens: University of Georgia Press, 1986.

Orth, John V. *The Judicial Power of the United States: The Eleventh Amendment in American History.* New York: Oxford University Press, 1987.

Paul, Arnold M. *Conservative Crisis and the Rule of Law: Attitudes of the Bar and Bench, 1887–1895.* Gloucester, Mass.: Peter Smith, 1976.

Pressly, Thomas J., and William H. Scofield, eds. *Farm Real Estate Values in the United States by Counties, 1850–1959.* Seattle: University of Washington Press, 1965.

Pulley, Raymond H. *Old Virginia Restored: An Interpretation of the Progressive Impulse, 1870–1930.* Charlottesville: University Press of Virginia, 1968.

Purcell, Edward A. *Litigation and Inequality: Federal Diversity Jurisdiction in Industrial America, 1870–1948.* New York: Oxford University Press, 1992.

Reed, S. G. *A History of the Texas Railroads.* Houston: St. Clair Publishing, 1941.

Ripley, William Z. *Railroads: Finance and Organization.* New York: Longmans, Green, 1915.

Rothman, David J. *Politics and Power: The United States Senate, 1869–1901.* Cambridge, Mass.: Harvard University Press, 1966.

Scott, Roy V. *Railroad Development Programs in the Twentieth Century.* Ames: Iowa State University Press, 1985.

Shaw, Barton C. *The Wool-Hat Boys: Georgia's Populist Party.* Baton Rouge: Louisiana State University Press, 1984.

Shaw, Robert B. *A History of Railroad Accidents, Safety Precautions and Operating Practices.* 2d ed. Potsdam, N.Y.: Northern Press, 1978.

Sheldon, William Dubose. *Populism in the Old Dominion: Virginia Farm Politics, 1885–1900.* Princeton: Princeton University Press, 1935.

Silverman, Robert. *Law and Urban Growth: Civil Litigation in the Boston Trial Courts, 1880–1900.* Princeton: Princeton University Press, 1981.

Sklar, Martin J. *The United States as a Developing Country: Studies in U.S. History in the Progressive Era and the 1920s.* Cambridge, Eng.: Cambridge University Press, 1992.

Skowronek, Stephen. *Building a New American State: The Expansion of National Administrative Capacities, 1877–1920.* Cambridge, Eng.: Cambridge University Press, 1982.

Spratt, John Stricklin. *The Road to Spindletop, Economic Change in Texas, 1875–1901.* Austin: University of Texas Press, 1955.

Stokes, Durward T. *Company Shops: The Town Built by a Railroad.* Winston-Salem, N.C.: John F. Blair, 1981.

Stone, Richard D. *The Interstate Commerce Commission and the Railroad Industry: A History of Regulatory Policy.* New York: Praeger, 1991.

Stover, John F. *American Railroads.* Chicago: University of Chicago Press, 1961.

———. *History of the Baltimore and Ohio Railroad.* West Lafayette, Ind.: Purdue University Press, 1987.

———. *The Railroads of the South, 1865–1900: A Study in Finance and Control.* Chapel Hill: University of North Carolina Press, 1955.

Summers, Mark W. *Railroads, Reconstruction, and the Gospel of Prosperity: Aid Under the Radical Republicans, 1865–1877.* Princeton: Princeton University Press, 1984.

Swaine, Robert T. *The Cravath Firm and Its Predecessors, 1819–1947.* 3 vols. New York: Ad Press, 1946–48.

Tilley, Nannie May. *The Bright Tobacco Industry, 1860–1929.* Chapel Hill: University of North Carolina Press, 1948.

Thimm, Alfred L. *Business Ideologies in the Progressive Era, 1880–1914.* Tuscaloosa: University of Alabama Press, 1976.

Thornton, J. Mills, III. *Politics and Power in a Slave Society: Alabama, 1800–1860.* Baton Rouge: Louisiana State University Press, 1978.

Trelease, Allen W. *The North Carolina Railroad, 1849–1871, and the Modernization of North Carolina.* Chapel Hill: University of North Carolina Press, 1991.

Waller, Altina L. *Feud: Hatfields, McCoys, and Social Change in Appalachia, 1860–1900.* Chapel Hill: University of North Carolina Press, 1988.

White, G. Edward. *Tort Law in America.* New York: Oxford University Press, 1980.

Woodward, C. Vann. *Origins of the New South, 1877–1913.* Baton Rouge: Louisiana State University Press, 1951.

Wright, Gavin. *Old South, New South: Revolutions in the Southern Economy Since the Civil War.* New York: Basic Books, 1986.

Zunz, Olivier. *Making America Corporate, 1870–1920.* Chicago: University of Chicago Press, 1990.

Articles and Essays

Adams-Weber, M. C. "The Interstate Commerce Commission and Southern Territory Freight Rates, 1887–1940." *Journal of Transportation History* 4 (September 1983): 63–74.

Beck, John J. "Building a New South: A Revolution from Above in a Piedmont County." *Journal of Southern History* 53 (August 1987): 441–70.

Binder, John J. "The Sherman Anti-Trust Act and the Railroad Cartels." *Journal of Law and Economics* 31 (October 1988): 443–68.

Boyd, J. Hayden, and Gary M. Walton, "Social Savings from Nineteenth Century Rail Passenger Services." *Explorations in Economic History* 9 (Spring 1972): 233–54.

Bratton, William W., Jr. "The New Economic Theory of the Firm: Critical Perspectives from History." *Stanford Law Review* 41 (1989): 1471–1528.

Carson, Robert B. "Railroads and Regulation Revisited: A Note on Problems of Historiography and Ideology." *Historian* 34 (May 1972): 437–46.

Crow, Jeffrey J. "'Populism to Progressivism' in North Carolina: Governor Daniel

Russell and His War on the Southern Railway Company," *Historian* 37 (August 1975): 649–67.

Daniels, Stephen. "Continuity and Change in Patterns of Case Handling: A Study of Two Rural Counties." *Law and Society Review* 19 (1985): 381–420.

———. "Ladders and Bushes: The Problem of Caseloads and Studying Court Activities over Time." *American Bar Foundation Research Journal 1984* (1984): 751–95.

———. "A Tangled Tale: Studying State Supreme Courts." *Law and Society Review* 22 (1988): 833–63.

Engel, David. "The Oven Bird's Song: Insiders, Outsiders, and Personal Injuries in an American Community." *Law and Society Review* 18 (1984): 551–82.

Escott, Paul D. "Yeoman Independence and the Market: Social Status and Economic Development in Antebellum North Carolina." *North Carolina Historical Review* 36 (July 1989): 275–300.

Fish, Carl R. "The Restoration of Southern Railroads." *University of Wisconsin Studies in the Social Sciences and History* (1919), no. 2.

Fleming, Walter L. "Immigration to the Southern States," *Political Science Quarterly* 20 (June 1905): 276–97.

Ford, Lacy K. "Civil Wrongs: Personal Injury Law in the Late 19th Century." *American Bar Foundation Journal* (1987): 351–78.

———. "Rednecks and Merchants: Economic Development and Social Tensions in the South Carolina Upcountry, 1865–1900." *Journal of American History* 71 (September 1984): 294–318.

Freyer, Tony. "The Federal Courts, Localism, and the National Economy, 1865–1900." *Business History Review* 53 (autumn 1979): 343–63.

Friedman, Lawrence M., and Jack Ladinsky. "Social Change and the Law of Industrial Accidents." *Columbia Law Review* 67 (1967): 50–82.

Friedman, Lawrence M., and Robert Percival. "A Tale of Two Courts: Litigation in Alameda and San Benito Counties." *Law and Society Review* 10 (1975–76): 267–301.

Friedman, Lawrence M., and Thomas D. Russell. "More Civil Wrongs: Personal Injury Litigation, 1901–1910." *American Journal of Legal History* 34 (1990): 295–314.

Galanter, Marc. "Reading the Landscape of Disputes: What We Know and Don't Know (and Think We Know) About Our Allegedly Contentious and Litigious Society." *UCLA Law Review* 31 (1983): 4–71.

———. "Why the 'Haves' Come Out Ahead: Speculations on the Limits of Legal Change." *Law and Society Review* 9 (1974): 95–160.

Gold, D. M. "Redfield, Railroads, and the Roots of Laissez-Faire Constitutionalism." *American Journal of Legal History* 27 (July 1983): 254–68.

Gordon, Robert. "Legal Thought and Legal Practice in the Age of American Enterprise, 1870–1920." In *Professions and Professional Ideologies in America, 1730–1940*, edited by Gerald Geison, 170–110. Chapel Hill: University of North Carolina Press, 1983.

Halliday, Terrence. "Six Scores and Ten: Demographic Transitions in the American Legal Profession, 1850–1980." *Law and Society Review* 20 (1986): 53–78.

Hersch, Philip L., and J. M. Netter. "The Impact of Early Safety Legislation: The Case of the Safety Appliance Act of 1893." *International Review of Law and Economics* 10 (May 1990): 61–75.

Hovenkamp, Herbert. "Regulatory Conflict in the Gilded Age: Federalism and the Railroad Problem." *Yale Law Journal* 97 (1988): 1017–72.

Hudson, Henry. "The Southern Railway and Steamship Association." *Quarterly Journal of Economics* 5 (October 1891): 70–94.

Hunt, James L. "Law and Society in a New South Community: Durham County, North Carolina, 1898–1899." *North Carolina Historical Review* 68 (October 1991): 427–60.

Jenks, Leland H. "Railroads as an Economic Force in American Development." *Journal of Economic History* 4 (May 1944): 1–20.

Johnson, Dudley S. "Early History of the Alabama Midland Railroad Company." *Alabama Review* 21 (October 1968): 276–87.

Kaczorowski, Robert. "The Common Law Background of Nineteenth Century Tort Law." *Ohio State Law Journal* 51 (1990): 1127–99.

Kagan, Robert, et al. "The Business of State Supreme Courts, 1870–1970." *Stanford Law Review* 30 (1977–78): 121–56.

———. "The Evolution of State Supreme Courts." *Michigan Law Review* 76 (1978): 961–1005.

Klein, Maury. "Competition and Regulation: The Railroad Model." *Business History Review* 64 (summer 1990): 311–325.

———. "Southern Railroad Leaders, 1865–1893: Identities and Ideologies," *Business History Review* 42 (autumn 1968): 288–310.

———. "The Strategy of Southern Railroads, 1865–1893." *American Historical Review*, 73 (April 1968): 1052–68.

Klein, Maury, and Kozo Yamamura. "The Growth Strategies of Southern Railroads, 1865–1893." *Business History Review* 41 (winter 1967): 358–377.

Krasity, Kenneth. "The Role of the Judge in Jury Trials: The Elimination of Judicial Evaluation of Fact in American State Courts from 1790 to 1913." *University of Detroit Law Review* 62 (1985): 595–632.

Kretzmer, David. "Transformation of Tort Liability in the Nineteenth Century: The Visible Hand." *Oxford Journal of Legal Studies* 4 (1984): 46–87.

Krislov, Samuel. "Theoretical Perspectives on Caseload Studies: A Critique and a Beginning." In *Empirical Theories About Courts,* edited by Keith Boyum and Lynn Mather, 161–87. New York: Longman, 1983.

Lewis, W. David. "Joseph Bryan and the Virginia Connection in the Industrial Development of Northern Alabama." *Virginia Magazine of History and Biography* 98 (October 1990): 613–41.

Lipartito, Kenneth. "Getting Down to Cases: Baker & Botts and the Texas Railroad Commission." *Essays in Economic and Business History* 6 (1988): 27–37.

———. "What Have Lawyers Done for American Business? The Case of Baker & Botts of Houston." *Business History Review* 64 (autumn 1990): 489–526.

McGuire, P. S. "Railroads of Georgia, 1860–1880." *Georgia Historical Quarterly* 16 (September 1932): 179–213.

McIntosh, Wayne. "A State Court's Clientele: Exploring the Strategy of Trial Litigation." *Law and Society Review* 19 (1985): 421–47.

Malone, Wex. "The Formative Era of Contributory Negligence." *Illinois Law Review* 41 (1946): 151–82.

Martin, Albro. "The Troubled Subject of Railroad Regulation in the Gilded Age—A Reappraisal." *Journal of American History* 61 (September 1974): 685–709.

May, James. "Antitrust Practice and Procedure in the Formative Era: The Constitutional and Conceptual Reach of State Antitrust Law, 1880–1918." *University of Pennsylvania Law Review* 135 (1987): 511–12.

Merkel, Philip L. "The Origins of an Expanded Federal Court Jurisdiction: Railroad Development and the Ascendancy of the Federal Judiciary." *Business History Review* 58 (autumn 1984): 336–58.

Moger, Allen. "Industrial and Urban Progress in Virginia from 1880–1900." *Virginia Magazine of History and Biography* 46 (1958): 307–36.

———. "Railroad Practices and Policies in Virginia After the Civil War." *Virginia Magazine of History and Biography* 59 (October 1951): 423–58.

———. "The Rift in the Virginia Democracy in 1896." *Journal of Southern History* 4 (August 1938): 295–317.

Munger, Frank. "Social Change and Tort Litigation: Industrialization, Accidents, and Trial Courts in Southern West Virginia, 1872 to 1940." *Buffalo Law Review* 36 (1987): 75–118.

———. "Trial Courts and Social Change: The Evolution of a Field Study." *Law and Society Review* 24 (1990): 217–26.

Odum, E. Dale. "The Economic Impact of Railroads on Denton County, Texas, 1880–1920." *East Texas Historical Journal* 29, no. 2: 54–60.

Palmore, Joseph R. "The Not-So-Strange Career of Interstate Jim Crow: Race, Transportation, and the Dormant Commerce Clause, 1878–1946." *Virginia Law Review* 83 (November 1997): 1773–1817.

Potter, David M. "Historical Development of Eastern-Southern Freight Rate Relationships." *Law and Contemporary Problems* 12 (summer 1947): 416–48.

Russell, Thomas D. "Historical Study of Personal Injury Litigation: A Comment on Method." *Georgia Journal of Southern Legal History* 1 (1991): 109–34.

Sanders, Robert H. "Progressive Historians and the Late Nineteenth-Century Agrarian Revolt: Virginia as a Historiographical Test Case." *Virginia Magazine of History and Biography* 79 (October 1971): 484–92.

Scheiber, Harry N. "The Road to Munn: Eminent Domain and the Concept of Public Purpose in the State Courts." *Perspectives in American History* 5 (1971): 329–402.

Schwartz, Gary. "Tort Law and the Economy in Nineteenth Century America: A Reinterpretation." *Yale Law Journal* 90 (1981): 1717–75.

Thomas, William G., III. " 'Under Indictment': Thomas Lafayette Rosser and the New South." *Virginia Magazine of History and Biography* (April 1992): 207–32.

Usselman, Steven W. "Air Brakes for Freight Trains: Technological Innovation in the American Railroad Industry, 1869–1900." *Business History Review* 58 (spring 1984): 30–50.

Wetzel, Kurt. "Railroad Management's Response to Operating Employees' Accidents, 1890–1913." *Labor History* 21 (1980): 351–68.

Woodman, Harold D. "Economic Reconstruction and the Rise of the New South, 1865–1900." In *Interpreting Southern History*, edited by John B. Boles and Evelyn Thomas Nolen. Baton Rouge: Louisiana State University Press, 1987.

Papers, Theses, and Dissertations

Asher, Robert. "Workmen's Compensation in the United States, 1880–1935." Ph.D. diss., University of Minnesota, 1971.

Axelrod, Bernard. "Railroad Regulation in Transition, 1897–1905: Walker D. Hines of the Railroads Versus Charles A. Prouty of the Interstate Commerce Commission." Ph.D. diss., Washington University, 1975.

Brockman, John. "Railroad Radicals and Democrats: A Study in Texas Politics, 1865–1900." Ph.D. diss., University of Texas, Austin, 1975.

Burt, Jesse C. "A History of the Nashville, Chattanooga & St. Louis Railway, 1873–1916." Ph.D. diss., Vanderbilt University, 1950.

Carlson, James A. "The Iron Horse in Court: Thomas Ruffin and the Development of North Carolina Railroad Law." Master's thesis, University of North Carolina–Chapel Hill, 1972.

Churchman, John H. "Federal Regulation of Railroad Rates, 1880–1898." Ph.D. diss., University of Wisconsin, 1976.

Cubby, Edwin Albert. "The Transformation of the Tug and Guyandot Valleys: Economic Development and Social Changes in West Virginia, 1888–1921." Ph.D. diss., Syracuse University, 1962.

Fuller, Justin. "History of the Tennessee Coal, Iron, and Railroad Company, 1852–1907." Ph.D. diss., University of North Carolina–Chapel Hill, 1966.

Gilliam, George Harrison. "Making Virginia Progressive: Courts and Parties, Railroads and Regulators, 1890–1910." Master's thesis, University of Virginia, 1997.

Henson, Stephen Ray. "Industrial Workers in the Mid–Nineteenth Century South: Atlanta Railwaymen, 1840–1870." Ph.D. diss., Emory University, 1982.

Hunt, James L. "Legislatures, Courts, and Nineteenth Century Negligence: Political and Constitutional Conflict over Standards of Liability." Paper presented at the American Society of Legal Historians conference, Minneapolis, October 1977.

O'Brien, Timothy. "Tracks to Progressivism: Railroad and Florida Politics, 1879–1891." Bachelor's thesis, University of Virginia, 1992.

Odum, Edwin. "Louisiana Railroads: A Study in State and Local Aid." Ph.D. diss., Tulane University, 1961.

Patterson, Robert Lewis. "State Regulation of Railroads in Texas, 1836–1920." Ph.D. diss., University of Texas, 1960.

Patterson, William H. "Through the Heart of the South: A History of the Seaboard Air Line Railroad Company, 1832–1950." Ph.D. diss., University of South Carolina, 1952.

Sanders, Albert Neely. "State Regulation of Public Utilities by South Carolina, 1879–1935." Ph.D. diss., University of North Carolina, 1956.

Sommers, Lawrence Edmund. "Lawyers and Progressive Reform: A Study of Attitudes and Activities in Illinois, 1890 to 1920." Ph.D. diss., Northwestern University, 1967.

Steelman, Joseph Flake. "The Progressive Era in North Carolina, 1884–1917." Ph.D. diss., University of North Carolina, 1955.

Thomas, William G. "Railroad Attorneys and the Issue of Segregation Before and After *Plessy*." Paper presented at *Plessy v. Ferguson* Revisited Conference, Howard University, Washington, D.C., November 1996.

Tinsley, James A. "The Progressive Movement in Texas." Ph.D. diss., University of Wisconsin, 1953.

Triplette, Ralph R., Jr. "One-Industry Towns: Their Location, Development, and Economic Character." Ph.D. diss., University of North Carolina, 1974.

Vogt, Daniel. "Problems of Government Regulation: The Mississippi Railroad Commission." Ph.D. diss., University of Southern Mississippi, 1980.

Wright, Charles Conrad. "The Development of Railroad Transportation in Virginia," Ph.D. diss., University of Virginia, 1930.

Jones, T. N., 64
Jones, Thomas Goode, 8, 171*n*10, 270
Judges. *See* State judges
Juries, in personal injury cases, 75, 76, 151, 151*n*26, 159

Kansas City, Memphis & Birmingham Railroad, 63–4
Kansas City Southern Railway, 240
Keeble, John B., 228, 232*n*, 261
Keller, Morton, 2*n*
Kentucky: lobbying in, 90, 105, 174, 175, 215; railroad legislation in, 105, 230; Progressives in, 168, 175, 197; free passes in, 180, 180*n*28, 181; L&N's political involvement in, 181, 182; railroad commission in, 203; jury trials in, 234; workmen's compensation law in, 238–9
Keystone Bridge Company, 120–3
King, Spalding & Little, 138*n*
Klein, Maury, 246*n*41
Knights of Labor, 110–1
Knoxville & Augusta Railroad, 166
Knoxville, Cumberland Gap & St. Louis Railroad, 64–5*n*8
Kolko, Gabriel, 210–1*n*26, 227*n*1
Kostal, R. W., xiii

L&N. *See* Louisville & Nashville (L&N)
Lane, Edgar, 84*n*, 169*n*
Lane, Taliaferro, Pearson, Webb & Tillman, 45
Larew, C. G., 250–1
Lathrop, Gardiner, 195, 261
Law departments of railroads. *See* Railroad legal departments
Law profession: and tension between

"ideal and actual in the law," 33–4, 38*n*, 49–50; corporation versus "anti-corporation" lawyers generally, 35–6, 36*n*6, 44–5, 59–60, 137, 197, 249–50; ethics of, 35–6, 276–8; and Cravath system, 36–7; and large law firm, 36–7, 38; emergence of corporate-client-based firm in South, 37–8; financial difficulties for young lawyers, 42; and associationalism, 262–3; discontent over corporations' place in, 263–6; amoralism of corporate lawyers, 276–8. *See also* Personal injury lawyers; Railroad lawyers; specific lawyers and law firms; and state bar associations, such as Alabama Bar Association
Lawton, Alexander R., Jr., 41–2, 44, 98
Lawton & Cunningham, 42
Lee, Fitzhugh, 184
Legal departments of railroads. *See* Railroad legal departments
Legal profession. *See* Law profession; Personal injury lawyers; Railroad lawyers; specific lawyers and law firms; and state bar associations, such as Alabama Bar Association
Letcher & Letcher, 126
Liability legislation. *See* Employers' liability legislation; Federal Employers' Liability Act (FELA)
Livestock-damage claims, 81, 125–7, 126–7*nn*
Lobbying: as corruption, 83, 84*n*; railroads' need for, 83–4; railroad lawyers' role as lobbyists generally, 84–85, 271, 273; economic development argument of, 85, 97, 106–8; in Texas, 85*n*46; by Bax-

of, 87, 98–9, 103–4, 169, 181–6;
public relations for, 99, 152; speed
of, 127*n*52; and segregation, 129–
33, 132*n*61, 194, 219–25; major
lines by 1900, 164–5, 165*n*1; capital improvements for, 187, 215–6,
245; nationalization of, 246, 272.
See also Accidents; Employees of
railroads; Personal injury cases;
Rates; Regulation of railroads;
headings beginning with Railroad;
and specific railroads
Raleigh & Gaston, 96
Rates: and pooling, 5, 210, 241, 244,
246; federal court decisions on,
87–8, 170, 187, 203; *Munn v. Illinois* on, 87; state regulation of,
87–8, 186–7, 193, 197; *Smyth v.
Ames* doctrine on, 170; *Alabama
Midland Railroad* case on, 203;
and Interstate Commerce Commission (ICC), 203, 207, 209, 210;
long-and-short-haul discrimination
in, 204, 206–9, 242, 262; local
protests against, 206–9; differential
rates on half-full carloads, 209;
and valuation, 213, 215, 216, 218;
and capital improvements for railroads, 215–6; railroad commissions' regulation of, 215–8; and
Mann-Elkins Act, 241–2, 262;
lowering of, by 1916, 245
Reagan, John H., 111–2
*Reagan v. Farmer's Loan & Trust
Company*, 170
Reath, Theodore W., 147
Rebates, 206, 209
Reconstruction, 25, 26, 83, 220
Redwine, Leonidas, 18
Regulation of railroads: rate regulation, 5, 87–8, 170, 186–7, 193,

197, 203; and engineers, 89–90;
and Georgia Pacific, 89–90, 100,
101; and Federal Employers' Liability Act (FELA), 153, 177, 178,
184, 226–39, 232*n*, 240, 259–61,
274–6; difficulties of, 202; railroads' support of federal regulation, 210, 210–11*n*26, 213–5,
235, 239–40, 275; confusions
about and inefficiency of, 239–40,
244; and Mann-Elkins Act, 241–4,
262; and Progressives generally,
245, 259, 275; and Wilson administration, 245–6; and Transportation Act of 1920, 246, 246*n*41.
See also Interstate Commerce
Commission (ICC); Railroad commissions; State legislatures; and
specific states
Removal to federal court: for right-of-
way cases, 31–2; for personal injury cases, 75, 75*n*30, 77, 80,
234; state legislation for preven-
tion of, 105, 230–1, 237; opposition to, 230–1; for FELA cases,
233, 235–7; southern attorneys'
preference for generally, 234–5,
234*n*17, 272
Republican Party, 25, 26
Retainer contracts, 43, 44, 45–7, 59
Retainers. *See* Salaries and retainers
Revenues of railroads, 204–5
Rice, Samuel F., 45
Rich, Edgar J., 243, 262
Richmond & Allegheny Railroad,
11–5, 17, 18, 268
Richmond & Danville (R&D): takeover of Oxford & Clarkesville Railroad by, 11; lawyers for, 47–51,
55–7, 64, 89; conflicts within,
48–9; reorganization of legal de-